THE SELF-CONCEPT

THE SELF-CONCEPT

REVISED EDITION
VOLUME ONE

*A Review of Methodological Considerations
and Measuring Instruments*

by

Ruth C. Wylie

UNIVERSITY OF NEBRASKA PRESS
LINCOLN AND LONDON

Publishers on the Plains

UNP

To my Mother

Copyright © 1961, 1974 by the University of Nebraska Press
All Rights Reserved
International Standard Book Number 0–8032–0830–8
Library of Congress Catalog Card Number 72–97165
Manufactured in the United States of America

First printing: 1974
Most recent printing indicated by the first digit below:
    2   3   4   5   6   7   8   9   10

Contents

Preface

A number of considerations entered into my decision to undertake the revision of my 1961 book, *The Self Concept: A Critical Survey of Pertinent Research Literature*. First, it is obvious that interest in the self-concept or some aspect of it has been high and widespread in a number of fields, probably even increasing during the twelve years since the 1961 book went to press. I infer this interest level from the innumerable allusions to the self-concept in many psychology, education, and sociology books, and from the overwhelming volume of research output indexed in the *Psychological Abstracts*.

A second consideration was the increase in methodological publications which presented ideas that self-concept researchers should know about and use. These ideas include critiques of once commonly employed methods, suggestions for improved methods, and current controversies about these more recently suggested methods. Third, an enormous number of substantive research studies have appeared; and it seemed that these need to be summarized, evaluated critically, and synthesized insofar as possible in order to be maximally available and useful to researchers and theorists. Finally, quite a few colleagues and friends encouraged me to undertake this revision because they shared my opinion that the above considerations imply that such a revision will be useful.

It is my hope that this volume will make three kinds of contributions. First and foremost, it may play a part in improving the quality of self-concept research in the future. Although methodological guidelines and critiques are available in many journal articles and books, these ideas are widely scattered. It requires considerable time and effort to find, evaluate, and synthesize them; and it is often not obvious from such sources just how the various methodological considerations are conceptually relevant and practically applicable to the particular problems with which the self-concept researcher wishes to deal. Perhaps the present overview and synthesis will be helpful along these lines. Moreover, I hope that my specific critiques of particular studies and lines of research may prove to be a helpful supplement to general methodological discussions, in that the more specific critiques may alert future self-concept researchers to the characteristic pitfalls they should avoid. Additionally, a quick entrée into what is available by way of instruments and what has been done thus far on given substantive topics may enable future self-concept researchers to choose their next steps more expeditiously and wisely.

Secondly, although the focus of this work is the self-concept, I hope that the methodological sections especially may make a valuable contribution to students of other aspects of personality, helping them to evaluate and improve research in their respective areas. Many of the methodological references brought together here and the methodological issues evaluated in this work are relevant to measurement of a variety of personality constructs and to testing a variety of propositions regarding personality.

The two potential contributions already mentioned could be rather briefly described, but clarifying the third requires somewhat more explanation—an exposition which is longer than the relative importance I assign it among the three potential contributions. I hope that this work may indirectly bring about an improvement in the education of beginning students of psychology. I have been deeply concerned about the possibility that unfortunate educational effects are being created by the way in which ideas about the self-concept have been presented in introductory psychology texts and in texts purporting to be intermediate-level treatments of personality psychology. For example, I looked at 15 introductory books published between 1968 and 1972. Of these, 4 did not index *self-concept* or any apparently related term, and with the omission of the topic I have no quarrel. Although the remaining 11 texts indicated in title and/or preface the intent to present a scientific approach to psychology, all made broad, unsupported, uncriticized generalizations about the self-concept. That is, the sections about the self-concept had one or more of the following failings which could seriously mislead the student and interfere with his acquiring a scientific attitude toward this topic: (a) No indication was given that the statements were intended to be theoretical propositions, as opposed to known relationships. The impression created is that these are obvious truths which may be validated by a reader's experiences, when in fact they are assertions from a most complex, inadequately explored area of psychology. (b) Either no study relevant to any of the general assertions was even mentioned, or one or two were briefly cited. (Sometimes even these were not actually self-concept studies!) (c) No doubts were expressed about the methodological adequacy of the cited study or studies. (d) No inkling was given that a large volume of research has been published and that serious controversy remains, partly because of unresolved methodological problems. Of course I do not believe that an introductory text should be a miniature critical exegesis of research literature and related methodology. But I do believe that such extreme departures from the scientific approach as those listed above can quite probably have one or more unfortunate effects: (a) Widespread credence is lent to unsupported common-sense statements and to the idea that making such assertions in the name of scientific psychology is acceptable among experts. (b) Brighter, more discerning students will develop a disrespect for psychologists' approach to this topic (thus alienating some of them from going on to learn more about the field and to make their own contributions). (c) The future psychologist beginning his exposure to the field by reading such texts will have to unlearn erroneous ideas before he can go on to attain an accurate picture of the field and perhaps to make a scientific contribution; or if he does not unlearn these ideas before undertaking his own research, the volume of uninterpretable research will be further increased.

The situation with regard to intermediate-level personality texts is much the same as with the introductory texts. Excluding those purporting only to present theories and those specializing in personality assessment, I examined eight personality texts published between 1962 and 1972. The seven of these which purported to represent a scientific approach and which discussed the self-concept gave more extensive treatment to the topic than was the case in the introductory books. Only two, however, cited an appreciable number of substantive and methodological research publications; and even here, critical evaluation of the studies themselves or their merits for supporting or refuting the stated generalizations was often superficial, sparse, or missing altogether. All in all, then, even the student who proceeds to the intermediate level of personality study is plausibly liable to suffer many of the same unfortunate educational effects as I suggested might result from his reading about the self-concept in introductory texts.

I am not, of course, suggesting that the present book should be read by beginning students. Rather, I should like to believe that authors of introductory or intermediate texts might be helped by this work to improve the educational effectiveness of their presentations of self-concept materials to introductory students, and that the state of contemporary texts being what it is, instructors may find this book a useful source for correcting or supplementing textual materials.

Every portion of the manuscript has been read by at least one of the following persons; and the clarity, accuracy, and comprehensiveness of the work were much improved by following their helpful suggestions: Katherine E. Baker, Peter Bentler, Robert Bills, Donald T. Campbell, Donald Fiske, David Hamilton, Kristina Pritchard, Barbara Long, Peggy J. Miller, Ellen Piers, Morris Rosenberg, Franklin Shontz, Julian Stanley, Susan Stevenson, and Alice W. Wilson. I am especially indebted to my friend and professional colleague Katherine E. Baker, with whom I have spent many profitable and enjoyable hours discussing psychology in general and the issues in this book in particular. Of course I take responsibility for whatever flaws remain in this manuscript despite all the help which has so generously been given me.

In regard to technical aspects of the preparation of this volume, I wish to thank Catherine Borland and Judith Parker for typing assistance; Stephanie Bernstein and Margaret Weigel for aid in various phases of reading and correcting proof; Mary Coughlin for assistance in bibliographic search; and Peggy J. Miller for aid in all these technical phases of the work as well as for intelligent and thorough aid in categorizing and excerpting the bibliographic references. Teresa Perella and Penelope Partlow of the Goucher College Library have been especially helpful in obtaining interlibrary loans.

Goucher College provided a half-year's leave and some financial support for early phases of the bibliographic search. Without these, this volume could not have been completed.

RUTH C. WYLIE
Goucher College

Preface to the First Edition

Some years ago, I became interested in the current trend toward rapprochement between personality theories and general behavior theories, and in the beginning which had been made in applying experimental and psychometric methods to the testing of some personality theories. One of the systems I examined from this viewpoint was self-concept theory, and I hoped to formulate some research of relevance to this and other personality theories which emphasize constructs concerning the self. As a background for such an undertaking, I began to examine the pertinent theoretical and empirical literature. It soon became obvious that this literature was growing in chaotic profusion and could profit from some sort of evaluative, organized summary.

At the outset I intended to limit myself to a critical summary of the available studies. However, appropriate comprehensive criteria for evaluation were not available in any one place, and so a major part of my task became the accumulation and systematic presentation of such criteria. Although there is much useful material in the methodological literature of experimental and psychometric psychology, the setting up of suitable criteria was not an entirely simple, straightforward job of compilation and application of ready-made standards. In fact, in the development of my own thinking, reflection on the basic rationale of research design and measurement in this particular area has proved to be the most interesting and potentially valuable aspect of the preparation of this book. I hope that these ideas, as well as the particularized criticisms and substantive overviews, will prove useful to graduate students and researchers who are interested in this and related topics. I believe that there are important lessons to be learned in exploring the issues involved in research in this area.

When this book was in various stages of preparation, several persons read substantial portions of the manuscript, or all of it. Thanks to these interested and perceptive critics, the accuracy, clarity, and comprehensiveness of the book are much greater than they otherwise would have been. These persons are: Katherine E.

Baker, Robert R. Blake, Mary Evans Collins, Lee J. Cronbach, Frank J. Dudek, Marshall R. Jones, Jane S. Mouton, James T. Russell, William Stephenson, and Georgiana R. Wylie. Throughout the preparation of the book I received especially valuable support and encouragement from Katherine E. Baker, Mary Evans Collins, and Georgiana R. Wylie.

Correspondence with a number of the authors cited in the book clarified certain questions I had about their theoretical or empirical work. Many of these correspondents encouraged me to feel that this arduous task needed doing. There are also numerous friends and colleagues with whom I have had helpful, informal conversations during the time when this book was being prepared. I wish to thank all of these persons collectively for their encouragement, kind cooperation, and contributions to my thought. Of course I must take final responsibility myself for any shortcomings of accuracy or interpretation in the book.

Thanks are also due to Shehbal Erdeniz and Vivian McCraven for their part in the search for titles, and to Edith Spoley, who did the major part of the typing.

The publisher and the author wish to express their gratitude to the copyright owners listed below for permission to quote from their publications: *Acta Sociologica*, American Psychological Association, Inc., Appleton-Century-Crofts, Inc., Basic Books, Duke University Press, D. Van Nostrand Co., Inc., *Educational and Psychological Measurement*, Houghton Mifflin Co., Inc., *Human Relations, Journal of Clinical Psychology, Journal of Counseling Psychology, Journal of Projective Techniques*, Journal Press, *Journal of Social Issues*, Ohio State University Press, *Personnel and Guidance Journal*, the Ronald Press Co., School of Aviation Medicine, United States Air Force, University of Chicago Press, and Yale University Press.

Part of the cost of the literature search, the critical reading, and the writing of this book was defrayed by funds from Grant No. M–1822 from the National Institute of Mental Health. The author wishes to thank that agency for making it possible to carry out this work.

THE SELF-CONCEPT

1

Introduction

A. A Brief Historical Overview of Psychologists' Interest in Constructs concerning the Self

In psychological discussions, the word *self* has been used in many different ways. It is often said that these usages may be roughly dichotomized into those which refer to *self as agent or process* and those which refer to *self as object of the person's own knowledge and evaluation* (English & English, 1958; Hall & Lindzey, 1970; Symonds, 1951). In the second category, psychologists have postulated that knowledge and evaluations of one's own characteristics or states may be available to one's conscious awareness, or may be partially or entirely unavailable to awareness.

Unfortunately, the apparently plausible and simple dichotomy of "self as agent" and "self as object" does not serve adequately to classify and characterize the usage of self-referent constructs by personality theorists. Self-concept theorists who appear to be referring to "self as object" are not interested in S's self-concept only as a cognition or evaluation of S's "self as object." Rather, they attribute behavior-influencing characteristics to the self-concept or the ideal-self concept, thus implying a more "active" role for these concepts than the simple phrase "self as object" might imply. Moreover, some personality theorists postulate processes which seem to refer to "self as agent" and "self as object," but which go beyond both senses and are not clearly related to either. For example, Horney (1950) suggests that growth tendencies of a "real self" are present in everyone; Maslow (1954) postulates an inborn motive to develop one's potentialities (self-actualization).

To what possible meanings of *self*, then, does this book refer? It seems fair to say that most of the measuring instruments and researches refer more closely to the second (self-as-object) meaning,

1

but that the self-concept variables under consideration are hypo-thetically assigned behavior-determining roles as well.

Early in the history of American psychology, there was consider-able interest in the self. For example, William James (1890) accorded this topic an important place in his psychological thinking, and to a certain extent the study of the self was pursued by introspectionists (Calkins, 1930).

During the second, third, and fourth decades of the twentieth century, constructs concerning the self did not receive much atten-tion from the behaviorist and functionalist psychologies which were dominating the American scene. As Hilgard (1949) points out, the introspectionists were unable to handle the self, and of course such a "mentalistic" construct as the self-concept was anathema to behaviorists. Meanwhile the psychodynamic postulates which were being developed by Freudians and neo-Freudians necessarily implied a self referent in order to make them plausible and understandable. For at least two reasons these theories did not immediately bring constructs concerning the self to the forefront of American psy-chology. First of all, Freud himself, in his early theorizing, strongly emphasized the role of the id, and he did not explicitly formalize a self construct or assign the closely related ego functions much importance, relatively speaking. Secondly, his theory was being denied or ignored by many American general psychologists who found it lacking in rigor, in susceptibility of empirical test, and in compatibility with the theoretical models then in favor.

Recently, however, there has been a marked proliferation of self theories, traceable to a number of influences: In his later writings, Freud (1962) himself assigned greater importance to ego develop-ment and functioning, and of course the neo-Freudians stressed the importance of the self-picture and the ego-ideal. At the same time, American psychologists who were beginning to work in clinical areas found behavioristic models apparently too limited to account for the phenomena they were observing, and they were ready to entertain psychoanalytic ideas, particularly of the revised variety. Since their interests were somewhat different from those of students of the general experimental psychology of cognition and motiva-tion, the clinicians may have felt less need for neat, philosophically sophisticated, operationally circumscribed theorizing. They may have been less distressed to depart from such theorizing in their search for conceptual schema to account for their observations.

Throughout this period the functionalists never gave up intro-spective methods, and the Gestalt psychologists injected their phe-nomenological methods and theories into the stream of general psychology. Meanwhile, the possibility of an operational behavior-ism involving complex cognitive and motivational intervening vari-ables was being explored within the domain of general psychology. All of these facts implied the possibility of fusing general psycho-logical theories of cognition and motivation with the psychoanalytic or psychodynamic theories originating in the clinic. And so we find that almost all the theories of personality which have been put forth within the last three decades assign importance to a phenom-enal and/or nonphenomenal self-concept with cognitive and moti-vational attributes.

Although there was much writing of such theories beginning in the 1940s, there was very little empirical work done prior to 1949. Since that time, however, there has been an increasingly large output of investigations, and it is with the review of this empirical litera-ture that the present work is concerned.

B. Purpose and Scope of This Work

The present volume is intended to be one of two which together will present a revised and extended consideration of the topics covered in Wylie (1961). This volume is concerned with a con-ceptual treatment of methodology relevant to self-concept research and an evaluation of extant research designs, procedures, and meas-urement techniques. The projected second volume will attempt to synthesize and evaluate the conclusiveness of the substantive studies in the light of the methodological considerations presented in the first volume. This division into two volumes seemed advisable in view of the explosive proliferation of references since the appearance of the original book in 1961.

The domain to be surveyed in the two volumes is broadly con-ceived to include methodological and substantive research publica-tions of pertinence to a wide variety of theories which accord an important or even central role to the self-concept (e.g., Adler [Ans-bacher & Ansbacher, 1956]; Allport, 1961; Angyal, 1941; Cattell, 1966; Erikson, 1950, 1959; Fromm, 1939; Horney, 1937; Jung [Progoff, 1953]; Lecky, 1945; Lynd, 1958; Maslow, 1954; McClelland, 1951; Mead, 1934; Rogers, 1951a, 1959; Snygg & Combs, 1949;

Sullivan, 1953). Some of these theorists (e.g., Lecky, Rogers, and Snygg and Combs) have been called phenomenological theorists because of their stress on the role of the conscious self-concept in determining a person's behavior. In the present work, major emphasis is given to empirical studies which pertain to this conscious self-concept, sometimes called the phenomenal self. To a lesser degree, attention is also given to investigations concerned with nonphenomenal constructs, for example, the unconscious self-concept.

The above-mentioned theories are in many ways ambiguous, incomplete, and overlapping; and no one theory has received a large amount of systematic empirical exploration. Moreover, a great many empirical studies relevant to self-concept do not address themselves to any one theoretical position. Therefore neither the present volume nor the projected second one is organized around the framework of any particular theory. Rather, the material in this volume is organized in terms of methodological issues, problems, recommendations, and critiques of extant measuring instruments, while the second volume will present clusters of empirical studies. Reference to theoretical ideas is made when discussing proposed operational definitions of constructs and empirical tests of principles; and the second volume especially will present some conclusions concerning the extent to which the principles of various theorists seem to have been explored and supported.

A more detailed preview of the present volume should be helpful to the reader at this point. Chapter 2 considers a number of aspects of methodology which are relevant to self-concept research. First, it examines the assumptions apparently made by some persons that self-concept or phenomenal personality theories cannot be scientific, or that there are unique problems of research design involved in testing theories about the phenomenal self, the nonphenomenal self, and self-referent constructs which have been proposed without reference to the phenomenal-nonphenomenal dimension. Second, a summary is presented of methodological flaws and questionable methodological practices which are avoidable but still commonly found in self-concept research.

An examination of empirical studies makes it apparent that ambiguities in the measuring instruments can be traced partially to inadequacies in the theorists' definitions of their terms. We cannot attempt in this book systematically to review, compare, criticize, or put in order the various nonoperational definitions in common use.[1] However, the general conceptual and methodological problems of defining self-concept variables operationally are considered at length in chapter 3.

Chapter 4 describes and criticizes some of the instruments which have actually been used in attempts to index aspects of the self-concept, especially some aspect of self-regard. Here are considered both instruments which explicitly purport to index the phenomenal self-concept and those which are presented as alleged self-concept measures without explicit reference to the conscious-unconscious dimension. A great problem in the self-concept area is the enormous proliferation of instruments, the great majority being used only once or twice, with little or no information about the methods of construction, reliability, or construct validity being given for most of them. Interpretation of individual studies and meaningful syntheses are therefore precluded. Since no useful purpose could be served by a superficial consideration or listing of each instrument which has ever been used, I selected a few for detailed description and criticism in chapter 4. In choosing, I kept in mind such factors as the frequency with which the instrument had been used and the desirability of representing a variety of theoretical positions, aspects of self-concept allegedly indexed, and formats. The critical evaluations of the instruments are made in the light of the methodological desiderata given in chapters 2 and 3.

From a theoretical standpoint, and from the standpoint of available research, the major discussion of measurement appropriately centers on problems and instrumentation in the measurement of the phenomenal self. However, even phenomenological personality theorists implicitly or explicitly admit nonphenomenological constructs (e.g., the unconscious self-concept). Measurement of these constructs is considered in chapter 5.

Apparently all theorists assume that the self-concept is not entirely "realistic" and that lack of "realism" may have psychodynamic significance and important behavioral consequences. To the degree that a person's self-concept is "realistic," he is said to have "insight" into himself. Chapter 6 first considers the general problems which one encounters when attempting to define *insight*

---

1. For extensive listing of such terms the reader is referred to Chein (1944), Combs and Soper (1957), English and English (1958), Hall and Lindzey (1970), Rogers (1951a), and Symonds (1951). For some attempted comparisons and contrasts, see Wylie (1968).

from this point of view. It then reviews and evaluates the various operational definitions in common use and points out the possibilities for artifact in measurement techniques and research design which render most "insight" research uninterpretable.

Chapter 7 summarizes the main conceptual and methodological implications of the detailed facts and evaluations presented in chapters 2 through 6. In chapter 7 I stress that these implications should be kept in mind and systematically applied in future conceptualizing and empirical work.

The second volume of this book will consider studies in which self-concept variables were related to alleged antecedent, consequent, or correlated variables. In many instances the variables were chosen for study on grounds of their supposed relevance to self, according to one or more versions of personality theory.

In selecting references to be included in either volume, some limiting criteria had to be established. From one viewpoint, any investigation in which S makes a report about himself, say, on a personality inventory or in an interview, might be regarded as suitable for inclusion. However, I have restricted myself largely to studies which appear to have received at least some of their inspiration from self theories. Most of the publications which are included here appeared between 1949 and 1971, inclusive. A few references of an earlier date and some which appeared in 1972 are also included. In the 1961 edition of this work, doctoral dissertations were listed in the bibliography for the sake of completeness and were occasionally referred to. I have omitted them from the present edition because the examination of the enormous number of published references left no time or energy to collect and evaluate the original dissertations; and *Dissertation Abstracts* contains too little information to sustain salient evaluations of research methods.

2

Self-Concept Theories and Problems of Research Methodology

A. Introduction

In this chapter I discuss the following points concerning the mutual relevance of research methodology and self-concept theory. First, I consider what methodological problems or weaknesses are introduced by the present vague and incomplete state of self-concept theories—problems which are not necessarily intrinsic to personality theories stressing phenomenal variables and self-referent constructs, but which could conceivably be minimized or eliminated by improved theoretical statements. Second, I evaluate the question whether there are any methodological problems or limitations which are necessarily intrinsic to this type of psychological theorizing, no matter how clear, refined, or sophisticated the theoretical statements may eventually become. An argument is developed that the methodological requirements and difficulties implied by this kind of theorizing are not unique in kind, although coping with them presents many more practical difficulties than is the case with general behavior theories. Third, an overview is presented of the most commonly encountered actual methodological flaws or questionable practices in research relevant to self-concept theories—weaknesses which are remediable within our present knowledge about research methodology and which must be remedied if important increments are to be added to our empirical knowledge relevant to self-concept theories.

7

B. Methological Implications of Vagueness and Incompleteness of Extant Theoretical Statements

1. Basic Constructs

The basic constructs as defined in the writings of self-concept theorists frequently seem to point to no clear empirical referents. Thus it is no wonder that a wide array of "operational definitions" of some of these constructs has been devised by various experimenters. And by the same token it is understandable that some constructs have received no empirical exploration. (For more detail concerning the vagueness and variety of "definitions" of self-referent constructs, see Wylie, 1968.)

2. "Postulates" or "Laws"

Sometimes these theories have been expressed in terms of a series of "postulates" or "laws" relating the inadequately defined constructs to each other, to antecedents, or to consequents. (See Rogers, 1951a, 1959; Snygg & Combs, 1949.) Such a form leads one to search for determinateness and internal consistency in the set of statements. However, the shape of the function, the range over which the relationship is supposed to hold, or the manner of interaction between joint determining factors is typically not specified. It appears to me that there are occasional contradictions between one proposition and another, but it is often impossible to be sure. As a consequence of these ambiguities, directional hypotheses are not always clearly implied, and plausible interpretations of trends which go against the predicted direction are often possible.

3. Phenomenal and Nonphenomenal Variables: Methodological Problems Stemming from Ambiguities in Their Relative Roles

One particular kind of ambiguity deserves more detailed attention, since it involves that class of variables which are assigned special importance in self-concept theories, namely, phenomenal variables. As is well known, self-concept theorists believe that one cannot understand and predict human behavior without knowledge of S's conscious perceptions of his environment and of his self as he sees it in relation to the environment. Because of this central role accorded to conscious perceptions, cognitions, and feelings, these theorists have often been labeled "phenomenological."

Not all writers have consistently reserved the term *phenomenology* to refer to the study of direct awareness, but I use the term with that meaning only. Most workers refer to a continuum of clarity in the phenomenal or conscious field, including the phenomenal self, and I apply the word *phenomenal* to all aspects of that continuum. On the other hand, attitudes, knowledge, motivations, and perceptions which are hypothesized to be definitely unconscious, I call *nonphenomenal*.

Like all psychologists who deal with inferred variables, personality theorists face many difficult problems in defining terms and achieving appropriate observable indices for their constructs. Chapter 3 is concerned with a detailed analysis of these difficulties, and it outlines the requirements for achieving appropriate measurement of self-concept constructs, especially phenomenological self-concept constructs. There it becomes clear that many of the measurement problems are not new or unique to this area, but researchers have not paid sufficient attention to previous relevant analyses or to parallel kinds of problems already discovered by workers in other fields of psychology. In addition, chapter 3 shows that, in some ways, uniquely difficult problems are encountered in achieving valid measurement of self-concept constructs, whether or not they are phenomenological.

Some of the most crucial difficulties seem to center around the degree to which self-concept theorists wish to be, and can fruitfully be, consistently phenomenological. Many examples of this unresolved dilemma can be found in the writings of phenomenological theorists. As one illustration I have chosen some quotations from Rogers's publications. At some points he seems to imply that *only* when a feeling or item of information about the self or environment comes at least dimly into awareness will it influence behavior. "The self-concept or self-structure may be thought of as an organized configuration of perceptions of the self which are admissible to awareness. It is composed of such elements as the perceptions of one's characteristics and abilities; the percepts and concepts of the self in relation to others and to the environment; the value qualities which are perceived as associated with experiences and objects; and goals and ideals which are perceived as having positive or negative valence [Rogers, 1951a, p. 136]." "This configuration . . . as Raimy says . . . 'serves to regulate behavior and may serve to account for uniformities in personality' [Rogers, 1951a, p. 191]."

"As long as the self-Gestalt is firmly organized, and no contradictory material is even dimly perceived, then positive self-feelings may exist, the self may be seen as worthy and acceptable, and conscious tension is minimal. Behavior is consistent with the organized hypotheses and concepts of the self structure [Rogers, 1951a, p. 191]." "[Although the individual whose self-concept is incongruent with reality may be vulnerable], the extent to which he dimly perceives these incongruences and discrepancies is a measure of his internal tension and determines the amount of defensive behavior [Rogers, 1951a, pp. 191–192]." However, it becomes obvious in other places that processes such as drives, unconscious motivation, repression, and denial are at least tacitly assumed to occur and to determine behavior, even though it is never clearly specified how such non-phenomenological constructs are to be articulated into the theoretical system. For example, "He may have some experiences which are inconsistent with this perception, but he either denies these experiences to awareness or symbolizes them in such a way that they are consistent with his general picture [Rogers, 1951b, p. 321]." "While these concepts are nonverbal, and may not be present in consciousness, this is no barrier to their functioning as guiding principles [Rogers, 1951a, p. 498]." In general, the problems and limitations of phenomenological theorizing have not been faced squarely by proponents of self-concept theories. (See Smith's, 1950, criticisms of phenomenological theories and Snygg and Combs's, 1950, rejoinder.)

From the research standpoint, two sorts of problems are created by theorists' use of both phenomenal and nonphenomenal variables, coupled with failure to face and resolve the attendant conceptual ambiguities: On the measurement side, the need for a peculiar kind of discriminant validity is created; that is, to test these theories one should have available two different classes of instruments or sets of operations which index the phenomenal and nonphenomenal constructs, respectively. On the hypothesis-testing side, one needs to know more explicitly whether the phenomenal, the nonphenomenal, or both classes of constructs are allegedly associated with the independent variables, the dependent variables, or the correlated variables to which the hypothesis refers. These matters are fully discussed in chapters 3 and 5.

In the face of this situation, most empirical workers have initiated their studies by circumventing these confusing issues. Some have said, in effect, "Let us see how much of the variance in Ss' behavior on X, Y, Z . . . we can account for on the basis of variance in Ss' self-report responses on instruments A, B, C. . . . We shall offer an interpretation of our findings based on the assumption that the self-report responses correlate with the other behaviors because Ss' phenomenal fields, as tapped by our measures A, B, C, have determined Ss' behaviors on X, Y, Z. We recognize that processes or attributes of which S is unaware may also be affecting his self-report responses and other behaviors. Some of these factors of which S is unaware may be relevant to our theory, some may not be. In any case we can face the problems of alternate interpretations and of unaccounted-for variance at some future time."

Those investigators who were interested in Ss' nonphenomenal selves and fields have, in effect, offered an exactly parallel argument based on assumptions concerning *their* instruments' validity and the alleged influences of nonphenomenal fields on Ss' behaviors.

Still others have either explicitly or implicitly denied the necessity or usefulness of trying to relate their self-relevant constructs to the phenomenological-nonphenomenological continuum. This, of course, does not excuse them from amassing pertinent evidence regarding the construct validity of their instruments, based on an explication of their theory and the characteristics and alleged place of the constructs in it.

Now one may grant that a researcher is not obligated to perfect his own or someone else's theory before attempting to test some aspect of it. However, careful scrutiny of empirical studies makes one conclude that measurement and hypothesis testing in this field are chaotic partly because these issues have not been explicitly recognized and systematically handled.

A review like the present one is not the appropriate place for a frontal attack on basic phenomenological theory building or for an evaluation of the merits of building new versions of self theory which explicitly or implicitly omit reference to the phenomenological continuum. Therefore, in considering instruments and studies presented in a phenomenological theoretical framework, I too bypass theoretical questions concerning nonphenomenal determinants in Ss' general behaviors. I take as my point of departure the fact that these theorists specify that S's phenomenal field "determines" at least a great deal, if not all, of his general behavior. The latter tenet implies that, regardless of how the questions of nonphenomenal determinants may eventually be conceptualized, we must develop instruments which validly index Ss' phenomenal fields, especially their phenomenal selves. Only then can we relate such responses to the other behavior of S which is allegedly a function of the phenomenal field.

Similarly, when evaluating instruments and research purportedly involving nonphenomenal self-relevant constructs, I bypass unresolved issues in theory and direct the criticisms to the question whether nonphenomenal variables, as distinct from phenomenal or unclassified variables, have been indexed with instruments of demonstrated discriminant validity for that purpose. In evaluating instruments based on a disavowal or ignoring of the relevance of phenomenology in self theory, I restrict myself to a critique of the cogency of the evidence for construct validity as each worker has presented such evidence and related it to his own verbal specifications for his particular self-relevant construct.

C. RESEARCH DESIGNS APPROPRIATE FOR TESTS OF SELF-CONCEPT THEORIES

It is important to consider in some detail the question whether any peculiar or unique methodological requirements or limitations are logically implied by self-concept theories of personality, as contrasted to, say, those implied by general behavior theory in psychology. There has been considerable confusion on this score, mainly involving questions about the scientific status of such theories, the implications of such theories' reliance on phenomenological variables, and the mistaken idea held in some quarters that such theories are ahistorical. In this section I consider these questions in the order just given.

1. Scientific Status of Self-Concept Theories

The discussions of methodology in this book are based upon the assumption that the scientific method can be fruitfully used to test phenomenological personality theories, including self-concept theories, in order to establish nomological (i.e., general scientific) laws, just as the scientific method is assumed to be applicable to testing theories in other areas of psychology. With some possible exceptions, the statements of Rogers, Lewin, Freud, and the neo-Freudians seem to imply acceptance of this assumption. Recently, however, some personality theorists, especially those interested in phenomenology and self-referent constructs, have been turning to existential psychology, which criticizes the assumptions and methods of modern behavioral science (May, 1958, 1969).

Existentialists point out that modern science is concerned with finding methods of isolating factors and observing them from an "allegedly detached" base and with selecting for investigation those phenomena which can be reduced to abstract general laws. As a result, according to the existentialists, the laws formulated have little relation to the person in his unique, changing, concrete world of experience. Not only does scientific method fail to do justice to the data, but it tends to hide rather than reveal what is going on in the person, since we try to see the person in terms of our scientific concepts. While existentialists "do not rule out the study of dynamisms, drives and patterns of behavior, . . . they hold that these cannot be understood in any given person except in the context of the overarching fact that here is a person who happens *to exist, to be*, and if we do not keep this in mind, all else we know about this person will lose its meaning [May, 1958, p. 12]."

In their recent evaluation of existentialist influences on modern personality theory, Hall and Lindzey (1970) point out that the scientific assumption of determinism is actively rejected by existentialist psychologists, and this point has especially appealed to certain personality psychologists in America. Of course, to the extent that free will or free choice occurs, the experiences and behaviors associated with it are not amenable to scientific description and conceptualization. One should note, however, that, contrary to the implied allegations in certain existentialist writings, no philosophically sophisticated natural or behavioral scientist believes that determinism is an empirically proven or provable assumption regarding events in his domain of inquiry. But if scientific method is not to be an absurd enterprise, scientists (including personality theorists) must assume at least enough order and lawfulness to make searching for it a reasonable activity.

There is also a third way in which the beliefs of existential psychologists apparently differ from the views of other psychologists. Existentialists seem to feel that it is possible and necessary for the observer to become directly aware of the conscious world of the subject. In this connection, they deplore the influence upon psychology of the historical dichotomy between subject and object in Western thought. May (1958) writes, *"The grasping of the being of the other person occurs on a quite different level from our knowl-edge of specific things about him* [p. 38]." And on pages 55 and 56 he says, "*Being together* means *being together in the same world*" and "the other person's world . . . cannot be understood as an external collection of objects which we view from the outside (in which case we never really understand it)."

Some of the psychologists whose work appears in the present volume have moved toward acceptance of one or another aspect of the existentialist view (e.g., Jourard, Leary, and Stephenson).

This book is not the place to evaluate the existentialist position. I am concerned with research methods and results; and these, with a few possible exceptions, appear to stem from the following two assumptions: (a) There is value in using modern scientific method to establish nomological laws. (b) Psychological processes occurring inside an organism cannot be directly observed, but must be inferred from observable behavior, in combination with other observables. In short, the status of self-concept theories is the same as that of theories in other areas of psychology, insofar as applicability of the scientific approach is concerned.

2. Do Self-Concept Theories Imply Intrinsic Limitations in Applicable Scientific Methods?

Among those who accept the idea that scientific method is appli-cable to testing self-concept theories, there are differences of opinion as to the scientific methodological requirements of phenomeno-logical theory and self-concept theory. Some persons feel that the methodological requirements of phenomenological theory are pecu-liar to that type of theory. That is, they feel that the scientific methods of the phenomenologist *must* differ from those which can be used and are appropriate to testing other kinds of psychological theory. (See Spence, 1944.) In fact, they would argue that these neces-sary differences in appropriate method also pertain to self-concept theories which assign importance to unconscious (nonphenomenal) perceptions of self and environment. In view of this unresolved controversy, one may profitably spend some time analyzing the situation in an attempt to determine the methodological possibilities and requirements which are appropriate to phenomenological and self-concept theories.

The three questions at issue are briefly stated below. The first two questions stem from the fact that phenomenological theorists and self-concept theorists assign crucial theoretical importance to inferred states of S, that is, to S's perception of self and environment. (a) Does this aspect of these theories necessarily imply that phenomenological and self-concept theorists can never meet behaviorists' requirements that theory-relevant variables be defined in publicly verifiable data language? (b) Does this also necessarily imply that true S-R (stimulus-response) research designs are impossible in principle, with only R-R (response-response) (correlational) designs being attainable? If so, *cause-effect* statements can never be tested, since R-R results will never suffice to sustain causal inferences. The third question follows from the emphasis of phenomenological theories (e.g., Lewin's) and self-concept theories in particular (e.g., Rogers's, and Snygg and Combs's) on contemporary or ahistorical relationships among theoretical variables: (c) If only ahistorical relationships are to be included in the theory, does this not imply a further intrinsic limitation on the applicability of scientific method, that is, the exclusion from consideration of past environmental and subject variables?

Relevant to these questions I argue below that none of these suggested unique methodological limitations or requirements is logically implied by phenomenological or self-concept theories. I agree with Campbell (1969a) when he says, "Such a phenomenology [of the other one] would occupy a status no more indirect, no more presumptive, no more difficult of verification, than a law-giving behaviorism. In addition, it should be unifiable with such a behaviorism once certain stubborn and wrong predilections for the mode of unification are overcome [p. 66]."

The development of my argument is made in terms of the *if-then* paradigm which can refer to purely contemporary *if-then* variables, or to temporal antecedent-consequent sequences ("cause-effect" sequences). Both the contemporary and the antecedent-consequent version of the if-then paradigm may refer solely to relationships between observables; or they may refer to relationships between inferred variables; or to relationships between observed and inferred variables. I assume that theoretical propositions in any area of psychology are always of the if-then variety, in which, ultimately, observable behavior is predicted or explained as a function of relevant variables that are external to the subject and/or characteristic of the subject.

Note that all psychological theory uses the antecedent-inferred-

consequent paradigm in several ways: (a) to define an inferred construct; for example, if S gives certain replies to standard questions
asked under specified conditions, a level of "intelligence" is inferred;
or if certain verbal replies are given to specified questions under
stated conditions, a level of self-regard is inferred; (b) to state propositions concerning influences upon inferred states allegedly dependent on these influences; for example, severe sensory deprivation
lowers intelligence; severe parental punishment lowers self-regard;
(c) to state propositions concerning the relationships between an
inferred state and consequent behaviors other than those used to
define that inferred state. These latter consequent behavior variables
may in certain instances be of interest because of their allaged connection with other inferred states; for example, behaviors allegedly
indicative of defensiveness are predicted to be a function of self-
concept (which has been independently inferred from behaviors,
as exemplified above).

(Here I think it is important to digress momentarily in order
to remind the reader that alleged relationships between an inferred
state or process and some behavior other than that used to define
the inferred state or process may sometimes involve associations
between contemporaneous variables rather than a temporal antecedent-inferred-consequent sequence.)

Most psychologists would probably agree that a complete science
of behavior must eventually determine which classes of observable
antecedents are relevant, and must eventually include all classes of
relevant antecedents in its behavior laws. At present we are far
from this point in any area of psychology, and the typical psychological theorist is aiming toward a more restricted set of laws which
are not intended to cover all the important if-then possibilities.
Such restricted intentions are characteristic of phenomenologists and
self-concept theorists as well as of other theorists.

For convenience the analysis below works through the if-then
sequence, beginning with behavior consequents referred to by *then*.
It must be recognized that the discussion of behavior consequents
necessarily involves foreshadowing the discussion of inferred variables to come later on.

OBSERVABLE CONSEQUENTS

Within any area of psychology (e.g., within the psychology of
learning or of motivation), psychological theorists differ from each

other regarding their preferences for kinds of behavior variables which will be useful (a) to define their inferred variables and (b) to postulate as being related to their defined inferred variables. This sort of difference of opinion, which also characterizes phenomenological personality theorists and self-concept theorists, does not set them apart from theorists in other areas of psychology.

As is pointed out in chapter 3, self-concept theorists seem bound to make much use of verbal behaviors to define their phenomenal self-concept variables and to serve as dependent variables when questions concern the determinants of self-concept. Moreover, verbal behaviors may also be useful to define other variables allegedly related to self-concept, as antecedents, correlates, or consequents. But self-concept theories are by no means restricted to verbal behaviors, since some of their hypotheses regarding relationships of self-concept variables to dependent-behavior variables contain some of the consequent nonverbal responses characteristically used in some studies in perception, learning, and motivation. Social behavior categories (e.g., sociometric status) and psychiatric behavior categories are also often examined as variables allegedly correlated with or consequent upon self-concept. As yet there is no systematic plan in any personality theory for designating the classes of behavior variables for which the theory wishes to account. In any event, observable behaviors of some kind, designated in some specifiable manner, must be the consequents in a scientific psychology, no matter what the school of thought. Naturally, then, in the case of self-concept theorists who aspire to be scientific, this general requirement is applicable and takes the usual forms of demanding specification of behaviors used to infer self-concept and phenomenal experience constructs and then designation of other behaviors theoretically said to be correlated with or consequent to the inferred self-concept and phenomenal world of S.

INFERRED CONSTRUCTS

As I have already implied, most psychologists consider it necessary to insert inferred variables or theoretical constructs into the predictive "equation." Views differ within psychology as a whole as to the kinds of constructs which will be most fruitful in developing a behavior science. For example, Hebb prefers neurophysiological constructs; Hull, mathematical intervening variables; and Gestalt psychologists, phenomenal field constructs. Personality theorists, of course, find inferred variables essential to their theorizing, too. As I have already pointed out, many of the inferred variables of self-concept theorists are phenomenal, but these theorists also use non-phenomenal constructs such as unconscious cognitions.

Regardless of the type of construct preferred, from the point of view of theory building, the theoretical constructs or inferred variables of the personality theorist fulfill the same role as the theoretical constructs in other psychological theory. That is, these constructs are introduced to help explain behavior variations which occur under constant external stimulation, and similarities of behavior which occur under varying external stimulating conditions. Specifically with reference to self-concept theories, individual differences in verbal responses to stimulus inputs (e.g., questions) seem to require the postulation of inferred individual differences in Ss' self-concepts or phenomenal views of the environment. Moreover, Ss' other behaviors supposedly cannot be accounted for solely on the basis of "objectively defined" stimuli or self-characteristics only. Instead, the introduction of such constructs as self-concept and phenomenal view of the environment seem necessary in order to increase accuracy and comprehensiveness in accounting for these behaviors.

Also, regardless of variations among theorists with respect to the type of construct preferred, every theorist must define his inferred constructs in terms of relationships between observables if they are to be scientifically useful.

Heider (1959) has discussed inferred constructs and their relationship to observable antecedents and consequents, with reference to Lewin's theory. His views are applicable to other phenomenal theorists and, of course, to self-concept theorists as well. Heider says that Lewin's concern with inferred constructs is greater than is the concern of behaviorists. This does not mean, however, that Lewin ignored, either theoretically or experimentally, the observed antecedents and consequents to which inferred variables are anchored. Heider (1959) writes,

> [Lewin's] primary concern is with what goes on in this life space; that is where he expects to find the relevant variables, the nodal points which he expects to follow exact laws without exceptions. In contrast to Lewin's concern with the life space, psychology today often considers input and output as the primary object of study; true enough, there are also intervening variables, but they play only an ancillary role.

The psychologist deals with them somewhat reluctantly and then only because otherwise the relations between input and output become unmanageable.

For Lewin these so-called intervening variables are the focus from the start, and input and output are relegated to a secondary role; they form the tools for observation which make it possible for us to get a glimpse of the processes in the life space which are the ultimate object of observation. [P. 5]

In short, although self-concept theorists may assign greater importance to their inferred constructs, the methodological requirement of anchoring constructs to observable antecedents and consequents is the same for self-concept theory as for any other.

OBSERVABLE ANTECEDENTS

On the antecedent side it is common in psychological theorizing to divide the observables into several classes:

1) observable characteristics of the environment, or stimuli
   a) contemporary environmental conditions or stimuli
   b) past environmental conditions or stimuli
2) observable characteristics of the subject
   a) contemporary observable characteristics of S
   b) past observable characteristics of S

As I have already implied in my discussion of observable consequents and inferred variables, one or another of the sorts of antecedents mentioned above might play one or more of the following roles in a psychological theory: (a) in the antecedent-consequent relations used to define the inferred variables in the theory; (b) in the laws describing influences upon the inferred characteristics of S or processes within S; (c) in laws relating S's behaviors to his inferred states or processes, given certain antecedent inputs. Since these possibilities characterize many psychological theories, including phenomenal and self-concept theories, it is clear that no unique methodological limitations or requirements for self-concept and phenomenal theories are implied here.

As on the behavioral (consequent) side discussed above, theorists in any area of psychology may differ with respect to the following points: (a) what kinds of antecedent variables they postulate as probably being important to study; and (b) what classification scheme they believe will prove to be the most fruitful and appropriate one to apply to antecedent variables.

That opinions within the field differ and that means for resolving these differences are not at hand are true of phenomenal and self-concept theories in a manner completely analogous to many other psychological theories. Accordingly, one cannot find in this respect any grounds for concluding that phenomenal and self-concept theories imply any unique methodological requirements or limitations.

Contemporary Stimulus Antecedents

Consider contemporary environmental conditions or "stimuli" first. Behaviorists, Gestalt psychologists, and personality theorists, especially self-concept theorists, have all assigned importance to contemporary stimuli. Problems arise in the definition of *stimulus*. To some (e.g., Spence, 1944) it has seemed that this is one point at which the appropriate method for self-concept and phenomenal theories becomes unique, although other analyses to be elaborated below (i.e., Jessor, 1956; and Verplanck, 1954) would refute this allegation.

Those following Spence's views make the following argument on this point: The self-concept theorist has made it clear that he is interested in the stimulus from self or from the environment *as the subject sees it,* consciously or unconsciously, rather than being concerned exclusively with the stimulus as it is physicalistically defined. This means that the stimulus *must* be inferred from S's response. The necessity of defining stimuli by means of response inferences seems to imply that the phenomenal and self-concept theorists must employ R-R (response-response) designs instead of the more usual S-R (stimulus-response) designs.

An overview of the studies actually done in the area of self-concept theory quickly reveals that R-R designs are, indeed, the most common. What does this situation imply?

1. Can one unequivocally infer cause-effect sequences from such R-R correlational designs? The answer is clearly negative. If self-concept theorists are limited by the nature of their theory to contemporary response-response correlations, their theory can never lead to the predictive cause-effect type of if-then laws.

2. Does the fact that stimuli must be response-inferred by self-concept theorists necessarily restrict these theorists to response-response correlational designs, so that they will never be able to

state cause-effect relationships in the same sense as the behaviorist does?

Reflection on the latter question leads one to realize that it entails two methodological problems, both of which plague any scientific phychological theorist, whether behavioristic or phenomenological. The first problem is whether postulated environment or subject antecedents can be specified in data language. Assuming the first problem is solvable, the second is whether the experimenter can control conditions of observation well enough to establish the temporal priority of the observable antecedents, that is, whether he can justify the interpretation that the observable antecedent "causes" the observable consequent.

Verplanck (1954) has offered an analysis of the stimulus which is helpful in comparing phenomenological theory and general behavior theory with reference to these methodological problems. He has outlined four definitions of *stimulus*: Stimulus I is a part of the environment or a change in part of the environment. Stimulus II adds to Stimulus I the qualification that the environmental change becomes a stimulus only when a response of some kind is produced. Stimulus III refers to a class of environmental events which cannot be identified independently from the observation of lawful activity of the organism. This is Skinner's *stimulus* term. Stimulus IV adds to Stimulus II hypothetical or inferential stimuli such as the movement-produced stimuli of Guthrie, or of Dollard and Miller. Verplanck (1954) remarks,

> Such inference-backward to quasi-independent variables in behavior seems to be characteristic of the work of many behavior theorists. . . . It is not impertinent to ask whether, since this is so regularly the case, will it ever be possible to develop a science of behavior in which laws relating data-language stimuli to data-language responses can be found. Is it necessarily the case that "stimuli" become response-inferred concepts, bearing no necessary relationship to what is put in front of the organism? [P. 286]

Verplanck's (1954) analysis of the stimulus in behavioristic learning theories makes it clear that the general phenomenological theorist and the self-concept theorist are not unique in having difficulties in defining their antecedents in terms of data language. Stimuli are, it seems, response-inferred constructs in all sorts of psychological theories. Thus, no fundamentally new methodological problems for phenomenology seem to be implied by the analysis of the antecedent up to this point.

Let us carry the analysis further, however. First let us note, as Jessor (1956) has pointed out, that stimulus characteristics can be defined (inferred) from the responses made by two classes of persons. (a) The experimenter defines the stimulus through his own observing responses (often entailing, of course, the use of instruments); and such defining observations can presumably be repeated by other experimenters. In this instance we customarily say that the stimulus antecedent is defined in data language. Let us call this stimulus inferred from the experimenter's response $Stim_E$. (b) When the experimenter varies $Stim_E$ and observes concomitant variations in the subject's responses, he may under certain conditions infer variations in perceptual processes within S. (Depending on his theoretical predilections, the experimenter may infer phenomenal percepts, physiological processes, or purely logical intervening constructs.) If the experimenter is a learning or motivation theorist, he recognizes that these inferred processes must be the direct antecedent of the subject's responses in his so-called S-R experiments relevant to laws of learning or motivation. Accordingly, it seems appropriate to label such inferred processes $Stim_S$. (Of course, the label $Stim_S$ is unique to the present analysis rather than being the notation used by any particular theorist to refer to such inferred processes.)

One way of looking at classical perception experiments is to say that they relate $Stim_E$ (stimulus as defined by the experimenter's response) to $Stim_S$ (stimulus as inferred from the subject's response). Both psychophysicists and Gestalt psychologists have done many experiments of this sort. It is obvious that we customarily call them "stimulus-response" experiments. Although the antecedent in such "stimulus-response" experiments is response-inferred, it is customarily called "stimulus" because it is inferred from the experimenter's, not the subject's, response. The subject's reaction to that "stimulus," that is, to $Stim_E$, is customarily called a "response" (but I am here repeatedly drawing attention to the fact that the theoretically oriented experimenter customarily assumes that this response indicates an inferred process which I call $Stim_S$). Regardless of customary terminology, we certainly have here a situation in which both the antecedent ($Stim_E$) and the consequent (subject's response from which $Stim_S$ is inferred) can be given in data language. The conclusion should be clear that both behavioristic and phenomenological stimulus variables are amenable to definition in data language.

If the experimentalist is a perception theorist, the establishment of a relationship between $Stim_E$ and $Stim_S$ is the main issue for him. However, if he is a learning or motivation theorist, he will be interested in going on, as I said above, to use $Stim_E$ (and, hence, response-inferred $Stim_S$) in further experiments involving other predicted behavioral consequences in which he is theoretically interested. For example, he can present S with one value of $Stim_E$ and condition him to give a galvanic skin response to it. From learning theory he predicts that, if he presents other values of $Stim_E$, the generalization of the galvanic skin response will follow a gradient of similarity along the $Stim_E$ dimension. He feels that it is sensible to make the prediction partly on the basis of the already established function which relates $Stim_E$ to $Stim_S$. If his prediction is confirmed, he feels that he has another stimulus-response, cause-effect law. Only to the extent that he has carried out such procedures can he correctly speak of cause-effect relationships between separately defined stimuli and responses.

As I said above, the Gestalt psychologist of perception, like other perception experimenters, has typically not been concerned with carrying his procedure beyond the first kind of stimulus-response experiments, establishing relationships between $Stim_E$ patterns and a percept (here $Stim_S$ inferred from S's response). Most of the actual experimental work of Gestaltists has been of this perceptual kind. However, in their more general theoretical discussions, Gestalt theorists have emphasized the principle that all behavior must be viewed as functionally related to he subject's perception of the situation (here labeled as $Stim_S$). A hypothetical example will illustrate how necessary it can be to establish a $Stim_E$-$Stim_S$ relationship before trying to predict relationships between $Stim_E$ and other behaviors. Suppose the experimenter has established a discriminative GSR to patterns containing curved lines as contrasted to patterns containing only straight lines. To test generalization, he presents two parallel straight lines with radiating additional straight lines. $Stim_E$ is defined in terms of the E's responses in preparing and measuring the stimulus pattern of straight lines. S gives a GSR to the straight-line pattern. Why? To explain or predict S's behavior in this instance one must utilize $Stim_S$, *not* $Stim_E$; that is, one needs to know that the S would say these parallel lines ($Stim_E$) look curved to him ($Stim_S$). If that had been established prior to the conditioning experiment, one could say that one had demonstrated cause-effect relationships between separately defined stimuli and responses. And in this case it would be particularly pertinent to use $Stim_S$ rather than $Stim_E$ as the basis of prediction.

But what about the self-concept theorist? Insofar as he is interested in the subject's phenomenal view of the environment, and its relation to theory-relevant behavior, it seems that the logic of the above experiments would apply to him. The difference lies in the practical difficulties in implementing this logic.

First of all, there are probably greater practical problems in establishing useful $Stim_E$ categories for the sorts of complex environmental patterns in which the phenomenological personality theorist is interested. Secondly, the practical difficulties of making the experimenter's stimulus-defining responses public and repeatable may be greater, due to the complexity of the environmental patterns which seem theoretically relevant (e.g., peers' treatments of the subject). And of course the practical difficulties of systematically presenting various values of any $Stim_E$ category would be much greater for the phenomenological personality theorist than for the psychophysicist or for the Gestalt psychologist who is interested in visual perception. Nevertheless, such studies should be undertaken. Nothing about the theory necessarily implies that such studies are theoretically irrelevant or impossible in principle.

Granted that the basic methodological logic of establishing $Stim_E$-$Stim_S$ relationships is the same in any *phenomenological* work, whether it be the experimental psychology of vision or phenomenological personality theory, what can one say about so-called unconscious perceptions of environment? Are there methodological parallels here, too, between self-concept psychology and the experimental psychology of perception, or does the former involve basically different methodological considerations?

On first thought, one might deem it appropriate to look at the experimental methodologies for defining *subception* or *perceptual defense*, since much of this work was based on the notion that S could somehow register "unconsciously" the emotionally upsetting nature of certain $Stim_E$ objects. As I said, an attempt is made in phenomenological work to find how $Stim_S$ is defined verbally, and to correspond such verbal reports with E's operational definition of

$Stim_E$. By contrast, "perceptual defense" was supposedly indicated by the *joint presence* of (a) correspondence between $Stim_E$ and $Stim_S$ when the latter was defined in terms of nonverbal indices such as GSR or size of duration threshold, and (b) a failure of correspondence between $Stim_E$ and $Stim_S$ when the latter was defined by S's verbal report. Personality theorists were particularly interested in this work insofar as it seemed to indicate what Eriksen (1958) called a "superdiscriminative unconscious" which somehow served a protective or defensive function. Unfortunately for those personality theorists, increasingly sophisticated analyses of this line of experimental work and its results render other explanations scientifically preferable to an explanation in terms of the operation of a superdiscriminative unconscious (Eriksen, 1958; Neisser, 1967). Accordingly, if a self-concept theorist wishes to hypothesize the operation of unconscious perceptual reactions to the far more complex $Stim_E$ objects presented to Ss by personality researchers, he will not find positive help in the experimental psychology of unconscious perception. He will, of course, be faced by the same unsolved methodological problems as face the experimentalist in that he must, in order to demonstrate unconscious perception in his own field, assume the burden of proof that the following conditions occur simultaneously: (a) verbal reports in reaction to $Stim_E$ fail to correspond with $Stim_E$, and (b) other behaviors show that S is reacting to $Stim_E$ in a manner different from his verbal reactions but congruent with E's definition ($Stim_E$).

When we turn to the kind of experiment in which $Stim_E$ antecedents (and therefore $Stim_S$) are related to theoretically relevant responses of the subject, we find again that the practical difficulties are greater for the self-concept and phenomenological personality theorist. For one thing, individual differences are expected to be much greater and to occur commonly in the $Stim_E$-$Stim_S$ relationships of the complex sort which interest the self-concept and phenomenological theorist. Furthermore, it is not clear how one can set up general criteria (comparable to the establishment of Ss' visual normality prior to the conditioning experiment described above), by which one can know that the $Stim_E$-$Stim_S$ function obtained on one subject will quite probably apply to another subject. It seems, therefore, that the phenomenological theorist must use the same subject in exploring the $Stim_E$-$Stim_S$ relationship that he uses in a further study which tests a hypothesis about the relationship between $Stim_E$ (therefore $Stim_S$) and a theoretically relevant response.

For example, the experimenter might first establish that Stimulus Person 1 ($Stim_{E1}$) and Stimulus Person 2 ($Stim_{E2}$) are regarded by the subject as, respectively, a friend of his ($Stim_{S1}$) and a mere acquaintance ($Stim_{S2}$). The experimenter could then test the hypothesis that a subject's self-rating behavior on a stated instrument is more affected by evaluations of him which allegedly come from Person 1 (friend) than by evaluations of him which allegedly come from Person 2 (acquaintance). One cannot safely assume that the same actual stimulus persons, $Stim_{E1}$ and $Stim_{E2}$, would be viewed as friend and acquaintance by another S. Therefore the $Stim_E$-$Stim_S$ relationship would have to be separately established for a second subject before going on to test the hypothesis with him.

Contemporary Characteristics of the Subjects

The behaviorist, if he wishes to, can enter into his if-then statements some observable characteristics of the subject such as age, sex, or IQ. In the learning equations of Hull (1951), for example, individual or species differences are to appear as constants. Such variables would be consistent with an objective, behavioristic approach.

The self-concept theorist, on the other hand, must use the subject's view of his own characteristics in his lawful if-then statements. Of course he may include objectively defined characteristics of S in his theoretical statements; but it is the use of S's view which has sometimes been said to differentiate the methodology required by self-concept theories from the methodology required by behavioristic theories. Does it?

First, we note that in either case an R-R design is implied; that is, a subject's characteristic or response is correlated with a behavior of that subject. But in the case of the objectively observable subject characteristic used by the behaviorist as an antecedent, it may seem that the experimenter defines it by his own responses; while the subject's view of himself which the phenomenologist uses as antecedent is defined partially in terms of the subject's responses. This differentiation cannot be defended, however, because in the last analysis, the operations used to define subject antecedents are essentially the same for the self-concept theorist and the behavior theorist. In both cases the experimenter specifies what observations of the subject he has made and under what conditions. For example, in determining an objective characteristic like IQ, the behaviorist asks specified questions and records and scores the subject's replies. In determining the subject's view of his own ability, the experimenter also asks specific questions and records and scores the subject's replies. If the behaviorist wishes to infer that IQ indexes ability, or if the self-concept theorist wishes to infer that the subject's description of himself indexes his self-concept of his ability, both are faced with the requirement of establishing the construct validity of their instruments. In any event, neither the R-R design of the behaviorist nor the R-R design of the phenomenologist is sufficiently controlled to permit the conclusion that cause-effect relationships have been established. Underwood (1957) has made very clear that the use of subject variables as antecedents necessarily involves ambiguities in interpreting the obtained results.

In addition to the ambiguities necessarily associated with R-R designs, there is much danger of artifactual contamination between the two measures being correlated. Probably such contamination has occurred frequently and is more difficult to avoid in the studies done by the self-concept theorists than in studies done by behavioristic psychologists. This merely implies the need for greater precaution in establishing operationally independent measures for the antecedent responses (from which S's self-concept is inferred), and the consequent responses. It does not seem to imply that a fundamental difference must obtain between behavioristic and phenomenological research.

Past Environmental Conditions, Stimuli, or Subject Characteristics

Self-concept theorists have sometimes been labelled "ahistorical," with the implication that studies involving past antecedents for present behavior are inappropriate to these theories. However, it is clear from an examination of these theories that they are by no means ahistorical, so genetic research designs are in order. The problems of defining past environmental or past subject characteristics in historical studies are in principle the same as those we have already discussed in connection with defining contemporaneous antecedent environmental or subject characteristics.

One fact about the studies which have actually been done to test genetic propositions should be noted. Most researchers who are interested in historical propositions have used R-R research designs

in which two *contemporaneous* responses are correlated. For example, the young adult's current view of his parents' opinions of hin.
is correlated with his present report of his self-concept. Such a design
is an inappropriate expedient for exploring the influence of the
parents' earlier opinions upon the child's self-concept. The design
may yield interesting exploratory information on S's current view
of parent and self, but it does not test a historical hypothesis in
which the researcher was primarily interested.

All in all, we do not believe that, *in principle*, the testing of
phenomenological or self-concept theories requires a methodologically distinct approach from that which is appropriate to testing
more behavioristic theories. Although R-R correlational designs may
be easier and may even be the only possible kind for a given proposition, controlled antecedent-consequent studies are as necessary
and appropriate in testing self-concept theory as in testing behavioristic theories.

3. Commonly Occurring Methodological Flaws or Questionable Methodological Practices in Self-Concept Research

Thus far I have considered methodological difficulties stemming
from the vague and incomplete state of present versions of self-
concept theory; and I have concluded that no methodological limitations are necessarily implied in principle by a more fully developed
self-concept theory, even though practical implementation of scientific method is much more difficult here than in some other areas
of psychology. I turn now to the question whether self-concept
research has been as methodologically sound as the present state of
theorizing and the availability of relevant methodological recommendations would permit. I argue that, although doing adequate
research relevant to self-concept theory is admittedly more practically difficult than in some other areas of psychology, there is
really no justification for the weaknesses found in a great many of
the studies.

Sources of Applicable Methodological Guidelines

Specifications for developing valid and reliable measurement
procedures and for controlled research design have been discussed
in numerous places. Among those which are relevant to self-concept
research and which appeared long enough ago to have been of pos-

sible guidance in the planning and execution of recently published studies are the American Psychological Association (1954, 1966), Campbell and Fiske (1959), Cronbach and Meehl (1955), Campbell and Stanley (1963), Underwood (1957), and Wylie (1961). The first four references are especially relevant to questions of measurement. Underwood (1957) covers a wide range of research designs and demonstrates effectively the limitations and difficulties encountered when trying to use subject variables as independent variables. Campbell (1957) and Campbell and Stanley (1963) do not deal with problems of control in R-R studies; but their analytical summaries of experimental and quasi-experimental designs have been developed with special reference to investigations performed in social and educational settings. Wylie (1961) focused particularly on methodological problems and requirements in self-concept research.

(More recent methodological recommendations which should be examined very closely by future self-concept researchers include Fiske, 1971, regarding measurement of theoretical constructs in personality study; Cronbach, 1971, regarding validity of measurement; Stanley, 1971, regarding reliability of measurement; and Campbell, 1969, regarding sources and control of methodological "artifacts," that is, those characteristics of method which provide plausible explanations of findings alternate to the explanation[s] E wishes to offer.)

COMMON METHODOLOGICAL SHORTCOMINGS IN EXTANT RESEARCH

Unfortunately much of the research in the area of self-concept has not shown the effects of studying and taking seriously whatever specifications and recommendations were available at the time of the execution of the research. There are so many particular ways in which research methods or research reports can be inadequate that space does not permit a detailed analysis here. However, one can make the general statement that, despite some improvements in published researches, the method in the majority of studies in the area of self-concept theory has been inadequate in one or more important respects. Unfortunately, the kinds of methodological shortcomings one finds are essentially the same as those I pointed out more than ten years ago (Wylie, 1961).

I list here the most commonly occurring kinds of shortcomings.

1. The method used is often so vaguely indicated as to prevent interpretation and analysis and to make replication impossible.

This is particularly unfortunate in a relatively new research area where well-known, standardized methods are not available. Since journal space is limited, more use should be made of the facilities of the American Documentation Institute. But even within the enforced limitations of journal space, more detail could and should be included.

2. There is very common use of measures having undemonstrated, inadequate, or even entirely unexplored construct validity. Problems include failure to take into account the requirements for establishing construct validity, and errors of omission and commission in validity-relevant research. These problems are considered in detail in chapter 3.

3. In practice there has been heavy reliance on R-R designs to test what are really antecedent-consequent hypotheses.

4. In some studies there are not enough different control groups to hold constant or account for all the important irrelevant variables. Frequently the inherent characteristics of the control Ss, their method of choice, and/or their treatment is inappropriate. Of course where control groups are inadequate in any of these ways, it cannot be concluded that the dependent variable is a function of the alleged independent variable. Factors left uncontrolled in one or another study include all those listed as extraneous by Campbell (1957) and considered in great detail by various authors in Rosenthal and Rosnow's (1969) recent book on artifacts in behavioral research. Frequently no information is given as to matching or randomizing of groups. Thus, in many studies one cannot pinpoint just which factors may afford alternate interpretations of the findings. The intrinsic methodological faults associated with matching groups rather than forming them randomly have not been sufficiently recognized.

5. In many studies there is a strong possibility of artifactual contamination between independent and dependent variables, due to such things as overlapping instruments, failure to use blind judgments, effects of common response sets, and use of verbal reports not only to index self-concept dimensions but to measure behaviors allegedly related to self-concept as well. Artifactual contamination is especially likely to occur when two-part scores are used to measure either or both variables.

6. Various types of overgeneralization occur. In their conclusions and discussions, Es sometimes do not respect the limitations im-

posed by their restricted hypotheses, measuring instruments, groups, and procedures. Worthy of special note is the tendency to use very artificial, brief, and often trivial laboratory manipulations in purported tests of propositions about the effects of long-term, systematic influences (e.g., social learning, peers' opinions) on the self-concept. Also especially noteworthy in self-concept research is the heavy reliance on self-report measures as indices of the essentially nonverbal behaviors E hypothesizes are related to self-concept. Thus E generalizes from verbal to nonverbal behaviors, with no empirical warrant for this.

7. In some studies it appears that psychological generalizations are based on findings of unclear statistical significance. This is due to E's failure to adhere to commonly accepted statistical conventions. (a) One-tailed tests have been used in situations where theoretical predictions are not unequivocal and where "reverse" trends are interpreted ad hoc by E. (b) Separate replicative interpretations of hypotheses are sometimes based on data which are nonindependent (e.g., repeated tests of the same Ss with correlated instruments). (c) Within any one study which yields many significance tests, five in one hundred such tests may be significant at the .05 level by chance only. Nevertheless, some Es have assigned psychological interpretations to such findings. (d) A special problem of this sort involves establishing a "chance" base line when trying to determine S's accuracy in predicting a particular person's behavior or when trying to determine the degree of similarity between S's self-concept and that of a theoretically relevant other person. What degree of correctness or similarity might be expected by "chance"? What degree of correctness might be expected if S predicts another unique person's behavior on the basis of his stereotype about others in general, or others in the predictee's age, sex, or social group? To what extent does the similarity between two particular individuals of special interest to E exceed the similarity to be expected between any two persons from the respective groups to which these individuals belong? Of course the latter two questions require control groups of predictees and are not simply questions of statistical interpretation, based on an assumption about "chance" base lines.

8. Most studies have been one-shot affairs with no replication or even cross-validation of instruments. It is probable that some of the statistically significant findings are actually due to chance and could not be replicated. Perhaps some of the significant findings may

depend on particular idiosyncracies of procedure and instrument which are theoretically irrelevant. And, of course, null findings obtained from a single study are uninterpretable.

Campbell (1957) has argued against exact replication on the grounds that replication continues the confounding of (a) theoretically relevant aspects of the independent variable and the observational techniques with (b) specific artifacts of unknown influence. On the other hand, he recognizes the fact that only confusion can result from trying to synthesize results obtained from heterogeneous, unreplicated results. He suggests that a "transition experiment" may be useful. In such an experiment, the "theory-independent" aspects of the independent variable and the observational techniques are varied in a multiple design, one segment of which exactly replicates the original experiment (Campbell, 1957, p. 310).

9. The use of demographic or sociological independent variables which have unknown relevance to psychological variables precludes clear psychological interpretation of obtained associations.

Use of Deception in Self-Concept Research

Finally, I consider in relation to self-concept research a group of methodological techniques which have received much recent attention, namely, the use of deception in one or more aspects of the research procedure (Argyris, 1968; Aronson & Carlsmith, 1968; Baumrind, 1964; Campbell, 1969; Golding & Lichtenstein, 1970; Kelman, 1967; McGuire, 1969; Milgram, 1964; Ring, 1967; Silverman, Shulman, & Wiesenthal, 1970; Stollak, 1967; Stricker, 1967; Stricker, Messick, & Jackson, 1967, 1969; Walster, Berscheid, Abrahams, & Aronson, 1967).

Stricker (1967) has shown that deception techniques have apparently been used more commonly in some kinds of personality and social-psychology research than in others. However, it has not yet been estimated how often deception has been used in self-concept research. My impression is that it has been used an appreciable number of times. Some of the deception techniques seem patently innocuous, but others have involved salient aspects of S's feelings and self-concept.

It is necessary to raise both ethical and methodological issues in the use of deception; but they cannot be discussed entirely separately because some of the ethical implications stem from the likelihood that common use of deception in psychological research will fundamentally alter the methodological nature of research situations in the future.

Several different ethical questions need to be considered:

1. Which deception techniques, if any, unreasonably violate the S's rights to privacy and to voluntary participation in decisions affecting their lives?

2. Will Ss be psychologically harmed by certain deceptions? For example, are Ss especially likely to be harmed by studies which give them false feedback about their personality characteristics or performances? May it be especially harmful to lead Ss to do things within the experiment which they would have preferred to believe they were incapable of doing, at least under such circumstances (e.g., to conform, be cruel, show gullibility, or exhibit prejudice)?

3. Does "debriefing" the subjects counteract all possible harmful psychological consequences induced in them by some aspect of the deception? Will debriefing create undesirable effects when Ss are thus brought to realize they have been gulled?

4. If debriefing is used, will the debriefing affect Ss in a way which will render them unsuitable to serve as Ss in future research studies (because they will now be suspicious rather than naïvely and wholeheartedly cooperative in following E's instructions)? These future studies might be deemed more important to science than the one in which Ss have been deceived. Moreover, the E performing these subsequent studies might not realize he was dealing with "suspicious" Ss, so that he might be misled in the interpretation of his findings.

5. Will debriefing and possible consequent communications from Ss to others concerning the deceptive nature of the experiment eventually debase the reputation of all psychological researchers, including those who have not used deceit? Will it therefore interfere with E-S relationships in future research and preclude execution of interpretable experiments in many areas of psychology, even those experiments not using deception techniques? May this even contribute to debasing the credibility of language in social interactions generally?

6. If one or more of the above unwanted effects are created, who is wise and impartial enough to determine whether possible benefits to scientific knowledge from a given study or line of research which might seem to require the use of deception may reasonably be expected to outweigh the unwanted side-effects of the deception?

Beyond these ethical questions, some primarily methodological and empirical queries must be given serious conceptual and research consideration. While one would like to be able to answer these questions on empirical grounds, the available methodological research on deceit and debriefing is sparse, not always capable of direct generalization to self-concept research, and in some instances seriously flawed methodologically, hence uninterpretable.

1. Have the deception techniques had the desired effect on *S*s, that is, have *S*s been deceived? Stricker (1967) showed that few *E*s have bothered even to try to answer this question about their experiments which employed deception. In these few researches, the post-experimental inquiry techniques and criteria for *S*s' having been deceived were inadequate for the purpose of inferring *S*s' state of deception. Golding and Lichtenstein (1970) used confederates to "tip off" some of their *S*s to *E*'s deceptions. They showed that *S*'s likelihood of revealing his knowledge of *E*'s deception techniques depended on whether *E*'s instructions before the postexperimental inquiry stressed the importance to *E* of the "scientific integrity" of his experiment or the importance to *E* of finishing his data collection soon. In either case, relatively few of the *S*s who know of *E*'s deception techniques "confessed" their knowledge. This clearly suggests that even under relatively ideal conditions, postexperimental inquiries overestimate the degree to which the deception techniques had the desired effects of fooling *S*s.

Intuitively one can think of various reasons why *S*s may pretend that they did not know of *E*'s deception; e.g., *S* may want to please *E* and he feels that *E* wishes to consider his techniques successful; or *S* does not want to admit that even for a portion of the experimental session he was gullible. Conversely, it seems plausible that *S* may avoid admitting naïveté by pretending he had been suspicious of deception throughout the experiment, even though it was only the postexperimental inquiry which aroused his suspicions.

2. Assuming that *E* decides to use deception techniques, what methodological recommendations can be made to increase the effectiveness of the techniques and to evaluate their effectiveness in misleading *S*? In the absence of empirical bases for answering this question, the reader may find helpful the suggestions by Aronson and Carlsmith (1968); Campbell (1969); and Stricker, Messick, and Jackson (1969).

3. How effective is debriefing in restoring *S*s to their preexperi-

mental state, which is what most *E*s seem to assume they have accomplished by debriefing? The term *preexperimental state* is vague and obviously covers a wide range of possibilities; but important aspects of it include *S*s' preexperimental levels of anxiety and self-esteem. There is virtually no empirical information on this question. One experiment by Walster, Berscheid, Abrahams, and Aronson (1967) suggested that a very thorough attempt to debrief *S*s following presentation of false feedback information regarding their social impressions may not be effective immediately and may for certain personality types be ineffective even after a longer time delay. In the absence of additional empirical information, it seems intuitively plausible to believe that debriefing quite often does not accomplish its purpose of restoring *S*s' original opinions of themselves. For one thing, when debriefing inevitably reveals *E*'s deception, the credibility of the debriefing itself may well be doubted by *S*, leading to *S*'s inability to be convinced by the debriefing. Also, Walster et al. (1967) have suggested a kind of situation in which *E*'s supposedly false feedback might be in the long run more credible to *S* than the supposedly true debriefing information. In this hypothetical kind of situation, *S*'s recent preexperimental real-life experiences might have raised serious questions in his mind about his standing on a certain psychological dimension (e.g., creativity) about which *E* is supposedly informing him during the course of the experiment. If *E*'s actually false evaluation of *S* accords with these doubts, *S* might find such false information more credible than the debriefing information. Certainly, if *S* was naïve and trusting before the experiment, debriefing cannot reasonably be expected to restore him to that state, which is probably the ideal condition needed by the next *E* who wishes him to serve as a subject.

That the combined experience of deception and debriefing may have effects on *S*s' behavior in later studies is suggested by the results of Silverman, Shulman, and Wiesenthal (1970), who experimentally deceived and debriefed one group and gave a second group a memory study without deception. In a second phase of the research, both groups were given the same series of standard personality tests. The obtained group differences in the second phase led the authors to suggest that "the deception experience sensitized subjects to possible ulterior purposes of experiments, increasing evaluation apprehension and their tendencies to present themselves as psychologically strong and stable [p. 209]." However, since *N*s were relatively small and it is not stated that groups were formed at random, there is a possibility that significant second-session differences on the personality tests may have represented consistent intergroup differences with respect to the personality variables rather than the effects of the alleged independent variable (deception-debriefing) on the personality-test scores.

4. In consideration of the many difficult methodological and ethical problems entailed in deception procedures, is it possible that the most defensible methodological approach would be to eliminate, or perhaps postpone, introduction of deception techniques?

Some would argue for eliminating deception even if this means seriously curtailing the number of problems which could then be examined scientifically. Alternately, others have argued that deception can be eliminated in at least some research by substituting role playing by Ss as a means to examine the influence of certain variables which had previously been studied with the use of deception. For example, Roger Brown (1962) wrote, "The role-playing design does seem to permit the testing of detailed implications in a model of attitude change without relying on elaborate techniques of deception. We believe that a role-playing subject will behave in a way that corresponds more closely to the life situation than a hoodwinked subject will [p. 74]." In 1965 he reaffirmed this view, saying, "Role playing offers an alternative to deception. Instead of concealing experimental manipulations one can reveal them and ask subjects to help [p. 580]." Kelman (1967) also suggested that the substitution of role playing for deception is a possibility worth exploring seriously.

Bem (1965) presented empirical results in which role-playing Ss reproduced the same data trends previously obtained from deceived Ss. However, empirical studies show that such replications are not always obtained (e.g., Greenberg, 1967; Jones, Lindner, Kiesler, Zanna, & Brehm, 1968). Therefore on empirical grounds alone, the defensibility of substituting role playing for deception must be questioned.

So far as the principle of using role playing as a substitute for deception is concerned, Bem (1968) stated, "No 'as if' methodology, including the technique of interpersonal simulation, is an adequate substitute for the intensive study of the actual situation being modeled [p. 273]." Thus he agrees with Jones et al. (1968) in their opinion: "Apparently, role playing does not offer a completely viable alternative to the study of involved subjects. The results of 'as if' experiments, while they may be most informative about processes of social perception . . . are not a substitute for the painstaking study of involved subjects [p. 268]." Freedman (1969) has developed a very cogent argument why the use of role playing in order to study problems not accessible to traditional methods (including those ordinarily studied by deception techniques) is futile in principle. He points out that such attempted use of role playing is based on the very assumptions which science rejects, namely, that anyone's *guesses* about the influence of a variable may never be safely assumed to be the same as findings resulting from the actual manipulation of the variable.[1]

If role playing cannot legitimately be substituted for deception techniques, can the use of deception techniques at least be postponed? That is, can we further our scientific knowledge by first exhausting the possibilities of testing our propostions by methods which do not involve deception? Then, perhaps, consideration of deception techniques might be more defensible for exploring the remaining propositions.

---

1. The reader who is interested in a detailed review of opinion and evidence regarding role playing as an alternate to deception should see Miller (1972).

3

Analysis of Problems in Measuring Self-Referent Constructs

The worth of research in any field obviously depends in large part on the success with which the investigator has measured the variables he is trying to relate. Accordingly, since it is the purpose of this book to evaluate self-concept research critically, we must consider the sorts of instrumentation problems one encounters, and we must set up some guidelines by which one can evaluate the state of measurement in this area. It is necessary to consider several aspects of measurement which, though inextricably intertwined, cannot be discussed simultaneously: construct validity, scaling, and reliability. For reasons that will become apparent in the course of developing these topics, I shall take them up in the order just stated.

Throughout this chapter I discuss problems common to measuring self-referent variables, including the phenomenal field, the phenomenal self, and self-referent attitudes not specifically related to a phenomenal dimension by those who postulate them. Later on I consider some particular problems encountered in trying to measure some of the more specific constructs, for example, self-esteem, self-consistency, and self-other orientation. All of the general comments in the immediately following paragraphs will be applicable to the evaluation of specific instruments when they are discussed in the next chapter.

A. Why Construct Validity is the Necessary Kind of Validity

Problems of measuring the phenomenal field and self-referent attitudes may be seen as essentially those of establishing *construct validity,* in Cronbach and Meehl's (1955) sense of this term. Construct validity is necessary because, by definition, S's cognitions and attitudes about himself (whether or not one considers their relationship to the phenomenal dimension important) are private and beyond direct observation by the investigator. It is *not* sufficient to demonstrate that one's self-referent measures have "predictive" or "concurrent" validity in the sense that an MMPI scale, for example, may be shown to discriminate nosological categories without an explanation of why the association is obtained.

In order to index constructs involving S's phenomenal fields or phenomenal self, E must use some form of self-report response made by S as a basis for his inferences. In practice, this self-report behavior has usually taken the form of a verbal response or some sort of a choice response when S is instructed to indicate specified conscious processes. Despite their many limitations, these methods seem to be the only kinds appropriate to this type of construct. That is, if we use projective test, autonomic, or other nonverbal responses from S without telling him of our intent to infer his conscious processes (as, for example, Combs, Soper, & Courson, 1963 have done), we have no way of knowing whether such responses reflect conscious or unconscious cognitions and feelings.

Phenomenologists would like to assume that S's self-report responses are determined by his phenomenal field. However, we know that it would be naïve to take this for granted, since it is obvious that such responses may also be influenced by (a) S's intent to select what he wishes to reveal to the E; (b) S's intent to say that he has attitudes or perceptions which he does not have; (c) S's response habits, particularly those involving introspection and the use of language; (d) a host of situational and methodological factors which may not only induce variations in (a), (b), and (c), but may exert other more superficial influences on the responses obtained. In later sections of this chapter these problems are considered in more detail.

Those who think it unnecessary and unfruitful to relate self-referent constructs to the phenomenal-nonphenomenal dimension presumably have justification for using behavioral indicants other than self-report, for example, muscular intensity of striving behaviors in level-of-aspiration situations, or proximity of circles chosen to represent self in relation to specified others. However, they, too, must face the probability that many of the irrelevant variables listed above may be determining Ss' responses, lowering their validity as an indicant of the theorist's construct. For example, intensity of motivation to succeed in a level-of-aspiration situation must be very imperfectly indicated by the single index, intensity of muscular activities, since it is well known that individuals differ in their characteristic patterns of arousal indicants when motivated. Moreover, individual differences in the muscular-tension measurements may be determined to an unknown degree by situational factors such as individual differences in Ss' responses to the instruments used for measuring tension and in their interpretations of the instructions E has given them in order to induce them to accept the task as relevant to their self-esteem. In short, problems of identifying, minimizing, and taking into account the influence of irrelevant response determiners must be dealt with whether or not the index purports to measure a self-referent construct specifically related to the conscious-unconscious dimension.

B. Obtaining Items for an Instrument to Measure Self-Referent Constructs

Obviously, item selection for any instrument designed to measure a construct must be based on the maker's (or others') expert judgments about the characteristics and scope of the construct. For example, in the case of *global* self-regard, there is at least implicitly involved a notion of *overall* self-evaluation. Presumably this is based somehow on S's synthesized self-appraisal across a wide range of attributes. In reaching this global appraisal, S must have been influenced by (a) the salience of each attribute to him; (b) his desired or tolerable standing on the attribute; (c) his actual standing on the attribute. The instrument maker must decide what range of attributes to try to include in his proposed measure. Or perhaps E is interested in some more restricted aspect of self-concept, such as S's judgments of the strength of one or more of his needs in Murray's rationally defined need system, or S's judgment of his own standing with reference to a factorially defined cluster of attributes. It is clear that considerable expert knowledge will be required to attempt to operationalize any of these sorts of self-referent constructs.

It is generally agreed that the problem of obtaining items which will acceptably represent any theoretical construct is extremely important, since the chosen items will determine in part the generalizability of the research based on the items. For example, Brunswik (1956) has argued that stimulus or test-item sampling in all areas of psychology is of equal importance to the more usual sampling of populations of persons. In his analysis of the way in which psychological research designs should be elaborated to include both kinds of sampling and thus become more "representative," he contends that stimulus or test-item sampling has been used in practice more than it has been explicitly accepted or analyzed in discussions of method. Specifically applying this point to personality testing and self-concept measurement, Mowrer (1953b, p. 358) states,

> Whereas much attention has been given to the logic of sampling universes or populations of persons, little attention has been given to sampling theory where test or occasions universes are concerned. . . . [and] the results obtained by the use of these (e.g., Q and O) techniques may vary widely with the nature of the universe of statements (or trait names) from which items are selected.

Guttman (1950, pp. 80–81), in connection with his theoretical development of problems of scaling, states,

> It is therefore essential to inquire into the nature of the *universe of all possible questions of the same content,* and to determine what inferences can be made about that universe that will not depend on the particular sample of questions used.

Although there is consensus as to the importance of the problem, no unequivocal solution can be presented. Some psychometricians (e.g., Cronbach, Rajaratnam, & Gleser, 1963) have argued that a test maker should define an item population covering the range of attributes involved in his construct, and sample randomly from the item population so that statistical procedures applicable to random sampling may be applied and the generalizability of the findings may be estimated with the use of this statistical model. Others (e.g., Stephenson, 1953; Neff & Cohen, 1967; Wittenborn, 1961) have recommended stratified sampling of test items from different factorial levels. Loevinger (1965), however, has argued cogently that defining a population of items is manifestly impossible. Accordingly, neither random nor stratified samples from such a population can be drawn. Cronbach et al. (1963) agree that these difficulties exist; but they seem to feel satisfied with the following practical recommendations similar to those of Loevinger (1965), Fiske (1966), and others: The best available procedure for the test maker is to *begin* by giving a "literary" definition of his construct, making it as unequivocal as he can, and specifying the boundaries between constructs as clearly as possible. Available factor analytic studies, "rational" systems such as Murray's, or E's own notions not necessarily referring to available research may be sources of ideas for these literary definitions. Stimulus-item pools thought to be relevant to those definitions should be prepared, evaluated by expert judges, and editorially culled and revised. A minimum requirement should be that the construct be defined explicitly enough so that experts can agree on whether or not specific items are exemplars of the concept. The results of such analyses may then be subjected to converging operations such as those outlined below, with revisions and reapplication of converging operations as appropriate.

C. SCALING

Let us assume that an investigator has succeeded in refining and making explicit his ideas about his construct and has decided upon an item or group of items which seem to have promise for eliciting responses indicative of the construct. He still must decide on that crucial step in the measurement process, the rules by which numbers will be assigned to Ss. Presumably Ss vary with respect to the construct, if only with regard to its presence or absence; so 1 and 0 would be the simplest possible level of measurement. However, if it is possible to differentiate among Ss along a multistep scale pertinent to the construct, information is thrown away when only a presence-absence measurement is made. E would wish to use as precise a scale as possible (i.e., ratio as opposed to interval; interval as opposed to ordinal; ordinal as opposed to nominal), because the more precise his scale, the better the chances of developing precise generalizations using the instrument as one of his measures.

In self-concept measurement, researchers assume that numerical values representing, for example, degrees of overall self-esteem, or degrees of self-perceived dominance, or degrees of overall self-ideal discrepancy, indicate at least ordinal positions of Ss along the hypothesized self-concept continuum. Statistical treatments applied to the data often imply that E believes he has made even more precise measurement than ordinal. However, two things make it questionable whether even the crudest ordinal measurement has been obtained by E's method. First, there is typically no assurance that Ss are actually using the same subjective dimension that E has in mind; and second, there is no assurance that successive scale steps have a uniform meaning from S to S.

The situation is far from simple; and presently no one can map a guaranteed road to interval scaling of self-concept continua. However, the fact that we cannot presently envisage how to attain perfection does not imply that we must give up hope of improvement and settle for the present highly inadequate state of affairs. Measurement of self-concept dimensions could be appreciably improved if Es developed and analyzed their instruments in the light of available information regarding scaling. The immediately following paragraphs clarify the situation with respect to what is desirable and possible to attain.

Many self-concept instruments have multiple items. For example, this is the case with Q sorts, semantic differential scales, graphic rating scales, rating scales with descriptive adjectives to demarcate scale ranges, questionnaires in which S says how frequently the item characterizes him, and Guttman scales. The scores obtained on such an instrument necessarily involve a composite of many items, each of which represents a separate scale on which S must rate himself. Thus it is necessary for E to decide how to assign a number to each S to represent S's position on the particular subjective dimension represented by that item. The constructor of the instrument defines the dimension verbally for S. E, then, in effect, asks S to regard himself as a "stimulus" and to place this "stimulus" on the subjective dimension E has described. To follow these directions, S has to do two things: (a) develop a conception of what content and situation the item refers to, and (b) develop some psychological metric of the dimension on which he is going to place himself.

In the typical instrument, unfortunately, S has to decide for himself the meaning of the wording of the item, for example, which of various meanings of *responsible* is intended by E. That individual differences in interpretation of the item's meaning play an important part in determining S's choice of where to place himself on E's scale has been demonstrated by Loehlin (1961, 1967) and by Kuncel (in press), using differing methods of studying the problem. Therefore, score differences which are usually interpreted as inter-S differences in self-perceived location along E's subjective dimension may instead be inter-S differences in the meaning of the subjective dimension upon which each S has scaled himself. This, of course, is a question of construct validity.

Moreover, in the typical instrument, S has to decide for himself to what situations the items refer. For example, is he supposed to rate his degree of self-confidence with reference to dating, participation in sports, or getting along on his job? Is he supposed to take into account both the situations where it would be appropriate and inappropriate to feel depressed? Since the instructions typically do not answer these questions for S, he supposedly places his self-rating on the item with reference to an unknown combination of situational referents. As I point out below, Fiske (1966) argues that lack of structure increases error variance, since each S makes his own, unknown interpretation of word meanings and situational referents. Hunt (1965) contends that omission of situational referents in personality measurement instruments is probably largely responsible for the low predictability from such measures to behavior, because $S \times$ Situation Interaction accounts for more variance in personality scores than does the main effect of Ss. Here, then, is another reason why score differences which are usually interpreted as inter-S differences in self-perceived location along E's subjective dimension may instead represent something else—in this instance, inter-S differences in situational referent. So again we have a question of construct validity.

An additional problem arises in the case of many instruments, namely, that S must, at least by implication, place himself on each scale with respect to how a hypothetical reference group would be distributed on the scale. The range of the subjective dimension covered by the scale obviously depends on the reference group S uses to anchor it. Again, unfortunately, the instructions given by the scale's constructor or by E usually do not suffice to assure that all Ss will choose their self-descriptive locations with respect to a common reference group. Accordingly, inter-S score differences which are usually interpreted as inter-S differences in self-perceived location along E's subjective dimension may instead be inter-S differences in the range of the dimension to which S is referring himself.

Assuming that the aforementioned ambiguities with respect to word usage, situations, and reference groups were at least fairly satisfactorily handled by means of much clearer, more structured communications from E to S, one would still need to explore further the quantitative meaning of the successive scale steps which S is asked to use for each item. How can E interpret in meaningful numerical terms S's placement of himself if E knows nothing of S's psychological metric for the dimension used? How can E interpret the difference between the self-placements of two Ss if he does not know they were using the same psychological metric? Similarly, how can *E* interpret a difference between *S*'s self-placement and his ideal-self placement if he does not know about *S*'s psychological metric?

Although Guilford (1954), Stevens (1957), Stevens and Galanter (1957), and Torgerson (1958) have discussed how psychophysical methods can be used to derive scales for subjective dimensions, only one of the instruments covered in the present review has been refined by the application of such techniques (Rosenberg's, 1965, Self-Esteem Scale). Perhaps the failure to try to make use of available techniques stems in part from the failure to understand how the problems of *S*'s metric manifest themselves in self-concept measurement, and how available scaling techniques could be applied in order to increase our precision of measurement.

Let us consider an example in order to show how ambiguities in *S*'s metrics arise and to examine possible ways of reducing such ambiguities. Suppose that we have an item involving a subjective dimension, the meaning of which has been adequately communicated to *S*. Suppose, also, that *S* is asked to use one of seven scale positions on a line to describe himself with respect to the given subjective dimension. The scale points may be equally spaced along the line with only the two ends marked, for example, *very characteristic of me, not at all characteristic of me.* Presumably the equal-appearing intervals along the visual rating scale are intended to induce *S* to imagine the corresponding subjective continuum to be divided into equal-appearing intervals. However, there is no assurance that *S*s are thus induced to imagine the subjective continuum to be equally divided, especially since the instructions typically do not ask them to try to do so. Thus, each *S* may develop his own interpretation of the quantitative meaning of the scale intervals. Here, then, is yet another reason why score differences which are usually interpreted as inter-*S* differences in self-perceived location along *E*'s subjective dimension may instead represent something else—in this case, inter-*S* differences in interpretation of the quantitative meaning of the scale intervals.

What steps should be taken to guide all *S*s to a uniform interpretation of the steps on the subjective continuum? As I have already indicated, it is not sufficient to provide steps that are equally spaced visually along a line. Labeling of each point on the line could be helpful in getting inter-*S* uniformity in interpretation.

If *S* is to compare himself to a specified hypothetical reference group, the labels might refer to percents, tenths, quarters, or halves of the group. In some instruments, however, *S* is asked, in effect, to consider the occasions relevant to the subjective dimension and report the degree to which the subjective dimension has characterized him, considering those occasions. For this purpose, *E*s sometimes employ probabilistic labels for the scales, for example, *frequently*, or *sometimes*. However, the use of such adverbial labels for scale points is not enough, since *S*s may differ regarding their quantitative referents for these labels unless more specific guidance is given. One way to improve uniformity of interpretations of the "degree" of the characteristic implied in a scale step is to supply more definite quantitative labels for the scale points, for example, *100% of relevant occasions, 50% of relevant occasions*.

An alternate way to increase precision in specifying the quantitative meaning of scale steps is suggested by the work of Cliff (1959), Dudek (1959), and Howe (1962). Cliff's and Dudek's work involved the scaling of the evaluative values which *S*s assigned to person-relevant adjectives when these adjectives were modified and when they were combined with each of nine common adverbs of degree (e.g., *somewhat, rather, quite, very*). Using the successive-intervals method, Howe (1962) scaled the pleasantness-unpleasantness values of person-relevant adjectives when these adjectives were (a) unmodified; or (b) combined with each of several probabilistic adverbs, for example, *doubtfully, certainly*; or (c) combined with each of several adverbs of degree (intensive adverbs), for example, *rather, quite*. Cliff (1959) found an almost perfect linear relationship between scale values obtained by the paired-comparison and successive-intervals methods, while Dudek (1959) reports that the sets of scale values resulting from successive-intervals and constant-sum methods were not linearly related. Nevertheless, at least the rank order correspondence of scale values Dudek obtained from successive-intervals and constant-sum methods was extremely high.

These researches are considered here because of their indirect implications for self-concept researchers rather than because the obtained scale values may be used directly to measure differences of degree to which *S*s see themselves being characterized by a self-concept item. The important point is that there is apparently considerable communality among *S*s with respect to the quantifying effects indicated by certain intensive or probabilistic adverbs. Therefore, such adverbs might be employed to label scale points on a scale which Ss are asked to use for self-description. Before such an application of Dudek's, Cliff's, and Howe's work is justified, however, the following points must be considered:

1. In the development of any given self-concept scale, the quantifying effects of the selected adverbs for the particular items used in the self-concept instrument must be established by appropriate pilot work.

2. If the selected adverbs prove to lead to unequally spaced increments in subjective degree, correspondingly unequally spaced points along the scale line might appropriately be provided to Ss in conjunction with the respective adverbial labels.

3. Since adverb-adjective interaction was found by Dudek (1959) and by Cliff (1959) (e.g., the adverb *pretty* had a different modifying effect on the degree of scaled favorability of the adjectives *good* and *bad*), there may be adverb-item interaction in self-descriptive scales as well. If pilot work shows this to be the case, adverbs yielding little or no such interaction should be chosen; or, if this cannot be done, the scale for each self-concept item may have to be marked off into intervals appropriate to the adverb-item interaction determined for that item.

4. Even though clearly discriminable scale steps may be represented by each chosen adverb, one must always remember that such steps represent *mean* scale values, and each individual S will not view the steps in exactly the same way. Serious confusion can arise if E fails to remember this point about scaling, as exemplified below in the section on social desirability. Nevertheless, if researchers take care to choose adverbs with highly different mean "degree" values and minimal inter-S dispersions about these means, they can bring about a great improvement in self-concept measurement, as compared to bypassing the problems of scaling altogether.

5. As indicated above, scales developed by the various alternate psychophysical methods of scaling intensive adverbs were not all linearly related. Therefore, it is plausible that this lack of linear relationship may occur in scaling the modifying effects of intensive or probabilistic adverbs in self-concept scales. If such lack of linear relationship is found, it implies that scales derived from at least one of these psychophysical methods must not be an interval scale. Until we determine why different methods lead to somewhat different scales, "a rigorous operational approach in interpreting and using

variously derived scales seems indicated [Dudek, 1959, p. 547]."
Nevertheless, the application of any one of these methods should,
at the very least, considerably increase the uniformity with which
Ss construe the metric with respect to which they are asked to locate
themselves. Any one of these methods should result in at least an
ordinal scale, and perhaps something more precise. They should
result in an appreciable improvement in the degree to which inter-S
differences in self-description indicate actual differences in Ss' subjective locations along a self-concept dimension.

All that I have said thus far pertains to improving the scaling
of a single self-concept item. As mentioned above, most self-concept
instruments have multiple items allegedly pertaining to a given
dimension, for example, self-esteem, self-perceived dominance; and
S places himself on a continuum pertaining to each item. Typically,
E sums the numerical values of S's self-placements across items to
obtain an overall score. No attention is paid to differences in dispersion of ratings from item to item, so items with maximal dispersion
automatically carry the most weight in determining inter-S differences in total scores. Moreover, no attention is paid to the fact that
Ss differ with respect to the salience of the various items in determining their overall self-conception with respect to the overall
dimension, for example, self-esteem or dominance. That is, a sum
does not take such differences into account by weighting items differentially according to their perceived salience for S. The sum is a simple expedient in the face of ignorance and should be so recognized.

Steps could be taken to weight item ratings differentially according to their perceived salience to S, but this has not yet been tried.
There would be, of course, no external validity criterion against
which the purported improvement produced by such weighting
could be tested. However, it seems reasonable to suppose that scores
developed on such a basis would relate more strongly than would
simple-sum scores to behaviors which are hypothesized to be a function of the construct the total score purports to index, for example,
self-esteem.

Although problems of summation impose limitations on the
interpretability of total scores, such summed scores could be much
more valid and reliable than they now are if the sums were based
on ratings for separate dimensions measured under the following
conditions: (a) there is uniformity among Ss regarding the meaning
of each subjective dimension and the situational and group refer-

ents relevant to it; (b) there is uniformity among Ss regarding the quantitative meaning of the scale steps S is to use in reporting his self-perceived location on the dimension. If progress is to be made in self-concept research, much can and should be done to improve our instruments in these two respects.

D. CONVERGING OPERATIONS FOR EXPLORING AND IMPROVING CONSTRUCT VALIDITY

As I mentioned in chapter 2, self-concept theorists could profit from examining and applying relevant analyses made by psychologists working in other areas. For example, the difficulties and requirements encountered in attempting to measure self-referent constructs validly seem to be similar to those already encountered, and to some extent analyzed, by experimental psychologists working in the field of perception. Garner, Hake, and Eriksen (1956) have noted the fundamental problem of identifying the influence of *perceptual* processes on responses made in perceptual experiments (as opposed to other influences on response availability and production). It is useful in the present discussion of processes influencing Ss' self-concept reports or other self-revealing behaviors to draw analogies with their analysis of processes influencing Ss' perceptual responses. Before going into details of this sort, however, we need to remind ourselves of pertinent general methodological requirements for establishing construct validity, as these have been stated by Garner, Hake, and Eriksen (1956), by Cronbach and Meehl (1955), and by Campbell and Fiske (1959), among others.

Garner, Hake, and Eriksen have pointed out that

> the necessary condition which makes possible the determination of particular characteristics of any concept (including the concept of perception) is the use of what have been called converging operations. Converging operations may be thought of as any set of two or more experimental operations which allow the selection or elimination of alternative hypotheses or concepts which could explain an experimental result. They are called converging operations because they are not perfectly correlated and thus can converge on a single concept. [1956, pp. 150–151]

In Cronbach and Meehl (1955) and Campbell and Fiske (1959) we find what amounts to more particularized specifications for appropriate "converging operations" for establishing the construct validity of measuring instruments.

One may make observational, including mathematical, analyses of the measuring process to determine what variables other than the construct in question might be influencing our results (Cronbach & Meehl, 1955). In the case of measures purporting to index a self-referent construct, such influences might include (a) other inferred processes or states, such as S's desire to give a favorable self-presentation; or (b) method factors, such as instrument form or scoring and statistical procedures.

In particular, it is pertinent to make internal item analyses and internal factor analyses of an instrument to suggest how many basic processes must be postulated to account for response variance on the instrument as a whole (Cronbach & Meehl, 1955). Not only might "irrelevant" variables be suggested by such analyses, but some insight may be gained into the degree to which complexity of the instrument corresponds to the hypothesized complexity of the relevant construct, and guidelines may be provided for building a more homogeneous measure of the intended construct.

One may ascertain that there are significant intercorrelations among measures presumed to measure the same construct (Cronbach & Meehl, 1955; Campbell & Fiske, 1959). Such *convergent validity* values should be not only significant, but sufficiently high to warrant further consideration of the instrument(s)' usefulness as an indicant of the intended construct.

Not only should one obtain evidence of convergent validity, but *discriminant validity* should be explored as well (Campbell & Fiske, 1959). Do scores from a particular measure of a specified construct correlate "too highly" with scores from a measure of an allegedly different construct? If so, there are no grounds for inferring that two different constructs are being measured. The correlation could depend on common method features, common construct features, or both.

Following Cronbach and Meehl's (1955) final suggested operations for exploring construct validity, one may examine results obtained from studies in which responses on the instrument in question are related to other stimulus and response variables. That is, a researcher may design a study on the basis of certain theoretical premises coupled with an assumption concerning the construct validity of the instrument he is using to measure one of the variables. Positive findings from such a study offer support simultaneously to the construct validity of the instrument and to the theory behind the study. In general, such investigations would involve (a) successful prediction of group differences and (b) studies of predicted changes over occasions (especially after controlled experimental intervention). We must bear in mind, however, that such findings offer ambiguous support at best, since the ratio of unknown to known variables does not preclude alternate interpretations. We are not, therefore, warranted in bypassing validating procedures of the other types mentioned above. The appearance of face validity of an instrument coupled with studies of the last-mentioned type will never suffice to establish the instrument's construct validity.

Thus far the stated requirements are applicable to the study and measurement of any sort of construct, and I have indicated particular similarity to the problems of psychologists studying perceptual processes. However, we face an additional problem not encountered by psychologists studying perception. In the case of a perception experiment, E usually is dealing with S's response to a stimulus, the properties of which can be agreed upon by a number of observers. Therefore, insofar as S's reports agree with E's independent knowledge of stimulus attributes, E can establish that S's verbal report is most probably validly indexing his percept. If S's report does *not* reveal that he has seen the stimulus characteristics E expects, E is faced with an ambiguous situation, thus: (a) S may be missing something, or experiencing something different from other observers who have examined the stimulus under comparable conditions, but his report is nevertheless a valid index of what *he* is seeing; or (b) S may be withholding what he sees, or may not have the necessary verbal skills to report accurately, etc. (i.e., his report is not a valid index of his percept). The self-concept researcher, although dealing with phenomenal fields in much the same way as the perception experimenter, has the disadvantage of having no way of independently checking S's reports, since there is no immediate stimulus and hence no way of getting agreement of other observers about what S should presumably be experiencing under specified conditions. So the self-concept researcher's method problems are much more complicated than those of the experimental psychologist studying perception.

E. APPLICATIONS TO SELF-CONCEPT MEASUREMENT OF SUGGESTED CONVERGING OPERATIONS FOR ESTABLISHING CONSTRUCT VALIDITY

In this section I expand on the specifications for converging operations I have just briefly listed, in order to present methodological developments in more detail, especially as they have been applied or could conceivably apply to evaluating and improving measurement in the self-concept field. Occasionally it is useful to keep in mind analogies between the methodological problems in self-concept research and those in general experimental psychology of perception and learning, especially as the latter remind us of variables which have been considered little, if at all, in the self-concept field. A general idea of the current status of self-concept measurement will become apparent; and some recommendations for self-concept researchers are made. Detailed critiques of specific measures in common use are presented in chapter 4.

1. Analysis of Irrelevant Response Determiners

SOCIAL DESIRABILITY

Ss' tendencies to respond in a "socially desirable" way on self-report instruments are quite probably irrelevant or contaminating variables which decrease the construct validity of self-concept reports. This potentially invalidating influence has received an enormous amount of conceptual and empirical attention (e.g., Block, 1965; Crowne & Marlowe, 1964; Crowne & Stephens, 1961; Crowne, Stephens, & Kelly, 1961; Edwards, 1957a, 1967a, 1967b, 1970; Jackson, 1967b).

Unfortunately, very little of this work can be applied to the validity problems with which the self-concept researcher is concerned. This is so for three reasons: (a) Validity issues which have interested social-desirability researchers are frequently different from those facing the self-concept researcher. For example, the former have often been occupied with the influence of social-desirability tendencies on the concurrent or predictive empirical validity of self-report instruments, as opposed to the construct validity of those reports as indicants of self-concept (e.g., Block, 1965; Dunnette, McCartney, Carlson, & Kirchner, 1962; Heilbrun, 1965; Heilbrun & Goodstein, 1961a). (b) Validity issues which have concerned social-desirability researchers have often been too vaguely specified to make the work of the former useful to self-concept workers. (c) The influence of social-desirability tendencies upon self-reports has often been explored by procedures inappropriate to the validity concerns of either group. To explain why this lack of applicability obtains, we need to examine some assumptions made (often only implicitly) by workers in the field of social-desirability tendencies.

Assumptions Underlying Available Social-Desirability Research

First, it is implicitly assumed that there are agreed-upon, obvious standards of what constitutes socially desirable behavior. Moreover, it is assumed that, because of social reinforcement, Ss have learned about these normative standards and have accepted them as their own personal ideals. A third assumption is that Ss are reinforced for guiding their conduct according to these socially and personally desirable standards, with the result that many Ss do develop many desirable behavior characteristics. (Although some Ss do not develop some of the desirable characteristics, the explanation of such exceptions is typically not considered by social-desirability researchers.) Regarding S's self-reports, it is assumed that one of several things may occur: If S's actual trait is desirable, it is assumed that the self-report will be favorable and accurate. (Little attention is given to the possibility that S's self-report will be inaccurately unfavorable to self.) If S's actual trait is less desirable or is undesirable, S may deliberately falsify, or he may defensively fail to recognize his shortcoming, or he may recognize his shortcoming and give an accurate report.

Empirical Status of Assumptions

Much work is based on the first assumption stated above, that the degree of social desirability of various behavior traits, as described in verbal-report items, is readily apparent and highly agreed upon. In an effort to support this assumption, many studies have been published showing very high correlations across items between mean Social Desirability Scale Values (SDSVs) obtained from groups of judges differing widely in age, sex, culture or nationality, sick-well status, and criminal status (e.g., Cowen, 1961; Cowen, Davol, Reimanis, & Stiller, 1962; Cowen, Staiman, & Wolitzky, 1961; Cowen & Stricker, 1963; Cruse, 1965; Edwards, 1957a; Klett, 1957a, 1957b; Klett & Yaukey, 1959; Lövaas, 1958, across Edwards Personal Preference Schedule [EPPS] item means; Stollak, 1965a, across EPPS scale means; Wahler, 1958; Zax, Cowen, Budin, & Biggs, 1962). However, this sort of evidence is an inappropriate test of the assumption because there are great individual differences in SDSVs for any given item, as shown by Messick and Jackson's (1961) standard deviations around each mean item SDSV. Scott (1963) showed that for 26 out of 30 items he studied, the standard deviations of individual Ss' judgments around the respective mean scaled SDSVs were greater than would be expected if these judgments reflected only random error about a true stimulus location. Borislow (1958) showed that the interprofile correlation (W) between Ss trying to fake the EPPS under social-desirability instructions was only .38, indicating that different item alternatives were chosen by different Ss as being socially desirable. Messick (1960), for the EPPS, and Wiggins (1966), for the Minnesota Multiphasic Personality Inventory (MMPI) items, demonstrated that the desirability domain is factorially complex; and they suggest the factors represent differences among individual points of view. Norman (1967) found in one study that 19.1% of the variance in social-desirability ratings of adjectives was due to interaction of Total Persons × Attributes, that is, to individual differences in the reactions of any given S to any given attribute. Obviously, then, the first assumption is false, and individual differences in Ss' judgments of what is socially desirable must be taken into account in any demonstration of or control for the alleged contaminating influence of social-desirability tendencies upon self-report behaviors.

Moreover, as stated above, much social-desirability research implicitly assumes high congruence between S's perception of what is socially desirable and his conception of what is personally desirable. But it has been empirically demonstrated that perceived personal desirability is not necessarily the same as either individually perceived social desirability or group norms regarding perceived social desirability (e.g., Borislow, 1958; Kenny, 1956; Martire & Hornberger, 1957; Rosen, 1956a, 1956b; Rosen & Mink, 1961). Even when a correlation of .98 *across item means* was obtained between SDSVs and mean personal-desirability values, the latter were significantly more variable (Cowen, Budin, & Budin, 1961). Presumably, personal ideals might operate upon behaviors, including self-report behaviors, in ways parallel to the alleged influence of perceived social desirability, so omission of consideration of the personal-desirability variable is a serious one in the arguments and empirical work of those concerned with social-desirability influences.

Researchers stressing the importance of social-desirability influences on self-reports further assume that there is an all-pervasive and very strong influence of group social-desirability norms upon Ss' behaviors in self-report tests along the lines described above. That is, it is assumed that Ss will describe themselves in statements which are socially and personally desirable, either because they are realistically characterized by these statements, or because they are deliberately falsifying, or because they have repressed awareness of their shortcomings. This assumption is allegedly supported by the very common finding of a high correlation *across items* in a heterogeneous item pool between mean frequency of endorsement for each item and mean SDSV for each item (Cruse, 1965; Edwards, 1957a, 1957b; Kenny, 1956). Whatever the truth of the assumption, such correlations across item means constitute inappropriate evidence for it; and the more appropriate *within-S* association between probability of endorsement and SDSVs (or, in some studies, Ss' individual judgments regarding the item's social desirability) is generally much lower (Block, 1965; Boe & Kogan, 1966; Milgram & Helper, 1961; Norman, 1967; Scott, 1963; Taylor, 1959). Heilbrun and Goodstein (1961b) found that, on pairs of EPPS statements showing discrepancies with respect to Ss' individual judgments of social desirability, an average of 67.16% of the endorsements were of the more socially desirable statements; while for pairs of statements imperfectly matched on mean SDSVs, an average of 55.8% of the endorsement statements were with higher mean SDSVs.

Norman (1967) has argued cogently for the application of analysis of variance (ANOVA) and analysis of covariance to bring out the appropriate kind of estimate of the typical degree to which a S's probability of endorsement of any particular item is a function of his perception of the item's social desirability. The obtained estimates of association would not then be based on inter-S variations or interattribute variations, but on Person × Item interaction.

Some Contradictory or Qualifying Assumptions

Some assumptions stated or implied by social-desirability researchers seem to contradict or qualify those I have just evaluated. Thus, on the one hand, there is supposedly the above-mentioned strong tendency for social-desirability considerations to distort the self-reports of all or many Ss on all traits, leading, as we saw, to a prediction of high correlations across items between mean SDSVs and probability of endorsement. On the other hand, it is also assumed to be possible that Ss may learn to deceive E regarding some shortcomings, give honest (though objectively inaccurate) favorable self-reports on other characteristics, and perhaps accurate reports of shortcomings on still other items. The methodological implications of this situation have never been worked out. An assumption which qualifies those I considered originally is that Ss develop *individual trait differences* regarding the following very general, "content-free" tendencies: (a) to evaluate the social desirability of many disparate trait descriptions in the specified normative way, and (b) to be generally honest or dishonest about deliberately falsifying self-reports, or (c) to be generally defensive or nondefensive to a specifiable degree about admitting shortcomings to self. Crandall, Crandall, and Katkovsky (1965); Crowne and Marlowe (1964); Edwards (1957a); and Jackson (1967b) have all developed scales which purport to measure individual differences in this supposed trait of "content-free," socially desirable responding in both test and nontest situations. One cannot conclude that these three scales are alternate measures of a trait, however, since intercorrelations among these scales are either low Edwards's SD vs. Crowne-Marlowe $SD = .35$, as reported in Crowne and Marlowe, 1964) or are not known.

Apparently both Edwards and Crowne and Marlowe regard the third possibility listed above as more descriptive than the second of the individual trait differences they are trying to measure by their respective social-desirability scales. Edwards (1967b, pp. 69–70) says, for example:

> I hope that you will not identify this [SD] trait with another trait, which might be defined as the tendency to falsify responses in self-description. . . . Nothing [in the definition of SD] implies that socially desirable responses are untruthful and that socially undesirable responses are truthful or vice versa.

Crowne and Marlowe (1964, p. 190) state:

> In presenting this interpretation, we have taken sides in a dialectic going back to the origins of personality testing, in which are pitted the opposing notions of conscious and deliberate faking or misrepresentation and a less frankly aware, defensive kind of self-depiction. The studies on the approval motive are not, of course, definitive at this point, but they do suggest the latter.

In contrast to Edwards and Crowne and Marlowe, Jackson (1967b, p. 12) recognizes that:

> Higher than average scores on the Desirability Scale implies [sic] that the subject either consciously or unconsciously has focused on this aspect of items, and has responded largely in terms of Desirability. High scores may thus indicate either conscious distortion or impression management, on the one hand, or the more subtle influences of atypically high self regard or of a high degree of conventional socialization. Conversely, very low scores may indicate possible tendencies toward malingering, or, more likely, atypically low self regard.

Certainly, as all these authors recognize, nothing in the measurement operations per se or the related validational studies of their scales rules out the possibility that between-S variance on their scales might be accounted for in part by conscious falsification of either the "fake good" or "fake bad" variety.

Implications for Validity of Self-Concept Measures

The following paragraphs examine the implications of the above arguments and lines of research for the validity problems facing the self-concept researcher.

Conceptually, one must ask how and to what degree could Ss' tendencies to respond in a socially desirable way invalidate *self-concept reports?* The answer depends on what sort of self construct we wish to measure. For example, if E wishes to measure some aspect of the phenomenal self, and S is deliberately trying to fool E by making a favorable self-presentation, obviously his self-description is an invalid index of his phenomenal self. Alternately, S may not be trying to deceive E, but may be reporting a socially desirable picture of himself which he believes to be true. Whether or not others' ratings or "objective measures" would agree with S's socially desirable report about himself is irrelevant here. *The point is, if S's self-reports are socially desirable, this high degree of socially desirable self-reporting does not ipso facto invalidate the report as an indicant of his phenomenal self.*

We may be interested in characteristics of S associated with his phenomenally honest, favorable self-report, in which case we have before us a different validity question, that, is, whether his self-report validly indicates his characteristics as judged or measured by others. It is possible that S may tend to endorse many socially desirable items because he believes they characterize him accurately, and they in fact do. As Heilbrun (1964), among others, has pointed out, if socialization has been successful, socially desirable traits will frequently characterize Ss. This being the case, for many Ss, socially desirable self-reports will not only be a valid index of S's phenomenal self, but will be a valid appraisal of his personal attributes as these might be assessed by an outsider or objective measure.

Suppose, as an alternate possibility, that S's honestly reported phenomenal self is more favorable than estimates made by objective observers. In this case, as I have stressed, the self-report is a valid indicant of S's phenomenal self, regardless of the above-mentioned discrepancy. But in such a case, E then sometimes infers that S has unconsciously defended himself against recognition of his own shortcomings. Moreover, E sometimes makes the additional inference that S's unconscious self-concept must be less favorable than his conscious self-concept. Obviously, a discrepancy between phenomenal self-report and an objective measure does not per se warrant such an inference, so yet another type of validity question is raised. Independent operations would have to be used to indicate the presence and degree of such defensiveness; and the validity of these measuring operations would have to be determined.

In their interpretation of the influence of defensiveness on self-report, Crowne and Marlowe (1964) argue that insecurity regarding his self-adequacy leads S unconsciously to need approval of others to an unusual degree in order to bolster his self-regard. Favorable self-presentation helps to get and keep that approval. Thus, if S gives a very socially desirable self-report on an alleged self-concept measure coupled with a high score on their scale of "need for social approval," Crowne and Marlowe would like to invoke the above explanation of the pattern of findings. However, as I indicated, they do *not* argue here that S's unusually favorable self-report is itself invalid in the sense of being a conscious distortion.

It is one thing to recognize conceptually all the possibilities we have considered above. It is quite another to devise satisfactory methods to answer the following empirical questions: To what degree do social-desirability tendencies decrease the construct validity of specific self-report measures as indicants of the *self-concept*? How can we minimize the invalidating influences upon our measures?

There is no satisfactory answer to the first question. Regarding the second, the matter of deliberate deception of *E* is probably best handled by establishing testing conditions which maximize rapport with *E* and make it worthwhile from *S*'s standpoint to be as honest as possible. There is no way, of course, to be *sure* that the desired optimum conditions have been obtained. It is well established that when *S* is asked to fake socially desirable self-reports consciously, different results are obtained than when *S* is instructed to respond honestly and/or under anonymous, nonthreatening conditions (e.g., Boe & Kogan, 1964; Borislow, 1958; Eisenman & Townsend, 1970; Jones, Gergen, & Davis, 1962). This sort of finding does not enable us to infer, however, that conscious distortion is eliminated under the latter conditions. No method sufficient for this inference exists!

Other methods of trying to prevent or minimize dishonesty or unintentional yielding to social-desirability tendencies have been tried. These methods boil down to one or more of the following: (a) attempts to fool or force *S* into being honest; (b) attempts to make *S* attend to and respond to item content without reference to its social-desirability value; (c) attempts to correct for *S*'s dishonesty and/or unwitting distortions. All such methods are open to several objections, and they do not solve the validity problems of the self-concept researcher.

For example, the EPPS uses a forced-choice format which requires *S* to choose one item within each pair of items when the pairs represent different "needs" but are closely matched on SDSVs. But it has been shown that this doesn't eliminate the ability of *S* to find and choose the more socially desirable item of the pair if he so desires (Corah, Feldman, Cohen, Gruen, Meadow, & Ringwall, 1958; Dicken, 1959; Edwards, Wright, & Lunneborg, 1959). Braun and Tinley (1969) have shown that Fricke's method of forcing *S* to choose from both good and bad items did not eliminate *Ss*' abilities to choose more or less socially desirable items within each list. In fact, pairing the items may make their normative SDSVs all the more discriminable to *S* (Feldman & Corah, 1960). Stollak (1965b), however, found a correlation of only .19 for male *Ss* when correlating perceived social desirability and probability of endorsement across the 30 items used by Edwards et al. and Corah et al. (Other drawbacks of the forced-choice format are discussed on pp. 76–80.)

In another approach, *E* includes in his instrument only items which are as close to the "neutral" range of the Social Desirability Scale as possible (Block, 1965; Cowen, Budin, Wolitzky, & Stiller,

1960). This may guarantee that no S can give a *highly* favorable or *highly* unfavorable self-report (in terms of SDSVs), either falsely or honestly; but it also has the effect of eliminating from the self-report (and hence from self-concept research based thereon) many important aspects of the self-concept. That this must be so is shown by Cruse's (1965) demonstration of extreme bimodality in SDSVs for (a) 1,647 concepts (1,575 of them originally chosen by Hilden, 1958, without reference to their SDSVs); (b) 2,824 personality statements as given by Edwards (1967b); (c) MMPI items as developed by Heinemann (published in Dahlstrom & Welsh, 1960) and by Messick and Jackson (1961). A very small proportion of the concepts or items fell within a "neutral" range. (So far as mean scores on different aspects of self-concept are concerned, Kogan and Fordyce's, 1962, data suggest that level of social desirability of items has little effect, at least in the various Q-sort forms of Interpersonal Check List [ICL] items they constructed.)

In a variant of this approach, items are deliberately chosen so that each trait-relevant item will have a high correlation with the corresponding trait-scale score and a relatively low correlation with a score from a specially devised Desirability Scale (Jackson, 1967b, p. 15). This helps to suppress correlations between trait scores which might depend mainly or solely on S's generalized tendency to choose desirable items regardless of their trait relevance, so that a kind of discriminant validity can be demonstrated, namely, that Ss can discriminate between a number of traits. Nevertheless, one wonders in this case, too, whether important trait content which is relevant to the self-concept may have had to be omitted in order to select items using Jackson's desiderata, since each total scale developed in this way had a fairly neutral mean (between 4.0 and 6.0 on a 9-point scale).

In a third approach, a separate desirability scale is included in the instrument and S's self-report scores may be "corrected" according to the degree to which he describes himself in terms of the rarely endorsed, highly favorable items and rejects the commonly rejected, highly unfavorable items (the item content in the scale being very heterogeneous) (Jackson, 1967b). Such a "correction" procedure is based on the unproven assumption that Ss who get a high desirability score on such a desirability scale have a generalized tendency to be deliberately dishonest and/or unwittingly swayed by favorability considerations in reporting their self-concepts with respect to socially desirable items, regardless of item trait content. (Jackson himself recommends against using a correction procedure.)

A questionable assumption underlying all these methods is the one mentioned earlier, that scaled group means regarding social desirability of items accurately reflect Ss' ideas regarding what is socially (let alone personally) desirable. As we have already shown, this assumption is not correct.

Cowen and Tongas (1959) thought they had found a way to retain very favorable and unfavorable items while eliminating the influence of social desirability upon the type of final scores which they recommended using (the summed [Self — Ideal] discrepancies from Bills's Index of Adjustment and Values [IAV]). However, their mistaken conclusion was based completely on artifact, as fully explained elsewhere (Wylie, 1961).

Furthermore, as I have frequently stated, none of these methods for controlling or minimizing the influence of social-desirability tendencies claims to improve the discriminant construct validity of a self-report instrument for inferring the relative contributions of accuracy in self-conception, conscious distortion, and unconscious distortion to the scores obtained. In some cases, the application of corrective techniques may improve concurrent empirical validity (as in the application of the K scale in making MMPI scores more accurately indicative of judged degree of pathology); but this is, of course, not the kind of validity relevant to the self-concept researcher. In other cases, variance among individual Ss' trait-scale scores in regard to social desirability is simply removed or minimized without explicit consideration of what the sources of those individual differences might be. In Jackson's (1967b) case, discriminant construct validity among trait scales may be fostered by the procedure used in item selection; but this is done at the cost of restricting the areas of self-concept the instrument is able to tap.

Regretfully, we must conclude that research thus far has been more useful in revealing blind alleys than paths to the goal of evaluating the distorting influence of tendencies to respond in a socially desirable way upon the validity of self-report instruments for evaluating the self-concept.

Supplementary Information on Social-Desirability Scaling

Some peripheral matters which may be of interest or use to self-concept researchers may be mentioned here. The following sets of items have been scaled for social-desirability values. Not all the social-desirability instructions given to judges were the same.

Set of 209 adjectives (Cooper & Cowen, 1962; Cowen, 1961; Cowen, Budin, & Budin, 1961)

Set of 100 Allport-Odbert adjectives (Crandall & Bellugi, 1954)

Butler-Haigh Q-sort items (Wiener, Blumberg, Segman, & Cooper, 1959)

California Psychological Inventory (Mees, Gocka, & Holloway, 1964; also in Edwards, 1970)

Edwards Personality Inventory (Edwards, 1970)

EPPS (Corah et al., 1958; Edwards, 1957a, 1970; Klett, 1957a, 1957b; Klett & Yaukey, 1959)

Hilden's Universe of Personal Constructs (Cruse, 1965)

IAV items (Cowen & Tongas, 1959)

Interpersonal Check List (Edwards, 1957b)

409 MMPI items (Rosen & Mink, 1961)

566 MMPI items (Messick & Jackson, 1961; also in Edwards, 1970)

Personality Research Form (PRF of Jackson) (Edwards, 1970)

96 Q-sort statements (scaled by Kogan, Quinn, Ax, & Ripley, 1957)

39 SD scale items of Edwards (DeSoto, Kuethe, & Bosley, 1959)

90 trait terms (Edwards, 1970)

Zimmer's (1954) 25 self concepts (scaled by Kenny, 1956)

There is a high correlation across item means between scale values obtained under instructions to judge the social-desirability values of the items and instructions to judge the items along the dimensions listed below. Presumably these correlations would occur only with certain item sets, since it is possible to scale items deliberately selected to be unrelated to psychopathology, as Crowne and Marlowe (1964) have done.

Feeling reactions of Ss to adjectives (Cooper & Cowen, 1962)

Well-being (DeSoto, Kuethe, & Bosley, 1959)

Health-sickness (Kogan, Quinn, Ax, & Ripley, 1957)

Adjustment (Heilbrun, 1964; Wiener, Blumberg, Segman, & Cooper, 1959)

Abnormality (Cowen, 1961)

SELF-PRESENTATION TACTICS AND SELF-DISCLOSURE

There has been a great deal of stress in the past 15 years on the fact that psychological research is a social situation and that the social-interaction characteristics of the research setup must be considered in interpreting the data (e.g., Friedman, 1967; Orne, 1962, 1969; Riecken, 1962; M. J. Rosenberg, 1969).

Orne (1962, 1969), for instance, has emphasized the "demand characteristics" of the experimental situation, in which S presumably wants to be a "good" subject by behaving in the way he perceives E wishes him to react. Although one might imagine that such a cooperative intent would promote S's honesty on self-report instruments, this is a naïve view. For example, S's particular hunch as to what E is actually trying to accomplish in the research may lead S to distort his self-report in an unknown way. Or in postexperimental inquiries, S might "collude" with E by failing to reveal (or even to remember) his hunches about the purpose of the experiment or his suspicions of E's manipulations and intentions, leading E to unwarranted complacency about his success in manipulating and controlling variables or his success in fooling S into believing that his self-reports will be anonymous. The very common use of deception has created not only severe ethical problems but a widespread suspicious attitude among supposedly naïve Ss with resultant unknown implications for all aspects of Ss' behavior, including self-report behavior (Kelman, 1967; D. T. Campbell, 1969; McGuire, 1969).

Relatively little has been done to try to explore empirically the implications of the social-psychological nature of the research situation for Ss' behavior in studies of the self-concept. However, some of the researches on *self-presentation* and *self-disclosure* have methodological implications for self-concept researchers. The studies suggest the importance of both stable and transient E and S variables, and of social-interaction variables which may affect Ss' behavior on self-report instruments administered in research settings. They also give some indication of the degree to which self-reports may show systematic intraindividual variation from time to time, yet be perceived by S to be unvarying so far as their phenomenological accuracy (honesty) is concerned.

The theoretical analyses made by these authors involve not only Ss' desires to present themselves as having favorable characteristics in order to gain approval or other rewards E can dispense (M. J.

Rosenberg, 1969; E. E. Jones, 1964), but also considerations such as maintaining power in a relationship and fending off dependency of others on the self (Gergen & Wishnov, 1965). It is by no means expected that a systematic trend toward phenomenologically inaccurate, but favorable, self-presentation would result from the operation of social-psychological variables in an experimental situation. For instance, Jones (1964) has argued that high-status Ss whose attributes are obvious will give especially modest self-presentations when seeking to ingratiate themselves with lower-status persons. And it is commonly accepted that emphasizing shortcomings is a possibility in the self-presentation of a person seeking counseling or help from E.

Self-Favorability in Self-Presentation

Schneider's (1969) study suggests that when the experimental situation is manipulated so as to increase S's need for approval from another person in the situation, his self-presentation will be affected. Ss gave two self-reports on a two-form modification of the Dickoff Triads Test, the first report under neutral instructions and the second with half the Ss being informed that their self-evaluation would be used as a basis for feedback evaluation from another person, half of them not being given these instructions. Between the first and second self-descriptions, Ss were told they had "failed" or "succeeded" on a separate test of an important self-attribute, "social sensitivity." Among "failing" Ss who thought their second self-evaluation on the Triads Test was to be used as a basis for evaluative feedback from others, favorability of self-presentation was greater on a repetition of the Triads Test than it was among "failing" Ss who did not expect evaluative feedback from the interviewer based on the Triads Test (second-test favorability scores having been adjusted for first-test score).

Another feature of a social-interaction situation which has been shown to affect self-presentation is the level of self-evaluations presented by others with whom S is interacting (Gergen & Wishnov, 1965). Each female S made self-ratings on the Dickoff Triads Test with the understanding that these self-evaluations would be presented to a partner who had previously given either high positive, average, or self-derogating reports about herself. Differences between these self-ratings made by S and those the S had made previously under "neutral" conditions were computed. Ss who expected their self-reports to be presented to partners with high-positive self-reports increased the number of favorable ratings in their own self-reports significantly, while the other Ss did not show changes in the number of favorable self-ratings. Ss whose self-reports were to be presented to high-positive partners also decreased the number of unfavorable ratings in their self-reports; while Ss whose self-reports were to be presented to average or low-positive partners *increased* the number of negative self-ratings. This finding may have relevance for self-concept studies in general, insofar as self-reports may be affected by the apparent competence and self-confidence of the E who collects Ss' self-reports in such studies. Of even more direct relevance would be studies directed explicitly toward looking at Ss' evaluative self-presentations under varying conditions of E's self-presentation.

In another study of the effects of intraexperimental social interaction upon self-evaluative reports (Sarason & Winkel, 1966), male and female Es who were high and low scorers on a Behavioral Hostility test obtained interview self-descriptions from male and female Ss who also scored either high or low on the BH scale. Dependent variables included ratings of 13 speech-content categories, 5 speech-disturbance categories, Ss' ratings of Es on an unspecified number of dimensions, Es' ratings of Ss on an unspecified number of dimensions, and observers' ratings of Es on 14 items! Insufficient information is given for evaluating the numerous "significant" F tests in the light of the total number of such tests made on the numerous dependent variables which were probably intercorrelated. Of greatest possible relevance to the present issue were the findings that Ss interviewed by male Es gave a significantly larger number of positive and a significantly larger number of negative self-references than did Ss interviewed by female Es. No main effects of E's BH score on S's self-references were found. Since male Es were more unfavorably rated by Ss, the authors suggest that "one, then, is left with the impression that a person's degree of comfort with and liking for another person may not be indicative of a willingness to 'open up' [Sarason & Winkel, 1966, p. 456]." This view is obviously different from that of Jourard in the studies cited below. Replication and cross-validation of this study, using larger numbers of Ss and Es, would be useful in view of the fact that the findings are suggestive but of questionable interpretability.

Many of the studies of self-disclosure behavior initiated by Jourard and his associates are methodologically relevant to self-concept research. Generally speaking, they involve, on the dependent-variable side, a number of measures of self-disclosure, including time spent talking about the self; range and type of targets Ss use for varying amounts and degrees of self-disclosure; degree of intimacy of topics for self-disclosure; and depth of self-disclosure. On the independent-variable side, researchers in this field have concerned themselves with stable individual differences in self-disclosing behavior (for which they have devised several purported measures) and with situational variables (including social interaction within the experiment) which possibly affect self-disclosure.

Individual Differences in Self-Disclosing Behavior

Pedersen and Higbee (1968) obtained some evidence of convergent and discriminant validity of the four "target scores" (disclosure to mother, father, best male friend, best female friend) of the long and short forms of Jourard's Self-Disclosure Scale. (The SD-60 is found in Jourard & Lasakow, 1958; and the SD-25 in Jourard, 1961).

However, there has been practically no success in showing that individual differences in *claimed* propensities for self-disclosure (as reported on one or more of the self-disclosure inventories) correlates with individual differences in some aspect(s) of *actual* self-disclosing behavior, as indicated, for example, by group-trainer ratings (Lubin & Harrison, 1964); amount of information revealed by graduate students making personal introductions in a classroom situation (Himelstein & Kimbrough, 1963); or peer-rated likelihood of confiding in others (Himelstein & Lubin, 1965). Pedersen and Breglio (1968) asked Ss in a classroom situation to describe themselves in writing in response to five sets of questions regarding interests, personality, studies, body, and money. The correlation between *depth* of this actual disclosure, as rated by two independent raters, and *total amount* of actual disclosure, indicated by word count, was .84. Although total depth and total amount of disclosure correlated significantly with scores on the short and long forms of the Jourard Self-Disclosure Inventory for two target persons (mother, father), the only particular content area in which actual disclosure correlated with claimed disclosure was "studies."

One study by Resnick (cited in Jourard, 1969) gave some indication that measurable individual differences predict to some extent the self-disclosure behavior of Ss. (This study is more fully discussed below.)

Of course, in all the above studies one can question the validity or relevance to self-concept research of the criterion scores (i.e., "actual disclosure" scores); but in any case, the various self-disclosure inventories do not as yet have firmly demonstrated validity for inferring any aspect of Ss' propensities to confide in others, including confiding in Es who are carrying out self-concept research. Either individual-difference factors are overridden by situational factors or the former have not been adequately measured. Thus the major findings from studies of self-disclosing behavior concern situational factors, as opposed to stable, individual-difference factors.

Situational Factors in Self-Disclosing Behavior

When each S was placed with two of E's confederates, Chittick and Himelstein (1967) found that the amount of information S revealed in introducing himself to the confederates was a positive, significant function of the amount the confederates revealed in their prior introduction. Overall, the material disclosed was quite innocuous, so the applicability of the study to self-concept research is limited. It might be relevant to such an instrument as the Who Am I? Test, however, if Ss were tested where they could sense how fully other Ss were responding.

In Resnick's (reprinted in Jourard, 1969) study, Ss were selected as high and low on a 40-item questionnaire asking them to indicate which topics they had fully revealed to somebody and which they would be willing to discuss with a same-sex partner they would meet in the course of the study. Pairs of Ss were formed to engage in dialogues on each of 20 topics, previously rated for degree of intimacy. On the basis of the self-disclosure inventory, high-high and low-low pairs of Ss were formed for the first experimental session, and low-high pairs for the second experimental session. Disclosure-output scores (weighting the items in terms of their rated intimacy) were the dependent-variable measure. Low Ss when paired with low Ss had a lower disclosure score than high Ss paired with high Ss, indicating some predictability from the inventory to an actual self-disclosing behavior situation. When paired with high Ss, low Ss obtained higher disclosure-output scores than when paired with other low Ss, suggesting that a situational variable was overriding the individual-difference variable. High Ss, on the other hand, did not obtain lower self-disclosure scores when paired with low Ss, suggesting that high scores on the self-disclosure inventory indicate stable tendencies not overridden in this experimental situation. Unfortunately for the interpretability of this study, the comparison of "like" and "different" dyads was confounded with order effects, since the same Ss were used in both phases of the experiment.

Whether "getting acquainted" with E can be a factor in what S discloses on a self-report instrument and to whom he discloses it was explored in Jourard and Kormann's (1968) study. At the beginning and end of a 2-week interval, E individually administered the EPPS and a modified Rivenbark Target Disclosure Scale in which S ranked 19 possible "targets" for his own self-disclosure, including "an interviewer for scientific purposes," "an *anonymous* questionnaire for scientific research," and "this experimenter." Control Ss had no contact with E between testing sessions, while experimental Ss had two 20-minute interviews "to get acquainted." Experimental Ss made slightly more changes on the EPPS (one-tail $p < .05$). No significant differences in pre-post changes in "target rankings" for scientific interviewer, anonymous questionnaire, or "this experimenter" were noted, however. (Unfortunately, the mean rank values of these targets are not published.) In a postexperimental inquiry, Ss who felt they had changed many answers on the EPPS reported various reasons for changing; but 20% of the experimental Ss and none of the controls listed as one reason a feeling that they could be more truthful in disclosing their preferences to E.

In another study combining individual-difference and situational variables, Jourard and Jaffe (1970) studied the effect of E's amount of disclosure on topics of greater intimacy than those used by Chittick and Himelstein. They obtained from undergraduate Ss indications of their past disclosure rates and the disclosure rate they anticipated for themselves in indivdual interviews on 20 disclosure topics rated by Ss for degree of intimacy. The number of seconds E disclosed herself on each topic followed this schedule for the first 10 and second 10 topics: Group 1, 20, 20; Group 2, 60, 60; Group 3, 20, 60; Group 4, 60, 20. In each group, Ss disclosed themselves on significantly more topics than they anticipated they would and more than they said they had disclosed in the past. Ss in all conditions tended to match their speaking time to that of the interviewer (E). This was even true within sessions for Groups 3 and 4.

In two additional studies, Jourard (1969) and Jourard and Fried-man (1970) explored the effects upon self-disclosure time of variations in E's behavior within the experiment. These variations were aimed at manipulating the psychological distance between S and the 22-year-old male E. In both experiments, Ss tape-recorded personal information on eight topics, previously scaled for intimacy. Experiment 1 involved three distance conditions: (a) E out of the room; (b) E in the room, but refraining from eye contact with S; (c) E offering continuous eye contact. No significant differences in total disclosure time was found for males, while females spent significantly more time in self-disclosure when E was absent. In the second experiment, distance was varied among four groups: Group 1, E told S nothing about himself; Group 2, E touched S while guiding him to his chair; Group 3, E spoke truthfully about himself on various topics for 3 to 5 minutes before S was asked to speak; Group 4, E both touched S and spoke about himself. A summed "feeling score" based on such ratings as being at ease with E, liking E, trusting E, and being understood by E showed Groups 3 and 4 reporting significantly more positive feelings than Groups 1 and 2. Also, before and after the session, Ss recorded their impressions of E on 40 evaluative traits; and Groups 1 and 2 showed significantly less impression change than did Groups 3 and 4, with Group 4 showing significantly more effect than Group 3. It is thus suggested indirectly that the experimental manipulation of "psychological distance" was effective. The number of seconds spent in self-disclosure increased from Group 1 to Group 4, with all differences significant except the 1-2 difference. Across all 64 Ss, the correlation between feelings toward E and duration of self-disclosure was .73.

This line of experimentation seems ingenious and important. For generalizability, however, more Es including both sexes and various ages should be used. And while time spent in self-disclosure is important, the self-concept researcher needs information about both the range of topics of the Ss' self-reports and the phenomenal veracity of them.

The variable of "intimacy" of self-disclosure topics seems intuitively to be of great methodological relevance to self-concept studies; it has been considered by no other researchers, so far as I know. However, for the same reason that scaled social-desirability values may be inappropriate to studies in that area, scaled intimacy values need supplementing in this line of research. That is, E should consider the individual S's view of the intimacy value of each topic on which dependent-variable measures are taken.

Furthermore, so long as self-concept researchers are going to rely on standard verbal-report measures, it would seem desirable to use one or more of them as dependent-variable measures in studies designed to look at self-disclosure as a function of social factors within the experimental situation.

Awareness of Distortion in Self-Presentation

A related set of questions concerns the degree to which S is aware of changes or distortions in his self-report. Is S's report of "honest" self-presentation to be taken at face value?

Jones, Gergen, and Davis's (1962) results seem to show that reinforcing conditions within an experiment can make Ss forget and/or distort the degree of dissimulation they engaged in while giving self-reports. Ss were instructed to present themselves either honestly or in a dishonest, "ingratiating" manner to an interviewer who gave them (as part of the interview) the Dickoff Triads Test, which purports to measure self-regard. Later they received positive or negative evaluations of themselves from the interviewers (the evaluations having been assigned by a predetermined schedule without reference to Ss' self-reports). When later questioned about the extent to which they had presented "their true picture of self" to the interviewer, those who had received positive evaluations from the interviewer were more likely than those receiving negative evaluations to claim their presentation to the interviewer had been accurate. Ss who supposedly had tried to present themselves honestly and then received negative evaluations from the interviewer, retrospectively reported slightly less accuracy in their self-presentations than did Ss who had received approving evaluation from the interview after giving him an inaccurate, "ingratiating" self-presentation.

Gergen and Wishnov (1965), in the experiment cited above, used a postexperimental inquiry to classify each S as high, medium, or low on awareness of changes in her self-report and/or feelings that her self-report truly represented her. They found no evidence that amount of change was related to "awareness," and concluded, "At least one implication of these results is that persons can vary markedly in the overt presentation of self and yet feel equally as honest across situations [p. 354]."

In summary, the researches presented in this section offer support to the idea that various characteristics of self-disclosing and/or self-reporting behaviors depend in part on such factors as the following: *E*'s self-presentation; imputed characteristics of other *S*s with whom the experimental *S*s expect to interact; other persons' behaviors in the experimental situation; experimental manipulations aimed at increasing *S*s' need for approval; and measurable individual differences in *S*s' self-disclosing propensities. Although these researches typically did not involve any of the usual self-concept measures, their suggestive relevance to interpretation of such measures is obvious. Research along these lines, using self-concept measures, would be very helpful in trying to evaluate the construct validity of responses made on such instruments under specified conditions.

CONTENT AREAS

Another possible factor which may be related in part to social desirability, self-disclosure, and self-presentation is the influence of areas of item content. Perhaps it is more socially acceptable to reveal oneself in certain areas than others, even when the factor of the self-favorability of the particular self-report content is held constant across content areas. Or perhaps areas of content may be differentially revealed, even with item self-favorability constant, because they are more or less salient to *S*'s self-esteem. This idea receives some suggestive support from the findings of Jourard and Lasakow (1958), whose *S*s reported that they voluntarily disclosed themselves to others more freely in certain areas than in other areas. For example, they reported that they revealed more about their attitudes, opinions, tastes, and interests than about their personality or body characteristics. (See also Jourard, 1958.) Also in suggestive support of the relevance of content areas to the construct validity of self-concept reports are findings reported by D. A. Taylor (1968). Male college roommate pairs reported quite different amounts of mutual self-disclosure during their first 13 weeks of acquaintance as a function of the scaled intimacy of the topic. It cannot be said in this study, however, that intimacy was varied independently of the social desirability or self-favorability of the contents of disclosure. *E* did not consider the social-desirability or self-favorability values of the disclosure areas.

Parenthetically, I note that D. A. Taylor and Altman (1966a, 1966b) have scaled 671 discussion topics as to intimacy value for college and navy male Ss. Although I must warn again here (as in the case of social desirability) that mean scale values are not necessarily relevant to the relation between judged intimacy and self-disclosure by individual Ss, some of the materials may be useful to self-concept researchers as a beginning basis for the study of the influence of intimacy of content areas on construct validity of self-report instruments.

KNOWN IDENTITY OF S

A number of investigators have taken the precaution to assure S's anonymity, on the theory that this would increase the validity of S's self-report as an index of his phenomenal field. While there is reason to believe that this is a desirable control (Davids, 1955), the influence of this factor on the availability of valid responses in self-report tests covered by this review has not been specifically demonstrated. Parker (1966) correlated self-concept measures from signed and unsigned self-reports; but unfortunately, order of task was completely confounded with signing, and no separate comparative estimate of test-retest reliability under either condition was obtained, so nothing can be concluded. Of indirect relevance is the demonstration by Kulik, Stein, and Sarbin (1968) that both high school and delinquent boys reported more antisocial behaviors on a written Delinquency Check List taken under supposedly anonymous conditions. However, the rankings of the boys' total DCL scores correlated .98 between the two administrations of the check list. Again, order of task and signing were confounded, thus limiting the conclusions.

Pending directly relevant, well-controlled research, it would seem wise to offer Ss anonymity wherever possible; but many investigators have not taken this precaution.

ACQUIESCENCE RESPONSE TENDENCIES

In its original meaning (Cronbach, 1946), the term *acquiescent-response set* referred to individual differences in the tendency to agree on true-false and "degree-of-agreement" questionnaires, especially where item content is ambiguous. It was later suggested that these individual differences may conceivably manifest themselves across a more or less broad behavior domain, ranging from (a) within-test-session consistencies, through (b) consistencies across specific test forms (the latter possibilities called *sets* by Jackson and Messick, 1962, as cited in Jackson, 1967a), through (c) consistencies across various test and nontest situations (called *styles* by Jackson and Messick, 1962, as cited in Jackson, 1967a).

Although there is some evidence that the consistent tendency to agree is not necessarily correlated with the consistent tendency to disagree (Peabody, 1961, and Martin, 1964, cited in Jackson, 1967a), most workers have provisionally assumed that the acquiescent-response tendency ranges from a positive to a negative pole.

If acquiescent-response sets or styles can be an important influence on self-report measures, the identification and control of such tendencies in self-concept research is important, both in measurement and in hypothesis testing. Of course, the possible influence of acquiescent tendencies complicates the interpretation of any single self-report item. Morover, when total scores are obtained by summing across items of heterogeneous content, the acquiescent component of variance accumulates while the construct (trait) component of variance accumulates to a lesser extent, depending on the degree of heterogeneity of item content. As a result, what may appear to be substantial reliabilities may actually reflect only or mainly the stability of acquiescence variance between test halves or across occasions. Or, in an instrument presuming to measure separately several different constructs (traits), correlations between traits could be spuriously high, preventing E from obtaining evidence of discriminant validity for the various subscales of his instrument. Finally, in hypothesis testing, one often correlates one or more self-concept measures with other scores which purport to indicate some personality attribute of theoretical relevance to a self-concept variable (e.g., Authoritarian-Scale F scores with self-esteem scores). If acquiescent-response tendencies influence each set of scores, the correlation between scores might be entirely or mainly artifactual.

The published literature of research and argument concerning acquiescent-response tendencies is enormous. The opinions of various authors regarding the occurrence and importance of acquiescent-response tendencies in personality testing cover all possibilities, from extreme importance (Jackson & Messick, 1958), to a moderate position (Campbell, Siegman, & Rees, 1967), to extreme unimportance (Block, 1965; Rorer, 1965).

As explained below, most of these publications are of only tangential relevance to a self-concept researcher. Some of them involve the question of how many "species" of acquiescent-response set there are, for example, for aphorisms and attitudes, information and ability tests, and personality-descriptive items (Jackson, 1967a). A great deal of the research concerns questions rather specific to the MMPI. For example, there is a controversy over whether the second largest factor repeatedly found in the MMPI should be interpreted as representing acquiescent tendencies, trait content, or both (Block, 1965; Jackson, 1967a; Rorer, 1965); or whether there may be two "species of acquiescence," one a *true* response-tendency and the other a tendency to accept many heterogeneous items as characterizing the self (Messick, 1967). Another line of research pursues the question whether acquiescent-response tendencies may co-vary with specifiable personality characteristics (e.g., Couch & Keniston, 1960; Messick, 1967).

Many of the above classes of research lead to equivocal results partly because of the very fact that Es use the MMPI or other similar, ready-made item pools from which it has been difficult or impossible to select item combinations so as to hold one variable constant while varying another (e.g., to hold constant pathological content, social desirability, or endorsement probability while varying the number of *true*-keyed responses). In any. event, MMPI scales and items are not especially to be recommended for self-concept research, where it would be far preferable to build items, scales, and instruments in a more rational, methodologically sophisticated manner. Therefore, one could argue for ignoring this literature. However, one should not ignore it, because MMPI items and scales have in the past been used as purported self-concept measures and also to measure variables such as adjustment with which self-concept variables are allegedly related. Accordingly, the self-concept researcher needs to be aware of the above-mentioned specific problems in MMPI interpretation.

What, then, of more direct relevance to self-concept measurement and research can be gleaned from the many publications on acquiescent-response tendencies? Since such tendencies are not per se of central interest to self-concept researchers, the main considerations are as follows: (a) to control for the possibility of the influence of acquiescent-response tendencies when designing research instruments and testing hypotheses; and (b) when interpreting results of self-concept studies, to scrutinize the measurement situation carefully for the possibility of alternate plausible interpretations in terms of acquiescent-response tendencies as opposed to substantive findings relevant to E's hypotheses.

Although it has not been demonstrated directly, it seems logically obvious that motivating S to pay attention to content will minimize the possible influence of acquiescent-response tendencies on self-concept scores.

So far as instrumentation is concerned, by far the best opportunity to minimize the influence of acquiescent-response tendencies is at the level of item writing and keying, rather than relying on highly questionable ad hoc statistical procedures applied to available item pools to try to "correct for" acquiescent-response tendencies (Jackson, 1967a). Obviously, if S's self-reports are to reflect as faithfully as possible his self-concept attributes, the chances of S's responding in such attributive terms are maximized if the content of each item is chosen for its carefully considered conceptual relevance (Fiske, 1966), and if both ends of supposedly bipolar attributes are represented in the item collection. And of course, items which are to enter into a total score for a stated attribute should be highly intercorrelated so that trait variance will accumulate faster than response-set variance when summing across items.

To assure communication of such content attributes to S so that he can respond in terms of them, familiar, understandable language should be used. Jackson (1967a) believes that acquiescent-response tendencies are maximized when the self-referent content dimension is of relatively low salience to S. For example, scales of average-judged desirability (saliency?) value tended to load highly on an "acquiescence" factor in the MMPI (Jackson & Messick, 1961). Unfortunately, if one attempts to minimize acquiescent-response tendencies by limiting oneself to highly salient items, one narrows the range of self-concept aspects one can explore with one's instrument, and one also tends to increase the possibility that social-desirability tendencies will distort self-concept reports on one's instrument, since salience and desirability quite probably co-vary.

Many researchers now prepare "balanced scales" as a means to control acquiescent-response tendencies. Here an approximately equal number of items relevant to an attribute are phrased so that *true* and *false* answers, respectively, increase S's attribute-score. Some researchers (e.g., Block, 1965) feel that such balancing is all

that one can hope to do, in practical terms. Jackson (1967a), however, points out that balancing per se by no means equates *true*-
keyed and *false*-keyed subsets with respect to other variables known
or thought to influence acquiescent responding, for example, item
ambiguity, the item's level of social desirability, or the item's probability of endorsement. Thus, even in balanced scales considerable
variance could conceivably be contributed to the total score by
acquiescent tendencies. Nevertheless, as Jackson (1967a) recognizes,
a dilemma is inherent in the fact that attempts to equate the subsets of balanced scales with reference to all these factors may seriously restrict item content of high relevance to E's purposes.

One possible way around these problems, Jackson (1967a) suggests, is to move to a forced-choice format. However, as is shown
in the next section, there are many serious and unresolved problems
associated with this format, and as yet there is no evidence that
the possible gain in avoiding acquiescent (or social-desirability) tendencies is not offset by other serious drawbacks.

So far as self-concept research to date is concerned, none of the
commonly used instruments has been evaluated and improved in
terms of the above considerations. The best recommendations for
the future seem to be: (a) to follow the best modern practices in
instrument construction, *but without* restricting attribute salience
or content for the sake of controlling acquiescent-response tendencies; (b) to arrange testing conditions so as to maximize Ss' willingness and ability to give an honest report of his self-concept; (c) to
consider in evaluating past and forthcoming studies the plausibility
of an interpretation in terms of acquiescent-response tendencies as
an alternate to a substantive explanation of the findings.

DEGREE OF RESTRICTION OF S's RESPONSE

The freedom of response allowed the S is evidently a pertinent
determinant of self-report responses, as it is of responses in perception experiments. For example, if S is allowed to give a free, unstructured report about his self-concept, in a manner comparable to
the Gestalt psychologists' techniques in eliciting reports from Ss
in perceptual experiments, it may be impossible to classify or
quantify S's responses in a way necessary to relate the response
index to other items in the "nomological net." For example, I found
that open-ended essays describing oneself and one's ideals for one's

own conduct were not codable for a number of the characteristics on which I had data from other instruments (Wylie, 1957). Ss' failure to mention certain characteristics on the essays occurred despite the fact that these characteristics had been shown by other investigators to be important parts of the self-concept, in the opinion of Ss who were similar in many ways to those I used (Diller, 1954). As indicated above, willingness to disclose oneself may vary with different content areas of self-disclosure (Jourard & Lasakow, 1958). This suggests one reason why open-ended self-reports may omit important aspects of the self-concept. Another reason is suggested by replies obtained by Spitzer, Stratton, Fitzgerald, and Mach (1966), when Ss were asked, "Which of the measures [IAV, TST, ACL, Fiedler Semantic Differential] allowed you to give the most (least) accurate description of yourself?" Forty percent of Ss felt the Twenty Sentences Test (TST, the open-ended instrument) was least accurate. Their reasons included its lack of structure and its tendency "to strain their powers of introspection."

On the other hand, when Ss' mode of reporting is circumscribed, as by a semantic-differential technique, Q sort, or any kind of inventory or rating scale, especially one of the forced-choice variety, one has no way of knowing to what extent the external limits imposed by the measuring instrument prevent S from giving an accurate report of his conscious cognitions or feelings. One is reminded here of the point made by Eriksen (1956) in connection with an operational analysis of "subception": the fact that a galvanic skin response was given along with an incorrect report of the visual stimulus may indicate *not* unconscious perception, but the fact that the range of responses which E permitted S to give did not include a means for him to specify his percept in all its relevant, but subtle, aspects. Few studies in the self-concept area have addressed themselves specifically to these important methodological difficulties. However, one study has shown that normal and abnormal Ss, when given free choice in a Q-sort setting, produce sorts more nearly U-shaped than normal (Jones, 1956). This of course implies that investigations using the conventional Q-sort procedure, which requires Ss to produce a quasi-normal distribution of item placements, have introduced some distortion into their instruments. Livson and Nichols (1956) found that unforced sorts (when Ss were describing others) yielded a composite distribution insignificantly different from rectangularity; and intrasorter as well as intersorter consistency in type of distribution was low. Although test-retest reliability was greater for forced sorts, Ss believed they could express their judgments better on an unforced choice.

Forced-choice (FC) techniques of the "paired statement" variety have received the closest methodological scrutiny. In this format, statements are presented in blocks of two to five; and, in a self-evaluative situation, S must indicate within each block the partial or full *rank order* of applicability of the statements to himself. He cannot say that he considers all of them applicable or all inapplicable (Waters & Wherry, 1961). Within each block, statements are supposedly matched on a measure of "attractiveness" to S (e.g., according to his preferences, or according to their social-desirability scale values); and they supposedly vary in respect to some validity index (e.g., correlation with job success or trait content). Purportedly, this technique reduces fakability (e.g., S cannot present himself in a socially desirable light or in terms of an ideal member of an occupational class); it minimizes intercorrelations among traits due to acquiescence-response set or extreme-response set; and it produces less skew in score distributions than is obtained by questionnaire or rating-scale formats. Thus, more valid discriminations among Ss are allegedly possible.

Counteracting the above arguments are a number of considerations, partly speculative, partly empirical. First, such techniques introduce spurious negative intercorrelations among traits. Then, as I have mentioned in the discussion of the social-desirability variable, Ss can discern within a supposedly matched pair which item has the higher social-desirability value. And, in any case, matching items on mean social-desirability value is an inappropriate way to control for Ss' individual judgments of the social desirability of items. Furthermore, it seems that Ss may resent a format which restricts them to ranking the applicability of traits which seem to them to be equally self-descriptive (or equally nondescriptive of self). Such resentment could lead to careless, unreliable, hence invalid, responding.

The occurrence of resentment was verified in a study by Waters and Wherry (1961) comparing Ss' reactions to the regular FC format and a format which allowed them to rate the absolute self-applicability of each statement. They found that Ss' reactions to the FC format were very unfavorable, for example, Ss disliked answering the items and found describing themselves difficult and objectionable; and they chose to discard the FC self-evaluation form when allowed to hand in the one form they felt gave the fairer description of them. (Ss were under the impression that the instrument was being used to predict drop rate in flight training for reasons other than lack of ability.) Further verification of resentment comes from another study (Waters, 1966) involving three tone levels of statements (negative, neutral, positive), and three instructional sets (FC "check least like me," FC "check most like me," and "rate applicability of both statements"). Again, Ss described the "rate both" procedure as the least objectionable format, while preferences between the two FC formats depended on whether items were positive, neutral, or negative in tone.

Edwards (1957a, p. 60) has reported that Ss sometimes express frustration when using his forced-choice EPPS. This may be due to thwarting of S's desires to put himself in a socially desirable light (since the items are paired according to their scaled Social-Desirability value). However, it may also be due to the frustration of having to represent the phenomenal field with an incongruent instrument. Supporting the latter interpretation are the findings of Levonian, Comrey, Levy, and Procter (1959). They factor-analyzed each of the 15 EPPS scales but found no large factors which were identifiable along the lines of the 15 major variables scored in the test. The correlations were low between items supposed to measure the same variables. They believe that this may be mainly due to the forced-choice form of the EPPS, which may easily lead to a negative attitude, promoting carelessness and unreliability. In their view, item form should make it possible for the respondent to express himself and his position as exactly as possible.

Most directly relevant to the above argument would be comparative tests of the effects upon validity of FC as opposed to other formats, both used in typical research conditions. Unfortunately, there is no definite evidence of this sort in the reviews of FC technique by Zavala (1965) and Scott (1968). The total number of researches they review is small, and almost all have one or both of the following limitations: (a) they do not involve direct comparisons of an FC form with another form of the *same* self-report instrument; (b) they use criterion scores which are inappropriate to exploration of the convergent and discriminant construct validity of self-concept reports as indices of self-concept.

There are some findings of suggestive relevance in Scott's studies

(1963, 1968). In his 1963 research, he correlated attribute (need) scores from the EPPS in its original form and a modified single-stimulus form with Ss' activity reports concerning the respective attributes. In his 1968 research, Scott correlated attribute scores from the Allport-Vernon-Lindzey Study of Values, the EPPS, and the Scott Values Questionnaire in their original FC form and in modified single-stimulus forms with friends' ratings, friends' rankings, and Ss' activity reports regarding the respective attributes. He found no evidence that validity coefficients varied as a function of the formats used. Null findings are always ambiguous, of course; and in considering the implications of these particular null findings, one should take into account the fact that these Ss were performing a laboratory exercise in introductory psychology in which they were told that the purpose of the research was to compare the validities of two test formats. This situation would, it seems, tend to minimize emotional involvement with test results, perhaps to a degree unrepresentative of much research on the self-concept. Becoming very involved in trying to give an accurate report of one's self-concept might produce one kind of effect, while becoming very involved in trying to produce a favorable impression on E might produce the opposite kind of effect, so far as relative validities of FC and other formats are concerned.

Probably the most reasonable conclusions from the assumptions and meager available data are these: (a) Construction of FC instruments entails much effort in attempting, unsuccessfully, to control the sorts of variables that forced-choice format was designed to control (e.g., judged desirability of statements). (b) The FC format arouses Ss' resentments, which may both indicate the impossibility of using the format for valid self-description and cause further invalidity through uncooperativeness or carelessness. (c) Other, less restrictive formats are preferable in self-concept research; and other ways of controlling the intended variables, such as invalidating effects of social desirability, should be found.

CONTEXTUAL EFFECTS

Helson's (1964) application of adaptation-level theory to personality measurement draws attention to the possibility that a rater's judgments of the degree of applicability of an individual item to a particular person may be affected by item context. This notion, obviously of importance in interpreting self-concept measures, has received little research attention, with mixed results. In the research summarized below, the referents of the term *context* are expanded to include both the position of one item or group of items among other items and the place of a group of items with reference to an induced *normative set*.

Young, Holtzman, and Bryant (1954) studied the effects of evaluative context upon item judgments made about others. Basic airmen rated well-known airmen peers, using all-favorable, all-unfavorable, or mixed lists of Allport-Odbert adjectives, with each list being given in an original and a reversed order. While position and order effects upon individual items were essentially negligible, striking context effects were found, namely, a negative adjective was more likely to be judged characteristic of a ratee if it appeared in a mixed than in an all-negative list; while a positive adjective was more likely to be judged uncharacteristic of a ratee if it appeared in a mixed rather than an all-positive context. It would be methodologically valuable to replicate this study with self rather than others as the object of ratings.

Although the *evaluative* level of ratings was not affected by order in either the Young, Holtzman, and Bryant (1954) study or that of Warr and Knapper (1967), the latter study showed that the total number of adjectives checked as "applicable" and "definitely inapplicable" declined across the 300 adjectives of the ACL, whether the adjectives were given in alphabetic or reverse-alphabetic order. This study, too, concerned ratings of others and might profitably be replicated, using self-ratings.

Affective Contexts for Self-Ratings

Aiken did the earliest study of the effects of affective context on actual-self ratings (reported in Osgood, Suci, & Tannenbaum, 1957). Three scales were used, one to represent each of the factors of semantic space: evaluation, activity, and potency. Self-ratings were made on these scales at the same time that other highly evaluative concepts, highly active concepts, or highly potent concepts were rated. Neither the evaluative, activity, nor potency value of the self-concept rating was affected by the type of context.

Two other studies of possible contextual effects on self-reports involved the effects of the affective referent of contextual items (anxiety or hostility) on self-report scores regarding the respective affects (anxiety or hostility) (Feldman & Siegel, 1958; Siegel & Feldman, 1958). Manifest Anxiety scores and Manifest Hostility scores seemed to be unaffected by the inclusion of the other type of affective items, as compared to the inclusion of contextual buffer items.

Self-Reports and Endorsement Probability of Contextual Items

In two studies involving self-report, the *endorsement probability* of contextual items was varied and the proportion of endorsed items within the varying contexts was observed. Haertzen and Hooks (1968) looked at endorsement rates for those items which overlapped between or among three inventories: Addiction Research Center Inventory, MMPI, and California Psychological Inventory. The inventories were known to yield respectively a low, greater, and greatest endorsement rate for the drug-addicted Ss used in this research. Reasoning from adaptation-level theory, they predicted that the probability of endorsement of the overlapping (embedded) items would be inversely related to the endorsement rates of the inventory which formed the context. Actually, the endorsement probabilities for any one embedded item were almost identical across the contextual conditions (inventories). Therefore the authors concluded that, for the group, the self-report responses were unaffected by adjacent items or by contextual items as a whole.

McGee (1967) also found no effects of contextual probability of endorsement on probability of endorsement of "key," or dependent-variable, items embedded in the varying "filler-item" contexts. His study involved 12 artificial-item lists from the MMPI, 4 each for high, medium, and low probability-of-endorsement key items. The 4 lists for high-key items, for example, involved mixtures of these items, with filler items of high, low, and medium probability of endorsement, and with no filler items.

Self-Reports and Contextual Salience of a Personal Ideal

Four studies concerned the effects upon self-evaluation scores of drawing S's attention to an ideal-self norm just before asking for an actual-self description.

In Milgram and Helper's (1961) study, some incoming male medical students ranked the applicability of Murray's 15 needs to "self" and then to "successful physician," while others ranked the needs with respect to "successful physician" and then "self." A correlation *across needs* was computed for each individual between his self-description and successful-physician description. Those Ss whose attention was directed toward the successful-physician ideal before giving self-descriptions showed higher correlations (median $r = .85$) than did those who ranked the needs for self before having their attention specifically drawn to the successful-physician ideal.

In the other study suggesting that self-reports may be changed by increasing the contextual salience of a personal ideal (Nakamura, 1959), experimental Ss expressed their opinions (ideals) regarding attitudes toward mental illness, then answered questions about the actual behavior of self and others in the area of difficulties they would experience in deciding to seek psychotherapy if they had severe problems. As predicted, significantly more Ss evaluated their own actions in a way congruent with their enlightened ideals when the self-referent question appeared immediately after the statement of ideals, as opposed to appearing after describing the actual behavior of others.

Both Milgram and Helper (1961) and Nakamura (1959) could plausibly interpret their findings as indicating "defensive" behavior which Ss engage in to bring self-reports more in line with their momentarily highly salient ideals. However, the following three studies give no support to the generality of such a phenomenon. All of them involve varying the order in which Ss report on ideal self and actual self. Using a modified form of the Butler-Haigh *Q* sort, Williams (1963) found no difference in "adjustment score" for self and no difference in self-ideal congruence as a function of whether the self-sort preceded or followed the ideal sort. Using a 50-item *Q* sort from Cattell's list of surface traits, Quarter, Kennedy, and Laxer (1967) obtained no difference in mean self-ideal r in two groups, one of which sorted in the order self-then-ideal, and the other of which sorted in the order ideal-then-self. Palermo and Martire (1960) correlated *across mean item rankings* on 26 adjective scales and obtained similar null results. It is questionable whether this type of correlation is an appropriate test of their order hypothesis, however.

In summary, there are many conceivable contextual effects on self-concept measures, and few methodological studies relevant to the estimation of such influences. Although effects of evaluative context were found in one study of ratings of others, no effects of evaluative or affective context have been found in studies involving self-report. Reconciliation or synthesis of the results of these studies is impossible because of wide variations in method. In some, but not all, researches, contextual order effects have been found; and there is no obvious way to reconcile the variations in results. The probability of endorsement of an item does not seem to depend on the probability of endorsement of the items forming its context. Further methodological research in the area of contextual influences should be done; and pending the results of such research, substantive studies of self-concept should be examined to see whether artifactual contextual effects could plausibly account in part for the results.

SET, EXPECTATION, TASK STRUCTURE

The effect of set or expectation has been found in perceptual experiments to influence S_s' responses, perhaps partly by way of influencing perceptual processes as such, but quite probably by way of influencing response availability to some degree without necessarily altering perceptual processes. As it is well known from general experimental psychology that manipulating instructions may induce changes in set or expectation, the influence of instructions may pertinently be considered here. There have been marked variations from study to study in the particular directions given to S to define a concept which was assigned the same label (e.g., ideal self). No one has systematically studied the influence of such variations upon self-report responses in self-concept studies. Sometimes within the work of a single investigator there appears to be a wide gap between what S is literally told and the set which E infers he has induced in S. For example, Cohen (1959, and with Stotland et al., 1957) sometimes asked his S_s to mark his instrument as "a person" would act or feel and sometimes as "I" would act or feel. But he infers that in either case the individual is revealing his *own* self-concept (or ideal self).[1] Experimental demonstration of the equivalence of such differently worded instructions is lacking. In fact, certain investigators using other measuring instruments have demonstrated that reliably differing responses are obtained when the two types of instructions are responded to by the same S_s (Arnold & Walter, 1957, using the Rotter Incomplete Sentences Blank).

---

1. Personal communication, January 5, 1959.

Although not concerned explicitly with the problem of set or expectation in self-concept measurement, Fiske's (1966) paper on "task structure" as a factor in adequate, theory-relevant tests has obvious applicability to this issue. As his best single index of adequacy he uses *remainder variance*, the proportion of total variance in a person-item matrix which remains after subtracting the variances of item means and person means. His aim would be to reduce the person-item-interaction component of this remainder variance and to increase valid person variance with regard to a homogeneous construct dimension. A priori considerations and an examination of the adequacy of a number of self-report instruments led him to hypothesize that test adequacy should be a direct function of the degree of structure of the task, structure which is established by instructions and the situation. He further hypothesizes that the adequacy of a test is a direct function of the degree of structure of the typical item-stimulus. It seems reasonable that irrelevant response determiners (as indicated by remainder variance) may be decreased by increasing task and item structure; but the interpretation of person variance which such structuring may increase obviously depends on additional considerations. One of these is how clearly one conceptualizes the construct he wishes to measure; another is how careful one is in preparing substantively homogeneous relevant items. Loehlin (1961, 1967) found that individual differences in the "meaning" attributed to adjectival concepts equaled consistent individual differences in Ss' use of the adjectives to describe themselves. This implies that person variance in self-concept scores would be more clearly attributable to individual differences in self-concept if one could be more sure that Ss agree on the meanings of the terms. We should note that he is using the term *meaning* in the sense of Osgood's semantic space, not in the dictionary or denotative senses, and his results must be viewed in that light. Nevertheless, his work suggests that an important aim of item structuring should be to communicate to Ss as clearly as possible the behavioral referents to which the item is supposed to apply. So far as individual differences in connotative meaning in Osgood's sense are concerned, at least the evaluative dimension may be taken into account partially by asking S to indicate his "ideal" with respect to the concept. Loehlin (1961) himself suggests that fuller descriptions such as are used in some rating scales may reduce inter-S variance in meanings assigned to the items.

Paradoxically, though structure may reduce remainder variance by minimizing *some* irrelevant response determiners, it may open the way for *other* irrelevant response determiners to increase person variance (e.g., faking or resistance to self-disclosure would be easier to do in a structured situation). But, as I have previously pointed out, to continue to use the approach of making tests "nonobvious" through ambiguous structuring may only assure a large amount of uninterpretable remainder variance rather than make a greater proportion of person variance attributable to self-construct variance per se. We are repeatedly led to see that there is no known substitute for establishing maximum rapport and cooperation in the experimenter-subject interaction if we wish to maximize the construct validity of self-concept instruments.

Response Frequency

The frequency of making a response in the past has been shown to be related to response availability in perceptual and learning experiments. We may find it pertinent to seek for analogies here, too, in the measurement of the self-concept and the phenomenal field through self-report techniques. With meanings held as constant as possible, to what extent would variations in the familiarity of words furnished to S on check lists or rating scales affect their probability of endorsement, the probability of choice of one member of a pair of items, or the scale value S assigns an item to express his self-concept? To what extent will free-answer self-reports be a function of the ease with which certain common words or cliché phrases come to mind? This problem in constructing instruments remains virtually untouched. Wylie found that open-ended essays describing the self (used in her 1957 study) gave the coder a strong impression of Ss' cliché-proneness. Using a Q-sort technique, D. M. Taylor (1955) found markedly increasing congruence between self and ideal on repeated testing over a short time interval. Quite plausibly this could be an example of the influence on S's responses of increasing familiarity with the response items, since no therapy or other theoretically relevant variable was known to have intervened which might have changed the phenomenal self as such. We must conclude, however, that there has been no formal study of the possible influence of response familiarity upon the validity of a self-report technique for revealing Ss' phenomenal fields; and that no means of minimizing the influence of this variable has been developed.

SCORING AND STATISTICAL PROCEDURES

Finally, as part of the search for the influence of irrelevant variables on our measuring process, we need to examine our scoring and statistical procedures to determine whether they may be affecting our findings in misleading ways.

Response Total and Response Length

The need to control for response total appears in any instrument in which S is allowed to give as many or as few responses as he wishes. For example, if the number of items chosen from an adjective check list is taken as S's score without allowance for the total possible number which could be chosen, group comparisons regarding aspects of self-concept may be confounded with tendencies to choose few or many items (e.g., in Sarbin & Rosenberg, 1955).

In various instruments, the attempt is made to control R total by using percent scores; but this is a dubious practice when the total number of Rs used as the basis for computing percents may be very few, as it often is in the Twenty Sentences Test (Mulford & Salisbury, 1964), for example.

A related problem concerns response length. Megargee (1966) has shown, for example, that response length is correlated with various response scores on the Holtzman Ink Blot Test. Thus, even if the number of Rs is held constant by asking for only one response per card, scores of a particular kind might be a function of the tendency to make lengthy responses rather than being a function of the construct the scores purport to measure.

Summation across Scaled Items

Some self-concept researchers use only one psychological dimension as a basis for their scores. The scaling problems which must be handled if construct validity is to be maximized are discussed in section C of this chapter. When Es add scores across scale dimensions, numerous opportunities occur for irrelevant influences on the sum to diminish its construct validity. Some of these also have already been considered in section C above.

Influence of Dichotomous Scoring

If each answer is scored dichotomously, the remainder variance (as opposed to person and item variance) is artifactually inflated, compared to what is obtainable with multistep scoring (Fiske, 1966). Also, limitations are set on the magnitudes of obtainable phi coefficients and Pearson r coefficients, depending on the item marginal splits. This can lead to possible misleading results, as explained, for example, by Block (1965).

Items Overlapping between Trait Scales

If two or more separate trait-scale scores are based in part on overlapping items, correlations between these scores or comparisons of correlations between each and an external variable are bound to be artifactual to some extent (Block, 1965).

Influences of Ipsative Scoring

Ipsative scoring of allegedly different trait scales which ordinarily results from forced-choice formats means that S cannot score simultaneously high (or simultaneously low) on two or more trait scales, even if he so judges himself. An artifactual tendency toward negative intercorrelations between trait scales is built in by this type of scoring, possibly leading to mistaken conclusions about the discriminability of the traits to the Ss. Also, correlations between ipsatively scored scales and external variables will quite possibly be very misleading as compared to counterpart correlations between nonipsatively scored trait scales and external variables. Finally, the degree of linear dependence among ipsative trait scores makes the application of factor analysis techniques inappropriate, and factor patterns especially hard to interpret (Jackson, 1967a).

Two-Part Indices

The most serious and frequently occurring scoring difficulties in the area of self-concept research seem to be those associated with two-part indices, for example, self-ideal discrepancies supposedly indicative of self-regard, and self-other discrepancies purporting to measure insight. Such two-part indices have been widely used without sufficient prior exploration of questions which are highly pertinent to their possible interpretation in terms of the construct which they purport to index. The many questions about the construct validity of these indices go beyond those which pertain to factors influencing the construct validity of each of two components—factors considered in the preceding sections of this chapter.

Conceptual Distinctions among Two-Part Indices. "Difference" and "gain" scores of all types, including the above-mentioned ones, have come under increasing methodological evaluation and criticism. Differences of opinion have been expressed as to which "corrected form" of obtained "raw" difference scores might be most appropriate (e.g., Cronbach & Furby, 1970; O'Connor, 1972a, 1972b). More basically, the question has been raised whether difference scores "are rarely useful, no matter how they may be adjusted or refined [Cronbach & Furby, 1970, p. 68]." In their general analysis of difference and gain scores, Cronbach and Furby (1970) imply that the same sorts of methodological criticism apply to a wide variety of such scores, including both self-ideal discrepancies supposedly indicative of self-regard, and self-other discrepancies supposedly indicative of insight. In fact, they argue that there is no justification for computing and using difference scores for individuals in order to operationalize individual differences in standing with respect to a construct's dimension. However, I contend that the self-ideal discrepancies and self-other discrepancies are conceptually different from one another and therefore require somewhat different kinds of methodological analysis, despite certain operational similarities. My argument stems from the fact that the self-ideal discrepancy is a phenomenal discrepancy, while the self-other discrepancy is not.

Specifically, a discrepancy between S's self-description and his ideal-self description on a psychological dimension involves a difference between two "points," both by definition in the phenomenal field of the S. Thus we are dealing with a discrepancy which we may conceptalize as being experienced directly by the reporting S and reacted to directly by him. This implies that a subtractive procedure is not the only conceivable way of operationalizing such a discrepancy, that is, that an alternate index might be taken in terms of S's reporting directly the experienced magnitude of the discrepancy. By contrast, a discrepancy between S's self-description on a psychological dimension and O's report about S's standing on that dimension, although also a "difference" score, does not define a discrepancy which is experienced by and reportable by S. Therefore the subtractive index of insight cannot conceivably be supplanted by an alternate direct report by S concerning this discrepancy, as was conceivable in the case of the self-ideal discrepancy.

Since these two types of two-part scores seem to be getting at quite different types of discrepancies, I give below a separate methodological consideration of each. The bulk of the present discussion is devoted to a consideration of self-ideal discrepancies. A more thorough analysis of the insight score is postponed until chapter 6, where its many complexities are reviewed in detail.

Regarding the self-ideal discrepancy scores, one should note that those who use them often interpret them as indices of self-regard without considering the many assumptions and possible complications briefly described below. (To simplify the immediately following discussion I direct my comments to self-ideal discrepancy scores obtained on a single psychological dimension. Complexities introduced by summing discrepancies across dimensions are considered later on.)

Cognitive Self-Ideal Discrepancies and Self-Regard. At the outset it is necessary to make a conceptual distinction which is typically completely ignored by Es who use this type of score—a distinction between the cognitively experienced magnitude of a self-ideal discrepancy and the degree of S's self-regard. Simply to assume a perfect correspondence between cognitive magnitude of the discrepancy and strength of affective reactions associated with it is unwarranted on both intuitive, conceptual grounds and empirical grounds.

Self-Ideal Discrepancies: Implications of the X-Y Subtraction. Cronbach and Furby (1970) argue that the use of differences between two values to define individual Ss' scores indicative of a construct should be discontinued in favor of multivariate approaches. However, they suggest that, if E is determined to use two-part subtractive scores, a number of methodological refinements may increase the construct validity of such scores. First, instead of subtracting raw X from raw Y, they suggest that E should subtract estimated "true" $\hat{Y}_\infty$ from estimated "true" $\hat{X}_\infty$. Moreover, they point out that the use of either of these subtractive procedures implies that the best way to operationalize a construct defined by a discrepancy between two values is simply to subtract one value from the other. That is, they say that the use of simple subtraction does not take into account the possibility that the discrepancy score might define the construct better if one used the expression $\hat{X} - a\hat{Y}$ (where a could take any value), as opposed to the usual procedure in which one simply takes $X - 1.00 \, Y$. On what grounds, however, could one choose that value of a which would lead to the best operational definition of the construct in question? According to Cronbach and Furby (1970), one should be guided by that function of X_∞ and Y_∞ which has the strongest relations with "variables that should connect with the construct [p. 79]."

However, in the case of phenomenal self-ideal discrepancies, I argue that neither the discontinuation of the subtractive type of self-ideal index in favor of multivariate approaches nor Cronbach and Furby's (1970) suggested empirical approach to weighting the X and Y variables in the discrepancy is necessarily appropriate to the theoretical status of this particular construct. That is, since the discrepancy is presumably something S can experience as a difference between his actual self-concept and his ideal for himself, there seems to be a theoretical reason to try to operationalize it by a subtractive score, as free as possible of irrelevant influences, of course.

The phenomenal status of the self-ideal discrepancy also implies that it would be open to being operationalized by an alternate method, that is, by a direct judgment by S of the size of the experienced discrepancy. So far as the cognitive phenomenal self-ideal discrepancy is concerned, it would be most interesting to see whether estimates of its magnitude obtained by the subtractive procedure correlate highly with values obtained when Ss are asked to give direct judgments of the magnitudes of these discrepancies. If the results of such explorations show imperfect correspondence between subtractive self-ideal discrepancies and self-ideal discrepancies judged directly by S, one might consider abandoning the discrepancy-score method altogether. Alternately, if one wished to retain the subtractive score and introduce "correction factors" into it, the value of a in the expression $X - aY$ might be made in terms of the respective functional relationships of "true" self score and "true" ideal score to S's direct estimates of discrepancy size. This approach in terms of alternate indices of the construct seems potentially more appropriate to the problem at hand than does Cronbach and Furby's (1970) more general approach of choosing the value of a in terms of the functional relations of "true" self score and "true" ideal score to "variables that should *connect with* the construct [p. 79, emphasis added]."

Additional Problems in Self-Ideal Discrepancy Scores. Returning to issues concerning the subtractive method of scoring, even if one can successfully build a defense for such an approach as being conceptually appropriate to operationalizing a self-ideal discrepancy experienced by S, one still must face many complications in addition to those already examined. These complications may finally lead to the advisability of abandoning this type of score.

For one thing, it should be realized that the attainment of highly reliable difference scores depends upon having a high average reliability of the two component scores and a low correlation between the component scores. For example, if the mean reliability of the components entering the difference score is .80 and the correlation between them was .80, the reliability of the difference scores would be expected to be zero. If the average reliability of the components was .80 but the correlation between the components was .00, the reliability coefficient of the difference scores might then be expected to reach .80 (Stanley, 1971).

Even if highly reliable self-ideal discrepancies are obtained, one must still hold open the question raised earlier: Do reported self-ideal discrepancies of various sizes merely indicate varying degrees of cognitively experienced discrepancy, or are they valid indicators of degrees of self-regard as well? If experienced self-ideal discrepancies do have some association with self-regard, one must still consider more specific questions: Are reported self-ideal discrepancies of a given size anywhere along a psychological dimension interpretable as indicating the same degree of self-regard? Does a large discrepancy from one part of the scale range necessarily indicate poorer self-regard than a smaller discrepancy from another part of the scale range? More direct demonstration than has been forthcoming thus far will be required to justify using size of reported cognitive self-ideal discrepancy as a basis for inferring degree of self-regard.

The Self Score as an Alternate to the Self-Ideal Discrepancy. It may appear that some investigators have gotten around some of these difficulties by using only the S's descriptions of self (which I call self scores). However, when Es do this, in effect they use the favorable end of the scale as the "ideal self" reference point, and each S's self score therefore amounts to a discrepancy between the self-descriptive scale point and this common ideal point.

One possible advantage of the self score of self-regard is that the only source of unreliability in it is the self score itself, since the ideal value is fixed for all Ss. At first glance it might appear that another advantage is gotten from the use of the self-score method: since each self score is, in effect, assigned its value by subtraction from a common ideal value, each successively larger self score, that is, each successively larger "discrepancy" between the self score and the fixed ideal end of the scale, includes the scale range of the next smaller "discrepancy" plus an additional part of the range. Accordingly, it might appear that one has by-passed troublesome questions as to whether successively larger "discrepancies" (self scores) involve successively larger experienced self-ideal discrepancies. Also, since there would be in the self-score approach only one way to get a "discrepancy" score of a given size, it might appear that one would not be troubled by the question whether "discrepancy" values of the same size from different parts of the psychological dimension indicate equivalent experienced discrepancies. Moreover, on an empirical level, the fact that there is considerable stereotypy among individual ideal-self reports—so that such ideal-self reports actually contribute relatively little to the variance in self-ideal discrepancies— might be used to support the argument that one might as well use only self scores rather than discrepancies computed by subtracting self from individually reported ideal values.

But possible objections to the use of self scores as indices of either cognitive self-ideal discrepancies or of self-regard must be considered. First and foremost, the phenomenological theorist would be concerned that his measures are consistently phenomenological, which means that the discrepancy between the scale value of S's own self score and his own stated ideal for self is more conceptually appropriate to phenomenological research than is a "discrepancy" between S's self-report and a fixed value set by external judges. Thus it is illustory to suppose that one has solved the problem of interpretation of discrepancy sizes simply by declaring without warrant that the ideal for self is seen by all Ss at the same point. Second, this approach still does not address the problem of whether or how cognitive self-ideal discrepancies and degrees of self-regard are related. Third, it is an empirical question of considerable theoretical interest whether and to what extent S's reported ideal for self is related to the self-report; and in addition, whether the ideal-self report is related to other variables to which the self score is also related, for example, to directly stated self-acceptance, to measures of defensiveness, or to measures of popularity. One cannot explore these questions if individual ideal-self reports are not obtained.

In short, a discrepancy between self and stated ideal for self seems plausibly to be an experience about which S should be able to report, and which phenomenologists should attempt to index and use in research, since such an approach is consistent with their theorizing. On the other hand, many unwarranted conclusions can be reached if insufficient attention is paid to the interpretational pitfalls in the use of two-part indices and to the relationships of each component to other theoretically relevant behavior measures. Moreover, if one's interest is primarily in predicting behavior accurately (that is, without regard for the theoretical implications or explanations of such accuracy), it may turn out that the self-report (as opposed to the self-ideal discrepancy report) should be used.

Problems of Summation of Self-Ideal Discrepancies. Thus far my comments have referred to a self-ideal discrepancy based on a single psychological dimension. It is obvious that trying to interpret even such a "simple" self-ideal discrepancy score is fraught with many hazards. But the most commonly used forms of self-ideal discrepancy score introduce even more complexities. For example, in Bills's (undated) IAV, Worchel's (1957) Self-Activity Inventory, or Leary's (1957) ICL, a self-ideal discrepancy is obtained for S for each of numerous trait scales. These separate discrepancies are then summed to yield a total self-ideal discrepancy score for S, supposedly indicative of S's "global" self-regard. I pointed out earlier that it is not known even within a single scale that equal-size discrepancies represent either equal-size cognitive discrepancies or equal degrees of self-regard. When one sums discrepancies across trait scales, one is, in effect, assuming that equal-size discrepancies *anywhere* on *any one* of numerous trait scales correspond to equal-size cognitive discrepancies or equal degrees of self-regard. Obviously, this much broader assumption is even farther from being demonstrated than is the case for a single scale.

Beyond the above-mentioned complexities introduced by summation across scales, there is also the question of handling "reverse discrepancies" when summing. The reader may imagine that it would be unlikely for S's rating of self to be more favorable (in terms of the culturally ideal end of the scale) than his rating of his ideal self. However, such "reverse discrepancies" do occur; for example, S may say that he is actually a more friendly person than he ideally would like to be. Worchel (1957), in connection with this problem on his Self-Activity Inventory, contends that "in any case it is the amount of discrepancy and not the direction that is important in the prediction of maladjustment [p. 7]." I question whether discrepancies in a "reversed" direction have the same meaning in terms of self-regard as do discrepancies in the more usual direction. For this reason, the common practice of absolute summing seems questionable without further relevant evidence regarding its effects on construct validity. On the other hand, it is not clear what defensible change could be substituted. That is, if algebraic summation is used and frequent "reversed" discrepancies occur, the positive and negative values could cancel each other, giving S a sum indicative of relatively little overall self-ideal discrepancy, when in fact he reported many such discrepancies on individual psychological dimensions.

Discrepancy Scores of Insight. Returning to the point that discrepancy scores of insight may involve somewhat different conceptual and methodological analysis than the self-ideal discrepancy scores, I must repeat the observation that, in the case of insight, the two values on which the discrepancy score are based come from different reporters, S and an other. That is, we are not dealing with a phenomenal state of S which presumably might be indexed alternately by subtracting values assigned to two of S's reports or by asking for direct judgments from S. The complications of discrepancy scores of insight are fully discussed in chapter 6, and the implications of the distinction I have just drawn are developed there. Meanwhile, suffice it to say that the pitfalls in trying to obtain a valid insight score in terms of a discrepancy are in many ways similar to those in deriving any two-part operational definition of a construct; but there is less reason to argue for the potential usefulness of individual discrepancy scores as possibly valid and appropriate individual-difference measures to use in the study of insight.

2. Correlational Analyses of Convergent and Discriminant Validity

INTERCORRELATIONS

It is somewhat useful to examine convergent validity by looking at intercorrelations between scores purporting to measure the same construct, for example, to intercorrelate alleged measures of global self-regard. If the correlations are considerably lower than the respective reliabilities would permit, this, of course, calls into question the construct validity of the noncorrelating scales which bear the same label. Unfortunately, if high intercorrelations are obtained, construct validity is only suggested, not definitively evaluated, because irrelevant factors could account for the high correlations. Many empirical intercorrelations among self-concept measures have appeared in the literature, most of them involving scores purporting to index global self-regard.

Cross-instrument correlations between purported measures of a global self-regard construct have run between essentially zero and +.81, depending on the sample and instruments involved. The typical r is about .40. Of 93 cross-instrument correlations we examined, only 7 were .7 or .8. There are too few replications of any particular combination to sustain generalizations about any instrument, but obviously the picture is not encouraging regarding the construct validities of most of the scores correlated. (For correlations between the IAV and other instruments, see Bendig & Hoffman, 1957, re IAV and Maudsley; Bills's undated manual, re IAV and Phillips's Self-Acceptance and Berger's Self-Acceptance; Cowen, 1956, re IAV and Brownfain's, 1952, scale; Crowne, Stephens, & Kelly, 1961, re IAV, Buss's adjectives, and ACL; Omwake, 1954, re IAV, Phillips' Self-Acceptance, and Berger's Self-Acceptance; Spitzer, Stratton, Fitzgerald, & Mach, 1966, re IAV, ACL, TST, and Fiedler's Semantic Differential; Stone & Winkler, 1964, re IAV Self-Acceptance and BHQ; Winkler & Myers, 1963, re IAV and BHQ; Viney, 1966, re IAV, Motivation Analysis Test, 16 Personality Factor Questionnaire [16 PF], CPI, Shlien's Abstract Apparatus, and Ideo-Q-Sort. For correlations between the CPI and other instruments, see Hamilton, 1971, re CPI, ICL, Janis-Field, and self-ratings; Schludermann & Schludermann, 1970b, re CPI, SAI, and Maslow's Security-Insecurity [S-I]; Vincent, 1968, re CPI, Tennessee Self Concept Scale [TSCS], 16 PF, Maslow's S-I. For other combinations, see Herbert, Gelfand, & Hartmann, 1969, re Bledsoe-Garrison and Sears's tests of children's self-esteem; Larsen & Schwendiman, 1969, re semantic differential, Janis-Field, and Barron's Ego Strength; Mayer, 1967, re Lipsitt and Piers-Harris self-concept scales for children; Perkins & Shannon, 1965, re Coopersmith's Self-Esteem Inventory [SEI], Machover's Draw-a-Person [DAP], and Shannon and Shoemaker's pictorial test; Sears, 1970, re self-criticism, ideas of reference, self-aggression and self-satisfaction [subscales of goodness of self-concept]; Silber & Tippett, 1965, re Rosenberg Self-Esteem, Heath's Self-Image, Repertory Test, and interview estimates.)

Some studies involve associations between corresponding subscales of two instruments which plausibly should correlate since they seem to be intended to measure corresponding constructs. The' results of these studies are complex, but typically, little if any support is given to the construct validity of the scores which purport to measure corresponding content dimensions of the self-concept. (See, for example, Gynther, Miller, & Davis, 1962, re EPPS and ICL; Megargee & Parker, 1968, re ACL and EPPS; Mitchell, 1963a, re 16 PF and CPI; Merenda & Clarke, 1968, re Activity Vector Analysis [AVA] and ACL; Parker, 1966, re questionnaires and Picture Story Test; Schlicht, Carlson, Skeen, & Skurdal, 1968, re Incomplete Sentences Blank [ISB] and modified BHQ.)

FACTOR ANALYSIS

Factor analysis is not a single technique, but a group of techniques designed to describe or interpret in more or less parsimonious terms the correlations in a matrix. By far the most common type of matrix involves correlations among items (or among tests) across persons; and the immediately following paragraphs concern only such matrices. (The reader who is unfamiliar with factor-analytic technique will find Eysenck's [1970, chap. 2] brief introduction helpful as a basis for understanding this section.)

In factor analysis, choices of type of solution, number of factors to retain, and rotation scheme are somewhat arbitrary, with concomitant limitations on the definitiveness of the results. (See P. A. Smith, 1962, and Norman, 1969, for direct comparisons of several solutions applied to the same set of data.) Interpretation of the obtained factors is also not dictated by the mathematical solution chosen, further limiting the usefulness of factor analysis as a tool. In fact, as Coan's (1964) review summarizes, there is a wide range of expert opinion as to whether any factor can justifiably be interpreted in any psychological terms, or should be considered merely one mathematical expression of correlational trends. However, if one *is* willing to assume that it is useful to theorize, using admittedly "invented" and provisional hypothetical constructs, then "a factor interpretation in the form of a hypothetical concept is useful if the entities or relationships to which it refers can be examined in the light of further research [Coan, 1964, p. 128]." In this argument, factor analysis does have some value in designing and evaluating new psychometric instruments as well as in evaluating the construct validity of extant measures.

One may apply factor analysis to several kinds of matrices: correlations between items, usually within an instrument or within a provisional item pool; correlations between scales within an instrument; or correlations between scale and/or total scores from two or more instruments.

Factor analysis may be employed in a number of ways to explore and improve convergent and discriminant construct validity. One can use it in an exploratory, inductive fashion to suggest plausible interpretations of items or item groups which "belong together" in terms of a factor solution. Follow-up by way of test construction, revision, or interpretation would depend on the purposes of the investigator. Lumsden (1961) has argued that factor analysis provides the only rational procedure for selecting items for constructing unidimensional tests. One extracts a single factor from the interitem correlations, culls out items having large residuals, and reanalyzes the intercorrelations among the remaining items until a satisfactory fit to a single-factor solution is obtained. Such a satisfactory outcome will probably occur only if items are carefully preselected with the aim of attaining interitem homogeneity and a sufficiently large proportion of homogeneous items is put into the item pool. Thus, factor analysis cannot guarantee success in unidimensional scale construction.

Another use of factor analysis is to test hypotheses about the construct validity of extant instruments. As one example of hypothesis testing, if the only purpose of an instrument is to measure a global construct (e.g., self-esteem), one should be able to attain a meaningful general-factor solution from an interitem correlation matrix involving semantically heterogeneous content; and the items should load acceptably on the general factor. Of course, success in obtaining a satisfactory general-factor solution does not suffice to demonstrate that irrelevant variables such as response set have been ruled out as an explanation of the intercorrelations (e.g., perhaps the factor could be interpreted in terms of response set rather than self-esteem).

As another example of hypothesis testing, if an instrument is alleged to measure several self-concept factors with several respective scores, but no group-factor solution can be found in which the items or separate scales load appropriately on the respective factors, the use of separate labels and scores for the scales is misleading. But again, the attainment of a satisfactory correspondence between factors and scales, or factors and item clusters, is only suggestive, not definitive with respect to whether the scores reflect the purported self-concept dimensions.

No matter what result is attained by a given factor analysis of an instrument purporting to measure some aspect of the self-concept, we should see under what circumstances, if any, it is replicable before we attempt to give more than a highly tentative interpretation of the factors in theoretical terms (Coan, 1964).

Finally, questions have been raised whether the factors ("psychological dimensions") which are suggested by analyzing correlations among scores across persons may be appropriately interpreted as characterizing any individual (Coan, 1964). This controversial question awaits further study of the relationships between the outcomes of the usual factor-analytic techniques and others which have been proposed. Such other factor-analytic techniques involve, for example, matrices of correlations among persons across items (Cattell, 1952; Fagan & Guthrie, 1959; Gorlow, Simonson, & Krauss, 1966; Guthrie, Butler, & Gorlow, 1961; Stephenson, 1952; Stricker & Ross, 1964); or intraindividual matrices of correlations from a Q sort (Edelson & Jones, 1954; Frisch & Cranston, 1956; Nunnally, 1955; C. R. Rogers, 1954a, 1954b); from a questionnaire regarding role variability (Block, 1961); or from a "personal construct" grid (Bannister & Mair, 1968).

Turning now to empirical output, we find dozens of factor analyses involving instruments which have been devised or appropriated by self-concept researchers. Some instruments have been developed on the basis of factor analysis, others analyzed ad hoc. Several conclusions emerge:

1. So far as *internal* factor analysis is concerned, interitem analyses are rare as compared to interscale analyses. This leaves the matter of *intrascale* homogeneity typically unexplored by factor analytic techniques (and usually unexplored by any empirical method other than E's or judges' opinions)!

2. Practically none of the instruments commonly used by self-concept researchers has been subjected to more than one *internal* factor analysis based on different sets of data, much less to internal analyses which are sufficiently similar to be considered cross-validations. Exceptions are Bills's Index of Adjustment and Values (IAV),

Gough and Heilbrun's Adjective Check List (ACL), LaForge and Suczeks's Interpersonal Check List (ICL), the MMPI, the California Personality Inventory (CPI), certain Osgood Semantic Differential scales (Smith, 1962), and self-rating scales used by Borgatta (1960a, 1960b, 1964) and by Norman (1969).

3. A number of self-concept instruments have been included among the variables in a factored battery (which may include other self-concept variables as well as other types of variables). But apparently there has been no replication of any of the battery combinations; so results cannot be compared from study to study.

4. Internal factor-analytic solutions typically have not supported the purported discriminant validity of separate scale scores. For example, numerous interscale factor analyses of MMPI reveal only two sizable factors (Block, 1965; Edwards, Diers, & Walker, 1962; Kassebaum, Couch & Slater, 1969; Jackson, 1967a; Welsh, 1956).

In the studies which factored correlations among the 18 scales of the CPI, only two to six interpretable factors were obtained (Crites, Bechtoldt, Goodstein, & Heilbrun, 1961; Mitchell & Pierce-Jones, 1960; Nichols & Schnell, 1963; Pierce-Jones, Mitchell, & King, 1962; Schludermann & Schludermann, 1970a; Shure & Rogers, 1963; Springob & Struening, 1964; Veldman & Pierce-Jones, 1964).

Three factor analyses of the eight basic variables of the ICL revealed that three factors were sufficient to account for most of the variance, one of them being perhaps methodological (Bentler, 1963; Briar & Bieri, 1963; one by LaForge cited in Foa, 1961).

Levonian (1961a) factored interitem correlations from the 16 PF test and obtained evidence that only four factors were needed to account for the variance. Moreover, Levonian (1961b) found that items within any one of the 16 PF factors are not at all homogeneous. In a factor analysis of the 16 PF and the 13 scales of the Guilford-Martin Inventory, W. C. Becker (1961) found eight distinguishing factors within the 16 PF.

A similar finding was obtained for the Edwards Personal Preference Scale, where 15 interitem factor analyses were performed, one for each of the separate need scales (Levonian, Comrey, Levy, & Procter, 1959). Interitem correlations within any one scale were extremely low, and no evidence was found of a large factor corresponding to the need purportedly measured by the scale. These authors and Stricker (1965) have both questioned the applicability of factor analysis to a forced-choice test which yields ipsative scores.

Milton and Lipetz (1968) attempted to circumvent these objections by intercorrelating scale scores from which they eliminated those items which forced S to choose between the two needs being correlated. Factoring matrices of such correlations for males and females, they obtained only five factors for each matrix.

In a factor analysis of a matrix of intercorrelations of twelve scores from the Tennessee Self Concept Scale, Rentz and White (1967a) found that all self-scores (three row and five column scores) loaded highly on only the first ("evaluative") factor. However, the application of factor analysis is inappropriate since row scores are completely redundant with column scores in this test. Working with correlations among 100 TSCS items, Vacchiano and Strauss (1968) obtained 20 factors; but the factors did not correspond respectively to the TSCS scales.

Using 24 ACL scales, Parker and Megargee (1967) found only three content-relevant factors in each of three factor analyses (observers' reports of delinquent Ss; self-reports of Peace Corps Ss; freshman Ss). The factors were comparable between matrices. From a factor analysis of the correlations among the 300 ACL items, Parker and Veldman (1969) obtained seven factors.

Petersen (1965) expresses the most extreme view about the possibility of obtaining many self-report factors having discriminant validity. He believes that, in general, only two factors will suffice to account for all the common matrix variance in verbal personality tests, regardless of the number of dimensions the test purports to measure. He argues that factor results are more replicable if only two factors are extracted and that these factors will be found to refer to perceived adjustment and introversion-extraversion. While Petersen's argument is based mainly on reexamination of Cattell's work, Eysenck (1970) presents relevant information in his evaluation of the factor-analytic work of a number of other researchers.

5. Factor-analytic studies of instruments purporting to measure "overall" self-esteem, self-acceptance, etc., lead one to believe that either there is no such measurable dimension as overall self-esteem, or at least some of the scales purporting to measure this construct are doing a poor job of it. For example, Schludermann and Schludermann (1969a, 1969b) factor analyzed interitem self, interitem ideal self, and interitem discrepancy correlations for Worchel's Self Activity Inventory (SAI). For the separate scores (Self, Ideal) the maximum amount of variance accounted for by any one of 16 to 19

factors extracted per matrix was 11% to 19%. They concluded that the SAI was not a unidimensional scale. Mitchell (1962) reports 7 factors for the 49 items of Bills's Index of Adjustment and Values (IAV). Bills, however, reports that he has factored each of the following four matrices of interitem correlations: Self, Self-Acceptance, Ideal Self, and [Self − Ideal]. In each matrix, the first factor accounted for 60% to 62% of the variance, leading him to believe that a general factor accounts for most of the variance in each matrix (Bills, personal communication, 1971).

Vincent (1968) factored intercorrelations among selected scales of the CPI, TSCS, and 16 PF. The scales were selected because they had been similarly labeled by their maker as purported measures of self-acceptance or a feeling of self-adequacy. After varimax rotation to orthogonal simple structure, the first of the two factors Vincent retained accounted for 48% of the variance; but the CPI variables showed little or no loading on this factor. Viney (1966), too, found no evidence of a general factor to account for correlations between scales, all of which purported to measure self-regard. Using [Self − Ideal] discrepancies on 40 items of a self-regard questionnaire, Guertin and Jourard (1962) found a large "self-esteem" factor for males, but not for females.

The total yield of information in proportion to the energy and time expended on factor analysis of self-concept measures seems limited. It is clear that factor analysis has been used more to test hypotheses about extant self-concept tests than as a tool in the construction of new ones. The consistent failure to support the maker's hypotheses, though disappointing, yields valuable information. To avoid such disappointments and make more constructive use of the factor-analytic technique, it is desirable to use the technique from the beginning of the test construction process; and as we discuss below in connection with the multitrait-multimethod matrix analyses of Campbell and Fiske (1959), especially devised variants of factor analysis will probably prove useful in exploring discriminant and convergent construct validity by the multitrait-multimethod approach.

For the benefit of readers interested in available factor-analytic information regarding particular tests used in self-concept research, I list here the articles which I have examined. (Further references regarding factor analyses involving some of these instruments may be found in Buros, 1970.)

List 1 is arranged according to the test which has been internally factor analyzed. List 2 involves factor analyses of varying combinations of tests (or scales therefrom) and is arranged alphabetically by author, with the tests indicated separately for each article. Publications involving the usual factor-analytic technique, inverse factor analysis, and intraindividual factor analysis are all included for the sake of completeness.

List 1: Instruments Subjected to Internal Factor Analysis

(For additional references prior to 1960, see Eysenck, 1970, chap. 5.)

Activity Vector Analysis (AVA)
  Merenda and Clarke (1959)

Adjective Check List (Gough) (ACL)
  See text references above

Butler-Haigh Q sort (BHQ)
  Butler (1968)
  McKenna, Hofstaetter, and O'Connor (1956)
  Rogers, C. R. (1954a, 1954b)

California Psychological Inventory (CPI)
  See text references above, and List 2

Clyde Mood Scale
  Klein and Parsons (1968)

Early School Personality Questionnaire
  Coan and Cattell (1959)

Edwards Personal Preference Scale (EPPS)
  See text references above

General Adaptability Adjective Check List (GAAL)
  Sciortino (1969b)

High School Personality Questionnaire
  Cattell, Wagner, and Cattell (1970)

Ideological Survey
  Pishkin and Thorne (1968)
  Thorne and Pishkin (1968)

Illinois Index of Self-Derogation
  Meyerowitz (1962)

Index of Adjustment and Values (Bills's IAV)
  See text references above

Intellective Adjective Check List (IAL)
  Sciortino (1969a)

Leadership Self Ratings
  Bartlett (1959)

Metaphor Scales
  Knapp (1960)

Minnesota Multiphasic Personality Inventory (MMPI)
  See text references above, and List 2

Mother-Child Relationships Questionnaire
  Mitchell (1963b)

Motivational Adjective Check List (MACL)
  Sciortino (1967a, 1967b, 1967c, 1968)

Picture Choice (for retardates)
  Guthrie, Butler, Gorlow, and White (1964)

Piers-Harris Children's Self-Concept Scale
  Piers and Harris (1964)

Q sorts, miscellaneous
  Baker (1968)
  Edelson and Jones (1954)
  Fagan and Guthrie (1959) (instrument relevant to Arieti and
    Sullivan)
  Frisch and Cranston (1956)
  Gorlow, Simonson, and Krauss (1966) (instrument relevant
    to Jung's typology)
  Klausner (1953)
  Kniss, Butler, Gorlow, and Guthrie (1962) (instrument for
    ideal self, retardates)
  Nunnally (1955) (instrument created from patient's state-
    ments, for her use)
  Pearl (1954)

Rosenberg Self-Esteem Scales
    Kaplan and Pokorny (1969)
    List 2

Self Activity Inventory (Worchel's SAI)
    See text references above, and List 2

Self-Concept Questionnaires, Miscellaneous
    Guertin and Jourard (1962)
    Gunderson and Johnson (1965)
    Washburn (1961)

Self-Concept Test for Retardates
    Guthrie, Butler, and Gorlow (1961)

Self-Ratings, Miscellaneous (See also Questionnaires, Miscellaneous)
    Block (1961a)
    Borgatta (1960, 1964)
    Elliott (1960)
    Engel and Raine (1963)
    Lorr and Rubenstein (1956)
    Norman (1969) (same scales as Borgatta)
    Richards (1966)
    Rubenstein and Lorr (1957)
    Storm, Rosenwald, and Child (1958)
    Zimmer (1956)

Self-Report Inventory
    Bown, Fuller, and Richek (1967)

Semantic Differential, Miscellaneous Scales from Osgood, or General Technique Applied
    Burke and Bennis (1961)
    Kingston and White (1967)
    Reece (1964)
    Smith, P. A. (1960, 1962)

16 PF (Cattell)
    See text references above, and List 2

Tennessee Self Concept Scale (TSCS)
    See text references above, and List 2

Word Rating List (academic self-concept)
Payne and Farquhar (1962)

Where Are You? (children's self-concept test)
Engel and Raine (1963)

List 2: Factor Analyses Involving Mixtures of Tests or Scales

Becker, W. C. (1960), potpourri of variables, including parental self-ratings

Berger (1968), mixture of Janis-Field and Eagly items re self-esteem

Cartwright, Kirtner, and Fiske (1963), MMPI, Q sort, Social Attitude Scores, posttherapy questionnaires

Cartwright and Roth (1957), 10 measures, including BHQ self-ideal r, Q-adjustment score, Willoughby therapists' ratings, E score, ratings from TAT

David (1968), 3 MMPI scales, Superego Test

Farley (1968), self-ratings, questionnaires re drive, anxiety

Forsyth and Fairweather (1961), 66 clinical variables, including self-ideal r from Q sort

Gibson, Snyder, and Ray (1955), 6 MMPI scores, 6 Rorschach indices, 8 interview measures

Gocka and Marks (1961), 11 MMPI scales; 16 PF

Grant (1969), TSCS, Forms A and B of 16 PF, personal data

Rentz and White (1967b), Osgood Semantic Differential Self and Ideal; TSCS, 16 PF

Rokeach and Fruchter (1956), 10 scales: Welsh A and Pa from MMPI, Dogmatism, F, Rigidity, E, PEC, Left Opinionation, Right Opinionation, self-rejection

Schludermann and Schludermann (1970b), CPI, SAI, Maslow's S-I

Singer (1969), Do of CPI, MCSD, Welsh A of MMPI, ACL, other variables

Stimson (1968), IAV (3 scores), BHQ (Dymond scores), SAI (Self), and other variables

Strong (1962), SAI, IAV, Dymond's adjustment score for BHQ

Vacchiano, Lieberman, Adrian, and Schiffman (1967), TAT, self-description, reputation, assessment

Vincent (1968), selected scales from CPI, Maslow S-I, 16 PF, TSCS

Viney (1966), selected scales from Motivational Analysis Test, IAV, 16 PF, CPI, and Shlien's instruments

MULTITRAIT-MULTIMETHOD TECHNIQUES

There has been universal acceptance in principle of Campbell and Fiske's (1959) argument that a "multitrait-multimethod matrix" is *required* in order to evaluate both convergent and discriminant trait (construct) validity. Using the word *method* to refer to variations in instrument form or procedure for collecting data, they point out that data from a given method can be used to infer different traits (constructs). For example, a questionnaire method can be used to reveal self-esteem or dominance. On the other hand, different methods can purport to measure the same construct (e.g., a questionnaire, a self-rating scale, or an interview might reveal self-esteem). As the name implies, a multitrait-multimethod matrix contains the correlations one obtains when each of supposedly different traits (constructs) is measured by each of several supposedly different methods and the obtained score arrays are intercorrelated.

So far as self-concept constructs are concerned, the multitrait-multimethod approach to exploring convergent and discriminant validity of any particular self-concept measure must entail the following as a bare minimum: (a) at least one self-concept construct measured in at least two ways; (b) at least one other construct measured in at least the same two ways. The latter might be a self-concept construct, or it could be some other kind of variable, depending upon whether E wishes to establish discriminant validity between respective purported indices of two aspects of the self-concept or between a self-concept measure and some other measure, for example, attitude toward others. Other measures, such as peer ratings of the same trait(s) regarding which S's self-concept is being measured, might be included in the matrix for various reasons; but convergence between self-concept measures and such other variables as peer ratings is, of course, not relevant to the convergent validity of the alleged measures of Ss' self-concepts per se.

To illustrate the approach, portions of Hamilton's (1971) matrix are given in Table 1. (The reader should note that Hamilton's study cannot be evaluated from the excerpts chosen for this illustration.) In the excerpted portions of this study, self-esteem was purportedly measured by each of three different methods: one of the scales of the California Psychological Inventory (CPI), a Likert-type scale (Janis-Field), and self-ratings. A supposedly different self-perceived characteristic, dominance, was purportedly measured by each of two of these measures: a second CPI scale, and self-ratings. A supposedly still different self-perceived characteristic, dogmatism-flexibility-openmindedness, was purportedly measured by each of the three measures: a third CPI scale, a Likert-type scale, and self-ratings. In the general discussion to follow I use only the construct *self-esteem* as an illustration.

Certainly, correlations involving the same method used to measure the same trait (construct) should yield the highest correlations in the matrix, since the correlated arrays are influenced by both construct and method variance. These, of course, are *reliability* coefficients which are not given by Hamilton, so there are blanks in the main diagonal of the illustrative matrix, Table 1.

As stated earlier, in support of *convergent construct validity* of one's measures, one would expect significant correlations between results of different methods purporting to measure the same trait or construct. Such correlations are called monotrait-heteromethod correlations. For example, in the case of self-esteem in the illustrative matrix, one finds convergent validity coefficients of .67, .58, and .60.

In support of *discriminant validity*, one would require that monotrait-heteromethod (convergent validity) coefficients exceed heterotrait-heteromethod coefficients; for example, correlations between self-esteem scores from two different purported methods of measuring self-esteem should exceed correlations between self-esteem scores obtained by one method and dogmatism scores obtained by another method. This requirement depends on the fact that neither common method nor a common construct supposedly influences the heterotrait-heteromethod coefficients. In the illustrative matrix, all correlations in the triangles bounded by dashed lines are heterotrait-

TABLE 1

CORRELATIONS AMONG MEASURES OF SELF-ESTEEM, DOMINANCE, AND DOGMATISM (OPENMINDEDNESS, FLEXIBILITY)

	CPI 1	CPI 2	CPI 3	Likert-Scales 4	Likert-Scales 5	Self-Ratings 6	Self-Ratings 7	Self-Ratings 8
CPI								
1. Self-esteem	---							
2. Dominance	.67	---						
3. Flexibility	.10	−.04	---					
Likert-type Scales								
4. Janis-Field (self-esteem) *	.67	.52	.13	( )				
5. Dogmatism (openmindedness)	.09	.12	.42	.39	( )			
Self-Ratings								
6. Self-esteem	.58	.55	.13	.60	.17	( )		
7. Dominance	.40	.54	.05	.36	.02	.44	( )	
8. Openmindedness	.04	−.02	.34	.14	.17	.14	.06	---

NOTE: Adapted from Hamilton (1971). This matrix contains only portions of Hamilton's published matrix. $r = .23$ is significant at the .05 level.

* No dominance measure was made by means of a Likert-type scale.

heteromethod *r*s. If we select those *r*s which involve self-esteem purportedly measured by one instrument and another trait purportedly measured by another instrument, we find 10 *r*s, none of which is as large as the convergent validity coefficients involving self-esteem, and most of which are much smaller than the convergent validity coefficients involving self-esteem. Arranged in order of size, the heterotrait-heteromethod *r*s are .55, .52, .40, .36, .17, .14, .13, .13, .09, and .04. Thus the illustrative matrix appears to satisfy this requirement so far as the discriminant validities of these three self-esteem measures are concerned.

Another indicant of discriminant validity occurs when monotrait-heteromethod (convergent validity) coefficients exceed heterotrait-monomethod coefficients. It is hoped that the latter will be the smaller because they would be determined to a large degree by method influences which ideally should be minimal; while it is hoped that the convergent validity coefficients will be larger because they should ideally be determined to a large degree by valid variance with respect to the construct, and relatively little by method influences. In the illustrative matrix, these heterotrait-monomethod values are given in the triangles bounded by solid lines. One value (.67) is as large as the largest convergent validity coefficient for self-esteem, while the remaining values are distinctly smaller (.44, .39, .14, .10, .06, −.04). Thus, in this regard, too, this matrix gives some support to the discriminant validities of the self-esteem measures; but the support is not as clear as in the first-mentioned discriminant validity comparisons. In general, however, this last requirement for discriminant validity may be too stringent. Humphreys (1960) argues that it is only a desirable specification, not a necessary one. Jackson (1969) agrees that this specification may be unrealistic, stating, "Even on logical grounds there seems to be scant justification for this universal requirement [1969, p. 33]." Consider, for example, a situation where two constructs, although conceptually and empirically discriminable, do in fact tend to be associated. The associative tendency, coupled with some common method variance, could yield a substantial heterotrait-monomethod *r*. By contrast, one or both of two different methods of measuring allegedly the same construct might be fairly unreliable, so that a relatively low convergent validity coefficient could result even if both measures were validly indicative of the alleged construct, within the limits of their respective reliability coefficients.

Yet another indicant of discriminant validity occurs when patterns of trait intercorrelations are similar in the heterotrait triangles of the matrix. In the illustrative matrix, for example, if one self-esteem measure correlates significantly with dominance but not with dogmatism, each such pair of correlations should follow this pattern. That this is true in the illustrative matrix is evident when one compares the six correlations between self-esteem and dominance (.67, .55, .52, .44, .40, .36) with the respectively corresponding correlations between these same self-esteem scores and dogmatism scores obtained by the same types of instruments as were used in the measurement of dominance (.10, .04, .14, .14, .13, .13).

The Campbell-Fiske ideas are of such importance and methodological developments have occurred so rapidly that we shall give some details here as a basis for guiding future researchers, as much as for evaluating the work of past investigators.

Obviously, Campbell and Fiske's (1959) specifications are vague on a number of important matters. For one thing, the degree of methodological variety among so-called different methods will be an important factor in determining and interpreting the matrix values. For example, heteromethod rs, supposedly determined largely or entirely by common trait variance, may be inflated by common method variance if extremely small differences in method are involved (e.g., if two ways of responding to a rating scale are considered to be different methods, as in Borgatta, 1964). The researcher is left to use his own judgment here. Furthermore, Campbell and Fiske deliberately avoided presenting statistical significance tests for evaluating evidence of convergent and discriminant validity in the pattern of correlations in the matrices. Various informal approaches have been used, such as finding by inspection the proportion of heterotrait-heteromethod correlations which are smaller than the relevant monotrait-heteromethod (convergent validity) coefficients (Norman, 1969; Dicken, 1963; Scott, 1963); or comparing the rs or the mean r in the convergent validity diagonal with the mean value of the heterotrait-heteromethod correlations (Tippett & Silber, 1965; Haley, 1970; Dielman & Wilson, 1970). Such informal approaches can have the disadvantages of being inconvenient and tedious in the case of large matrices, and equivocal in any matrix (Jackson, 1969; Kavanaugh, MacKinney, & Wolins, 1971). Also, informal approaches preclude comparisons of effects within and between studies (Kavanaugh et al., 1971).

To aid the researcher in evaluating multitrait-multimethod matrices more fruitfully (both with respect to the validity applications we are presently considering and with respect to other questions), several statistical approaches have been developed quite recently. Self-concept researchers would do well to examine them closely. Basically, these methods involve either analysis of variance or some form or modification of factor analysis applied to the matrices.

Following Stanley's (1961) proposal, Boruch and Wolins (1970) and Kavanaugh, MacKinney, and Wolins (1971) have developed a mixed ANOVA model which analyzes sources of variance into subject, trait, method, and error. From application of this model one can evaluate the following effects of particular relevance to the convergent-discriminant validity issue: (a) subject variance, that is, convergent validity or overall agreement regarding Ss across methods and traits (constructs); (b) Subject × Trait Variance, that is, discriminant validity or the amount of discrimination on traits across Ss; (c) Subject × Method Variance, indicative of method bias confounding the first (convergent validity) result. F ratios and estimates of variance components can be simply calculated directly from the correlation values. The advantages of this technique are:

> (a) it is a more efficient manner to summarize and interpret the evidence for discriminant and convergent validity, particularly if the matrix is fairly large; (b) the validity information is more explicit (less judgmental) and quantifiable by this method; (c) it allows the estimation of method bias and the amount of sampling variance in the research; (d) the relative strength of the effects can be obtained. [Kavanaugh et al., 1971, p. 39]

In addition, a method is given for making meaningful comparisons between studies. Of particular interest for exploratory work are suggestions for partitioning large matrices in light of the results of the initial ANOVA and applying the ANOVA technique to each submatrix separately to determine what methods and/or traits one wishes to retain for further development in order to maximize convergent and discriminant validity.

This model does not lead to the answers to all the validity questions the self-concept researcher should be asking, however. For one thing, the ANOVA permits statistical inference about the matrix as a whole (or any particular submatrix as a whole) and does not provide a statistical test applicable to the evaluation of any one instrument the researcher may be developing. Furthermore, the ANOVA model is the familiar linear one of classical test theory which assumes, among other things, that methods factors do not interact multiplicatively with trait factors. Thus, the model's usefulness depends on how well its assumptions fit the empirical case. There is growing agreement that the lack of fit may be serious; and in fact, Campbell and O'Connell (1967) have presented empirical evidence from several multitrait-multimethod matrices showing that method factors do seem to interact multiplicatively rather than additively with trait factors. This has led them to question whether factor analysis and also ANOVA may be fundamentally inappropriate for the analyses of such matrices.

Despite these doubts about the applicability of assumptions of linearity, several investigators have proposed factor analysis models for evaluating multitrait-multimethod matrices (Boruch & Wolins, 1970; Boruch, Larkin, Wolins, & MacKinney, 1970; Conger, 1971; Jackson, 1969; Norman, 1969). The area is complex and controversial; and the reader may wish to consult Jackson (1970, p. 9, and 1971) for a classification of the models and one view of the controversy; Boruch (1970) for a comparison of Jackson's and his factor analytic models; and Boruch et al. (1970) for a comparative empirical application of their ANOVA model and one factor analysis model.

The factor analysis modifications suggested do not aim for maximum parsimony, that is, to "explain" the observed matrix with a minimum number of factors. This is so because E is generally using his technique to search for support for his ideas about discriminant validity of a number of scores which allegedly measure respectively discriminable constructs. Accordingly, he would hope to attain at least as many factors as there are allegedly discriminable constructs; and all alternate methods purporting to index a given construct should have their highest loadings on the factor representing the construct. As in the ANOVA model, one should note that the factor analytic techniques are directed toward evaluating the matrix as a whole, and statistical tests of the adequacy of any particular measure are not involved.

Despite some reservations, it seems highly desirable that self-concept researchers should not only produce relevant multitrait-multimethod matrices, but they should apply one or more of the foregoing formal modes of analysis in the process of developing their instruments and exploring the convergent and discriminant construct validity of these instruments. Boruch et al. (1970) have made a helpful beginning in comparing interpretations derived from ANOVA, one type of factor analysis, and informal inspection according to Campbell and Fiske's desiderata. It will be useful if their recommendations are followed that "relations among the various techniques of assessing multitrait-multimethod matrices and their efficacy . . . be investigated [Boruch et al., 1970, p. 851]."

As I said earlier, a multitrait-multimethod approach to validation of self-concept instruments must involve at least one self-concept construct measured by at least two methods *and also* at least one other construct measured by at least the same two methods. The latter construct may or may not be a self-concept construct, depending on whether E wishes to (a) establish discriminant validity between measures of allegedly different aspects of the self-concept; or (b) establish discriminant validity between a self-concept measure and a measure of some other construct, such as S's views of his parents' ideals for him.

I have examined well over 2,000 published researches appearing between 1961 and 1971 which used at least one measuring instrument which can be construed as a possible indicant of some aspect(s) of Ss' self-concepts; and a great many of these studies employed more than one such instrument. With all this amassing of self-concept data after the appearance of the Campbell-Fiske (1959) article, one might expect numerous applications of the multitrait-multimethod technique. Instead, I have located only 18 matrices in which even one self-concept measure has been included. Of these 18 matrices, 4 contained only one self-concept measure (Dicken, 1963; Dielman & Wilson, 1970; Kavanaugh, MacKinney, & Wolins, 1971; Lawler, 1967), because they were directed toward validating certain measures as indicants of traits per se rather than toward validating of instruments as indices of aspects of Ss' self-concepts. Thus, correlations between self-ratings and ratings by others were appropriate to the authors' purposes.

In 6 other matrices, although more than one self-concept measure was involved, these measures were not purporting to tap exactly the same self-concept constructs. They showed that Ss were apparently discriminating among specified traits in somewhat the same way when using the same instrument under instructions to respond from two standpoints: self and desirable self on the Personality Research Form in the Kusyszyn and Jackson (1968) study; self-ratings and predicted peer ratings in 2 matrices presented in Norman (1969); and absolute self-ratings versus self-rankings in specified types of groups in Borgatta's (1960a, 1964) 3 matrices. This information is valuable; but it is not, of course, the same as establishing convergent and discriminant validity of two different methods of allegedly indexing the *same* specified self-concept variable(s).

Of the remaining 8 matrices, 2 were specifically directed toward evaluating convergent and discriminant validity of several scores allegedly indicative of two discriminable aspects of the self-concept: self-esteem and self-image stability (Silber & Tippett, 1965; Tippett & Silber, 1965). These two are based on overlapping data from the same *S*s and could be presented as one matrix. They were able to find evidence for convergent validity among their self-esteem measures, but not much evidence for their self-image stability measure. They obtained some evidence of discriminant validity of self-esteem measures, as opposed to measures of self-image stability. (The fact that the two sets of measures were drawn from the same instruments raises interpretive problems in this study, as the authors note.)

The most extensive application of the multitrait-multimethod technique (Hamilton, 1971) intercorrelated five alleged measures of self-esteem, four alleged measures of dominance, and four alleged measures of dogmatism-openmindedness. As I noted in the excerpts of this matrix discussed above, three of the self-esteem measures showed convergent validity coefficients of .58 to .67. The convergent validity coefficients involving his other two measures of self-esteem were much lower (.33 to −.02). Considering the entire matrix, the evidence for discriminant validity between the self-esteem measures and dominance measures was unimpressive. Only in terms of Campbell and Fiske's final criterion (consistency of interrelationships among traits in the heterotrait triangles) did some evidence of such discriminant validity occur.

The 6 remaining matrices were not intended by their authors as tests of validity of self-concept indicants; but they can be so interpreted (Jackson, 1969, pp. 41–42, regarding Forms AA and BB of the Personality Research Form; Jackson & Guthrie, 1968, regarding Form AA and self-ratings of the 20 traits of the Personality Research Form; Norman, 1969, pp. 433–434, regarding self ratings and questionnaire responses concerning factorially determined traits; Scott, 1963, regarding forced-choice and single-stimulus forms of EPPS versus self-ratings on the EPPS need variables; Megargee & Parker, 1968, regarding two matrices involving Murray needs indexed by ACL and EPPS; and Haley, 1970, regarding eight personality scales and corresponding self-ratings). All of them obtained some evidence of convergent and discriminant validity of different methods of measuring different aspects of self-concept, although the evidence obtained in some instances was limited and weak.[2]

Altogether, the proportion of research time in the self-concept field which has been devoted to this indispensable type of validational work is miniscule; and the continued use of instruments without this type of work seems indefensible. The work which has been done suggests that this approach can have salutary effects in instrument development and in inducing caution in interpreting the results of extant studies.

3. Studies Based on Assumed Validity: Theoretically Predictable Relationships of Alleged Self-Concept Measures to Other Variables

So far as most researches pertaining to the self-concept are concerned, the only evidence which might be adduced for the construct validity of their self-concept measures is that implied by Cronbach and Meehl's fourth criterion—positive findings in studies relating alleged self-concept measures to some other variables in a manner predicted by theory. Since most investigators have proceeded to use their self-concept instruments for such studies without systematically applying any of the other previously mentioned forms of analysis, the results of their studies can be considered to support, rather than to demonstrate unambiguously, the construct validity of their self-concept measures. Moreover, Cronbach's (1971) recent statement is too frequently applicable to studies exemplifying Cronbach and Meehl's fourth type of converging operations:

---

2. F. Baker (1971) has published a matrix of correlations among four aspects of Eriksonian "ego identity," each aspect measured by Likert-type scales and by sentence-completion responses. Since he conceived of ego identity as involving self-attitudes, this matrix might be considered to be relevant here. Although significant convergent validities were found for each of the four aspects of ego identity, only one, "inner sameness and continuity," showed evidence of discriminant validity.

Merely to catalog relations between the test under study and a variety of other variables is to provide a do-it-yourself kit for the reader, who is left to work out his own interpretative theory. Construct validation should start with a reasonably definite statement of the proposed interpretation. That interpretation will suggest what evidence is most worth collecting to demonstrate convergence of indicators. A critical review in the light of competing theories will suggest important counter-hypotheses, and these also will suggest data to collect. Investigations to be used for construct validations, then, should be purposeful rather than haphazard. [P. 483]

Chapter 4 gives details concerning this type of study with respect to each of the instruments evaluated there.

F. Reliability of Measurement of Self-Referent Variables

In the construct-validity sections above, we stress the importance of obtaining discriminating, construct-relevant items to be presented under appropriately controlled conditions. The aim of this, of course, is to maximize the proportion of variance which is not only *dependable between-S variance* (as opposed to unsystematic or "random" variance); but is also *construct-valid between-S variance* (as opposed to dependable, between-S variance from systematic distortions such as response sets). No form of reliability coefficient or ANOVA technique for appraising reliability can assure us per se that our dependable between-S variance is to any specified degree construct-valid variance. This is so because systematic, irrelevant influences such as response sets or instructions will inflate reliability coefficients or "true-score" variance. Problems of identifying, eliminating, controlling for, or accounting for such systematic irrelevant influences are problems of improving construct validity.

Nevertheless, proper applications of reliability-estimation techniques can throw light on what proportion of variance between persons is unreliable, that is, random error; and hence, not even possibly interpretable as construct-valid variance.

The word *dependable* is vague. More specifically, when we are dealing with dependable variance we refer to various possible kinds of generalization: Can we generalize from one part of the task to another? From this task to various others of the same class? Across time, upon repetition of the same task or another task of the same class? To what conditions of testing can we generalize? Stanley (1971,

p. 359) points out regarding reliability: "The empirical procedures are very closely bound up with the logical aspects of the problem, so that one must first determine what is to be accomplished and what purposes are to be served by a measure of reliability. The empirical operations must be planned with these purposes in view and evaluated in the light of them."

For a modern summary of theory and applicable techniques, the reader is referred to Stanley (1971). Here we consider briefly some points particularly relevant to evaluating self-concept research.

It is often important to know to what extent there is consistency within the test with regard to what is being measured. The split-half technique is useful to estimate the reliability of comparable forms with zero time interval between forms; but of course the obtained estimate pertains to the particular groups of items E allots to each half. Reliability in the sense of the degree of homogeneity among all the items may be estimated by Hoyt's (1941) procedure, Cronbach's coefficient alpha, or (in the case of dichotomously scored items) by the Kuder-Richardson KR-20 formula (Stanley, 1971). Null or weak associations between self-concept variables or between a self-concept variable and another variable could easily stem from unreliable measurement of one or both variables, as opposed to a lack of association of importance to theory. Also, the inference concerning discriminant validity between two purportedly different instruments may become quite confused if two instruments vary greatly in reliability. For the great majority of self-concept instruments in common use, a Cronbach alpha, KR-20, or Hoyt coefficient could be computed; but a large proportion of workers report few or none of these, unfortunately.

A test-retest coefficient involving the same test, or appropriately timed testing with comparable forms, may be necessary to clarify interpretations of results in certain studies. For example, it some-times happens that groups of Ss allegedly differing in self-regard are drawn from a large pool of Ss who had been routinely tested with a self-regard instrument at a previous time. There is no assurance, however, that, at the time of the study, the Ss' self-regard status corresponds to that at the previous time of testing. Accordingly, if weak or null results are obtained with respect to the alleged inde-pendent variable, self-regard, or with respect to interactions between self-regard and another independent variable, one could rule out unreliability of the self-regard measure as one explanation of these null findings only if test-retest or comparable-forms reliability of the self-regard test were known to be high. In another version of the same problem, theoretically relevant correlations may be computed between previously obtained self-regard scores and currently obtained measures on another variable such as anxiety. Clearly, one could rule out unreliability of self-regard measurement as one possible explanation of weak or null correlations only if test-retest or comparable-forms information were available.

Often E does not wish to repeat the self-regard test or give a comparable form of it because he wishes Ss to see no connection between self-regard testing and the other variables in the current study. In such a case, a test-retest or comparable-forms control group should be used to ascertain the degree of test-retest unreliability characteristic of this type of S.

Another kind of situation requiring test-retest information occurs when there is a possibility that certain self-regard scores at any one testing time could represent a confounding of (a) randomness of responding, and (b) S's intentional choice of response to represent poor self-regard. For example, a zero self-ideal r in a Q sort could result from random responding and/or from S's expression of phenomenal lack of congruity between his actual self and his ideal self. If, on retest, self-self rs and ideal-ideal rs are high for Ss having low self-ideal rs, interpretation of the latter in terms of random responding is obviously ruled out.

Similar problems arise with scores from multiple rating scales in which an individual S's self-regard score is the sum of rating-scale values on numerous subscales. We know that, in actual practice, distributions of self-ratings on any one scale tend to pile up at the favorable end and are extremely skewed toward the unfavorable end. It thus happens that, when a total score of an S which is among the lowest self-regard scores actually obtained by Ss is divided by the number of scales, the mean score value of such an S lies near the middle of the scale range used for each self-judgment. Now such a middle-of-the-range mean for an individual S could have arisen in any particular case mainly from random responding; that is, if S were randomly marking the rating scales on a page, his mean should be about the middle of the scale range. (This would be true of *random* responders, whether or not the evaluative ends had been varied from left to right on the page to counteract position response set.) On the other hand, such a low self-regard score could arise by deliberate choice. Very high scores, on the other hand, would be unlikely from random responding, though they might conceivably represent a confounding of position response set and valid influences if scale ends have not been varied from right to left on the page; or they might represent a confounding of social-desirability response set and valid influences even if the scale ends have been varied from left to right. Again, test-retest reliability coefficients would help to counteract the random-responding interpretation of low self-regard scores. So far as I have been able to find, this sort of inter-pretational problem has not been recognized even in principle by researchers in the self-concept field.

This kind of ambiguity in interpreting low self-regard scores is particularly important in self-concept studies because some of the variables that one might hypothesize to be associated with self-regard (e.g., lack of success in school, delinquent behavior patterns) could also be expected to be associated with careless responding in a test situation. Accordingly, any interpretation of the association of low self-regard with such a variable would have to be viewed skeptically until the proposed alternate explanation of the association in terms of careless responding had been ruled out.

Unfortunately, ruling out the "careless responding" interpreta-tion is easier said than done in the case of rating-scale measures of self-regard. As I said, presenting a relatively high test-retest correla-tion is somewhat relevant; but perhaps this relatively high r is de-termined considerably more by test-retest consistency among high-self-regard Ss than by test-retest consistency among low self-regard Ss. In other words, a high test-retest r does not suffice, per se, to counteract completely the argument that delinquents, poor readers, disturbed Ss, etc., attain their lower self-regard scores partly or entirely because of their greater proneness to careless, unreliable responding. Inspection of the scatter diagram of test-retest scores might visually counteract such an argument, if the Ss with high self-regard test scores showed equal or more variability on retest in comparison to the Ss with low self-regard test scores. Going further, examination for each S of the total number of item shifts on retest and the absolute sum of shift values on retest might reveal that the low self-regard Ss were at least as consistent as the high self-regard Ss. To my knowledge, no such explorations have been attempted, probably because the existence of the problem has not been recognized.[3]

Some researchers seem to assume that split-half or other internal reliability coefficients can be offered in lieu of test-retest or alternate-forms coefficients when the evaluation of research findings actually requires an evaluation of Ss' consistency over time. This assumption is based on the idea that internal reliability coefficients can be used as rough estimates of the required test-retest or alternate-forms coefficients. However, the latter idea is not true. Regardless of what basis is used for obtaining split-half or internal reliability coefficients, workers agree that such coefficients may well overestimate the total reliability of a test over time (since the total unreliability of the latter includes instability errors as well as intra-S inconsistency errors and, if parallel tests are used, a lack-of-equivalency error as well). Dudek (1952) has demonstrated empirically that this is the case under specified conditions of test length and difficulty. Gulliksen (1950) has cited several studies appearing before 1950 which also demonstrated empirically that corrected odd-even coefficients overestimate both test-retest and parallel forms correlations. Cureton (1965) states that for 30- or 40-item forms given at intervals of a week or two, the test-retest coefficients may be of the same magnitude as consistency coefficients, with interform reliability appreciably lower. With longer time intervals, test-retest and parallel forms coefficients become smaller.

For some purposes it is useful to have equivalent forms of the same test, for example, when E wishes to rule out the influence of specific memory for items. Stanley (1971) gives detailed instructions

---

3. As this volume was going to press, an article appeared which is relevant to my argument about this problem (Gorsuch, Henighan, & Barnard, 1972). These authors reported that internal-consistency reliability coefficients on Bialer's and Miller's Locus-of-Control Scales increased linearly across verbal ability groupings in fourth- and sixth-grade samples. They pointed out that their obtained positive correlation between locus-of-control scores and verbal ability scores could have been a function of the unreliability of the low-verbal children's locus-of-control scores rather than representing a true relationship between ability and locus-of-control. They also point out, "Naturally, if the locus-of-control scales have a spurious correlation with verbal ability, *they will also have spurious correlations with all variables which normally correlate with verbal ability* [p. 588]." They conclude, "Since it is possible for *any* scale to have the problems found here with the . . . locus-of-control scales, systematic examination of reliabilities can be recommended for every questionnaire [p. 589]."

for building parallel forms. Of course a test and retest (whether with the same or alternate forms) will reflect "instability errors" dependent on time-associated factors as well as Ss' inconsistency errors.

No matter what type of coefficient is appropriate to the logical and empirical requirements of a study, one must also know whether the coefficient was computed from scores of Ss who properly represent the groups whose results we are trying to evaluate in the study. Thus, for example, to cite reliability figures for aviation cadet Ss in a study where prisoners are the Ss only gives a misleading impression.

In summary, so far as actual self-concept research is concerned, far too little attention has been paid to determining and reporting reliability figures, and to evaluating alternate explanations of obtained results of studies in the light of the degree of reliability of instrumentation. For the great majority of self-concept instruments in common use it is possible to compute split-half or internal consistency coefficients; but a large proportion of workers report few or none of these. Test-retest reliability estimates (whether using the same or alternate forms) are even rarer in the published literature. For many studies they are the only appropriate basis for evaluating results; and estimates from split-half coefficients are not an appropriate substitute. Even test-retest coefficients may not suffice, per se, to rule out certain artifactual explanations. The reliability figures should be, but often are not, relevant to the groups whose results we are trying to interpret in a particular study.

G. SUMMARY AND RECOMMENDATIONS CONCERNING GENERAL PROBLEMS OF MEASUREMENT OF SELF-REFERENT VARIABLES

Many of the specific points made in the preceding sections may be viewed as special cases of the general question: To what extent do random errors and method variance account for response variance on indices purporting to index S's self-concept? A minimum program of constructive procedures needed in future research in order to maximize construct-valid variance and minimize systematic and random error variance includes the following steps.

1. Research should focus on the use and development of a small number of instruments. When one surveys research in this area, one is struck with the great amount of effort expended, but scat-

tered much too widely and thinly. It seems doubtful whether any present instrument should continue to be used in exactly its present form.

2. We very much need a rational program of instrument development in the light of sophisticated modern standards, especially regarding (a) the assembly of theoretically relevant, well-constructed item pools; (b) formats to minimize response sets and maximize S's opportunity to present a description of himself which he considers valid; (c) application of scaling techniques; (d) use of factor analysis for item culling and scale construction; (e) application of multitrait-multimatrix techniques for exploring and refining convergent and discriminant construct validity; (f) avoidance of sources of artifacts in setting up the scoring system; (g) execution of *planned* groups of studies which simultaneously explore construct validity and theoretically relevant hypotheses.

3. Situational variables which we have reason to think *may* influence response output on our measures should be systematically considered and controlled in designing, applying, and interpreting scores from our instruments. Some of these variables are suggested by research in other areas, for example, perception; others are suggested by research done so far regarding the social psychology of the research situation and research in the self-concept area itself. Many of these variables need to be studied further as independent variables in their own right in the self-concept research area, with results of such methodological research used to guide further refinements of the measurement situation. Self-concept researchers must not be content with empirical or face validity of their measuring instruments.

Although progress has been made in the last decade, no investigator has satisfactorily conceptualized or coped with all the difficult measurement problems in the self-concept field. Quite a few have indicated that they make no claims for having tried to support the reliability or construct validity of their instruments, and they are content to "let the reader beware," as it were.

4

Description and Evaluation of Extant Self-Concept Measures

A. SELECTION OF INSTRUMENTS FOR CRITICAL EVALUATION

In the preceding chapter, I have considered general problems of measuring the self-concept. I turn now to descriptions and analyses of specific instruments which have been used as self-concept indices. This information should be useful to researchers and to those who wish to evaluate critically the results of studies in the area of self-concept.

The time has long passed when substantive studies based on unevaluated instruments should be considered publishable. Unfortunately, however, one still finds that a very wide range of instruments has been used to measure various aspects of the self-concept, most of these measures having been used in only one or a few studies. Many of the articles give incomplete descriptions of the instruments or no real description at all. Too often, no publicly available source is given for the reader to follow up, should he wish to know more about specific instructions to Ss, the item content, or even the rationale for item choice. Consequently, it is difficult or impossible for the critical reader to make any firm inferences as to what variables might be influencing Ss' responses. In the majority of studies, no reliability estimates are given; and those estimates that are presented are mostly of the split-half or interjudge variety, giving no indication of stability on retest. The problem of any kind of validity is often bypassed entirely, being replaced by assumptions of face validity or reliance on the reader to infer what he will from whatever statement of operations is given. Sometimes inappropriate (i.e., theoretically irrelevant or theoretically inconsistent) validity criteria are offered, for example, another's judgment of S or S's school achievement.

In the first edition of this book (Wylie, 1961), I tabulated whatever information I could find about each of the many instruments which had been used by one or more self-concept researchers. My reasons for being so thorough were to document the critical generalizations I made about the extent to which available instruments and relevant published information fell short of acceptable standards, and to provide possible leads to investigators who might wish to pick up for research and development one or another of the undeveloped ideas. To present such a tabulation for the even larger number of instruments I have encountered in this survey would be an enormous job which could not be defended in terms of providing leads to those who might wish to develop an instrument further. The reader might better choose among certain ones of the instruments considered below or "start from scratch," using the most sophisticated modern approaches to instrument construction.

I have selected for separate evaluation certain instruments which I thought warranted such attention for one or more reasons. First, any purported self-concept measure which I found to have been used in 12 or more studies is reviewed here, and a few used less frequently are also briefly considered. (The inclusion of a measure does not necessarily imply that it is a meritorious instrument; indeed, in some instances I argue that further use seems to be unjustified.) Second, it seemed worthwhile to represent instruments which arose from various theoretical orientations, for example, from Rogers's self-concept theory and from Kuhn's symbolic-interaction theory. Third, I wished to represent not only instruments which purport to measure overall aspects of self-concept such as "global self-regard" and "self-consistency," but also those which purport to obtain self-descriptions and/or self-evaluations along a number of separate dimensions such as body cathexis or dominance. Fourth, I have selected instruments which represent each of the following approaches to getting an evaluative index (regardless of whether the index pertains to global self-regard or to more restricted dimensions of the self-concept): (a) scoring each item with reference to an objectively judged favorability value; (b) asking S to state directly how well satisfied he is with his status on the characteristics in question; (c) asking S to state a self-description and an ideal-self description, using the discrepancy between the two as an evaluative index. Fifth, because researchers need instruments suitable for use with various age levels, I have selected some which purport to be

useful measures of children's self-concepts, as well as some of the
more numerous instruments aimed at adults. Sixth, I chose instruments so as to represent different formats which have been tried,
because I wished to display the intrinsic limitations and possible
assets of each. By format I mean whether the instrument uses a *Q*
sort, rating scale, adjective check list, yes-no questionnaire, semantic
differential, nonverbal, or open-ended approach to eliciting *S*'s
responses.

The reader may well wonder why all widely used self-report
personality tests were not included in the above selection, since
operationally they are essentially the same as many of the tests
which are evaluated here. My somewhat arbitrary basis for excluding these instruments from individual analysis is as follows. All those
which I have included purported, in whole or in part, to be self-
concept indices. By contrast, in the case of excluded ones such as
the MMPI or EPPS, the validity toward which the test constructors
aimed was of an "objective" kind. That is, they wished to devise
and use the instrument as a quick, efficient way to evaluate *Ss*'
"objective" characteristics which should be alternately assessable in
principle by such information as psychiatric diagnoses, supervisors'
ratings, or grades in school. In certain studies in which an *E* used
one of these instruments with the avowed purpose of measuring
S's self-concept, the study is included in the respectively appropriate
section—in some cases it is one of the studies attempting to vali-
date other self-concept instruments, in other cases it is included
among studies purporting to associate a self-concept variable with
some other variable(s).

Several of the instruments which are evaluted here meet more
than one of the stated criteria, and no mutually exclusive categories
can be set up for organizing the presentation of the evaluations.
Arbitrarily, therefore, I have chosen to present the evaluations in
the following order:

Instruments Mostly Aimed at Measuring Overall or Global
   Self-Regard:

   Q sorts, especially the BHQ set (Butler & Haigh, 1954), and the
      Hilden (1958) sets
   Index of Adjustment and Values, Adult Form (IAV) (Bills,
      Vance, & McLean, 1951)
   Self Activity Inventory (SAI) (Worchel, 1957)

Children's self-concept scales, especially the Coopersmith (1967)
   Self-Esteem Inventory (SEI) and the Piers-Harris Children's
   Self-Concept Scale (PH) (Piers & Harris, 1964)
Rosenberg's (1965) Self Esteem Scale (RSE)
Social Self-Esteem Scale (SSE) (Long, Henderson, & Ziller, 1970)

*Instruments Intended to Measure Self-Concepts Regarding More
Specific or Limited Dimensions (as well as global self-regard, in
the case of some of those listed):*

Adjective Check List (ACL) (Gough & Heilbrun, 1965)
Interpersonal Check List (ICL) (LaForge & Suczek, 1955)
Semantic Differential (SD) (Osgood, Suci, & Tannenbaum, 1957)
Tennessee Self Concept Scale (TSCS) (Fitts, 1964)
Body Cathexis Scale (BC) (Secord & Jourard, 1953; Jourard &
   Secord, 1954)
Who Are You? (WAY) or Twenty Sentences Test (TST)
   (Bugental & Zelen, 1950; Kuhn & McPartland, 1954)

B. Terminology in the Measurement of Self-Regard

The most commonly studied class of aspects of the phenomenal
self includes such attitudes as self-satisfaction, self-acceptance, self-
esteem, self-favorability, congruence between self and ideal self, and
discrepancies between self and ideal self. All these terms are not
synonymous, even in the literary sense. For some authors, self-
acceptance means respecting oneself, including one's admitted faults,
while self-esteem or congruence between self and ideal self means
being proud of oneself or evaluating one's attributes highly. In
fact, to some theorists, optimum self-esteem or self-satisfaction is
manifested by moderately small (rather than by very small or zero)
discrepancies between S's descriptions of self and ideal self on Q
sorts, rating scales, or adjective check lists. That is, self-acceptance
is presumed by some to be the conscious (realistic) recognition of
some falling short of the ideal.

If these terms had more clearly differentiated literary meanings
and correspondingly differentiated operational definitions, it would
be desirable to organize the discussion of the instruments according
to the construct involved (e.g., self-esteem as contrasted to self-
acceptance). However, the terms are so intertwined and overlapping
in the literature that the constructs must be discussed as a group.

This chapter is devoted to instruments which purport wholly or partly to measure an overall or very general evaluative attitude toward self. *For convenience of discussion I use the words "self-regard" or "self-regarding attitudes" as generic terms to include self-satisfaction, self-acceptance, self-esteem, self-favorability, congruence between self and ideal self, and discrepancies between self and ideal self.* If the authors have specifically labelled their instruments or the inferences they are drawing from their scores, this is indicated in the text.

For purposes of clarity, the following conventions are observed in regard to language usage. *Unless otherwise indicated, self means S's view of his actual self or real self, that is, his concept of himself as he actually is.* Unless otherwise indicated, the word *ideal* refers to S's view of his ideal self; his concept of the kind of person he would like to be. When *self sorts* are correlated with *ideal sorts* (as explained immediately below, under Q sorts), I refer in a general discussion of this kind of score to self-ideal correlations, or to self-ideal congruence. The expression *self-ideal* will *not* be used to refer to the person's ideal self. When indices of self-regard are obtained by subtracting self-ratings from ideal-self ratings, these will be referred to as [Self − Ideal] discrepancies (to be read "self minus ideal discrepancies"). Occasionally the general idea of such discrepancies will be referred to as self-minus-ideal discrepancies.

C. Instruments Mostly Intended to Measure Overall or Global Self-Regard

1. Q Sorts, with Special Reference to Butler and Haigh's and Hilden's Items

General Description of Q-Sort Procedure

One of the most commonly used techniques for assessing individual differences in phenomenal self-regard is the Q sort or slight modifications thereof (Stephenson, 1953). In the typical application of this technique, a large number of personality-descriptive items are sorted by S into nine piles which are arranged on a continuum according to the degree to which they are characteristic of S's self. S usually is forced by the instructions to place specified numbers of items in each pile so as to yield a quasi-normal distribution of items. S then sorts the same items once more into nine piles which are arranged on a continuum according to the degree to which they are characteristic of his ideal for himself. Again, the instructions usually force him to produce a quasi-normal distribution of the items.

Each item in the self-description may be assigned a value from one to nine, according to the pile in which S has chosen to put it. Correspondingly, each item in the ideal sort may be assigned a value from one to nine, according to the pile in which S has chosen to put it. For the individual S, a correlation coefficient may then be computed between the pile values of the items, as sorted by that S to describe his self, and the pile values of the same items, as sorted to describe his ideal self. It should be pointed out that Pearson r may be used even when quasi-normal sorting is not required of S (Nefzger & Drasgow, 1957; Livson & Nichols, 1956). Such a correlation coefficient between placement values assigned by a single S is usually called a self-ideal correlation, or self-ideal r, and these are the labels we shall use throughout our discussion. The self-ideal correlation may be considered to be a score for the S, and from the magnitude of that score the degree of that S's self-regard is inferred. Thus, although each forced sort made by a given S results in a set of ipsative item values for that S, the self-ideal r is clearly a normative value which, in the typical application, is compared from S to S.

(Q-sort correlational techniques may be used to relate other sets of descriptions than S's self-description and his ideal self-description. For example, S could be asked to sort the same items according to another set of instructions, such as "how I *should* be," or "how my friends regard me," or "how my mother wishes I were." A correlation coefficient for an individual S can be computed between item-placement values for any two sorts of the same items. For example, if S's ideal-self sort is correlated with his sort done under the instructions "how my mother wishes I were," one could infer the degree of agreement between the S's personal ideal for himself and the ideal he feels his mother holds for him. A matrix of correlations among a number of sorts made by one S may be internally factor analyzed [Nunnally, 1955; Rogers, 1954a, 1954b]; but of course, this process does not lead to a normative self-regard score. Alternatively, the item placement values assigned by one S may be correlated with the item placement values assigned by any other S [e.g., S_1's self-sort may be correlated with S_2's self-sort to infer the degree of similarity in the self-concepts of the two subjects].[1] Matrices of such correlations may be subjected to inverse factor analysis in an effort to establish types [Gorlow, Simonson, & Krauss, 1966]. Again, of course, normative self-regard scores do not result.)

SCORES BASED ON OBJECTIVELY JUDGED IDEALS

Returning to measures of self-regard, we should note that there is another less frequently used way of obtaining a self-regard score from an individual S's self-descriptive Q sort. In this alternate procedure, one compares the pile number of each statement, as S has sorted it, with the independently judged self-favorability (social desirability or positive tone) of each item. This type of score introduces a possible theoretical confusion. To be consistently phenomenological, a self-concept theorist must be concerned with the relationship between S's phenomenal self and his phenomenal ideal self, rather than relating S's phenomenal self to an objective judgment or cultural stereotype of the ideal person. Of course, S's idiosyncratic ideal self may overlap considerably or entirely with the culturally accepted view of an ideal person. (In later sections of the book considerable evidence of this overlap will be presented.) If this is the case, results from the use of the individual and cultural ideal will be highly similar. Nevertheless, it is not empirically safe to assume that individual Ss' phenomenal ideals for themselves are equivalent to culturally accepted standards for the ideal person. And if Ss do vary from one another with respect to the coincidence between the phenomenal ideal self and the cultural norm, scores

---

1. Mowrer (1953b) has suggested that the Q technique as defined by Stephenson is a loose designation for a number of distinct though functionally related procedures which need to be more precisely defined. He and Cattell (in Mowrer, 1953a) have said that there are three series of fundamentals among which the relations of correlation can be established in psychology: organisms, behavioral performances of any kind, and occasions. On Mowrer's modified and expanded version of Cattell's covariation chart, showing correlation techniques in terms of these three dimensions, self-ideal correlations are regarded as examples of Q technique in Cattell's and Mowrer's restricted sense (i.e., correlation of results obtained from two or more persons taking many tests on one occasion). To make this classification, the person sorting items under "self" instructions is considered to be a psychologically different person from himself sorting items under "ideal" instructions. The correlation of a self-sort before therapy with a self-sort after therapy is separately classified as O technique (correlation of the results obtained from one person taking many tests [items] on two or more occasions).

based on objectively judged ideals cannot be interpreted in a theoretically consistent way from S to S.

We need systematic research involving items which are separated according to (a) whether or not there is a cultural norm; (b) whether or not S has a personal phenomenal ideal; and (c) the extent to which the cultural norm and S's phenomenal ideal coincide.

It may turn out that one can, in some instances, predict behavior better when one uses a score in which E evaluates S's self-report in terms of an objectively judged cultural norm rather than in terms of S's reported phenomenal ideal self. However, such empirical validity is not equivalent to the construct validity one attempts to attain by comparing S's self-report with his report of his ideal self. Also, such superior empirical validity, if attained, would raise important theoretical questions for self-concept theorists; that is, it might suggest that the importance of the phenomenal self in predicting behavior has been overemphasized.

BUTLER AND HAIGH'S SELF-REFERENT ITEMS, PROCEDURE, AND ASSUMPTIONS

The set of Q-sort items which has been most extensively used as an index of self-regard is the group of one hundred self-referent statements employed in the research on nondirective psychotherapy described in Rogers and Dymond (1954).[2] This instrument, hereafter called BHQ, is therefore given the most detailed discussion, with the understanding that most of the comments made are generally applicable to the Q-sort techniques which are more briefly considered later.

BHQ items were to be sorted into nine piles, either according to the degree they were "like me," or (in another sort) according to the degree "I would most like within myself to be," or (in a third sort) according to the degree to which they characterize the "ordinary person." As is usually true in Q-sort work, S was forced to assign a certain number of items to each of the piles so that a quasi-normal distribution resulted.

Butler and Haigh (1954, p. 55) state that the use of forced sorting and of the self-ideal correlation as an index of self-regard was

---

2. Many later studies use only 76 or 80 of these items, selected as explained in Shlien (1961).

based on the following assumptions: (a) The self-concept consists of an organized conceptual pattern of the "I" or "me," together with the values attached to these concepts. (b) This pattern of organization can be mirrored, respectively, in terms of ordinal scale placements of the statements according to the degree to which they are "like me," ordinal scale placements of the statements according to the degree to which they are like "I wish to be," and in terms of discrepancies between the scale value assigned to an item on the self dimension, as contrasted to the ideal-self dimension.

The items used in the instrument were an "accidental" (rather than random) sample of statements from "available therapeutic protocols," reworded for clarity (Butler & Haigh, 1954, p. 57). Most, but not all, of the items appear on pages 78, 275, and 276 of the Rogers and Dymond book (1954) and on pages 76 and 77 of Robinson and Shaver (1969). They are mostly very general assertions, not situationally specified, such as: I am shy, confused, a failure, disturbed, hopeless, unreliable, worthless, optimistic, impulsive, rational, poised, tolerant.

We have no way of knowing how representative these statements may be of the self-esteem construct envisaged by Rogers and his co-workers because this construct was not explicitly defined by them.

DYMOND ADJUSTMENT SCORE FOR THE BUTLER AND HAIGH ITEMS

Dymond (1953) found that trained clinical psychologists could agree well that 37 of the characteristics were ones which a "well-adjusted" person should say are at least somewhat "like me"; that another 37 of them were ones which a "well-adjusted" person should say are at least somewhat "unlike me"; and that 26 items were unclassifiable as indicating "adjustment." (All the items which apparently are nowhere listed in the book fall into this third category. A number of investigators use only the 74 Dymond items.) She obtained an adjustment score by finding how many of the 74 items relevant to adjustment are placed on the "like me" or "unlike me" side of the distribution, as respectively appropriate. Dymond, of course, does not imply that the adjustment score necessarily reflects S's phenomenal picture of his own clinically defined adjustment, since he was not instructed to use this dimension as a basis for sorting. As stated above, it is the size of the self-ideal correlation which is assumed to index "self-dissatisfaction," that is, maladjustment as personally experienced by S.

In a study mentioned earlier (Wiener et al., 1959), 28 clinical psychologists sorted the Butler and Haigh items to describe how they thought "a well adjusted person would sort these cards." Mean adjustment values were obtained for each item. Then the 37 items most like the "well-adjusted" person and the 37 items least like the "well-adjusted" person were determined. Only 33 of the 37 "most adjusted" items and 29 out of the 37 "least adjusted" items were common to the lists compiled by Dymond and by Wiener et al. Of the 26 items found by Dymond to be irrelevant to adjustment, twelve were judged in Wiener's study to be reliably assigned to the adjusted or maladjusted side of the continuum. Wiener et al. (1959) concluded, "The failure to find greater consistency of item placement with the two methods of judgment raises some question about the need to investigate further the problem of establishing an Adjustment scale by either method [p. 320]."

RELIABILITY

Various kinds of questions should be asked concerning the consistency and reliability of the possible measures obtainable from this, or from any, Q-sorting procedure. In the Q sort we have several levels from which we could obtain quantitative data. These may be arranged in order of increasing complexity as follows: (a) individual item placements; (b) scores based on sorts made under a single set of instructions (e.g., on self-sort, *or* ideal-sort, *or* average-other-person-sort); Dymond's adjustment score applied to the self-sort would be an illustration; (c) scores which consist of intraindividual correlations obtained between sorts (e.g., self-ideal correlations). In the immediately following paragraphs, I consider problems of reliability and consistency which one encounters at each of these levels of complexity, respectively, and report relevant data.

At the most molecular level one may pay attention to the *individual item placements* made by S. Which items discriminate significantly between individual Ss at any one time? To what extent is each given item assigned the same pile number by the same S from time to time with no known systematic influence intervening between test and retest? Phillips, Raiford, and El-Batrawi (1965) tabulated item shifts upon retesting, but they reported only in terms of item-median self-self shifts and item-median ideal-ideal shifts.

Moving toward more global measures, one should consider *indices based on a single sort* (e.g., Dymond's adjustment score based on the self-sort). Do these scores discriminate significant individual differences at any given testing time? How stable does the rank ordering of individuals remain over time, with no known systematic influence intervening between test and retest? Stimson (1968) reported a 6-months test-retest reliability coefficient of .74 for Dymond scores from 35 college males. Livson and Nichols (1956) present evidence that unforced sorting, or better yet, forced sorting into a rectangular distribution results in higher test-retest reliability than does quasi-normal sorting of personality-descriptive items.

Of pertinence to group studies is the question whether the mean score of the control (untreated) group remains stable over time, which it might do even though the rank order of individuals changed considerably. A number of therapy studies (e.g., Cartwright & Vogel, 1960; C. R. Rogers, 1967; Rudikoff, 1954) suggest that Dymond adjustment-score means are essentially unchanged in untreated controls or in patients during their pretherapy waiting period.

Are there logical or empirical grounds on which sets of items constituting equivalent halves or alternate forms could be chosen or constructed? The existence of rationally devised alternate forms would be helpful in appraising test-retest reliability of scores based on a single sort, if one wanted to get a retest score which is free of specific memory influences. There was no attempt to establish equivalent halves or alternate forms of the Butler and Haigh items. (Hilden's, 1958, alternate sets of Q-sort items are considered separately below.)

The most complex type of score is the one typically employed in Q-sort studies, namely, the *r* obtained between *two sorts made by the same S under two sets of instructions* (e.g., the self-ideal correlation). If we consider the self-ideal *r* from each *S* as a normative "test score," we need to consider the following questions:

1. Do such scores yield significant individual differences at any one testing time? If so, what could such differences mean? Here we run into a troublesome interpretational problem, already mentioned in chapter 3, section F: if the self-ideal *r* of a given *S* at a given time is low or zero, does this represent random responding on *S*'s part, or does it accurately represent *S*'s perception of incongruence between his self and ideal self? *Randomness of responding and poor self-ideal congruence are completely confounded in such*

a score. If, when *S* is retested, the self-self correlation is high and the ideal-ideal correlation is high, while the self-ideal *r* remains low or zero, one would feel more confident in inferring phenomenal self-ideal incongruence for that *S*, as opposed to random responding. But either self-self or ideal-ideal correlations might be relatively low on retesting, indicating validly that *S*'s self- or ideal-concept has shifted for some reason. In such a case, the confounding of unreliability of responding and poor self-ideal congruence is impossible to untangle. No investigators seem to have recognized this problem. Butler and Haigh (1954) report that both client *S*s and control *S*s exhibited significant individual differences in self-ideal *r*s within their respective groups. This indicates that the self-ideal *r*, considered as a test score, was discriminating in some way among individuals. No other investigators have presented any evidence on this point.

2. To what extent is the rank order of the *S*s' self-ideal *r*s stable over time? Butler and Haigh (1954) give no information on this point. However, I was able to compute a test-retest *rho* for the 16 control cases whose initial and follow-up *r*s are tabled on page 66 of Rogers and Dymond (1954). The obtained value was .78. No other information on this aspect of reliability is available, to my knowledge, regarding either the BHQ or other *Q*-sort sets.

3. As pointed out earlier, the degrees of self-self and ideal-ideal consistency are relevant to the problem of interpreting low or zero self-ideal *r*s. It is also important to ask: What are the respective contributions of self-self consistency and ideal-ideal consistency to the reliability in rank orders of self-ideal correlations over time? Perhaps one of these sorts is more stable than the other. For example, we have no direct way of knowing the respective contributions of self-sorts and ideal-sorts to the above-mentioned test-retest *rho* of .78. The following data suggest very obliquely that self-sorts, being less consistent across time than are ideal-sorts, must play the greater role in lowering a *rho* between two sets of self-ideal correlations across time. For clients who waited 60 days for therapy, the correlations between initial and pretherapy self-sorts ranged from .57 to .78, and for ideal-sorts, from .56 to .90. Five of the ideal-ideal correlations exceeded the highest self-self correlation, implying that ideal-sorts may have greater consistency over time.

4. To what extent are the group mean self-ideal *r*s of specified groups consistent over time, with no known systematic influence

intervening? In Butler and Haigh's (1954) study, the control group
of Ss who did not have counseling, but who volunteered for "research on personality," showed a mean initial self-ideal r of .58, as
compared to a mean follow-up r of .59. The times between initial
and follow-up testing varied from S to S because testing times for
each control S were made to correspond with his matched experimental (counseled) counterpart. The client group showed a mean
self-ideal r of −.01 both in the initial test and in the test following a
60-day pretherapy waiting period. Shlien, Mosak, and Dreikurs
(1962) and Butler (1968) report essentially similar findings. Although
Phillips, Raiford, and El-Batrawi (1965) and C. R. Rogers (1967)
found lower self-ideal rs in their no-therapy groups (as compared
to findings of the other investigators), the mean self-ideal rs were
essentially unchanged over a waiting period. Taylor (1955) did not
use the BHQ, so his results cannot be considered to contradict
directly those given above; but he did find that Ss who repeatedly
did Q sorts once a day or oftener showed significant increases in
positiveness of self-concept.

Considering that the BHQ has been used in at least 15 studies
in addition to the Rogers and Dymond (1954) research, and dozens
of other studies have employed modifications of the BHQ or entirely
different Q-sort sets, we must conclude that consideration of reliability problems and the output of reliability information concerning Q sorts have been badly neglected.

Construct Validity of BHQ Scores

The construct validity of a Q-sort instrument for indexing S's
self-concept may be viewed from two aspects: (a) its usefulness as
an indicant of S's self-regard; and (b) the degree to which it reveals
"organization" or "patterning" in S's phenomenal self. Since actual
uses of BHQ assume (a) much more often than (b), and since (b) is
an indefensible inference (as shown below), I focus here mainly on
(a). I include Dymond's adjustment score and self-ideal rs in the
discussion of the construct validity of BHQ for inferring self-regard.

Construct Validity for Measuring Self-Regard

Irrelevant Response Determiners. Following the outline given in
chapter 3 of ways to evaluate construct validity, I consider first
the possible irrelevant determiners of responses or scores. Questions

can be raised about almost all the kinds of irrelevant determiners listed in the outline. Note particularly that the question of social-desirability influences remains unevaluated and uncontrolled. Stone and Winkler (1964) and Winkler and Myers (1963) found significant correlations of .36 and .30 between BHQ self-ideal rs and scores on the Marlowe-Crowne Social Desirability Scale. Of course, for reasons discussed above, this does not necessarily demonstrate that social-desirability considerations have distorted BHQ self-ideal rs as indices of Ss' phenomenal self-regard.

A second irrelevant response determiner of particular applicability to BHQ is the forced-choice format and its limitations on S's ability to present his self-concept accurately. As I have noted (Jones, 1956; Livson & Nichols, 1956), Ss do not spontaneously choose a quasi-normal distribution.

The wording of some of the items presents difficulties which can and should be avoided. In the case of Q sorting, if the dimension along which S must sort is "more or less like me," S may reasonably assume that the relative frequency with which he reacts in the specified ways is the dimension along which he is to array the items. If this is so, then the items should be uniformly phrased with respect to the variable of frequency. For example, items like "I put on a false front" or "I feel helpless" have no frequency of occurrence specified within them. Therefore S's job seems clearly to be one of ordering the items according to the frequency with which he would react or feel in these ways. However, confusion arises if S tries to apply the frequency dimension to a literal reading of such items as "I usually like people" or "I often kick myself for the things I do." This is so because a degree of frequency is already built into the statement itself. How can S say whether he more frequently "usually likes people," "often kicks himself," or "puts on a false front"? It is not possible to know from published information just how many of the sets of Q-sort items which have been used by various other authors contain this error in item phrasing. In future construction of sets of items, it would seem wise to keep this issue in mind.

If frequency ratings are to be used, it would also seem pertinent to make the referents comparable for all items by asking S, "How often do you do such-and-such a thing when it is a relevant response?" Otherwise differences in frequency ratings made by Ss concerning their own responses may reflect, to unknown degrees, differences in frequency of occurrence of appropriate opportunities for manifesting the respective behaviors.

The biggest problems of score interpretation arise in the areas of scaling and scoring procedures. First, we do not know definitely the meaning of any given size of discrepancy between self and ideal for any item. That is, the objective observer infers that whatever discrepancy exists between the pile number of the item as sorted under *self* and *ideal* instructions represents *S*'s conscious intention to express that particular experienced relationship between what he is like and what he would ideally wish to be like. However, we must realize that this discrepancy score was derived by the *experimenter* and that the *S* may or may not have been consciously aware of a discrepancy involving that item. This is true because, with one hundred items to arrange, *S* may easily forget the exact scale placement of an item under one set of instructions. Thus, despite his intentions to indicate a discrepancy of any given size, he may be unable to reveal his feelings accurately. If he were allowed to make his ideal-sort with a duplicate set of cards, while keeping the self-sort before him for reference, we might be safer in inferring that the size of the observed discrepancies reflects his consciously experienced discrepancies more accurately. However, if this method were to be used, we would perhaps foster both response sets and deliberate falsification, as we shall point out in connection with certain rating scale instruments to be discussed later.

A second problem in score interpretation is that discrepancy scores and global indices obscure individual differences which ought to be considered. Thus the self-ideal correlation as such gives no information as to (a) the patterning of individual items along the self-sort dimension; (b) the patterning of individual items along the ideal-sort dimension; and (c) the patterning of individual item discrepancies between self and ideal placements. A very large number of unique arrangements could yield similar or identical self-ideal correlation coefficients. The importance of this point is emphasized by considering a few examples in which discrepancies having probably different psychological meaning carry the same weight in determining the size of the self-ideal coefficient.

Example 1. Consider the following two discrepancies: (a) Item X is reported to be "somewhat like me," but "somewhat unlike my ideal." (b) Item X is reported to be "quite like me," but only "somewhat like my ideal." Surely these two discrepancies do not warrant comparable psychological inferences, though they may be of equal scale magnitude, and each involves a *self* pile number higher than the *ideal* pile number.

Example 2. Dymond has shown that 26 of the 100 Butler and Haigh items are judged by clinical psychologists to be irrelevant to adjustment. We do know that self-concept theory assumes that low self-ideal correlations are indicative of and/or lead to experienced discomfort and maladjustment. Suppose that we work from these two premises when computing an index of "discomfort" or "experienced maladjustment." Is it logical to assign equal weight to each of the following discrepancies? (a) A self-minus-ideal discrepancy on an item relevant to adjustment. (b) A self-minus-ideal discrepancy on an item irrelevant to adjustment.

Example 3. Imagine two subjects: (a) One places a certain item in a "wish it were much like me" pile and in a "not actually like me" pile. (b) The other places the same item in the "wish it were not like me" pile and in an "actually much like me" pile. These two types of discrepancies are possibly quite different in psychological meaning, even though the scale magnitude of the discrepancies could be the same.

One must conclude that the self-ideal correlation coefficient buries in a global index some individual differences which ought to be identified for study. In addition, I agree with Cronbach and Gleser's (1953, p. 459) statement that "combining many traits into any sort of composite index, whether it be a *D* measure, a *Q*-correlation or a discriminant function, or any of the other methods presently used, involves assumptions regarding scales of measurement which cannot usually be defended."

Correlational Analyses. Another way to explore construct validity is through correlational analyses relevant to convergent and discriminant validity. No multitrait-multimethod analyses have been published, so one must glean what he can from scattered sources. One might first inquire whether there are any published correlations between BHQ scores and scores from other instruments also purporting to measure self-regard. Although no such data are published in Rogers and Dymond's (1954) book, Shlien (1961) presents a matrix of correlations across Ss among self-ideal rs taken from the following: the original 100-item BHQ; 80 items, almost all from BHQ; Q sorts of the 49 adjectives from Bills's IAV; Q sorts of 25 self-referent statements respectively prepared by each S as important to himself; and *Q* sorts of one of Hilden's (1958) 50-item *Q* sets. The obtained *r*s range from .82 (between the 80-item BHQ and the 100-item BHQ) to .50 (between the 100-item BHQ and IAV-Q). Shlien invented two "abstract apparatuses," in which *S* represents his self-ideal congruence in terms of the amount of overlap between circles, and the overlap between squares. Self-ideal congruence scores from these apparatuses correlated with the 80-item BHQ self-ideal *r*s .39 and .48 (only the latter being significant). Stone and Winkler (1964) and Winkler and Myers (1963) obtained significant correlations between BHQ and IAV scores: .71 with IAV Self-Acceptance and .57 with IAV [Self—Ideal] discrepancies.

Thus, when we survey correlations among indices of self-regard, we find some evidence for convergent validity. However, a question of discriminant validity must be raised, since Winkler and Myers (1963) found as high or higher *r* between BHQ and Taylor's Manifest Anxiety Scale (−.68) as between the two alleged measures of self-acceptance. Perhaps offering some support to discriminant validity of BHQ is the finding of no association between Thematic Apperception Test (TAT) self scales and BHQ self-ideal *r*s in the Rogers and Dymond (1954) study. This null finding is relevant to discriminant validity only if one assumes that the authors intended the TAT measure to index the unconscious self-concept in contrast to the measurement of the conscious self-concept by BHQ.

Another sort of discriminant validity problem is raised when we ask whether the self-ideal correlation demonstrates dissatisfaction with self or perhaps more general dissatisfaction. It is a thorny issue, because self-concept theorists predict on theoretical grounds that there will be a correlation between satisfaction with self and satisfaction with others, for example. This makes very difficult the task of trying to establish discriminant validity of one measure as an index of phenomenal self-regard and of another as an index of regard for other persons or situations. The problem has not been directly attacked in the Rogers and Dymond (1954) book. Levy (1956) showed that low self-ideal correlations were associated with low actual-ideal correlations on one hundred statements of general applicability to *S*s' real and ideal home towns. Kornreich, Straka, and Kane (1968) extended Levy's findings by showing in three separate replications that low actual-ideal government correlations were associated with low actual-ideal self correlations. These findings raise the question whether low self-ideal correlations have discriminant validity for reflecting low self-regard rather than generally negative attitudes.

Studies Based on Assumed Validity. The final and necessarily most ambiguous kind of support for construct validity comes from positive findings in studies which assume the construct validity of an instrument while testing a theoretically relevant hypothesis using the instrument. Several such studies involving the BHQ found predicted differences between groups presumed to vary in phenomenal self-regard. In the Rogers and Dymond (1954) study, for example, the client group applying for therapy showed a mean initial self-ideal correlation of −.01, while the control Ss who volunteered to take part in research on personality showed a mean initial self-ideal correlation of .58. The experimental and control groups were satisfactorily matched for age, but only moderately satisfactorily matched with respect to sex, occupation, and socioeconomic status. The lack of perfect matching does not seem sufficient to account for the obtained differences in self-ideal congruence on any obvious basis other than that proposed by the experimenters, however. Cartwright (1963) also reports a significant difference in Dymond adjustment score between help-seekers and control Ss on a college campus. Shlien, Mosak, and Dreikurs (1962) report significant differences in self-ideal rs between normal controls and those seeking counseling. However, as Mowrer (1953b) has pointed out, such differences in self-ideal r between groups might be due to test-taking attitudes. For example, a candidate for practically free therapy may wish to show he has high standards but is inadequate in order to demonstrate that he deserves as well as needs help.

On theoretical grounds, Es have predicted positive association between self-ideal rs and "adjustment." In support of this prediction is the report by Hanlon, Hofstaetter, and O'Connor (1954) of a highly significant correlation between self-reported "adjustment" on the California Test of Personality and BHQ self-ideal rs. Winkler and Myers (1963) found a significant negative correlation between BHQ self-ideal rs and Taylor Manifest Anxiety Scores. Truax, Schuldt, and Wargo (1968) obtained numerous significant rs between self-ideal correlations from BHQ and scores from Truax's Anxiety Reaction Scale and from the MMPI. Their Ss were hospitalized mental patients and psychoneurotic outpatients. As shown in detail later, however, serious methodological problems preclude relying on correlations with self-reported adjustment to support construct validity of self-regard measures.

In accordance with theoretical expectations, negative associations have been found between BHQ self-ideal rs and "fear of failure" as measured by Hostile Press (Smith & Teevan, 1964); and a significant negative association has also been found between self-ideal rs from the BHQ and underachievement among bright students (Quimby, 1967).

Studies of psychotherapy are based on the theoretical prediction that self-ideal rs should increase with therapy; and early studies gave positive results. In the Rogers and Dymond study, no change in mean self-ideal correlation was found for the control group from initial to follow-up tests. Similarly, no change was found during the pretherapy period for the therapy clients who had to wait 60 days before undertaking therapy. On the other hand, a significant increase in mean self-ideal correlation was found between pretherapy and posttherapy sorts made by the clients. While such results are congruent with the assumption that self-ideal correlations validly index phenomenal self-esteem, we must note that S may be consciously malingering because he is too polite to admit to the therapist that he has not been helped (Mowrer, 1953b). The "adjustment score" for the self-sort, derived by Dymond, increased in the therapy group as the mean self-ideal correlation for that group also increased. Both of these scores were derived from the same instrument, however, so that one cannot say that independent measures have been related. That is, it may be that untrained Ss' opinions of what constitutes adjustment corresponds at least fairly well with the judgments of the trained clinicians who assigned adjustment scores to the items. In that event, an S who felt like disparaging himself would tend to place "well-adjusted" items in the "unlike me" side of the distribution when sorting for self-description, and in the "like me" side of the distribution when sorting for ideal description. This could result in both low self-ideal correlations and in poor adjustment score on the self-sort alone. The reverse outcome would hold true for Ss wishing not to disparage themselves.

Greater increases in self-ideal r in a therapy group as compared to a control group were also found by Shlien, Mosak, and Dreikurs (1962), using 80 items, almost all from BHQ, and by Butler (1968). On the negative side, several failures to find such increases have been noted. Phillips, Raiford, and El-Batrawi (1965) reported no increase in seven separate therapy groups. Truax, Wargo, Carkhuff, Kodman, and Moles (1966) found no significant changes in either delinquents or mental patients, either in self-ideal r or Dymond adjustment scores. C. R. Rogers (1967), using 80 items from BHQ, similarly found no change in schizophrenic patients in either self-ideal rs or adjustment scores. Ends and Page (1957) found no significant increases in self-ideal congruence or adjustment score on BHQ in any of four groups of hospitalized male inebriates treated respectively by learning-theory, client-centered, analytic, or social discussion (control) psychotherapeutic techniques. (In fact, a significant decrease in self-ideal congruence occurred in the learning-theory group.) Although J. M. Rogers (1960) expected to find increases in Dymond adjustment scores following operant conditioning in a "quasi-therapy" setting, no significant changes were obtained in either experimental or "no reinforcement" control groups. It seems, then, that this line of support for the construct validity of BHQ scores is not firmly established.

When shifts in self-ideal r *are* found as a function of therapy or other experimental treatment, we cannot tell without further analysis the contributions of shifts in self and in ideal self to the shift in self-ideal r. Some light is thrown on the problem by Rudikoff's (1954) analysis of data from eight of the client cases who waited 60 days prior to therapy. She found that in every case there was more shift in the self-sorts than in ideal-sorts from pre- to posttherapy. Only one ideal-ideal correlation was as low as the highest self-self correlation. When she obtained Dymond's adjustment scores on all sorts, she found no significant difference in the mean adjustment score of ideal sorts across the four testing points: (a) initial (prewait); (b) pretherapy; (c) posttherapy; and (d) follow-up. In contrast to this, the mean adjustment score of the self-sorts was different enough between pre- and posttherapy tests to be significant at better than the .001 level. Butler's (1968) results, although expressed in factor-analytic terms, suggest also that the major change over therapy occurs in the self-sort.

Overall, there is some support for the idea that BHQ self-ideal rs have some construct validity for indexing self-regard. Dymond adjustment scores seem sometimes to indicate clinically diagnosed differences in adjustment; but they may alternately be construed as a kind of self-regard index, since social desirability, personal desirability (ideal self), and rated adjustment have been shown to be correlated concepts (Wiener, Blumberg, Segman, & Cooper, 1959).

Construct Validity for Measuring Patterning or Organization within the Self-Concept

In self-concept theory, much importance has been assigned to the Gestalt, patterned, or integrated character of the self-concept. This is undoubtedly one of the reasons why Q sorts have appealed to investigators of that theoretical bent, since obviously many items can be included and they are arranged by S into a "pattern." For example, Mowrer (1953b, p. 374) says that correlations between sorts obtained from one person on two (or more) occasions are "admirably suited in theory to show personality changes (especially of an organizational kind)." Butler and Haigh (1954, p. 62) specu-late, "In brief, certain patterns of the self-ideal Gestalt may be discovered to indicate certain patterns or types of personality integration."

As we have shown, self-ideal rs probably do index self-regard. To contend that qualitative "patterning" or "organization" is also indicated is to say that one score can yield two separate pieces of information. This is manifestly impossible. Moreover, as we have argued above, a given r could come from many different item-place-ment combinations, so r is unsuited to indicate individual differ-ences in patterning. The idea of pattern or configural scoring is especially appealing to personality theorists; and presumably some type of pattern scoring might be developed for BHQ or another Q sort. Experience with pattern scoring in other areas of personality testing have not been encouraging, however, even when validity criteria are available (D. Campbell, 1963).

Studies Involving BHQ or Modifications of It, Not Cited in Text

The reader may find useful a list of references for studies involv-ing the BHQ and modifications thereof which I did not cite above because they were not explicitly pertinent to evaluating the reli-ability and construct validity of BHQ.

Those involving BHQ per se are: Farson (1961); Gruen (1960); Jacob and Levine (1968); and Lesser (1961).

Those involving some modification of BHQ, usually the use of BHQ items in a different format are: Bennett (1964a); Catron (1966); Crowne, Stephens, and Kelly (1961); Harmatz (1967); Harrow, Fox, Markhus, Stillman, and Hallowell (1968); Harrow, Fox, and Detre (1969); Hatfield (1961); Hills and Williams (1965); Isaacson and Landfield (1965); McCarthy and Brodsky (1970); Martin (1969); Schlicht (1967); Schlicht, Carlson, Skeen, and Skurdal (1968, 1969); Simmons and Lamberth (1961); and J. E. Williams (1962, 1963). Inasmuch as the items used in these studies overlap greatly with those in BHQ, the confirmations of theoretical predictions which were obtained in some of these studies offer some support to the construct validity of BHQ items as indices of self-regard.

OTHER Q-SORT SETS, ESPECIALLY HILDEN'S SETS

In addition to Butler and Haigh's Q sort, I have found allusions to about 70 other sets of Q-sort items published between 1950 and 1970. No set has been used in more than one or a very few studies. Although some information about the rationale for item selection is usually given, information about specific item content, reliability, and/or relevant construct validity is almost always missing. It is obvious that a great deal of work and thought has gone into the choice of items for some of these instruments, and researchers with similar rationales may wish to build on what has been done thus far. Accordingly, the following list provides references to Q-sort sets classified according to specified categories. Direct communication with the authors or acquisition of ADI documents will be necessary to get the items and instructions for Ss.

Q-Sort Sets Other than BHQ and Hilden's Sets, Categorized According to Rationale for Item Selection

Developmental level
 children: Cangemi (1966)
            Caplan (1957)
            Perkins (1958a, 1958b)

 adolescents: Anderson & Olson (1965) (similar to Engel, 1959)
            Constantinople (1969) (same as Wessman & Ricks, 1966)
            Engel (1959) (similar to Anderson & Olson, 1959)
            Stewart (1959, 1962)
            Wessman & Ricks (1966) (same as Constantinople, 1969)
            Wessman, Ricks, & Tyl 1960)
            White (1959)

Drives, needs, reactions to
frustration (See also Theo-
retical, below):   Cohen (1959) (Same as Stotland et al., 1957)
                                    Kelman & Parloff (1957) (drives)
                                    Stotland, Thorley, Thomas, Cohen, & Zander (1957)
                                        (same as Cohen, 1959)

Illness types: Lieberman, Stock, & Whitman (1959) (ulcer patients)
                                    Rosen (1966) (alcoholics)
                                    Dykstra (1969) (depressives)

Occupational categories:
    mathematicians,
    creative: Helson & Crutchfield (1970)

    mathematics teachers: Englander (1965–66)

    naval officers: Nahinsky (1958)

    nurses: Morrison (1962)
                                    Pallone & Hosinski (1967)

    research scientists: Gough & Woodworth (1960)

    industrial supervisor
    and subordinate: Vroom (1959)

Projective tests (Q sets
with purported corres-
pondence):   Chodorkoff (1954a, 1954b, 1956) (Rorschach, TAT)
                                    Friedman (1957) (TAT)

Self-regard; personality
description; or
adjustment: Akeret (1959)
                                    Block (1961b)
                                    Block & Thomas (1955) ⎱ nonprofessional Q sort
                                    Block & Turula (1963) ⎰
                                    Bower & Tashnovian (1955)
                                    Carroll & Fuller (1969) (Corsini SAQS, 1956)
                                    Cassel & Harriman (1959)
                                    Cohen (1959)
                                    Cowen, Budin, Wolitzky & Stiller (1960)
                                    Edelson & Jones (1954)
                                    Fairweather et al. (1960)
                                    Forsyth & Fairweather (1961)
                                    Foulkes & Heaxt (1962) (Corsini, 1956, sort)
                                    Frank (1956)
                                    Frisch & Cranston (1956)
                                    Goldman (1969) (same as Block's, 1961, CQ)
                                    Goldstein (1960)
                                    Graham & Barr (1967) (similar to Block & Turula,
                                        1963)
                                    Hatfield (1961)
                                    Hendrick & Page (1970)
                                    Klausner (1953)

Kogan, Quinn, Ax, & Ripley (1957)
Lepine & Chodorkoff (1955)
Mohanty (1965)
Pearl (1954)
Pyron & Kafer (1967)
Roth (1959)
Sappenfield (1970a) (photographs)
Sappenfield (1970b) (adjectives)
Smith (1958)
Stotland (1961)   ⎫ modification of
Stotland & Cottrell (1961, 1962) ⎬ Weinberger
Stotland & Dunn (1963)   ⎭
Sweetland & Frank (1955)
Taylor (1955)
Walker & Linden (1969)
Wallen (1969)

Speaking effectiveness: Ferullo (1963) (Wallen's *Q*)

Theoretically based
  Bion's group inter-
  action concept: Parloff (1961)

  Cattell: Hollon & Zolik (1962)
                         Quarter, Kennedy, & Laxer (1967)
                         Thompson & Nishimura (1952)

  Erikson: Constantinople (1969) ⎫ same instrument
                         Wessman & Ricks (1966) ⎭

Jungian types: Gorlow, Simonson, & Krauss (1966)

Murray needs: Baker (1968)
                         Fiedler, Warrington, & Blaisdell (1952) ⎫ same in-
                         Fiedler & Wepman (1951)   ⎬ strument
                         Rodgers (1959)

Psychoanalytic
theory: Krieger & Worchel (1960)

One set of items merits description here because it represents a systematic attempt to build alternate forms of *Q*-set items. From the Thorndike Century Senior Dictionary Hilden (1958) drew every word of a specified difficulty level which was suitable for formulating a statement about human reactions. For each word in this universe he composed a sentence appropriate for use in Q sorting. These sentences (items) constitute what he calls the Universe of Personal Concepts (UPC). By means of a table of random numbers he drew twenty sets of fifty items each from the serially listed sentences of the UPC. This procedure meant of course that there was some overlap of items from set to set; and approximately 600 items were used in no set.

As an empirical check on the equivalence of these randomly drawn sets, four graduate students made 20 self-sorts, then 20 ideal-sorts, using the 20 sets. Then they sorted all 1575 sentences in the UPC for self and for ideal. Since Hilden's procedure did not involve matching items (sentences), he had no rationale for inter-correlating the various self-sorts of a given S (or intercorrelating the various ideal-sorts of a given S) to determine whether alternate forms yielded comparable self-sorts (or comparable ideal-sorts). However, he could see whether the mean of a given S's 20 self-ideal correlations differed significantly from that S's self-ideal correlation obtained from the Universe of Personal Constructs. In the case of each of the four Ss, there was no significant difference between the mean of the 20 self-ideal correlations obtained from the 20 sets of items and the S's self-ideal correlation from the UPC. This suggests that the sets were essentially equivalent with respect to the degree to which self-ideal correlations obtained from them represented the specified universe, and that deviations from set to set could be attributed to sampling error.

What light do the results shed on the capacity of the sets to discriminate differences among Ss in self-ideal r? Inspection reveals that on 19 out of 20 sets, Subject C's self-ideal r was lower than that of any of the other three Ss, as was his self-ideal r on the UPC. Subjects A, B, and D had quite similar self-ideal rs on the UPC (.76, .71, and .76, respectively). These three Ss also tended to fall close to one another in the self-ideal rs obtained from each set and to exchange rank orders vis-à-vis one another on succeeding sets. This suggests that each separate set of sentences may be capable of discriminating reliable differences between individuals. It of course does not provide a basis for deciding how large a difference between two Ss must be on a given set in order to indicate a "true" (UPC) difference between the self-ideal correlations of the two Ss.

The attempt to define a universe, or item pool, so explicitly and operationally seems commendable, both in terms of coverage and provision for alternate forms. There is an apparently unresolvable problem (pseudoproblem?) as to whether the descriptive words in the dictionary adequately cover or proportionately represent the attributes which self-concept researchers need to be studying. It seems plausible that this approach optimizes such coverage. Of course, broad coverage and item selection on atheoretical grounds are definitely not appropriate to building an instrument with relevance to a delimited theoretical construct; and in this instrument one must remember that the sentences constructed (as opposed to the words drawn from the dictionary) definitely do not represent a random selection from any known pool. But so long as the instrument is used as a measure of overall self-regard, Hilden's approach may be somewhat defensible; and for a global self-regard measure it is important that a wide range of social-desirability values be included in the population of items. That this is the case is shown by Cruse's (1965) Social-Desirability values for the items of UPC. (It is interesting to note that these items, chosen with no reference to social-desirability considerations, yield an extremely bimodal frequency distribution of Social-Desirability scale values.)

The existence of alternate forms of known degree of empirical equivalence should be very helpful in studies requiring "before and after" or even more frequent test repetition. This is true because it seems likely that memory or other factors associated with retesting can affect such self-ideal correlations under certain conditions (D. M. Taylor, 1955). It seems regrettable, therefore, that more construct-validity studies of this instrument have not been made.

Of the seven published studies using one or more of the Hilden item sets, only Gildston's (1967) gives reliability information: a coefficient of .83 between self-ideal rs from Sets 14 and 15 in an almost immediate test-retest situation.

Convergent validity data on self-ideal rs are presented by Shlien (1961) for an unspecified Hilden set: with 100-item BHQ, $r = .65$; with 80-item BHQ, $r = .69$; with a Q-sort form of IAV, $r = .66$; with a Q-sort of statements which each S made up for his own use, $r = .75$.

No data relevant to discriminant validity seem to have been published.

Three investigators have reported that Hilden self-ideal rs discriminate between "known groups" in a theoretically predicted manner. Chase (1957) found significantly better self-ideal congruence in "normal" controls than in hospitalized mental patients, with the source of the difference lying in the self-sorts; Gildston (1967) reported significantly lower self-ideal congruence in stutterers as compared to nonstutterers; Manasse (1965) found significantly lower self-ideal congruence in improved schizophrenic patients in a day care center as compared with patients matched on illness status but functioning in the protected environment of the "best" hospital ward. Fuster (1963) obtained a significant positive association between self-reported adjustment (inferred from the California Test of Personality and Masani Problem Check List) and self-ideal *r*s from a Hilden set. (As I have already noted, such correlations between self-report instruments are especially open to alternate interpretations in terms of artifact.)

In one therapy study (Baymurr & Patterson, 1960), individually counseled student *S*s showed a "*Q*-adjustment score" improvement, while untreated controls and *S*s treated by group counseling or admonition showed no such change. Hansen, Moore, and Carkhuff (1968) found a significant positive association between improvement in self-ideal congruence and favorability of group-therapeutic conditions which were independently rated from tape samples by outside experts.

In summary, the very small amount of available evidence gives some support to the construct validity of Hilden's *Q*-sort sets as alternate-form measures of global self-regard.

2. Bills's Index of Adjustment and Values, Adult Form (IAV)

RATIONALE AND GENERAL DESCRIPTION

Some self-report instruments utilize a self-minus-ideal discrepancy score as well as a direct self-acceptance score to index self-regard. Bills's Index of Adjustment and Values (Bills, Vance, & McLean, 1951), a well-known example of this type of instrument, was designed to measure variables of importance to self-concept theorists. One hundred and twenty-four trait adjectives were selected from Allport's lists of 17,953 traits as representative, in the opinion of the test's designer, of items which occur frequently in client-centered interviews. Forty-nine items showing greatest test-retest stability on pretesting were retained in the final form, 40 are "desirable" and 9 "undesirable." Naturally, the adequacy with which the 49 chosen adjectives represent the Allport-Odbert list is unspecifiable.

In regard to himself, *S* gives three answers to each item: Column 1: How often are you this sort of person? (to be marked on a 5-point scale from "most of the time" to "seldom"). Column 2: How do you feel about being this way? (to be marked on a 5-point scale from "very much like" to "very much dislike"). Column 3: How much of the time would you like this trait to be characteristic of you? (to be marked on a 5-point scale from "seldom" to "most of the time"). The sum of Column 1 (with negative traits reversed) equals the Self score. The sum of Column 2 is taken as a direct measure of Self-Acceptance. The sum of the discrepancies between Columns 1 and 3 is taken as the [Self — Ideal] discrepancy, from which self-satisfaction is inferred. (The S also answers these same questions about other people, defined in terms of a relevant peer group. Items and directions for the entire procedure may be found in Bills, Vance, and McLean, 1951, and in Robinson and Shaver, 1969, as well as in Bills's undated mimeographed manual.)

RELIABILITY

Since Ss mark their responses to the three questions in columns on the same sheet, unreliability due to S's inability to remember previous column ratings could not enter into discrepancy scores which are computed across columns, nor into correlations computed between column scores. In this respect the IAV is superior to a Q-sorting technique. However, Bills's procedure may enhance the effects of response set upon discrepancy scores or upon correlations between column scores. Therefore, while reliability may be increased, construct validity is not necessarily increased accordingly.

For Self scores (Column 1), corrected split-half reliabilities range from .53 for 100 college students (Bills's undated manual) to .92 for 155 factory workers (Lefkowitz, 1967); while test-retest coefficients range from .90 (Bills's undated manual, 6-week interval, 160 college students) to .81 (Stimson, 1968, 6-month interval, 35 college males).

For Self-Acceptance scores (Column 2), corrected split-half rs were .91 (Bills, Vance, & McLean, 1951) and .93 (Brophy, 1959, 81 female nurses); while test-retest rs were .83 for a 6-week interval, and .68 and .79 for two samples after a 16-week interval (Bills's undated manual, total of 568 college Ss); and .70 (Stimson, 1968, 6-month interval, 35 college males).

For [Self — Ideal] discrepancy scores (between Columns 1 and 3), corrected split-half rs were .88 and .87 (Bills's undated manual, 237 and 100 college students); .92 (Brophy, 1959, 81 female nurses); and .88 and .93 (Windholz, 1968, 1969, 54 and 76 male college students); while test-retest rs were .87 for a 6-weeks interval; .69 and .52 for a 16-week interval (Bills's undated manual); and .61 (Stimson, 1968, 6-month interval, 35 male college students).

As fully explained on pages 119 to 121, low self-regard and randomness of responding are confounded influences on the score of any one *S* on this type of scale. Therefore, further information is needed as to whether response consistency among low self-regard *S*s is comparable to response consistency among high self-regard *S*s.

CONSTRUCT VALIDITY

Analysis of Irrelevant Response Determiners

Social Desirability. It is clear that social-desirability values of IAV adjectives are evident to *S*s and that high correlations *across item means* occur between rated social desirability and Self ratings, and between rated social desirability and Ideal ratings (Cowen & Tongas, 1959; Spilka, 1961). Spilka (1961) obtained an *r* of .57 between rated social desirability and Bills's Self-Acceptance. However, as explained in the section on social desirability (pages 52 to 62 above), this type of correlation is completely inappropriate evidence for arguing that construct validity of IAV scores as measures of self-regard is lowered by irrelevant or untrue social-desirability considerations. Cowen and Tongas (1959) found negligible correlations *across item means* between rated social desirability and [Self − Ideal] discrepancy scores, concluding that such scores are relatively free of distorting influences of social desirability. However, as explained in detail elsewhere (Wylie, 1961, p. 28), their conclusion is based on a methodological artifact.

Edwards's Social Desirability Scale scores have been reported to correlate *across S*s with IAV scores, as follows:

Self	.14 (n. s.)	Spilka (1961)
Self-Acceptance	.33 (n. s. males)	
	.35 (females)	Crowne, Stephens, and Kelly (1961)
[Self − Ideal]	−.47 (males)	Crowne, Stephens,
	−.57 (females)	and Kelly (1961)

Marlowe-Crowne Social Desirability scores correlated .28 with [Self − Ideal] discrepancies in Winkler and Myers's (1963) study. But these *r*s, too, prove nothing about whether the construct validity of IAV self-regard scores has been lowered by irrelevant or untrue social-desirability considerations.

In Bills's own work, favorable testing conditions and the stressing of the importance of honesty was assumed to induce frank reports. Conditions were unreported or less than optimal in many of the other studies cited below. As is the case with all self-regard instruments, nothing definite can be said about the degree to which irrelevant and untrue social-desirability considerations invalidate IAV scores as measures of self-regard.

Acquiescence Response Set. Acquiescence response set is inadequately controlled in the IAV since 40 of the 49 traits are "desirable."

Scoring Procedures. In the absence of any relevant information, it is unfruitful to speculate about the possible invalidating influences of most of the other possible irrelevant determiners of responses or response scores which I considered in general terms on pages 52 to 95 above. The implications of IAV scoring procedures for the instrument's construct validity do deserve some attention here, however.

As in all instruments involving summation across items, a given total Self-Acceptance score on the IAV could result from any one of many item combinations. Thus, summation across items in order to obtain a global Self-Acceptance score implies comparability among items with respect to their perceived salience for S's self-acceptance and their psychological metrics. There is no information to support these assumptions.

The second major purported self-regard score on the IAV is the [Self − Ideal] discrepancy. On pages 88 to 95 I have discussed the many methodological complexities and interpretational pitfalls of such [Self − Ideal] discrepancy scores; and the reader who wishes to evaluate the possible difficulties in inferring self-regard from the IAV [Self − Ideal] score should examine those pages carefully. Not only does a [Self − Ideal] discrepancy on a single psychological dimension present many complexities, but, as I point out in detail on the above pages, the problems of valid inference become compounded when [Self − Ideal] discrepancies are summed across scales to obtain an overall [Self − Ideal] discrepancy score.

Of particular empirical interest in regard to influences on the [Self − Ideal] scores from the IAV are data regarding the relative contributions of the Ideal and Self components to the two-part [Self − Ideal] score. It seems plausible that the Ideal scores are stereotyped and contribute little to the two-part score. Inspection of frequency distributions of college Ss for each of Bills's 49 adjectives reveals that, on 39 of these items, at least half the Ss fall at identical, extreme points on the 5-point Ideal-rating scales. For 23 out of the 49 adjectives, at least 66% of Ss fall at identical, extreme Ideal ratings. For 12 out of the 49 adjectives, at least 75% of Ss fall at identical, extreme points on the Ideal-rating scale. In contrast to this, only 4 of the 49 adjectives show 59% or more of the Ss falling at an identical point on the 5-point Self-rating scale.

Internal Correlational Analyses

Internal factor analyses should clarify the degree to which summing across disparate items to obtain a total self-regard score is justified by the presence of a general evaluative factor on which all items load appreciably. Mitchell's (1962) analysis of the 49 Self ratings yielded seven factors accounting for an unreported amount of the variance. He concludes that use of a global score is unjustified in view of his findings; but the information about variance accounted for by each factor is not given, and the number of Ss used was small for factoring a matrix of this size. In a personal communication (1971), Bills reports separate factor analyses of Self, Self-Acceptance, Ideal Self, and [Self – Ideal] discrepancy scores, based on 888 college Ss. In the case of each matrix, the first factor accounted for 60% to 62% of the variance, and the second, from 9% to 13%. No factor thereafter accounted for more than 6%. He concludes that "it is clear that one general factor accounts for most of the variance."

Of interest is the fact that item-total rs for the negative items are almost all in the .20s and .30s, while well over half of the item-total rs for positive items are in the .50s and .60s (Bills, personal communication, 1971). Inspection of Mitchell's (1962) factor matrix reveals that all the negative items load appreciably on one and only one factor, and that that factor is defined only by the negative items.

Convergent Validity

Correlations among scores purporting to measure the same construct are, of course, relevant to convergent and discriminant validity. First of all, convergence among the three IAV scores is to be expected and is relevant to the evaluation of their respective convergent validities, as explained below. However, use of three different scores to infer three allegedly different self-regard constructs is warranted only if there is sufficient evidence of their *lack* of convergence to suggest the possibility of discriminant validity. Secondly, correlations between IAV scores and those from other instruments which also purport to measure self-regard are relevant to convergent construct validity of IAV scores. We consider these two approaches immediately below.

The IAV yields three possible alternate indices of self-regard: (a) Self (by assuming that S has accepted a cultural stereotype at the good end of each rating scale, one can infer self-regard from the Self score alone, since the subtraction of Self from the constant steoreotype value would not modify the score essentially); (b) Self-Acceptance; (c) [Self − Ideal] discrepancy score (Bills evidently intended only the Self-Acceptance and [Self − Ideal] discrepancy scores as measures of self-regard. I am responsible for including the Self score in this list).

Several investigators have correlated *Self* scores (Column 1) with *Self-Acceptance* scores (Column 2), and the results were as follows, all *r*s being significant:

Bills (undated manual)	.90
Kania (1967)	.81
Spitzer et al. (1966)	.71

This implies that the two scores overlap greatly, which therefore renders questionable their discriminant validity and any uses based on the assumption of discriminant validity.

Self scores (Column 1) have also been correlated with [Self − Ideal] discrepancy scores (between Columns 1 and 3), yielding the following results. Of course these correlations are inflated by the common Self values.

Bills (undated manual)	.83
Kania (1967)	.75
Spitzer et al. (1966)	.70

Although *Ideal* scores (Column 3) are not used per se as self-regard measures, it is of parenthetical interest to note a reported r of .37 between *Self* (Column 1) and *Ideal* (Column 3) (Bills's undated manual, $N = 301$). This "across-S" r should not be confused with the "within-S" correlations between self and ideal which one obtains with Q-sort techniques. The modest size of this r is quite probably due in part to the restricted range of the Ideal ratings already noted above.

The following correlations have been obtained between *Self-Acceptance* scores (Column 2) and [Self − Ideal] discrepancy scores (Column 1 minus Column 3). All *r*s are significant unless marked n. s.

Bills (undated manual)	−.67
Crowne, Stephens, and Kelly (1961)	−.85 (males)
	−.62 (females)
Kania (1967)	−.76
Korner et al. (1963)	−.53
Medinnus and Curtis (1963)	−.57
Spitzer et al. (1966)	−.57
Viney (1966)	−.25 (n. s.)

These values suggest that the [Self − Ideal] discrepancy and the Self-Acceptance scores may be revealing somewhat different things, especially since the moderate-size *r*s were obtained despite the facts that each score has high split-half reliability and method variance probably is contributing to the size of *r*.

In the second kind of approach to convergent validity, each IAV score has been correlated with a number of other scores from other instruments which also purport to measure self-regard.

Self scores (Column 1) have been found to correlate as follows with various other self-regard scores, all *r*s being significant unless marked n. s.:

ACL Self Acceptance (Gough, 1960)	.57 (males); .47 (females) (Spitzer et al., 1966)
ACL Self Criticality (Gough, 1960)	−.60 (males); −.48 (females) (Spitzer et al., 1966)
Self-Derogation from TST (Kuhn & McPartland, 1954)	−.37 (males); −.32 (females) (Spitzer et al., 1966)
Self-Satisfaction from TST (Kuhn & McPartland, 1954)	.36 (males); .39 (females) (Spitzer et al., 1966)
Coopersmith (1967) SEI	.46 (males); .17 (n. s.) (females) (Ziller et al., 1969)
Cutick's Self Evaluation (Diggory, 1966)	.60 (males); .29 (females) (Ziller et al., 1969)
Nonverbal SSE ("horizontal self-esteem") (Ziller et al., 1969)	.10 (n. s.) (males); −.14 (n. s.) (females) (Ziller et al., 1969)

IAV Self-Acceptance scores (Column 2) have been correlated with scores from other instruments which also purport to index self-regard, with the following results. All correlations are significant unless marked n. s. Regardless of sign, the correlations indicate positive associations of degrees of self-regard.

Acceptance of Self (Berger, 1952)	.49 (Omwake, 1954)
Acceptance of Self (Phillips, 1951)	.24 (Bills's undated manual)
Acceptance of Self (Phillips, 1951)	.55 (Omwake, 1954)
Acceptance of self, coded from interviews	.84 (Bills, 1954a)
Worst realistic self-concept from Brownfain (1952)	.44 and .34 (Cowen, 1956)
Best realistic self-concept from Brownfain (1952)	.43 and .34 (Cowen, 1956)
Self-ideal r from Butler-Haigh Q sort (1954)	.71 (Stone & Winkler, 1964) −.43 (Strong, 1962)
Self Acceptance on ACL (Gough, 1960)	.48 (males); .31 (females) (Crowne, Stephens, & Kelly, 1961)
Self-Criticality on ACL (Gough, 1960)	−.51 (males); −.44 (females) (Crowne, Stephens, & Kelly, 1961)
Self-ideal discrepancy (Buss and Gerjuoy, 1957)	−.35 (males); −.18 (n. s.) (females) (Crowne, Stephens, & Kelly, 1961)
Self-Derogation from TST (Kuhn & McPartland, 1954)	−.27 (Spitzer et al., 1966)
Self-Satisfaction from TST	.33 (Spitzer et al., 1966)
Self-ideal discrepancy on Fiedler's adjective scales (Fiedler et al., 1959)	−.44 (Spitzer et al., 1966)

Self-ideal congruence, Shlien's Abstract Apparatus (1961)	−.02 (n. s.) (Viney, 1966)
Self-ideal r, Shlien's Ideo-Q (1961)	.37 (Viney, 1966)
Crowne's Self-Acceptance	−.35 (males); −.58 (females) (Crowne et al., 1961)
Semantic Differential Self-Acceptance	−.57 (Medinnus & Curtis, 1963)
Self and [Self − Ideal], SAI (Worchel, 1957)	−.43 and −.37 (Strong, 1962)

IAV [Self − Ideal] discrepancy scores (Column 1 minus Column 3) have been correlated with scores from other instruments purporting to measure self-regard, with the following results. All correlations are significant unless marked n. s. Regardless of sign, the correlations indicate positive associations of degree of self-regard.

Worst realistic self-concept from Brownfain (1952)	−.62 and −.29 (Cowen, 1956) (See also Cowen, 1954)
Best realistic self-concept from Brownfain (1952)	−.43 and −.44 (Cowen, 1956)
Self-ideal r from Butler and Haigh Q sort (1954)	.71 (Stone & Winkler, 1964) .57 (Winkler & Myers, 1963) .62 (Strong, 1962)
Self-Acceptance on ACL (Gough, 1960)	−.35 (males); −.53 (females) (Crowne et al., 1961)
Self-Criticality on ACL (Gough, 1960)	.34 (males); .51 (females) (Crowne et al., 1961)
Self-ideal discrepancy (Buss & Gerjuoy, 1957)	.32 (n. s.) (males); .39 (females) (Crowne et al., 1961)
Self-ideal discrepancy on Fiedler's adjective scales (Fiedler et al., 1959)	.56 (Spitzer et al., 1966)
Self-Derogation on TST (Kuhn & McPartland, 1954)	.25 (Spitzer et al., 1966)

Self-Satisfaction on TST   −.28 (Spitzer et al., 1966)
(Kuhn & McPartland, 1954)

Self-ideal congruence, Shlien's   −.12 (n. s.) (Viney, 1966)
(1961) Abstract Apparatus

Self-ideal r, Shlien's (1961)   −.23 (n. s.) (Viney, 1966)
Ideo-Q

Crowne's Self-Acceptance   .57 (males); .65 (females)
                                  (Crowne et al., 1961)

Semantic Differential Self-   .53 (Medinnus & Curtis, 1963)
Acceptance

Self and [Self − Ideal], SAI   .49 and .60 (Strong, 1962)
Worchel (1957)

For several reasons, it is impossible to synthesize conclusively the information regarding the correlations of IAV self-regard scores with other purported tests of self-regard. First, the other tests vary regarding their reliability, format, and other aspects of method (e.g., verbal-nonverbal). Secondly, number and types of Ss on which the rs are based vary widely, although all Ss were late adolescents or adults. Unfortunately, no multitrait-multimethod matrices are available to furnish a basis for systematic comparisons.

Inspection of the data presented above suggests the following very tentative generalizations:

1. Any one of the three self-regard scores of the IAV (Self, Self-Acceptance, [Self − Ideal] discrepancy) correlates moderately with a wide variety of verbal self-report instruments which also purport to measure self-regard. The size of the correlations does not seem to depend on similarity of format between instruments. For example, IAV scores which come from a rating-scale format give correlations of about the same size with scores from Q-sort, semantic differential, or adjective-check-list formats.

2. From the very small amount of available data, there is no evidence that any IAV score correlates with any nonverbal measure purporting to index self-regard.

3. There is no evidence that any one of the three IAV self-regard scores correlates best with other purported measures of self-regard. This, coupled with the sizable correlations between IAV scores, calls the discriminant validity of the three IAV self-regard scores into serious question.

Studies Based on Assumed Validity

By assuming the construct validity of the IAV scores as indices of self-regard and by adopting certain theoretical premises, predictions may be made concerning relationships which should be obtained between IAV self-regard scores and other variables. To the extent that the predictions are confirmed, some support is offered to the inference of construct validity, as well as to the theoretical premises being tested.

At best, even when individual studies are well designed and properly executed, and successive researches have been chosen in such a way as to extend systematically our knowledge of an instrument's construct validity, this type of research offers only equivocal support to construct validity. Unfortunately, although many studies of the IAV have been published, they are much less than optimally helpful in evaluating its construct validity. For some studies, the prediction which one should make from theory is not clear; in many there are serious methodological flaws. In a number of reports, the presentation of numerous significance tests within a single study makes evaluation of significance levels of particular associations impossible. And the total group of studies consists more of a miscellaneous than an integrated collection.

All the studies reported immediately below looked at associations between one or more IAV scores and other psychometric measures of *S. Lower* IAV self-regard scores have been found to be associated with the following variables.

1. *"Underachievement."* Among bright high-school students, differences in Self and Self-Acceptance were significant for males, but not for females (Shaw & Alves, 1963).

2. *Less Affect and/or More Dysphoric Affect.* In several studies, scores on self-report *anxiety* scales are larger for *S*s with lower IAV self-regard scores (Ohnmacht & Muro, 1967, Self-Acceptance vs. Cattell scales contributing to second-order factor of anxiety; Winkler & Myers, 1963, Self-Acceptance vs. Taylor Manifest Anxiety Scale, $r = .71$; Cowen, Heilizer, Axelrod, and Alexander, 1957, Self, Self-Acceptance, and/or [Self − Ideal] discrepancy scores vs. Taylor Manifest Anxiety Scale). Some question concerning the role of test-taking defensiveness is raised by the finding that *S*s in the latter study who showed high and low lie scores respectively differed in Self, Self-Acceptance, and [Self − Ideal] discrepancy scores; while

Kania (1967) found significant correlations between K scores from the MMPI and Bills's Self and [Self — Ideal] scores. One study found no association between Cattell's Q3 factor (which loads highest on his second-order factor of general anxiety) and [Self — Ideal] discrepancies (Viney, 1966).

Bills (1954b) found a higher incidence of five out of six Rorschach *depression* signs among Ss low on self-regard in terms of [Self — Ideal] discrepancies. Renzaglia (quoted in Bills's undated manual) found less optimism with respect to future college success, less satisfaction with the present period of life, and higher MMPI profile, especially D, Pt, Sc, and Si, among Ss low on Self-Acceptance. Brophy (1959) found significant associations between "general satisfaction" (indexed by three questions from a published happiness scale) and [Self — Ideal] discrepancy scores; but no relationship with Self-Acceptance scores. He also found "vocational satisfaction" (indexed by three questions from a published scale) significantly associated with [Self — Ideal] discrepancies. Mitchell (1963b) found a significantly greater factor loading of the IAV Self-Acceptance score on a "satisfaction-with-life" factor than on an "academic motivation" factor. (The factors were obtained from another questionnaire.)

Bills (1953a) reports more perceptual accuracy and less degree of affect on the Rorschach among Ss low on Self-Acceptance.

Using male Ss, Windholz (1968, 1969) obtained a significant r of .21 between [Self — Ideal] discrepancy scores and a daydream-frequency measure, and a significant partial r of .24 with a Hostile daydream score (the Hero daydream score being partialed out). However, Gardiner (1970) was unable to replicate the first finding with female Ss.

Bendig and Hoffman (1957) found small but significant trends for low self-regard (Self-Acceptance, [Self — Ideal] discrepancies) to be associated with introversion and neuroticism on the Maudsley Personality Inventory; but Crowne, Stephens, and Kelly (1961) found no association between "adjustment" inferred from an incomplete-sentences test and [Self — Ideal] discrepancies.

In Bills, Vance, and McLean's (1951) study, when Ss were explaining their own unhappiness, those with low Self-Acceptance scores gave more reasons coded by judges as indicative of self-blame. Boshier (1968b) found essentially no relationship between IAV scores and Ss' reported liking for their names.

3. *Psychosomatic Symptoms and Dissatisfaction with Body.* Ss
lower in Self-Acceptance reported more psychosomatic symptoms
(Bills's undated manual). Zion (1965) found larger actual-ideal discrepancies in a measure of body concept among Ss with high [Self —
Ideal] discrepancies on IAV; but she obtained ambiguous relationships between IAV Self-Acceptance scores and "body acceptance"
scores. Meissner, Thoreson, and Butler (1967) found no significant
main effects on the Self and Self-Acceptance scores when sex and
self-reported "obviousness" and "impact" of physical disabilities
were the independent variables. A significant triple-order interaction was obtained; namely, among Ss who reported high-obvious
high-impact physical disabilities, adolescent females (as predicted)
showed more negative Self and Self-Acceptance scores, while males
(contrary to prediction) showed more positive Self and Self-Acceptance scores. Korner, Allison, Donoviel, and Boswell (1963) failed to
confirm their prediction that the three IAV "self-acceptance" scores
would correlate with Draw-a-Person (DAP) scores allegedly indicative of "conflicts in body image," or with Ss' ratings of their own
unrecognized silhouettes.

4. *Lower Acceptance of Others.* As predicted, mothers studied
by Medinnus and Curtis (1963) showed significant association between degree of child acceptance (measured by semantic differential)
and Self-Acceptance on the IAV. Mitchell (1963b) found a significant correlation between college students' IAV Self-Acceptance
scores and their scores on a "satisfaction with home and family"
factor (based on a specially devised inventory). Among 300 college
students, self-regard scores correlated with scores attributed by self
to others as follows: Column 1 (Actual Self) vs. Actual Others = .78;
Column 2 (Acceptance of Self) vs. Acceptance of Others = .56;
Column 1 and 3 (Actual-Ideal discrepancy for Self) vs. Actual-Ideal
discrepancy for Others = .43 (Bills's undated manual).

Practically no investigators have tried to demonstrate theoretically relevant associations between IAV self-regard scores and "objective" characteristics or behaviors of S. Those studies in which
total self-regard scores were used have yielded null results which
are, of course, uninterpretable. (See Grande, 1966, regarding rated
performance of Peace Corps volunteers; Carson, 1967, regarding
welfare recipients as compared to other clients also applying for
rehabilitation services; and Boshier and Hamid, 1968, regarding
final examination scores.) Some theoretically predicted results were

obtained in three studies which looked for an association between (a) the size of [Self − Ideal] discrepancies for individual items and (b) reaction times and learning speeds involving the respective items. Roberts (1952) determined, for individual Ss, which words yielded some and no reported [Self − Ideal] discrepancies, and which yielded high and low reported Self-Acceptance. He found significantly longer free-association times to words which showed some [Self − Ideal] discrepancy or low Self-Acceptance, as contrasted to words which showed no [Self − Ideal] discrepancy or high Self-Acceptance. In a replication study, Bills (1953b) obtained nonsignificant trends similar to Roberts's findings. In a second part of his study, Bills predicted that changes over time in [Self − Ideal] discrepancies and Self-Acceptance would be associated with corresponding changes in reaction time. His significant results refuted rather than supported his hypothesis, however. Cowen, Heilizer, and Axelrod (1955) used a paired-associate learning technique with nonsense syllables as response words. The stimulus words were Bills's adjectives, which had been identified for the individual S as having high and low [Self − Ideal] discrepancies, respectively. Significantly elevated learning thresholds were associated with words thus identified as conflictual, when other variables (e.g., frequency) were well controlled.

Apparently few experimental studies involving predicted changes in IAV scores have been done. Bills (undated manual) cites Weider's findings that Ss having been taught by a "group therapy method" in a mental hygiene class showed significant increases in Self and Self-Acceptance scores (although [Self − Ideal] discrepancies showed no significant change). Changes did not occur in Ss taught by a "traditional classroom method." Grater's (1959) study of Ss in leadership training had no control group, so no conclusions can be drawn.

Discriminant Validity

In conjunction with the convergent-validity studies of IAV scores which we previously discussed, the researches considered immediately above add a limited amount of rather equivocal support to the contention that Self, Self-Acceptance, and/or [Self − Ideal] scores have construct validity as indices of self-regard. There is no clear demonstration that the three self-regard scores have discriminant validity for indicating, respectively, different kinds of self-regard, however. It is particularly interesting that the empirical findings obtained with the Self score (which is in principle only partly phenomenological) seem to be quite similar to those obtained with the Self-Acceptance score and with the [Self — Ideal] discrepancy score (which are in principle entirely phenomenological).

Beyond this we must still ask about discriminant validity between any one of these alleged self-regard scores and other scores which supposedly indicate some other variables, for example, more general dissatisfaction and anxiety. Although theory would predict that self-regard scores should correlate with such variables as dissatisfaction with others and anxiety, if the correlations between any IAV self-regard score and scores purportedly measuring one of these other variables is as high or higher than correlations between the IAV and other self-regard scores, the discriminant validity of that IAV score as an indicator of self-regard is called into question. A multitrait-multimethod matrix is needed; and one cannot glean from the presented studies any clear evidence for this type of discriminant validity. In fact, a few of the available findings suggest that IAV self-regard scores do not have discriminant validity in this sense. As reported above, for example, an r of .71 has been obtained between IAV Self-Acceptance scores and Taylor Manifest Anxiety Scores (Winkler & Myers, 1963); and an r of .56 has been obtained between Self-Acceptance scores and Acceptance-of-Others scores on IAV (Bills's undated manual).

Persons interested in using or evaluating the IAV may find helpful the following studies which were not included in the validity section because I did not consider them to be clearly relevant to the question of construct validity of the IAV: Bills (1953c), Boshier (1969), Corfield (1969), Dyson (1967), Folds and Gazda (1966), and Neuringer and Wandke (1966).

Another group of studies were not specifically cited in the discussion of the IAV because they employed one or another *modification* of the IAV: Archibald (1970), Bledsoe (1964), E. Horowitz (1962), McAfee and Cleland (1956), Pannes (1963), Rabinowitz (1966), Renzaglia, Henry, and Rybolt (1962), and Rivlin (1959).

CONCLUSIONS AND RECOMMENDATIONS

It is evident that the IAV has been used by many researchers. Reliability is quite high. Evidence for convergent validity includes correlations with many different purported measures of self-regard—a wider range of such instruments than is the case for any other self-regard measure. Although the degree of convergent validity of any of the self-regard scores from IAV is quite moderate, it is probably as good as for any extant instrument which purports to measure global self-regard with the use of numerous items; and the IAV is shorter and less cumbersome for S and E than is true of a number of the other instruments, for example, the Butler-Haigh Q Sort (BHQ), the Tennessee Self Concept Scale (TSCS), and Gough's Adjective Check List (ACL). Although variations in Ss and techniques do not permit definitive comparisons, there is some suggestion that the convergent validity of the simpler Rosenberg Guttman scale of self-esteem (RSE) may equal or exceed that of IAV.

Discriminant validity among the IAV self-regard scores and between any one IAV self-regard score and other conceptually distinguishable variables remains undemonstrated because multitrait-multimethod techniques have not been applied. Such evidence as is available suggests that discriminant validity of both kinds is lacking.

Keeping in mind Bills's original aim to create an instrument yielding one or more global self-regard scores, it could be fruitful to develop the IAV further toward this goal, using modern techniques of test development, namely: (a) improving the item set through addition of rationally selected items, application of internal factor analysis for evaluation and weeding of items, and the balancing of items to control for acquiescence response set; (b) using multitrait-multimethod matrices for exploration of convergent and discriminant validity of purported self-regard scores; and (c) carrying out a systematic program of exploration of construct validity in which IAV scores are used in testing theoretical hypotheses.

It appears that eventually a more valid general self-regard score could be based on a smaller number of selected items. However, available factor-analytic information suggests that valid measurement of separate, psychologically meaningful dimensions of self-concept will not be possible with IAV unless the item set is changed systematically and drastically from the present one.

3. Worchel's Self Activity Inventory (SAI)

When the 1961 edition of this book was in preparation, Worchel's (1957) Self Activity Inventory (SAI) was considered in detail because more information about it was available than for most other self-concept scales. Although a fair number of additional references have appeared since that time, they have not answered some of the critical questions raised earlier, nor have they yielded proportionate increases in much-needed knowledge about the reliability and construct validity of the scale. Accordingly, only a brief description and evaluation is given here.

RATIONALE AND GENERAL DESCRIPTION

The SAI is a self-concept measure which purports to describe ways of coping with hostility, achievement, sex, and dependency needs, and their frustration. The rationale for choosing item content was that these four need areas were apt to be major sources of conflict for men adapting to military life. No information is given concerning procedures by which the items were determined to have face validity for their respective purported need referents. Almost all the items seem to be negatively worded, that is, to attribute the stated characteristics to oneself would be to derogate the self. This fact means that possible acquiescence or negation response sets have not been adequately controlled. For each of three categories (Self, Ideal Self, Other), S is asked to use a 5-point frequency scale for each item to indicate how applicable the item is.

RELIABILITY

Even regarding the most-used score (the [Self − Ideal] discrepancy), reliability information is meager: a split-half r of .91 is reported by Byrne, Barry, and Nelson (1963) for college student Ss. Worchel (1957) gives 8-week test-retest rs for college students of .79 for Self; .72 for Ideal; and .78 for Other.

CONSTRUCT VALIDITY

Irrelevant Response Determiners

The analysis of possibly irrelevant response determiners is virtually untouched. As we said above, the possible influence of acquiescence response sets has not been ruled out.

G. Becker's (1968) correlation of .37 between the Marlowe-Crowne Social Desirability Scale and [Self − Ideal] discrepancies proves nothing, of course, about the distorting influences of social desirability upon the construct validity of the [Self — Ideal] score as a measure of phenomenal self-regard. No procedural means to control for faking or more subtle social-desirability effects are reported. Wilkinson (1970) purported to show a significant inverse relationship between "extremity response set" and measured intelligence; but average level of favorability was apparently not controlled between extreme and less extreme responders, so nothing can be concluded.

Regarding possible influences of scoring procedures upon construct validity, we note first that the [Self — Ideal] discrepancy is assumed to index "self-ideal congruence," while [Self — Other] discrepancy is assumed to index "self-depreciation." However, it is obvious that these scores cannot be independent of each other or of Self, since each discrepancy score contains Self. I have discussed the many methodological complexities and interpretational pitfalls of [Self — Ideal] discrepancy scores; and the reader who wishes to evaluate the possible difficulties in inferring self-regard from SAI [Self — Ideal] scores should examine pages 88–95 carefully. Not only does a [Self — Ideal] discrepancy on a single psychological dimension present many complexities, but as I point out in detail on the above pages, the problems of valid inference become compounded when [Self — Ideal] discrepancies are summed across scales to obtain an overall [Self — Ideal] discrepancy score. Considerable evidence supports the idea that the Ideal scores are more stereotyped and less related to other variables than are the Self scores (Byrne, Barry, and Nelson, 1963; Schludermann and Schludermann, 1969b; Worchel, 1957).

Internal Correlational Analyses

Schludermann and Schludermann's (1969a, 1969b) internal factor analyses of SAI scores yielded a large number of specific factors. Their results fail to support Worchel's implied assumption that Self scores or [Self — Ideal] scores refer to a global self-regard construct.

Convergent and Discriminant Validity

Convergent validity information is limited. Strong (1962) reports correlations of .60 between SAI and IAV [Self — Ideal] discrepancy scores, and .58 between SAI [Self — Ideal] discrepancies and Dymond scores from BHQ.

Strong's (1962) factor analysis of BHQ, IAV, and SAI involved none of the discrepancy scores from these instruments. It yielded four factors, one of which was a "definite Worchel self-concept factor," but which could have been a methods factor. Stimson's (1968) factor analysis of 19 variables found SAI Self scores loading highest on Factor I (favorable self-description), on which the following self-regard scores also received their highest loading: Bills's IAV Self, Self-Acceptance, and [Self — Ideal]; and Dymond adjustment scores from the BHQ. The other variables in this analysis did not load appreciably on Factor I, nor were they self-regard scores. This result offers some support for the discriminant validity of SAI scores.

Studies Based on Assumed Validity

I have examined 17 studies which bear indirectly on the construct validity of SAI inasmuch as they test simultaneously the construct validity of the instrument and some theoretical assumptions of the authors. Unfortunately, the researches give exceptionally spotty and weak support to the construct validity of any SAI score. This is so for several reasons: they cover a rather narrow range of other inferred variables; certain combinations of positive, negative, and null findings cannot be compared, synthesized, or reconciled, partly because of methodological variations; and many of the studies are open to serious methodological criticisms which space precludes presenting in detail. The main classes of variables looked at in relation to [Self — Ideal] discrepancies were aggression-hostility-derogation and adjustment.

1. Aggression-Hostility-Derogation. Since parts of the SAI were developed specifically to refer to self-concepts about management of hostility, researches in this area are especially appropriate. Three studies found predicted associations between *small* [Self — Ideal] discrepancies and some *behavioral* measures plausibly indicative of aggression (Worchel, 1958; Worchel & Hillson, 1958; Worchel & McCormick, 1963). On the other hand, Veldman and Worchel (1961) and Worchel (1966) obtained null findings. *Self-reported* hostility was associated with large [Self — Ideal] discrepancies in Rothaus and Worchel's (1960) study. Of some possible indirect relevance to this area of concern is Schludermann and Schludermann's (1970b) finding that Real Self on SAI correlated negatively and highly significantly with such California Psychological Inventory variables as self-control, tolerance, good impression, and achievement by conformity.

2. *Adjustment.* The SAI was developed especially as a predictor of "maladjustment," but studies which might be classified under this heading are relatively few and inconclusive: Hillson and Worchel (1957); Nebergall, Angelino, and Young (1959); and three studies reported in Worchel (1957) and criticized in detail by Wylie (1961).

3. *Miscellaneous.* Despite theoretical predictions of linear functions, null or curvilinear findings were found between [Self — Ideal] discrepancies and other variables, as follows: Null relationships were obtained with field-dependent behaviors (Young, 1959) and attraction to others (Griffitt, 1966, 1969); curvilinear relationships were found with performance decrements under threat (Miller & Worchel, 1956); and complex curvilinear relationships were obtained between parents' and children's [Self — Ideal] discrepancies (Wilkinson & Worchel, 1959).

Not supporting a predicted curvilinear relationship was Becker and Dileo's (1967) null association between [Self — Ideal] scores and scores on Rokeach's Dogmatism Scale.

Summary and Recommendations

In summary, although the SAI has continued to be one of the more frequently used self-regard measures, its further use for such a purpose cannot be defended in the light of the quantity, quality, or outcomes of research relevant to its reliability and its construct validity as a measure of self-regard.

4. Children's Self-Concept Scales, Especially the Coopersmith Self-Esteem Inventory (SEI) and the Piers-Harris Children's Self-Concept Scale (PH)

Because many investigators are interested in studying self-evaluations in children, there is a need for satisfactory instruments for measuring children's self-regard. Long, Henderson, and Ziller (1970), whose SSE is discussed on pp. 190–200, have presented considerable information on this nonverbal test; but no verbal self-concept measure has received wide use in published researches. The four instruments which have been most discussed, and might, therefore, be considered for analytical attention here, are Lipsitt's (1958) Self-Concept Scale for Children; Coopersmith's Self-Esteem Inventory (SEI) (1959, 1960, 1964, 1967); Bills's (undated manual) test for children (CIAV), and Piers and Harris's Children's Self-Concept Scale (PH) (Piers & Harris, 1964; Piers, 1969).

I have chosen to give some attention to the Coopersmith SEI, but to consider the PH scale in the most detail, omitting separate consideration of the other two. This choice is based on the following comparisons.

COMPARISON OF AVAILABLE INFORMATION ON FOUR SCALES

Rationale for item choice is most fully explained for PH and CIAV, somewhat explained for SEI, and not explained for the Lipsitt scale. The PH and SEI scales control somewhat for acquiescence-response set by including an equal or approximately equal number of favorably and unfavorably worded items, while CIAV and the Lipsitt scales do not. The split-half and test-retest reliabilities of all four scales seem to be approximately comparable insofar as information is available and comparisons are plausibly warranted, so decisions about the relative merits of the instruments cannot be made on grounds of reliability. Item analyses are more extensive or more fully described in the case of the PH scale as compared to the other three. Only PH has been internally factor analyzed. Convergent validity studies, that is, researches correlating scores from the instrument in question with scores from other instruments also purporting to measure phenomenal self-regard, are entirely absent for CIAV, and virtually so for SEI, PH, and Lipsitt scales, although the latter two have been correlated (Mayer, 1967). Studies which are relevant to construct validity because they test theoretical predictions are extremely few for all these instruments, but they are slightly more numerous for PH than for CIAV and SEI.

Readers interested in Bills's new test for children (CIAV) should consult his memeographed undated manual. Those interested in published research involving Lipsitt's (1958) scale should consult F. D. Horowitz (1962); Humes, Adamczyk, and Myco (1969); McCallon (1966a); Mann (1969); Mann, Beaber, and Jacobson (1969); Mayer (1966, 1967) Reese (1961); and Zunich and Ledwith (1965).

COOPERSMITH'S SELF-ESTEEM INVENTORY (SEI)

Coopersmith (1959) developed his Self-Esteem Inventory for children (SEI), beginning with items from the Butler-Haigh Q Sort (Butler & Haigh, 1954), reworded for children. He then added and eliminated items according to expert judgments. All the items in the final scale were agreed upon by five psychologists as indicating either high or low self-esteem; and repetitious, ambiguous items were eliminated. Items were "tested for comprehensibility," using 30 children. Although Coopersmith always refers to a 50-item scale, the only published version (Coopersmith, 1967) gives 58 items, presumably because 8 lie-scale items are included. Apparently no item analyses or internal factor analyses have been performed by Coopersmith.[3] No key is given for total scoring. Mikesell, Calhoun, and Lottman (1970) showed that high-school Ss obtained higher mean scores when instructed to "fake good," but this kind of analysis proves nothing, of course, regarding the invalidating influences of social desirability under normal or ideal research conditions.

Coopersmith applied the test to two samples, 102 Ss in New York State and 1,748 public-school children (further characteristics unspecified) in central Connecticut. Unfortunately, none of the quantitative information about the test except means and SDs is based on these total groups. In the studies which might have some relevance to the construct validity of SEI by relating SEI to other theoretically associated variables, highly restricted groups were used. For example, in the New York sample (Coopersmith, 1959, 1960), Ss who were high and low on SEI were further subdivided according to whether they were high and low on a Behavior Rating Form (BRF) by which teachers evaluated Ss' self-esteem, as this was presumably manifested in Ss' behaviors ($N = 48$, 12 per group). In the Connecticut sample (Coopersmith, 1964, 1967), five groups were formed, four as in the New York sample plus one in which both SEI and BRF scores were medium ($N = 85$, 17 per group). Thus, the research cannot tell us about relationships between SEI and other variables across the entire range of SEI scores. Furthermore, many of the comparisons Coopersmith reports with respect to the variables hypothetically related to *self-esteem* were actually made among four or five groups

---

3. White and Richmond's (1970) two factor analyses are based on relatively small Ns, and the published report gives no information about relationships of the items to the obtained factors.

which differed from each other regarding *discrepancies* between two alleged measures of self-esteem, SEI and BRF. Of course, these comparisons are not relevant to assessing the construct validity of SEI per se. Parenthetically, it is interesting to note that variations according to these discrepancies did not apparently prove to be significantly related to variations on many of his other variables, inasmuch as only about 10% of the *chi*-square values reported in the 1967 book were based on this breakdown, while about 85% of the reported *chi*-square values were based on a breakdown into high, medium, and low SEI scores among the 85 Ss, disregarding the discrepancy scores.

Presumably the teachers' BRF ratings might be expected to correlate to some extent with SEI scores, since the teachers were rating how Ss seemed to feel about themselves, as manifested by their behavior. On the other hand, on Coopersmith's assumption that behaviors evident to teachers may reveal individual differences in unconscious self-esteem levels, the correlation between SEI and BRF should not be as high as the respective reliabilities of the instruments would permit. Although he reports "substantial agreement" between the two scores, Coopersmith gives no interpretable statistical information about the relationship between these two measures for his Ss. Wiest (1965), however, reports correlations of about .40 on several samples. Other correlations relevant to convergent validity are reported by Ziller, Hagey, Smith, and Long (1969), namely, $rs = .46$ for males and .17 (n. s.) for females between IAV and SEI.

With his New York group of Ss, Coopersmith (1959) obtained significant rs of .36 with Iowa Achievement Test scores and .29 with a sociometric rating. With these same Ss, he failed to support a predicted association between self-esteem and measures of selective recall, and between self-esteem and desire to repeat tasks in a situation where Ss were made artifically to fail or succeed.

The bulk of Coopersmith's research, in which 85 Ss were studied intensively, is reported in his 1967 book. Groups were set up according to three types of classification: (a) SEI (high, medium, low); (b) discrepancies between SEI and BRF (five groups, as explained above); and (c) absolute size of discrepancy between SEI and BRF. There is no way to tell from the book whether Coopersmith tested the association of each other variable with each of these breakdowns. Moreover, there is no way of knowing to what extent other variables relevant to the dependent variables were held constant between comparison groups.

So far as the other variables were concerned, many scores were obtained from other self-report instruments (Rosenberg's questionnaire, subject interview, and a prejudice test); from Ss' "experimental behavior" (in level-of-aspiration, perceptual defense, recall of success and failure, and public and private conformity); from "creativity" tests (DAP, unusual uses, and circles); from Wechsler Intelligence Scale for Children (WISC); from sentence completion; and from TAT. Additional items were provided by mothers of Ss in interview and on Parent Attitude Research Instrument (PARI) scales which were apparently analyzed both by scale and by separate question.

It is impossible to tell from examining the book how many scores resulted from all these measures, or how many different scores were used in significance tests, although not reported in the book. Obviously, many of the scores used must have been intercorrelated. An enormous, but unreported and unspecified, number of significance tests was apparently made. All these considerations mean that there is no way of telling how many reached the .05 level, and certainly no way to estimate how many of the "significant" ones would be expected to occur by chance alone.

It is obvious, then, that Coopersmith's research cannot appropriately be used to support the construct validity of SEI as a measure of self-regard because the research is uninterpretable for all the reasons mentioned above.

Only six other publications using the SEI have come to my attention. Connell and Johnson (1970) found that for early adolescent males, but not females, high sex-role identification inferred from Gough's *Fe* Scale was associated with high SEI scores. Thus his theoretical prediction was supported for males only. Like Coopersmith, P. B. Campbell (1967) reported an association between SEI scores and Iowa Achievement Test scores ($r = .31$ for Ss in Grades 4 through 6). Boshier (1968a) found correlations about .8 between SEI and liking for one's first name. Confirming his prediction from Heider's balance theory, Wiest (1965) reports a significant r of .22 between SEI and a "congruency score," indicative of correlation, within each S, between S's report of how he liked others and how others liked him. Contrary to her expectation, Trowbridge (1970) found a significantly higher mean SEI among socioeconomically disadvantaged elementary-school children (as compared to more advantaged children). Confirming her prediction, mean SEI scores were higher in classrooms taught by teachers who had had a 1-year training program directed at "humanizing and individualizing the activities of the classroom." In the same vein, Purkey, Graves, and Zellner (1970) compared SEI scores of third- through sixth-grade children in school systems using a "humanistic" and "traditional" approach. They found higher SEI score means in the former group, except at Grade 3, which did not follow their prediction. Sixty-four intact classrooms equated for school grade and degree of cultural advantage were used.

Morse (1964) used SEI, but gave little information and no significance tests. Three other studies (Katz & Zigler, 1967; Lekarczyk & Hill, 1969; and Perkins & Shannon, 1965) are not relevant because they used modifications of SEI rather than the original instrument.

Altogether, the state of development of this inventory and the amount of available information about it do not make it an instrument of choice for self-concept research on child Ss. If further research and development were to be undertaken, this conclusion might be modified, depending on the results of such research.

PIERS-HARRIS CHILDREN'S SELF-CONCEPT SCALE (PH)

General Description

The PH scale has gone through several revisions (Piers & Harris, 1964; Piers, 1969), and in its present form it is comprised of 80 simple declarative sentences, worded at the third-grade reading level, to be answered yes or no, according to the way S *generally* feels.

With two exceptions, items are scored according to judges' ratings as to what constitutes a self-favorable reaction. The original item pool was Jersild's (1952) collection of children's statements about what they liked and disliked about themselves. Items were chosen from the pool according to the following criteria: those items which were included discriminated between Ss who were high and low on total scores; included items were answered in the expected direction by at least half of the Ss who had high total scores; with a few exceptions, the yes-no split on any included item was no more uneven than 90:10; and an equal number of positive and negative statements were to be selected for inclusion in the final form in order to control for acquiescence-response set.

Item elimination resulted in uneven coverage of Jersild's categories, putting the emphasis on his classes called "just me, myself" and "personality characteristics, inner resources, emotional tendencies," as opposed, for example, to "enjoyment of recreation" and "special talents." However, Piers (1969) thought that the categories covered by the items were probably most salient for "general self-concept."

Reliability

Kuder-Richardson reliabilities for an intermediate, 95-item form for six samples, from Grades 3 to 10, ranged from .78 for Grade-10 girls to .93 for Grade-3 boys (Piers & Harris, 1964). For three samples, Grades 3, 6, and 10, 4-month test-retest rs from the 95-item form ranged from .71 to .72 (Piers & Harris, 1964); While the 2- and 4-month test-retest r for fifth-grade Ss taking the 80-item form was .77 (Wing's unpublished data, cited in Piers, 1969).

These reliabilities seem satisfactory for research purposes. However, we must raise the same question here as we have in connection with rating scales, namely, to what extent are low scores indicative of poor self-regard and to what extent indicative of unreliability of responding? With an 80-item scale which has an equal number of positively and negatively keyed statements, random responding on S's part would result in a score of about 40, that is, 40 coincidences between S's choice of yes or no and the judges' rating of yes or no as indicative of desirable reactions. According to the norms given in Piers (1969), 20% of Ss attain scores this low or lower. Thus, there is a strong possibility that unreliable responding and poor self-regard are confounded to some unknown extent in many of the low individual scores. This is of special importance, inasmuch as some construct-validity studies compare "known groups" who would be expected to vary not only with respect to self-regard but also with respect to reliability of responding (e.g., delinquents vs. normals, retardates vs. normals, poor achievers vs. normals, emotionally disturbed Ss vs. normals). In another type of study, extreme groups of Ss who are high and low on self-concept scores are compared. For example, in the Morse and Piers (mimeographed manuscript) study, the mean PH values of high and low self-concept groups were 67.73 and 35.53. If scores on the "dependent" variable, for example, "word meaning," could conceivably be a function of unreliable responding, the association between "self-concept" and this measure of achievement could then be due to the common influence of unreliability of responding rather than to an association between low self-regard per se and poor achievement.

As explained fully on pages 119–120, neither Kuder-Richardson rs nor test-retest rs suffice to rule out this possibility. What is needed is a study of test-retest item stability among Ss with high, medium, and low PH scores.

Construct Validity

Irrelevant Response Determiners. Very little information is available regarding possibly distorting influences of irrelevant response determiners on the construct validity of this scale.

While item structure and wording are commendably simple, implying a favorable influence on construct validity, some items include a frequency modifier, for example, "often," while most do not. This kind of mixture, in conjunction with a "frequency" answer scale (e.g., yes = "generally how I feel"), yields unnecessary ambiguity in the task, with probably deleterious influences on construct validity.

Acquiescence-response set has been controlled to some extent by inclusion of equal numbers of positive and negative statements. It must be noted that the scale is not consistently phenomenological inasmuch as Ss' responses are scored against judges' conceptions of the desirable rather than against Ss' own conceptions of the desirable. Some research on Ss' ideal-self responses and on self-ideal discrepancies would be valuable.

As is true of all self-concept instruments, the problem of controlling or even evaluating the possible influence of social-desirability tendencies is unresolved. In five large samples, from Grades 4 to 12, rs between total PH scores and scores on the Children's Social-Desirability Scale (Crandall, Crandall, & Katkovsky, 1965) ranged from .34 to .45, all significant, according to Millen's unpublished data cited in Piers (1969). As fully discussed on pages 53 to 58, however, such information proves nothing about the degree to which faking or more subtle self-favorability influences distort the responses on this kind of scale. The directions given in the manual explicitly attempt to maximize Ss' willingness to be candid and to avoid responding in terms of how they think they ought to respond. Piers (1969) recommends that Ss be explicitly guaranteed anonymity wherever possible.

Internal Correlational Analyses. One internal factor analysis of the 80-item form is available (Piers & Harris, 1964; Piers, 1969). Ten factors accounted for 42% of the variance and six were "large enough to be interpretable": behavior, intellectual and school status, physical appearance and attributes, anxiety, popularity, and happiness and satisfaction. Presumably no evidence for a general factor was found, then, although the authors apparently intended their test to reflect a child's "general self-concept." On the other hand, in his generally favorable review of PH in Buros (1971), Bentler has argued that a principal-components analysis of binary items tends to lead to too many factors; and he speculates that PH may be more unidimensional than the available factor analysis suggests. In any case, further factor analytic work should be done, using Ss of the same and other ages. If stable factors appear, the question of the discriminant validity of respective cluster scores should then be explored.

Convergent-Discriminant Validity. With respect to the convergent validity of the total self-regard score from PH, virtually no information is available. Mayer (1967) reports an r of .68 with Lipsitt's (1958) Self-Concept Scale for Children for 98 retarded Ss, aged 12 to 16. The multitrait-multimethod matrix technique is, of course, indispensable for evaluating convergent and discriminant validity, and this test has been included in no such matrix. Regarding any of the cluster scores based on items which load highly on the respective factors, no information on convergent validity is available.

The main question of discriminant validity is whether total PH scores indicate self-regard as differentiated from other variables such as ability, achievement, anxiety, or general dissatisfaction. For the most part, low and insignificant rs with IQ are reported (Piers, 1969). For 11 samples from Grades 3 to 10, involving several IQ tests, rs ranged from −.04 to .48, only three of the rs being significant. In six groups from Grades 3 to 6, rs between achievement scores and total PH scores range from .06 to .43; five are significant. Thus it appears that rs between total PH scores and IQ or achievement scores do not approach the one available convergent validity value of .68 (between the PH and Lipsitt scales).

The fact that achievement does show some tendency to correlate with the total PH score may be indicative of the confounding of unreliability and low self-regard in determining low PH scores, as explained in the discussion of reliability above.

One would theoretically expect anxiety to be negatively correlated with overall self-regard. But what is implied if the numerical values of the correlations between "anxiety" scores and purported self-regard scores (here, PH scores) equal or exceed the convergent validity correlations between the purported self-regard measure under study (here, PH) and other purported self-regard scores? Obviously, such findings would call into question the discriminant validity of the purported measure of self-regard which is being studied. In five large groups from Grades 4 through 12, rs between PH and the Children's Manifest Anxiety Scale (CMAS) (Casteneda, McCandless, & Palermo, 1956) ranged from $-.54$ to $-.69$ (unpublished data by Millen, cited in Piers, 1969). The numerical values of these correlations approach or exceed the one reported convergent-validity coefficient of .68 between PH and Lipsitt's Self-Concept Scale for Children. Accordingly, these findings raise questions regarding the discriminant validity of total PH scores as indicative of Ss' "general self-concept." Piers (1969) suggests that the large rs are due to the fact that one factor of PH is "anxiety" and the CMAS and PH contain "similar items."

A secondary question of discriminant validity concerns the extent to which cluster scores (based on items loading highly on the respective factors) indicate respectively discriminable aspects of self-concept. The only available information here concerns cluster scores based on Factor II items. Although total PH scores do not typically correlate significantly with IQ, the subscore regarding "intellectual and school status" yielded rs of .43 and .50 with full-scale and verbal WISC scores. This is far from being the full complement of rs needed in the relevant multitrait-multimethod matrix.

Studies Based on Assumed Validity. Oblique evidence about the construct validity of total PH scores is provided by a few studies which test theoretically predicted associations between PH and other variables. Thus far, the accumulation of such evidence is small, and it gives spotty support to the construct validity of total PH scores as a measure of self-regard.

The following findings *support* theoretical predictions:

As mentioned above, total PH scores correlated significantly with scores from the Children's Manifest Anxiety Scale (Millen, cited in Piers, 1969).

Black children, ages 7 to 8, who showed Negro preference in terms of puppet choice had significantly higher PH scores (Harris & Braun, 1971).

Total PH scores correlated significantly with Ss' perceptions of their parents as loving, as opposed to rejecting ($r = .56$ for Grades 6 to 9, Cox's unpublished data cited in Piers, 1969).

In Piers's (in press) study of 8- to 14-year-old children, a group of Ss who were being diagnosed in a clinic obtained a mean PH score which was slightly but significantly lower than the mean score of a group of normal control children. (Both means were well within the "normal range," however.)

The following sets of findings are *variable in their support* for theoretical predictions and, hence, for construct validity:

As predicted, institutionalized retardates obtained significantly less favorable mean PH scores on the 95-item version of PH (Piers & Harris, 1964). However, we must note two reservations: (a) to some extent the institutionalized retardates' lower scores may be due to unrelability of responding as opposed to low self-regard; (b) Mayer (1966) found that mean self-concept scores of retardates in special classes did not differ from the norms.

As predicted, a "four-year average score on peer acceptance-rejection" was correlated with PH scores ($r = .61$ for 97 Ss in Cox's unpublished study, cited in Piers, 1969). Among sixth-graders, Guardo (1969) found total PH scores to be correlated in the predicted direction with number of nominations as "most popular," "least popular," "liked most," and "disliked most." All these *r*s were significant for girls, but only one was significant for boys. Among black, disadvantaged, sixth-grade boys, Ss' PH scores were significantly positively associated with the number of peer nominations "liked most," and significantly negatively associated with the number of peer nominations "liked least" (Morse & Piers, in press). On the other hand, Mayer (1967) found sociometric status to be unrelated to total PH scores. Unfortunately, since types of Ss and types of sociometric measures both varied among studies, no conclusive synthesis of these findings can be made; collectively they probably offer some support to the construct validity of total PH scores.

Failing to support the author's prediction, neither socioeconomic status nor earlier placement as opposed to later placement in a special class for retardates was associated with PH scores in Mayer's (1966) study. Also failing to support the authors' predictions, counseling did not affect PH scores of educable, mentally retarded adolescents (Humes, Adamczyk, & Myco, 1969; Mann, 1969; Mann, Beaber, and Jacobson, 1969).

Contrary to very commonly held expectations, but consonant with a number of recent findings, the PH mean of black, disadvantaged sixth-grade boys was slightly above the mean for white, normative samples (Morse & Piers, in press). Harris and Braun (1971) also reported median PH scores for black children to be above the norms reported by Piers (1969). Black Ss' medians were 77th percentile for the middle-class and 66th percentile for the lower-class Ss.

Summary and Recommendations. In conclusion, the Piers-Harris test seems worthy of further research and development. Studies of item stability among Ss who score low, medium, and high on total scores are needed in order to evaluate the possibility that unreliable, random responding is confounded with low self-regard in determining low PH scores. The convergent and discriminant validity of the total score needs much more exploration, especially by the use of the multitrait-multimethod technique. Replications of the factor analysis are needed if cluster scoring is to be continued; and again, appropriate explorations of convergent and discriminant validity of each subscore are needed, especially by way of multitrait-multimethod techniques.

5. Rosenberg's Self-Esteem Scale (RSE)

RATIONALE AND GENERAL DESCRIPTION

As I have frequently pointed out, most theorists and researchers have been explicitly or implicitly concerned with some version of the hypothetical construct *global self-regard*. This is evident partly in the widespread practice of building instruments by compiling a list of items which have heterogeneous, somewhat specific, content referents, and summing S's responses across items to obtain a total score. Although Es usually mention some of the criteria they used for item selection or construction, the importance of the item to each S's global self-regard is not known, and probably varies. Moreover, the psychological metric used by Ss in evaluating themselves doubtless varies among Ss and among items. Summation of item responses, as I have noted earlier, ignores these problems and, to a certain extent, assumes that global self-regard is somehow "content free" or "content general." This assumption is further evidenced by the commonly made prediction that the total score from one such instrument will correlate with total scores from other such instruments which include quite different assortments of item content. For the relatively few instruments which have been internally factor analyzed at the item level, the results give little or no support to the idea that inter-S differences in total score on the instrument represent inter-S differences along a unitary global self-regard dimension. (See pp. 101 to 102.)

There is an alternate and seemingly more straightforward way to build a measure of global self-regard which will have the desired unidimensionality. This is to construct a Guttman scale (Torgerson, 1958, chap. 12).

Rosenberg (1965) is apparently the only person who has tried to achieve a unidimensional measure of global self-regard (called by him "self-esteem") through the method of Guttman scaling. Since this approach has several possible merits, his scale will be evaluated here even though publications based on its use are not numerous.

The considerations which led Rosenberg to apply Guttman scaling were ease and economy of time in administering a short scale, and the hope that the desired unidemensionality could be achieved through the application of Guttman-scaling techniques coupled with satisfactory face validity for the scaled items. In addition, as I have already pointed out, this technique avoids the problems entailed in trying to select appropriate items referring to heterogeneous content areas; and it allows S to select and weight as he sees fit whatever specific behavioral referents seem appropriate to him as bases for responding to the very general items in Rosenberg's scale.

A brief description of Guttman scaling will help the reader to understand why such a self-regard scale might have the advantages just mentioned. Ideally, a Guttman scale is comprised of items drawn from the same "universe of content," more specifically, from the domain of one hypothetically unified construct. (Although Guttman, 1950, argues for the usefulness of the notion of "universe of content," I have contended on pp. 41 to 42 that such a conception does not seem to be defensible or useful in test construction generally. In any case, fulfilling the model of "sampling from a universe of content" is not necessary to the attainment of unidimensionality as defined in terms of factor structure).

In the idealized Guttman scale, successive items represent differing degrees of strength of the hypothetical construct, in Rosenberg's case, "self-esteem." These increasing degrees are defined in terms of increasing proportions of Ss who endorse each successive item. In such an idealized scale, if items are arranged in rank order of percentage of Ss who endorse them, one can know from any S's rank position among Ss which particular items he endorsed, because he will have endorsed all items up to a certain one and will have endorsed no item ranking higher than that one.

In practice, of course, such idealized outcomes do not occur; but Ss who do not respond in the ideal manner can be assigned the rank position of the most similar "ideal scale type." Several more or less arbitrary methods have been proposed for dealing with the assignment of Ss who are not most similar to any one scale type (Torgerson, 1958). After Ss have been assigned by one of these methods, errors can be counted. An error is a response by S to an item in a manner incongruent with the scale type to which he has been assigned. Then an index of error for the entire scale is obtained thus:

$$\text{Coefficient of Reproducibility} = 1 - \frac{\text{total number of errors}}{\#\text{ items} \times \#\text{ subjects}}$$

A coefficient of reproducibility (Rep.) of .90 or more has been taken as an arbitrary minimum for a possible inference that one is dealing with a satisfactorily reliable, unidimensional scale. If a satisfactory Rep. cannot be obtained with a certain number of items, Rep. can be improved by combining items to form "contrived items," as described in Stouffer, Borgatta, Hays, and Henry (1952).

Although a Rep. $\geq$ .90 is taken as a primary and necessary criterion for inferring that one's items comprise a unidimensional scale, it is not a sufficient criterion for that inference. Not only may Rep. be high for a number of statistically artifactual reasons, but a high Rep. can be obtained with items which are obviously *not* representative of the same construct, as Torgerson (1958) shows.

Following Suchman's (1950) argument that only a judgment of

content can determine what belongs to a "universe" and, hence, what should yield a unidimensional scale, Rosenberg explicitly chose items which seemed to him to have face validity. This gave him a basis in addition to Rep. for inferring that his scale had unidimensionality. He stated that, while the reader may question one or another of his items, there is little doubt that the items generally deal with a favorable or unfavorable attitude toward self.

However, achievement of face validity *and* a satisfactory Rep. value still do not suffice to produce a unidimensional scale. This is evidenced in the RSE by the internal factor analysis performed by Kaplan and Pokorny (1969) on a matrix of intercorrelations of all ten original Rosenberg items. They obtained two uncorrelated factors which accounted for 45% of the total variance. In correlating factor scores from each factor with other variables, they found that Factor 1 scores frequently correlated in an expected fashion, essentially replicating some of the correlations Rosenberg had obtained with the total scale. Factor 2 scores did not correlate with these other variables.

The items with "appreciable" loadings on Factor 1 and insignificant loadings on Factor 2 were: "On the whole I am satisfied with myself" (disagree); "I wish I could have more respect for myself" (agree); "I certainly feel useless at times" (agree); "At times I think I am no good at all" (agree). This factor they called self-derogation. Factor 2 appeared to them to "reflect a posture of conventional defense of individual worth, a stance which (in view of the statistical independence of the two factors) is apparently compatible with either high or low scores on the self-derogation factor." (Kaplan and Pokorny, 1969, p. 425.) This factor was defined primarily in terms of the following items: "I feel that I'm a person of worth, at least on an equal plane with others" (agree); "I feel that I have a number of good qualities" (agree); "I am able to do things as well as most other people" (agree).

RELIABILITY

To a certain extent, of course, the Rep. value may be taken as one index of reliability. Rosenberg (1965) reports a Rep. for his New York high school Ss of .92; and in a private communication he states that he obtained a slightly higher Rep. in a group of about 560 British adolescents. Silber and Tippett (1965) obtained a 2-week test-retest reliability coefficient of .85 for 28 college Ss.

CONSTRUCT VALIDITY

Irrelevant Response Determiners

Social Desirability. As is the case with all self-concept measures, nothing definite can be said about the degree to which deliberate distortions or more subtle desirability considerations affect responses. It appears that Ss could easily discern the desirable answers. However, in Rosenberg's research, Ss were guaranteed anonymity. In Silber and Tippett's (1965) study, which gives convergent-validity coefficients, Ss were volunteers for a long-term project who may plausibly be assumed to be well motivated toward cooperating in research. Furthermore, Ss were assured of confidential treatment, and care was taken to establish rapport with each S and to reduce test-taking defensiveness through the manner of presenting the tests.

Acquiescence Response Set. Acquiescence response set is somewhat controlled by the fact that there is an equal number of items for which "agree" and "disagree" responses indicate high self-esteem, and these were presented alternately.

Item Wording. One might question whether some of the combinations of item wording and response-scale possibilities create unnecessary interpretive difficulties for Ss. That is, some of the items have degrees of intensity or frequency built into the stem, some do not. For example, compare the items "On the whole I am satisfied with myself" and "I take a positive attitude toward myself." When each item is evaluated by S on the same 4-point scale from "strongly agree" to "strongly disagree," comparisons between items may be unnecessarily confusing. Since Rosenberg in fact used only an agree-disagree dichotomy in his scoring, this difficulty may be partly counteracted.

There is essentially no basis for evaluating the influence of the other possible irrelevant response determiners which were discussed in general terms on pp. 52 to 95.

Internal Correlational Analyses

The internal factor analysis by Kaplan and Pokorny (1969), based on 500 community adults, has already been discussed. In an interview study involving 223 sections, Kohn (1969) factor analyzed 57 of the items, including 6 RSE items or modifications thereof. Two of the resulting 12 factors were defined primarily in terms of RSE items. These factors appear to be similar to those of Kaplan and Pokorny (1969); and Kohn's division of 5 of his 6 items between factors replicates the comparable division made by Kaplan and Pokorny. While these findings offer support to the idea that RSE is not unidimensional, we still need a replication of Kaplan and Pokorny's analysis involving all 10 RSE items.

Convergent and Discriminant Validity

Silber and Tippett (1965) correlated RSE scores against three other measures of self-esteem:

Kelly Repertory Test, sum of [Self — Ideal] discrepancies, on 20 bipolar dimensions, $r = .67$

Heath Self-Image Questionnaire, sum of 20 selected items, $r = .83$

Interviewers' ratings of self-esteem, $r = .56$

Their Ss were 44 college students who volunteered for extensive research participation: 7 were hospitalized for emotional disturbances, 37 were normal volunteers. These convergent validities are among the highest we have observed in cross-instrument correlations.

Silber and Tippett (1965) present an evaluation of the discriminant validity of RSE scores as part of a multitrait-multimethod matrix. Besides including the self-esteem scores from three measures, as mentioned above, the matrix also included four self-image stability measures: a 5-item Guttman scale by Rosenberg aimed at changeability of S's self-view; interviewers' ratings of S's self-image stability; and the amount of change in 2 weeks on the Heath and Repertory tests mentioned above. As already indicated, the convergent-validity values, that is, the rs between Rosenberg self-esteem and self-esteem measured by three other methods, were .67, .83, and .56. All of them exceeded the correlation of .53 between two different "traits" (self-esteem and self-image stability) measured by the same method (Guttman scales). Moreover, the three convergent-validity values also exceeded the three heterotrait-heteromethod rs, that is, those between RSE and Repertory Test self-image stability, Heath self-image stability, and interview self-image stability (.40, .34, .21). The problem with this matrix, as the authors note, is that the "different trait" (self-image stability) is not entirely different operationally from self-esteem in that the same instrument is used in the case of the Heath and Repertory tests to get both self-esteem and self-image stability scores. However, it seems plausible that even lower heterotrait-heteromethod rs would have been obtained if this were not true, so the evidence for discriminant validity may be conservative.

Studies Based on Assumed Validity

There are many published data concerning the relationships between RSE scores and other variables to which self-esteem is theoretically expected to be related. In Rosenberg's major study, involving 5,024 high-school Ss, a great many associations were explored using the same Ss and involving dependent variables which were doubtless intercorrelated among themselves. One cannot tell how many significance tests were made altogether. As a result, it is difficult to evaluate how many "significant relationships" might have been expected to occur by chance. Moreover, not all the associations for which significance tests were made were intended as a test of a theoretical prediction. Thus, until cross-validation of significant, theory-relevant associations is done, one must view the findings and interpretations with caution.

A strong point of the study (too rarely characteristic of research in this field) was the attempt to control for other possible influences on the dependent variable when examining relationships between hypothetical independent and dependent variables. It was possible to accomplish this to some extent because of the large number of Ss in the New York study. On the other hand, since certain data (e.g., IQ) were unavailable, some controls could not be run. The method used was "standardization" as described in Rosenberg (1965, pp. 33 to 34).

I shall not list all the variables which Rosenberg and others have studied in relation to Rosenberg's self-esteem score. The most conservative case can be made for the construct validity of this scale by emphasizing the theoretically predicted associations which were obtained with the large New York group and apparently "cross-validated" by the same or apparently similar findings with other Ss. These are given in paragraphs 1 through 4 below.

1. Depressive Affect. Among 50 normal volunteer Ss at the National Institute of Mental Health who were rated by nurses, Ss with low RSE scores were significantly more often rated as gloomy and frequently disappointed (Rosenberg, 1965). In the New York study, self-reports on a Guttman scale of depressive affect were significantly associated with self-esteem; and in Kaplan and Pokorny's (1969) study with 500 community adults in Texas, Rosenberg's Guttman scale of depressive affect was significantly associated with factor scores based on the authors' self-derogation factor from the Rosenberg scale.

2. *Anxiety and Psychosomatic Symptoms.* In the New York group (Rosenberg, 1965) and in Kaplan and Pokorny's (1969) study using self-derogation factor scores, low RSE was significantly associated with a larger number of psychosomatic symptoms reported. The New York Ss with low self-esteem reported more tendencies to daydream and to be concerned with their own problems.

3. *Interpersonal Insecurity.* Among the 50 normal volunteers mentioned above, nurses significantly more often rated Ss with low RSE scores as touchy and easily hurt, and not well thought of (Rosenberg, 1965). Rosenberg's New York Ss with low RSE scores significantly more often reported themselves as having difficulty in making friends, being sensitive to criticism from others; being lonely, shy persons; and being bothered to find others having a poor opinion of them. From 1,800 Washington, D.C., seniors who took the Rosenberg scale, 18 with very high and 18 with very low RSE scores were selected to fill out the questionnaire used with the New York Ss and to be interviewed. These data, though based on small Ns, gave strong impressionistic support to the more quantitative findings (Rosenberg, 1965).

4. *Participation in Activities; Leadership.* Self-reported participation in such things as extracurricular activities, club memberships, elected positions, and discussions were significantly associated with high RSE scores in Rosenberg's (1965) New York group. In a separate group of 272 high school seniors, Ss with high self-esteem were significantly more often nominated by peers as someone they would vote for as "leader of English class today" (Rosenberg, 1965).

5. *Parental Disinterest.* A combined index of Ss' reports of parental disinterest and Ss' reports of lack of interest of other family members in what they said was significantly associated with low RSE scores in Rosenberg's New York group (Rosenberg, 1965).

6. *Participation in Upward Bound Program.* Among many other measures, Hunt and Hardt (1969) obtained RSE scores at six points

in a 2-year longitudinal study of a sample of 303 students in the Upward Bound program which is intended to "generate the skills and motivation for college success among young people from low income backgrounds and inadequate secondary school preparation [Upward Bound Guidelines, 1966, as quoted by Hunt and Hardt, 1969, p. 117]." In both Negro and white groups, RSE scores increased steadily and significantly across the six testing points, while no differences between control Ss at comparable younger and older ages were observed. It must be noted, however, that the control observations were made cross-sectionally, so that possible effects of retesting in the Upward Bound sample are not accounted for in this comparison.

Tippett and Silber (1965) present further data on their college Ss who took the RSE; but the analyses involving RSE are not clearly relevant to evaluation of the construct validity of the instrument. The same is true of most of the additional data analyses presented by Kaplan and Pokorny based on the same 500 Ss mentioned in the discussion of construct validity (Kaplan, 1970a, 1970b, 1971; Kapian and Pokorny, 1970a, 1970b, 1971). For other studies which used the RSE or selected items from RSE, see Bachman (1970), Brookover, Erickson, and Joiner (1967), Herman, Sadofsky, Bensman, Lilienfeld, and Manos (1967), Nocks and Bradley (1969), Schooler and Tecce (1967), and Yamamoto and Wiersma (1967). For various reasons, these studies, too, are not clearly relevant to evaluating the construct validity of RSE.

CONCLUSIONS AND RECOMMENDATIONS

It would be highly desirable if comparisons could be made of degrees of association between two or more self-esteem measures (one of them being Rosenberg's scale) and the degree of association between self-esteem (RSE) and other variables measured by the same and by different methods. However, the data presented in Rosenberg do not permit this, since no other self-esteem measure was used; and associations are given in terms of chi-square comparisons.

Finally, additional studies which relate non-self-report measures to the self-report self-esteem scores would be useful in evaluating the degree to which the reported significant associations are not artifactually resulting from response sets. Rosenberg does give associations of this kind, some of them testing theoretically expected relationships; but generally speaking, they are less numerous and weaker than the associations between self-report measures. (See, for example, his results concerning social class, ethnic status, religious status, and birth order).

All things considered, it seems that this scale deserves more research, development, and application. One merit of its brief, direct approach is that it does not assume that a group of items with heterogeneous content, chosen by E, and of variable and unknown salience to Ss may be summed to indicate global self-regard.

It is impressive that such high reliability is attainable with only 10 items and that such a short scale has yielded relationships supporting its construct validity.

Of course, the construct validity of the scale is quite vulnerable to deliberate distortion, and such distortion may artifactually inflate some of the validity-relevant findings which are based on two self-report instruments. This is probably no more true of RSE than of most multiitem scales. As is true of all measures which purport to indicate conscious self-concept, unconscious distortion does not constitute an invalidating influence. As I have repeatedly stressed, no theoretical or practical solution to the problem of detecting and controlling deliberate distortions has been found for any self-concept scale. Probably the best way to minimize this kind of invalidating influence is by procedural arrangements which enlist S's maximum cooperation and which structure the task as clearly as possible so that S can cooperate and direct his responses to the dimension E is trying to study.

Kaplan and Pokorny's (1969) and Kohn's (1969) findings suggest that the factorial structure of even this brief scale is complex. Their internal factor analyses should be repeated on other samples. If cross-validation supports their interpretation that variance in RSE scores involves the two factors "self-derogation" and "conventional defense of individual worth," the convergent and discriminant validity of each of these factor scores should be separately explored by multitrait-multimethod and other techniques. Moreover, it appears that, if their two-factor interpretation proves supportable, the present scale might usefully be expanded to include statements of especially high self-regard. Then explorations should be undertaken to see whether these new items constitute an extension of either of the continua presumably represented by Kaplan and Pokorny's factors, or whether they define a third orthogonal factor.

6. The Self-Social Symbols Tasks, Especially
Self-Social Esteem (SSE)

RATIONALE AND GENERAL DESCRIPTION

Among those tests which have been used in a large number of studies is a series of tasks by Long, Henderson, and Ziller (1970), employing an unusual nonverbal approach to measuring a variety of important self-relevant constructs, namely:

Self-Esteem: "person's perception of his worth . . . assumed to derive from . . . self-other comparisons [p. 10]."

Social Interest: "degree to which a person perceives himself as part of a group of others [p. 12]."

Identification: "the placement of the self in a 'we' category with the other person [pp. 13–14]."

Group Identification: "the number of other persons with whom the person identifies [p. 14]."

Egocentricity: "perception of the self as 'figure' rather than 'ground,' . . . directing of attention toward the self to the exclusion of others [p. 17]."

Power: "a conception of the self as consistently superior, equal, or inferior to specific other persons [p. 16]."

Complexity: "the degree of differentiation of the self concept, . . . the number of parts comprising the whole [p. 18]."

Individuation or Minority Identification: "whether the person thinks of himself as similar to or different from other persons [p. 15]."

Realism: (of size of self).

Preference: (essentially similar to identification).

The authors argue that the listed constructs are to be related to relevant personality theories and given their initial, preoperational definition in terms of these theories. However, in their development of theoretical background, Long, Henderson, and Ziller (1970) allude to the ideas of many theorists. These allusions are vague and incomplete, comprising an eclectic mixture so that it is impossible to articulate the measuring operations and results from any task with the views of any one theorist or combination of theorists.

Regarding one issue which has concerned self-concept theorists (the phenomenal dimension), the authors take no explicit stand (Long, Ziller, & Henderson, 1970; Ziller, Hagey, Smith, & Long,

1969). On the one hand, they list Rogers and Adler among the relevant theorists (Long, Henderson, & Ziller, 1970) and refer to their theory as "phenomenological" (Ziller, Long, Kanisetti, & Reddy, 1968, p. 317). Thus they imply that the conscious-unconscious dimension may be important in their constructs and therefore in their instruments. On the other hand, they eschew verbal reports in favor of a nonverbal task because they believe Ss may not realize what they are communicating; that is, the authors imply that Ss' unawareness may be important to their thinking about the relationships between the self-concept and behavior.

These unique, nonverbal methods are based on several assumptions (Long, Henderson, & Ziller, 1970, pp. 2–4): (a) "Arrangements of test symbols in a test booklet are veridical with self-other relationships in a person's life space." (b) "There are common and easily translatable meanings [for these spacial arrangements, including] interpretation of physical distance as psychological distance, positions from first to last as value, positions above or below another as power." (c) "A nonverbal response will often reveal a clearer picture of the person's self-conceptions than will a verbal response," because verbal reports are influenced by verbal fluency, vocabulary, and individual and cultural differences in word meanings, and because S can "see through" and manipulate verbal tests more than nonverbal ones. The authors bring some evidence which can be construed as congruent with the first two assumptions; but they by no means convince one that there are "common and easily translatable meanings" for the nonverbal, spacial responses. Carlson (1970), for example, has suggested that a symbolic spacial ordering of experience, especially spacial representations of self-esteem in terms of height or in terms of degree of left-right location on a page, may be a masculine characteristic, and may depend in part on variations across cultures. (Long, in a personal communication, and Long and Henderson, 1971, point out that there is great similarity between sexes and between cultures in the frequency distributions of Ss' horizontal placements of "unsuccessful person," suggesting that Carlson's point is invalid.)

Unfortunately, no evidence is brought to show or even suggest whether responses on these nonverbal tasks are less determined by various distorting influences than are the verbal Rs commonly employed by other investigators and criticized by Long, Henderson, and Ziller. We shall return to this issue after considering the tests.

Space precludes a review of the tasks, so some generally applicable comments will be made, and particular attention will be given to self-esteem.

In measuring most of the constructs, arrangements of circles representing self and others are used. For example, in a horizontal line of six circles or in a vertical line of five circles, high self-esteem is inferred in terms of the proximity of S's choice of a "self circle" to the left side of the horizontal line or to the top of the vertical line of circles. The first methodological problem concerns the overlap of these operations with those used to infer other constructs. For example, self-perceived power is inferred from S's designation of the location of specified others in the small circles of the following configuration, in which S is represented by the center dot.

But why is middle location in the vertical dimension indicative of less power in one configuration and of less self-esteem in another? In the identification measure, as in the horizontal self-esteem measure, a horizontal row of circles is presented. This time, either the right or left circle is designated by E as, say, "Mother." Identification is measured in terms of the proximity of S's choice of "self circle" to "Mother circle." But if the left-right dimension is "clearly translatable" as self-esteem, two interpretations are confounded for some Ss, or are pitted against one another for other Ss.

An additional problem in test operations occurs when E designates persons or types of persons the circles are to represent. Here E typically presents to S a mixture of types who vary in their realistic likeness to S (e.g., salesman, dancer), and who also vary in regard to their stereotyped social desirability (e.g., unsuccessful person, kind person). This seems to complicate the interpretability of the spacial-nearness dimension for both S and E.

RELIABILITY

Reliability information for the Horizontal Self-Esteem score is given in the manual (Long, Henderson, & Ziller, 1970) as follows: Corrected split-half rs for high-school Ss were .80; for fifth-grade Ss, .84; for third-grade Ss, .53. A 4-month test-retest r for sixth-grade Ss was .54.

As I have explained fully in the general discussion of reliability (pp. 119 to 121), a special kind of reliability problem occurs with this kind of test. In a test of this kind with a 1- to 6-point scale, if Ss randomly mark the scales, a mean of about 3.5 will result, given the method of scoring used on the test. Since much evidence shows that self-esteem distributions are very skewed toward the "bad" end, a score near 3.5 would be among the "lower self-esteem" scores actually obtained. Thus, if any given S obtains a mean score near 3.5 on a given occasion, two possible determinants of his score are operationally indistinguishable: unreliability and low self-esteem. In group comparisons, if there is a "lower self-esteem" mean for one group, it could be because there was a higher proportion of unreliable responders in that group. The importance of this fact for interpreting validity studies (e.g., known-group comparisons) and other findings will be brought out below. The difficulties in ruling out this alternate interpretation in terms of artifact is more fully discussed on pages 119 to 121. We note here that test-retest coefficients for the groups compared are necessary but not sufficient to establish that group differences in "self-esteem" are not actually group differences in reliability of responding.

Construct Validity

Support for Circle Position as an Esteem Indicant

The self-esteem measures have been applied to male and female samples ranging from preschool to adolescent, and to Ss in Canada, Israel, and India, as well as in the United States.

The general idea that position indicates esteem is supported by the following findings (Long, Henderson, & Ziller, 1970, pp. 26 ff.): (a) In 15 studies, persons described by E in favorable terms tended to be assigned by Ss to circles toward the left end. (b) Absolute distance of the self-circle from a negatively described person's circle correlated with the left-right position of the self-circle. (c) Children tended to place the self-circle farther to the right in a group of adults than in a group of peers. (d) Patients tended to arrange labeled circles in the following order: psychiatrist, psychologist, social worker, nurse, nurses' aide, other patients, self (Ziller, Megas, & DeCencio, 1964).

However, the data of Froehle and Zerface (1971) clearly indicate that systematic factors other than esteem may influence the ordinal placement of significant others within the line of circles. Responses from sixth-grade students, tenth-grade students, and adults were obtained with the significant others listed as in the original form for half of each age group, and in exactly the reverse order of that on the original form for the other half of each age group. A great many significant differences between mean "esteem" scores for significant persons were obtained when results from the two modes of presentation were compared. Of particular interest to self-concept researchers is the fact that these significant mean differences included those for "esteem" scores for "yourself." Froehle and Zerface (1971) conclude that "much more information is needed in regard to the 'ordering phenomenon' before it can be employed efficiently and effectively in the measurement of self-esteem [p. 74]."

Convergent Validity

Convergent validity receives limited support from correlations ranging from .42 to .50 between Horizontal and Vertical Self-Esteem scores (Van Arsdell, Roghman, & Nader, 1970, whose unpublished data are cited in Long, Henderson, & Ziller, 1970; Ziller, Hagey, Smith, & Long, 1969). Also relevant is an r of .35 between teachers' ratings of retarded Ss' self-esteem and Ss' horizontal self-circle position (unpublished study by Boyd, 1968, cited in Long, Henderson, & Ziller, 1970). If one is willing to assume that self-report measures purporting to measure self-esteem are "aimed at" the same construct(s) as those Long, Henderson, and Ziller are trying to measure, significant associations between such indices and the nonverbal measures may be taken as evidence of convergent validity. It is interesting to note that, despite questioning the validity of verbal report in self-concept measurement, the authors do cite in support of the convergent validity of their instruments two associations with verbal measures, both obtained with elementary-school Ss: (a) significant associations between self-descriptive adjectives and horizontal self-circle position (Long, Henderson, & Ziller, 1970); and (b) significant positive relationships between semantic-differential self-ratings and vertical height of Ss' self-circle (Long, Henderson, & Ziller, 1970).

Of particular interest is the fact that these heteromethod (verbal-nonverbal) correlations appear to be of the same order of magnitude as the correlations between Horizontal and Vertical Nonverbal Self-Esteem scores where much greater similarity of method prevails.

Discriminant Validity

Although the authors seem to assume sometimes that correlations between their nonverbal index and verbal self-esteem measures are relevant to convergent validity, at other times they seem to be saying that null correlations should be expected. They seem to imply that such null correlations should add a little support to the discriminant validity of the nonverbal (as opposed to the verbal) self-esteem measures. Thus, Ziller, Hagey, Smith, and Long (1969) cite insignificantly low correlations between their nonverbal Self-Esteem score and (a) Bills's IAV Self scores; (b) Coopersmith's Self-Esteem Inventory scores; and (c) Diggory's Self-Esteem scores. The whole interpretive issue needs to be clarified.

There is *no* evidence for another kind of *discriminant validity*, that is, among the scores on the nonverbal test which purport to measure different aspects of self-concept or even other variables. In fact, "identification-with-mother," "identification-with-teacher," and "social-interest" scores correlate significantly with self-esteem scores. Therefore, we need to know whether the two self-esteem scores intercorrelate even more highly and whether self-esteem scores (in contrast to identification or social-interest scores) have a distinctive and theoretically reasonable pattern of correlations with other variables. Similarly, in Dimas's (1969) unpublished study (cited in Long, Henderson, & Ziller, 1970), when "power" was raised through experimental treatment, negative self-image was also allegedly raised; so a problem of discriminant validity persists here as well.

Studies Based on Assumed Validity

A large group of studies is in oblique support of construct validity of Horizontal and Vertical Self-Esteem measures. The great majority of these studies involved the Horizontal measure. We say "oblique" because the relevance of these studies to the self-esteem measure depends on varying chains of assumptions; and interpretations in terms of the alleged construct validity of the tasks are not the only interpretations these studies would sustain. Additionally, in a number of studies, results different from those obtained could also have been encompassed by theory and assumptions about the alleged construct. As the authors usually noted, in most of the studies involving "known-group comparisons," the groups differed in several respects relevant to the self-esteem variable, not simply on the factor the study was intended to explore. Accordingly, interpretations must be equivocal.

Higher Horizontal and/or Vertical Self-Esteem scores have been found, *sometimes* at least, to be associated as postulated with the following variables:

1. *White as opposed to Negro status* in school beginners (Long & Henderson, 1968, 1970). In both studies, Negroes were lower in IQ, father presence, and previous school experiences, and were tested by white *E*s. In the 1968 study, Negroes were also lower in social class. Negro-white differences were not replicated in a different setting, using other age groups (unpublished study by Scheiner, cited by Long, Henderson, & Ziller, 1970; Taylor's unpublished study, cited in Ziller, 1969).

2. *Higher socioeconomic level* (unpublished studies by Richards, 1970, cited in Long, Henderson, & Ziller, 1970; and Ziller, Hagey, Smith, & Long, 1969). This relationship was not replicated, however, by Long and Henderson (1968, 1970).

3. *Tangible enrichment of the home* (unpublished study by Richards, 1970, cited in Long, Henderson, & Ziller, 1970).

4. *Oldest sibling status* (Long & Henderson, 1968; unpublished study by McCandless, 1969, cited in Long, Henderson, & Ziller, 1970).

5. *Higher grade level in school* (Long, Henderson, & Ziller, 1967a; Long, Ziller, & Henderson, 1968).

6. *Higher n Ach in Negro Ss* (Harootunian, 1968, cited in Long, Henderson, & Ziller, 1970).

7. *Higher rated social maturity* in Negro Head Start pupils (Long & Henderson, 1968).

8. *Higher Ilg-Ames test maturity* in white, middle-class kindergarten children (Long, Henderson, & Ziller, 1970).

9. *Higher teachers' ratings of speech quality* in nursery-school children (unpublished study by Richards, 1970, cited in Long, Henderson, & Ziller, 1970).

10. *Lower test anxiety* (Harootunian, 1968, cited in Long, Henderson, & Ziller, 1970).

11. *Lower originality on Torrance Lines Test* of creativity (Long, Henderson, & Ziller, 1967b).

12. *Better study habits* (Harootunian, 1968, cited in Long, Henderson, & Ziller, 1970).

13. Greater popularity (unpublished studies by McCandless, 1968; Ziller, Alexander, & Long, 1966; and Richards, 1970, cited in Long, Henderson, & Ziller, 1970).

14. Higher sociometric status (unpublished study by Ziller, Alexander, & Long, 1966, summarized in Ziller, Hagey, Smith, & Long, 1969).

15. Higher identification with mother (six studies cited in Long, Henderson, & Ziller, 1970).

16. Winning a political election (changes in self-esteem before and after the election; Ziller & Golding, 1969).

17. Frequent and consistent participation in a therapy discussion group (Mossman & Ziller, 1968).

18. Normality vs. institutionalization for behavior problems in adolescents (Long, Ziller, & Bankes, 1968; 1970).

19. Patient status (neuropsychiatric) as opposed to normal volunteer, staff status (Ziller & Grossman, 1967; Ziller, Megas, & DeCencio, 1964).

20. Younger as opposed to older adults (Ziller & Grossman, 1967).

21. Mesomorphy (unpublished study by McCandless, 1968, cited in Long, Henderson, & Ziller, 1970).

22. Higher scores on a Body Attitude Scale (Kurtz, 1971).

23. Indian adolescent status as opposed to U.S. adolescent status (Ziller, Long, Kanisetti, & Reddy, 1968).

A number of associations were *not* as predicted, namely: (a) Higher Self-Esteem scores were associated with lower caste in Indians (Ziller, Hagey, Smith, & Long, 1969). (b) More Asch-type conformity occurred among children with high-esteem scores (unpublished study by Foster & Ziller, 1966, cited in Long, Henderson, & Ziller, 1970; Ziller, Hagey, Smith, & Long, 1969). (c) There was no relationship between Self-Esteem scores and geographic mobility in children (Long, Henderson, & Ziller, 1970). (d) There was no association of reading achievement and Self-Esteem scores (Henderson, Long, & Ziller, 1965). (e) There was no association of high Self-Esteem scores and "internal orientation" as measured by Rotter's (1966) Internal-External Control Scale (Platt, Eisenman, & Darbes, 1970). (An additional study not involving specific predictions is Henderson and Long, 1967, regarding Ss with differential achievement in reading and arithmetic.)

Many of the obtained associations lend plausibility to the assertion that self-esteem is a determinant of the Horizontal and/or

Vertical scores, especially the Horizontal ones, since most of the studies involved this measure. Conclusive, integrative evaluation of the studies is impossible, however, because the pieces of information come from so many different groups varying in many respects, tested with a number of task variations and under a number of varying conditions.

Some of these findings are puzzling, as they do not conform to the associations found between certain variables (e.g., age, grade in school, older sibling status) and other measures of self-esteem. Some of the obtained associations may reflect an increase in ability to follow directions (i.e., increased reliability) with increasing age, grade in school, social maturity, and adequacy of study patterns.

Special Validity Problems

Particular attention must be given to the authors' contention that their method is less susceptible than are verbal-report measures to influences which lessen the validity of the response as an indicant of self-esteem. For one thing, variations in possible word interpretations which plague self-report instruments are allegedly avoided or minimized here. But, in fact, this cannot be so for two reasons: (a) *E* uses the same kinds of words to designate circles in this test (e.g., unsuccessful person, cruel person) as are commonly used in self-report instruments; (b) no demonstration has been made that *S*s interpret the types of nonverbal symbols used in SSE more uniformly than they interpret words or phrases in a self-report test. Furthermore, Long, Henderson, and Ziller (1970) repeatedly assert that their instrument has "low visibility," so that there is less possibility of its being biased by deliberate faking or social-desirability tendencies in the way a verbal report is "visible" and vulnerable. Unfortunately, neither their logic nor their evidence gives support to their premises. As indirect evidence that their instruments are not as readily influenced by distortions associated with high visibility, they cite insignificantly low correlations between their self-esteem scores and those obtained with Bills's IAV, Coopersmith's SEI, and Diggory's Self-Evaluation instrument. But the null associations are based on small samples of one age group (college); and aside from this limitation on their generalizability, null results are always open to many speculative interpretations. Thus there could be many other reasons for these null associations besides SSE's low visibility and consequent freedom from distortion. What is needed is direct testing of S's interpretation of the self-esteem instrument. For example, if Ss were told to "fake good" or "fake bad" in the sense of placing their self-circle in the position which represents most appropriately a socially desirable or socially undesirable person, or a good or bad person, or a person with high or low self-esteem, what would happen? If comparable groups of Ss were either run under standard conditions or told that someone was going to know how well they regarded themselves by where they placed their circles, would group means differ? Or if Ss were simply asked to state what for them was the "good" end of the line of circles, without reference to themselves, to adjectives, to people, or to any "concrete" term, what would happen? If Ss were given sets of adjectives allegedly used by other Ss to describe themselves on, say, Bills's IAV, and were asked to choose a circle location for each of six such persons making widely different self-reports, respectively, what would happen? At a minimum, this kind of evidence is a necessity for examining the "visibility" and the varieties of Ss' interpretations of the stimuli. Findings of high inter-S agreement on the properties of the item-stimuli would undermine the argument that this instrument is not "visible." On the other hand, it would strengthen the argument that the instrument is uniformly interpretable. Fiske (1966), in a cogent analysis of requirements for personality measurements which purport to index theoretical constructs, has argued that the adequacy of a measurement procedure directly depends on the degree to which the item-stimulus situation is clearly structured, so that variance due to individual differences among persons on the alleged construct dimension can be increased while variance due to unknown and idiosyncratic interpretations of the item-stimulus situation can be decreased. Although he concedes that obviousness of a test's content permits defensive self-presentation, he feels that such tendencies should be coped with in other ways than by allowing the test situation to remain ambiguous to Ss so that its results are uninterpretable by Es.

RECOMMENDATIONS

What is presently needed is an extensive, systematic program of research which would throw light on the convergent and discriminant construct validity of each type of score. It seems obvious that the great overlap between measuring operations for allegedly different constructs should be eliminated through dropping or drastically revising some of the tasks. Use of the multitrait-multimethod technique is definitely in order as one basis for such weeding, as well as for exploring convergent and discriminant validity. Each matrix should deal with a restricted age and culture group, and perhaps with only one sex. Each matrix should contain all the present measures which the authors feel presently show promise. Since the authors claim that these methods are superior to verbal report measures and measure something different from verbal measures, each multitrait-multimethod matrix should include several of the currently available measures of verbal self-regard for children of the ages used (e.g., Bills's IAV forms for Grades 3 to 12, undated manual; Piers-Harris Children's Self-Concept Scale, Piers, 1969). In addition, some nonverbal methods, such as those of A. H. Rogers (1958) or Shlien (1961) might be included. Teachers' or judges' ratings of Ss' supposed self-concept dimensions would also be relevant to include in such a matrix. It is interesting to note that many of the predicted and obtained associations of Horizontal Self-Esteem with other variables are the same as have been predicted and obtained using self-report self-esteem measures (e.g., sociometric status, illness status). It would be very worthwhile to make more systematic comparisons of this sort by incorporating some of these other variables into the multitrait-multimethod matrix.

In conclusion, considerable information is on hand regarding this ingenious, unique, and purportedly simple approach to the measurement of self-relevant constructs across a wide range of ages, cultures, and competence levels. Because it may be so widely applicable, its potential contributions warrant its being explored and developed further. These researches should be much more systematically planned than those presented thus far, however.

D. Instruments Intended to Measure Self-Concepts Regarding More Specific Dimensions (As Well As Overall or Global Self-Regard in Some Instances)

1. The Adjective Check List (ACL)

The Adjective Check List (ACL), a commercially available personality test, does not purport to be mainly a self-concept test (Gough & Heilbrun, 1965). In fact, much of the discussion of development, validation, and application of this instrument shows the authors' intentions to assess actual characteristics of Ss (or even of cities, historical personages, etc.), rather than to assess Ss' self-concepts concerning the characteristics purportedly covered by ACL. Buros (1970) gives 102 references concerning this test, but in my search of the literature involving avowed self-concept measurement I came across about 40 articles, showing that the ACL is being used as a self-concept indicant by an appreciable number of investigators and, therefore, deserves evaluation here. My comments are based on the manual and on those references which I have found in my search of self-concept literature.

RATIONALE AND GENERAL DESCRIPTION

In the most recent version of ACL described in Gough and Heilbrun (1965), 300 adjectives are presented in an alphabetized list, and Ss are directed to check those which apply to the object they are describing. Constructs were not clearly defined as a basis for item selection; and in general, sources of adjectives were vaguely specified. The authors began with a list of 171 items which Cattell had derived from factor analyses based on the Allport-Odbert list of 17,953 trait-descriptive adjectives. They added "words thought to be more or less essential for describing personality from different theoretical vantage points (e.g., those of Freud, Jung, Mead, Murray, etc.) [Gough & Heilbrun 1965, p. 3]." They also added words on the basis of their judgment as they continued to use the original list and found additional adjectives which they deemed important. There is no mention of which adjectives came from which of the sources and, accordingly, no recommended way of using any particular clusters to refer to such things as the Cattell factors or Freudian concepts.

Rather than subdividing the test according to factor structure or according to the various theories mentioned, they developed 9 empirical and 15 rational scales, as follows: The empirical scales included Total Number of Adjectives Checked, Defensiveness, Self-Favorability, Self-Unfavorability, Self-Confidence, Self-Control, Lability, Personal Adjustment, and Counseling Readiness. Of these, Self-Favorability and Self-Unfavorability are considered in detail below. The 15 rationally developed scales are intended to represent Murray needs.

Gough (1960) and Gough and Heilbrun (1965) recommend a variety of scoring procedures of possible interest to self-concept researchers; and other users of ACL have employed additional scores. In the first approach suggested by Gough and Heilbrun (1965), individual adjectives which significantly differentiate "known groups" are given psychological interpretations, according to the researcher's purpose in comparing the groups. In a second approach, one or more of the 9 empirical scales or the 15 Murray need scales may be used to obtain up to 24 different scale scores.

The present review is directed mainly to (a) two of the empirical scales, Self-Favorability and Self-Unfavorability, as these are the ACL counterpart of overall self-regard scores derived from other instruments; and (b) the rationally derived Murray need scores. The latter, as a group, should be shown to have convergent validity with respectively appropriate other measures of self-perceived Murray need dimensions and to have discriminant validity among themselves as indices of respectively different aspects of S's self-concept. A few studies involving individual adjectives are considered briefly.

This limited evaluative task is large enough, but it is further complicated by the fact that Gough and Heilbrun themselves have used two different ways of scoring self-favorability and self-unfavorability, while others have added still other variants. Some studies involving need scores have used one or a few need-scale scores; others have used all the scales. The result of all these variations is that strict comparability among researches is at a minimum and firm synthesis of information is impossible.

In the case of either type of favorability-unfavorability score suggested by the authors, only 150 adjectives are involved, 75 judged most favorable and 75 judged least favorable (or most unfavorable) by 97 undergraduate psychology students. Thus, Ss' self-concept scores on this variable are not entirely phenomenological, since their own ideas of what constitutes favorable or unfavorable do not enter into their scores.

In Gough's (1960) article, Self-Acceptance (SA) was determined as a ratio of the number of self-favorable adjectives checked to the total number of adjectives checked; while Self-Criticality (SC) was determined as a ratio of the number of self-unfavorable adjectives checked to the total number of adjectives checked. In the Gough and Heilbrun (1965) manual, however, separate tables are provided for Ss who fall into each of four different ranges of total number of adjectives checked; and one determines Ss' standard scores for self-favorability (Fav) and unfavorability (Unfav) in the respectively appropriate norm table.

RELIABILITY

Self-Favorability, Self-Unfavorability Scores

Apparently no reliability information is available about any favorability or unfavorability score except the Fav and Unfav scores described in the manual (Gough & Heilbrun, 1965). The test-retest reliability coefficients given in the manual imply that the reliability of these scores is not especially good, particularly in comparison with some of the measures of overall self-regard obtainable from other instruments.

In summary, these coefficients are as follows:

	Fav	Unfav
10 weeks, male college students	.76	.84
10 weeks, female college students	.67	.77
6 months, adult males	.31	.38
5½ years, medical students	.52	.41

Murray Need Scale Scores

For the same groups, test-retest reliability coefficients for the Murray need scale scores ranged from .25 to .90.

CONSTRUCT VALIDITY

Analysis of Irrelevant Response Determiners

Social Desirability. So far as I know, there is no published information about the judged social-desirability values of all 300 ACL adjectives. The 75 adjectives rated most favorable and the 75 adjectives rated most unfavorable by college Ss are given in the manual (Gough & Heilbrun, 1965). Rehm and Marston (1968) report that four male graduate clinical psychology students reached complete agreement on 123 adjectives as indicating positive self-concept and on 138 as indicating negative self-concept. Presumably the remaining 39 were either neutral or controversial. There is no way of knowing the amount of overlap between Gough and Heilbrun's and Rehm and Marston's lists.

Gough and Heilbrun (1965) give correlations between scores for 100 male Ss on Edwards's Social-Desirability Scale and ACL scale scores. These are .36 for Fav and −.31 for Unfav. Correlations involving the other scales range from .45 (Dominance) to −.41 (Succorance). Correlations between Ss' scores on Edwards's Social-Desirability scale and the ACL SA and SC scales ranged from .45 to .58 in four samples studied by Crowne, Stephens, and Kelly (1961). As I have repeatedly pointed out, however, such correlations prove nothing about the extent to which faking or more subtle social-desirability influences diminish the construct validity of ACL as a measure of Ss' phenomenal self-concept. As is true of all self-concept instruments at the present time, there is no way of evaluating the distorting effects, if any, of social-desirability influences.

Acquiescent-Response Tendency. Gough and Heilbrun (1965) recognized that the tendency to check many or few adjectives might represent a response tendency which has an irrelevant, distorting influence on Ss' scale scores. They assumed that the score Number of Adjectives Checked was a measure of acquiescent-response tendency. However, their assumption can be questioned because we do not know the number of desirable and undesirable adjectives in the list, and therefore, a social-desirability response set, if present, could be confounded with a content-free acquiescent-response tendency in their measure Number of Adjectives Checked.

In any event, there is obviously a need to control for individual differences in number of adjectives checked when using Ss' other scale scores as purported indices of aspects of self-concept. That this is so is shown by the following correlations between "number checked" and the raw scores on various scales: Fav = .76; Unfav = .55; and for other scales, *r*s ranging from .78, down through zero, to −.48 (Gough & Heilbrun, 1965).

As explained in an earlier section, they used two different ways to control for number of adjectives checked, the second being to get each S's standard score on any given scale within the appropriate one of four tables, each table being based on Ss whose number checked fell within a specified range. These corrected standard scores then correlated with scale scores as follows: Fav = .21; Unfav = .20; and for other scales, no *r*s exceeded .21 (Gough & Heilbrun, 1965).

Contextual Factors. Obviously, when S is instructed to check only applicable adjectives, a blank may mean a definite denial of the applicability of the adjective or S's feeling that the item is irrelevant. Warr and Knapper's (1967) study did not use the ACL for self-description, but their findings as a result of clarifying the instructions are of indirect relevance to this issue. In one group, their Ss marked each adjective *yes*, if descriptive, or *no*, if definitely not descriptive; or they left it blank if they considered the adjective inapplicable to the well-known public figure they were all rating. In another group, the standard instructions were used. They found no increase in the number of *yes* responses as compared to the number of checks in the group following the standard instructions; and they felt that they got useful information from the *no* responses. As part of the same study, these investigators looked at another contextual influence, the order of presentation of the adjectives. Half of each of the above groups was presented the adjectives in the usual alphabetical order, while the other half was given them in the reverse order. There was a definite decline in both *yes* (or check) and *no* responses as a function of ordinal position, within each order. Thus it seems clear that position of the adjective is an irrelevant determiner of S's likelihood of checking it; and the implications of this for affecting any of the scale scores or determining the exact content of adjective clusters which differentiate known groups cannot be evaluated without a detailed analysis of the distribution of scale items across positions.

Degree of Restriction of S's Responses. In Spitzer, Stratton, Fitzgerald, and Mach's (1966) study, Ss were asked which of four self-regard instruments had enabled them to give the most accurate description of themselves. The ACL was so chosen more frequently than were the IAV, Fiedler's Semantic Differential, or the Twenty Sentences Test (although only 35.2% of Ss chose ACL). The reasons for preferring ACL referred almost exclusively to the scope of the instrument; that is, the number and range of choices on the ACL were large enough so that some adjectives could be endorsed as pertaining to self. Furthermore, to some Ss, the instrument did not seem as undesirably unstructured and indefinite as the TST. When asked which instrument allowed them to give the least accurate description of themselves, 19.4% chose ACL. Reasons for this choice most frequently concerned the lack of situational specificity of the adjectives and the failure of the instrument to include any mechanism for expressing variations in intensity. Thus they felt that their

response possibilities were restricted by having to make dichotomized, unqualified choices. Whether Ss' opinions of the instruments
were related to the actual accuracy with which they expressed themselves is not known, of course.

Scoring and Statistical Procedures. So far as the Favorability and
Unfavorability scales are concerned, the ACL shares with many
other instruments the implicit assumption that S's total number of
keyed responses, regardless of item content, is an indicator of his
level of self-regard. That is, there are innumerable combinations of
particular adjective choices which could yield a given score, but
this is assumed to be irrelevant to interpreting that score as indicative of a certain level of self-regard. Furthermore, simple summation
implies that the chosen traits carry equal weight in determining S's
overall level of self-regard. We have often had reason to question
these assumptions.

In contrast to some other instruments in which direct self-
acceptance scores or self-minus-ideal discrepancy scores are commonly employed, the use of ACL scores assumes that S will regard
each adjective as self-favorable (or self-unfavorable) because a judge
so rated it. This assumption needs further exploration, comparing
more phenomenological ACL scores with the more usual ACL
scores.

The need-scale scoring scheme is based on the implicit assumption that need strength (or self-perceived need strength) is indicated
by the total number of keyed adjectives S chooses, without regard
to the particular combination of adjectives which went into making
his total. Moreover, the need-scale scoring scheme introduces still
further complications, in that some adjective choices are interpreted as "contraindicative," and a point for each such choice is
subtracted from the total number of adjective choices which are
said to be "indicative" of the need. This procedure is based on implied assumptions about the bipolarity of the need dimension.
Obviously, such assumptions need to be made explicit, and the
empirical relationships between positive and negative items need to
be explored.

Finally, it should be noted that overlap of items between scales,
while perhaps justified on rational grounds, complicates the interpretation of scale intercorrelations and patterns of correlations
between scale scores and other theoretically relevant variables.

Convergent and Discriminant Validity

Scale Intercorrelations. A table of scale intercorrelations based on 400 males and 400 females is given in the manual (Gough & Heilbrun, 1965). Inspection reveals many more significant correlations than would be expected by chance alone; but the authors feel that "most of the coefficients are low enough to indicate an adequate degree of independence among the scales [Gough & Heilbrun, 1965, p. 15]." Some of the high correlations come from scales which have an appreciable number of items in common, and this artifact has not been removed as yet because "to date it has not been possible to reduce overlap without at the same time impairing validity [Gough & Heilbrun, 1965, p. 15]." (They do not specify what type of validity is impaired.)

Factor Analyses of Scale Intercorrelations. Parker and Megargee (1967) did three factor analyses of ACL scale intercorrelations, two of them involving self-report data (Peace Corps Ss, 93 males, 103 females; freshmen at the University of Texas, 2,484 males and 1,935 females). They got the same factors out of each matrix, and the pattern of factor loadings was reported to be "remarkably alike." Factor I (Positive-Negative Evaluation) accounted for most of the variance for each group; Factor II (Ascendancy-Obsequiousness) accounted for about one-fourth of the variance for each group; Factor III (Emotionality-Stolidity) accounted for 11% to 15%; and Factor IV (Number Checked) for 5% to 7%.

These findings call into serious question the discriminant validity of the separate scale scores. It appears from this kind of analysis that a single positive-negative dimension is the most important construct indicated by this instrument.

Factor Analyses of Item Intercorrelations. The most basic way of determining how many constructs may have to be postulated to account for variance on a measuring instrument is, of course, to factor a matrix of item intercorrelations rather than a matrix of scale intercorrelations. This has been done by Parker and Veldman (1969), who factor analyzed the entire 300-item pool, using 5,017 college freshmen as Ss. They extracted and rotated seven major orthogonal factors. Based on this work, they chose 56 adjectives, the 8 which loaded highest on each of the seven factors; and 713 teacher trainees rated themselves on each of the 56 adjectives, using a 5-point scale. Factor analysis of these self-ratings replicated the original factor structure; and simple scale sums, as opposed to factor scores, yielded internal consistency coefficients ranging from .64 to .88; test-retest coefficients for a 1- or 2-week interval ranging from .80 to .92; and item-subscale correlations ranging from .48 to .81 (Veldman & Parker, 1970).

Of interest are the facts that (a) their factor structure is not congruent with that obtained from factoring the matrix of scale intercorrelations; (b) they did not obtain factors which correspond to the scale scores recommended by Gough and Heilbrun (1965); and (c) a drastic shortening of the number of items seemed to yield much the same dimensional information as Parker and Veldman (1969) had obtained from the much larger pool of 300 adjectives.

Convergent and Discriminant Validity of Favorability and Un-favorability Scores. Crowne, Stephens, and Kelly (1961) correlated the earlier SA score of Gough (1960) with Buss's Self-Acceptance score, Crowne's Self-Acceptance score, Bills's Self-Acceptance and [Self — Ideal] scores from the IAV, and a semantic differential score, all of which purport to measure overall self-regard. Pearson *r* values ranged from .3 to .6, suggesting some degree of convergent validity. However, we must note that ACL SA scores correlated with other variables just as highly as they did with alternate alleged self-regard measures: namely, with Incomplete Sentences Blank "adjustment" scores for three groups, *rs* ranged from .3 to .6; with Incomplete Sentences Blank "dependency" scores, *rs* were .4 and .3; and with Edwards's Social-Desirability Scale scores, *rs* were .4 and .6. Therefore, the discriminant validity of the ACL SA score is highly questionable, according to these results. Also relevant to the convergent validity of the ACL SA score are Spitzer, Stratton, Fitzgerald, and Mach's (1966) correlations between ACL SA and other alleged self-regard indicators, namely, Twenty Sentences Test Self-Derogation score, Bills's Self, Self-Acceptance, and [Self — Ideal] scores from IAV, and Fiedler's Semantic Differential Self-Acceptance and [Self — Ideal] discrepancy scores. As in the study by Crowne et al. (1961), *rs* ranged from .4 to .5. Spitzer et al. (1966) give no information relevant to the discriminant validity of ACL SA scores.

Pedersen (1969) correlated ACL SA scores with other purported self-regard indices, the Self-scores and the [Self – Ideal] discrepancies from a semantic differential instrument. Pearson *rs* ranged from .3 to .4, offering additional limited support to the convergent validity of ACL SA scores. However, as in the Crowne, Stephens, and Kelly

(1961) study, correlations of ACL SA scores with some of the other variables were of the same magnitude as correlations of ACL SA scores with other purported indices of self-regard, again calling into question the discriminant validity of ACL Self-Acceptance scores. The other variables included such things as semantic differential ratings of generalized other and of father, and Taylor Manifest Anxiety Scale scores.

Crowne, Stephens, and Kelly (1961) also correlated Gough's (1960) SC scores with the other alleged indicators of self-regard and with the other, non-self-concept variables listed above. The correlations supportive of convergent validity of SC scores ranged from .3 to .6; but as with SA scores, the correlations relevant to discriminant validity of SC scores were of about the same magnitude as the convergent validity of this score as an indicator of self-regard.

Since two sets of scale scores, Fav and Unfav, and SA and SC, are recommended, it is important to inquire whether respective pair members have discriminant validity as measures of two respectively different aspects of overall self-regard. According to Crowne, Stephens, and Kelly (1961), SA and SC scores correlated $-.9$ for each of two samples; while according to the Gough and Heilbrun manual (1965), Fav and Unfav scores correlated $-.31$ for males and $-.57$ for females. Why these values differ so markedly between the two sets of pairs is not clear. In any event, a serious question is raised about the discriminant validity between the pair members of either set as measures of two different aspects of overall self-regard.

The only other information relevant to the discriminant validity of the Fav and Unfav scores is given in Gough and Heilbrun's (1965) manual. The Fav and Unfav scales correlated very highly with some of the other scales, for example, in the range of .5 to .8 with the scales of Personal Adjustment, Dominance, Achievement, Endurance, Order, Intraception, Nurturance, and Affiliation. Two things prevent interpretation of these coefficients, however. First, they may be inflated by overlapping adjectives. Second, there are no convergent validity values for either Fav or Unfav scores with which to compare these heterotrait correlations so as to evaluate discriminant validity.

Convergent and Discriminant Validity of the Murray Need Scores. Megargee and Parker (1968) correlated Murray need scores obtained from the ACL with those from EPPS, producing a separate multitrait-multimethod matrix for male and for female Peace Corps

Ss. Among the females, 12 of the 15 ACL need scales yielded significant convergent validity coefficients, that is, significant correlations with the corresponding EPPS need scale; for males, only four such significant convergent validity coefficients were obtained. Megargee and Parker determined for each of those ACL scores which yielded a significant convergent validity coefficient how many rs between that ACL need scale and *different* EPPS need scales exceeded the convergent validity for that particular ACL need scale. If no such heterotrait r exceeded the corresponding convergent validity value, they considered the ACL scale to show both convergent and discriminant validity. This was the case for only four scales for female Ss and three for male Ss, with only one scale (Order) common to both the male and female list. A second test of discriminant validity was that the correlation between a given ACL need scale and corresponding EPPS scale should be larger than the correlations between the given ACL scale and other ACL need scales (heterotrait-monomethod rs). No ACL scale fulfilled this criterion of discriminant validity.

These results are congruent with the outcomes of intercorrelation and factor-analytic studies mentioned earlier, which also called the discriminant validity of the ACL need scales into serious question.

Studies Based on Assumed Validity

When an instrument has received a great deal of attention in the psychological journals, one normally finds that a substantial group of studies may be construed as relevant to the construct validity of the scores in that the studies test a theoretical prediction while using the instrument in question as one of the measuring tools. With the ACL this is not true, however; and very few studies qualify as examples of this oblique but somewhat useful approach to assessing construct validity. The lack of such a useful collection of studies is a function of two things. First, many different procedures and/or scoring schemes have been applied, and for no one of these is a group of studies available. This is true even for the overall self-regard scores, where at least three approaches have been used. Some investigators have invented very complex schemes without regard to the many sources of artifact such scores introduce. Second, many of the studies I looked at were avowedly exploratory rather than purporting to test any theoretical predictions; and no cross-validation work was done to test any theoretical hypotheses which might have emerged from the exploratory work.

In the studies which looked at individual adjectives, for example, the authors typically offered psychological interpretations based on the small number of adjectives which yielded significant differences in endorsement frequency between "known groups" such as groups of architects varying with respect to levels of rated creativity in MacKinnon's (1963) study. (See also Gough, 1960; Gough & Heilbrun, 1965; Joesting & Joesting, 1969). None of these authors has taken care of the problem of the number of "significant" differences to be found by chance alone among 300 comparisons, especially among 300 comparisons of nonindependent items such as adjectives of overlapping meaning. So far as I have found, there has been no cross-validation of any of these clusters of differentiating adjectives.

Only Korman (1969) seems to have designed his study of individual adjectives to test theoretical predictions. He hypothesized that Ss with high self-esteem, as measured by Ghiselli's Self Description Inventory, would describe themselves with those ACL adjectives which were hypothesized to characterize members of their chosen profession more often than would low self-esteem Ss with the same career choice, and more often than would a random sample of Ss. He confirmed this with business-student Ss with the adjectives *practical, rational, responsible*; with accounting-student Ss with the adjectives *precise, self-controlled, organized, thorough;* and with sales-student Ss with the adjectives *initiative (sic), aggressive, sociable, talkative.*

Thus, the entire area of reliability and construct validity of separate adjective self-descriptions is essentially unexplored.

At the level of need scales, MacKinnon (1963) predicted directional differences on 15 of the need scales among architects of three levels of creativity, the latter trait being determined by expert nominations. Pearson *r*s across all Ss between level of creativity and 22 ACL scale scores yielded 15 significant values; all involved the scales on which he had made directional predictions, but 2 of these significant differences were against his prediction. The 15 correlations, generally speaking, were quite low (up to .40) and MacKinnon did not take care of the problems of interpreting multiple significance tests made on correlated dependent-variable measures applied to the same Ss.

Working with high-school Ss who had been classified by nomination and test as creative in art, writing, or science (as compared to matched controls), Schaefer (1969) stated hypotheses regarding directional differences for 14 of the ACL scales. With his various subgroups he made 96 t tests, of which 56 tested the directional hypotheses. Of these 56 tests, 2 turned out nonsignificantly opposite to his predictions, while 36 reached $\leq .05$ level of significance. Again, the problem of evaluating multiple significance tests was not handled. For 2 scales for which MacKinnon had no definite predictions, Schaefer did predict, while for 5 scales Schaefer made no prediction but MacKinnon did. Thus, even though both researchers were working in the field of "creativity," their predictions, their definitions of creativity, and their findings varied so much that no clear implications for the construct validity of the ACL scales can be drawn from a synthesis or comparison of their two studies.

SUMMARY AND RECOMMENDATIONS

Although an appreciable number of researchers have used one or more ACL scores as self-concept indicants, and although this is one of the uses recommended by the authors in their manual (Gough & Heilbrun, 1965), information about the reliability of the scores is not particularly encouraging; and information is either absent or discouraging regarding the convergent and discriminant validity of the suggested scores.

Altogether, the published studies I have examined do not offer encouragement for the use of ACL, either as a measure of overall self-regard or as a measure of Ss' self-concepts about Murray's need areas. The factor analysis and multitrait-multimethod work clearly imply that the need-scale scores and the two self-regard scores do not have discriminant validity for the purposes suggested by their labels. Of course, I have considered only the construct validity of ACL scores as self-concept measures; and this is only one of the types of validity the authors aimed to attain.

Some readers may wish to make their own evaluations of the publications which formed the basis for my appraisal of the usefulness of the ACL as a self-concept instrument. Others may wish to look at one or more of the scoring schemes and/or instructional variations which have been devised and used only once or twice. For these purposes I list here whatever references I used but did not specifically cite in the text.

SUPPLEMENTARY REFERENCES

Bohn and Stephenson (1963); Brunkan and Shen (1966); Davis (1969); Fink (1962); Flynn (1966); Graves and Shearer (1971); Grigg and Thorpe (1960); Heilbrun (1961, 1962, 1965, 1970); Helson and Crutchfield (1970); Hess and Bradshaw (1970); Isabell and Dick (1969); Ivanoff, Layman, and Von Singer (1970); Langer (1962); Markwell (1965); Mason, Adams, and Blood (1966, 1968); Nidorf (1966); Norfleet (1968); Rosen and Ross (1968); Silverman, Shulman, and Wiesenthal (1970); Stimson (1968); Suinn, Osborne, and Winfree (1962); Vanderpool (1969); Williams (1965, 1967); Woolington and Markwell (1962).

2. The Interpersonal Check List (ICL)

RATIONALE AND GENERAL DESCRIPTION

The Interpersonal Check List (ICL) was developed by LaForge and Suczek (1955) to measure a number of variables defined by the Interpersonal Personality System of Leary (1956, 1957). The check list is used to get (a) a self-description; (b) an ideal-self description; and (c) a measure of "self-acceptance" in terms of discrepancies between self and ideal-self descriptions.

In the Interpersonal Personality System (Leary 1957, pp. 81–82) and his co-workers distinguish five "levels" of personality, which we may briefly identify thus: Level I = Public Communication (interpersonal impact of the subject on others); II = Conscious Descriptions (subject's view of self and world); III = Preconscious Symbolization (subject's autistic and projective fantasy productions); IV = Unexpressed Unconscious; V = Ego Ideal (subject's view of his ideal self and his standards).

They wished to develop several measures for each level which could be mutually compared and/or combined across levels, as well as within levels. To make such intra- and interlevel comparisons possible it was necessary to score each and every one of their instruments along the same interpersonal behavior dimensions.

As a point of departure in setting up such dimensions of interpersonal behavior, they examined many behavior terms and inductively established a 16-variable classification scheme. They report that this scheme seems to accommodate most of the words in the English language having a social connotation. In diagraming their classification plan, they ordered the 16 variables around a circle which is divided into four quadrants by the main axes, dominance-submission and hostility-affection. Each quadrant is subdivided into four parts, yielding 16 subdivisions of the circle. The successive sixteenths of the perimeter of the circle refer to interpersonal behavior characteristics which are considered to be psychologically adjacent to one another along a circular continuum. For example, *docile-dependent* is next to *self-effacing-masochistic*. Opposite points on the perimeter stand for psychologically opposite interpersonal behavior characteristics. For example, *self-effacing-masochistic* is placed directly across from *managerial-autocratic*. The radius of the circle indicates the intensity of the characteristic, from normal, moderate, or appropriate (at the center) to extreme (at the periphery).

Level II appears to refer to the phenomenal self-concept, and Level V to the phenomenal ideal for self. We should note, however, that Leary (1957, p. 132) specifically denied that he and his co-workers were measuring "level of consciousness." They preferred instead to say that Levels II and V are "conscious descriptions" of self and ideal self, because measures at these levels reflect how S chooses to present himself, rather than how he sees himself. In a personal communication Leary has said that he does consider Level II measures to be like other investigators' measures of the self-concept.

The ICL is one of the instruments used to index both Level II (conscious self-description) and Level V (conscious description of the ideal self). In its most recent form, the Interpersonal Check List contains 128 items, 8 for each of the 16 variables in the theory's classification scheme. The 8 items for any variable include 1 of least "intensity," 3 for each of 2 intermediate intensity levels, and 1 of highest intensity. Items are serially listed on the sheet which S uses, with those from the 16 categories intermingled within the list. The S describes his actual self and then his ideal self by checking as many items as he wishes.

The ICL has undergone successive revisions, involving "several thousands" of Ss. Clarity of meaning was a consideration in choosing adjectives (or brief phrases) to be included in the successive revisions. In the final form of the ICL, intensity values were assigned on the basis of a combination of two criteria: (a) whether psychologists had judged the item to be good, neutral, or bad from the viewpoint of the subject's culture; (b) the frequency with which subjects had checked the item in earlier forms (for example, the lowest intensity value was assigned to an item checked by 90% of persons, the highest intensity value to an item checked by 10% of persons).

Since scaled desirability and frequency of endorsement are known to correlate highly, both in general and for these items in particular (Edwards, 1957b; Levinger, 1961; Sperber & Spanner, 1962), these two criteria for item selection would be empirically highly redundant, and the resulting scaling would more appropriately be called social desirability than intensity.

In scoring the ICL, items representing successive pairs of the 16 interpersonal behavior characteristics are grouped together, dividing the circle into octants. For any given description, for example, of self, eight raw scores are obtained for each S by finding the total number of items S has checked which belong in each octant of the circle. A circular profile can then be plotted, with the radius of each octant determined by the number of items S checked belonging in that octant.

[Self — Ideal] discrepancies for each octant and a [Self — Ideal] discrepancy for all 128 items may also be computed. To obtain overall [Self — Ideal] discrepancies, differing scoring methods have been used by different investigators (e.g., Guerney & Burton, 1963; Hamilton, 1971).

Finally, some investigators have used only two scores, Dominance (Dom) and Love (Lov), either as self-descriptions or in terms of [Self — Ideal] discrepancies. Dom and Lov are not defined in the same way by all users, some employing intuitive formulae (e.g., Guerney & Burton, 1967; Hamilton, 1971), and others using scores based on factor analyses (Bentler, 1963). This kind of variation is one of the reasons why validity studies of the ICL cannot be constructively synthesized or unambiguously compared.

The reader may wish to consult LaForge (1963) for more detailed information about scoring techniques.

RELIABILITY

Two-week test-retest correlations are given for 77 obese women. When the data were grouped by octants, the average of the eight test-retest rs was +.78. This reliability coefficient may be somewhat inflated, since Ss' sets to check many or few items regardless of content were not controlled (LaForge & Suczek, 1955).

R. G. Armstrong (1958) reports Kuder-Richardson internal-consistency coefficients of .95 and .96 for Self ratings of normal and alcoholic Ss. It seems likely that the uncontrolled response set to check many or few items regardless of content must have inflated these coefficients, too. Altrocchi, Parsons, and Dickoff (1960) report that octant scores "were not stable enough" for complex analyses of variance.

CONSTRUCT VALIDITY

Irrelevant Response Determiners

Virtually nothing can be said about irrelevant response determiners.

Social Desirability. Boe and Kogan (1964) found high correlations among various SD scores based on seven methods of deriving a social desirability score for 64 selected ICL items; and high correlations across items have been obtained between rated social desirability and probability of endorsement (Edwards, 1957b; Levinger, 1961; Sperber & Spanner, 1962). Leff and Lamb (1969) found that higher scores on Octants 7 and 8 and on Lov for both Self and Ideal were associated with high Marlowe-Crowne Social Desirability. But, as fully explained on pages 53 to 58, all the preceding findings prove nothing about the influence of faking or more subtle social-desirability considerations in invalidating ICL scores as measures of conscious self-regard. No procedures for attempting to minimize this influence have been reported for the 128-item form. Kogan and Fordyce (1962) have selected 64 items from the original ICL such that each of the octants is represented by 8 items with a mean SD value of near 5.00 (neutral social desirability), and standard deviations of SD for each set of octant scores are nearly comparable. Although this doubtless tends to make octant sets more nearly equivalent with respect to possible desirability influences, it does not prevent individual differences in any score or in total [Self — Ideal] scores from being influenced by faking or more subtle social-desirability considerations.

Item Clarity. According to Leary (1957), "clarity of meaning" to patients as well as psychiatrists was a criterion in retaining items.

Variations in Response Totals. As indicated above, the tendency to check many or few items may distort correlations between variable scores, with implications for discriminant validity, and between

ICL-variable scores and other variables which depend on total response output, with further implications for validity.

Scoring and Statistical Procedures. I have discussed the many methodological complexities and interpretational pitfalls of [Self — Ideal] discrepancy scores; and the reader who wishes to evaluate the possible difficulties in inferring self-regard from ICL [Self — Ideal] scores should examine pages 88–95 carefully. Not only does a [Self — Ideal] discrepancy on a single psychological dimension present many complexities, but, as I point out in detail on the above pages, the problems of valid inference become compounded when [Self — Ideal] discrepancies are summed across scales to obtain an overall [Self — Ideal] discrepancy score.

In general, the Ideal score seems to be stereotyped and to correlate less well than the Self score (or to correlate not at all) with theoretically relevant variables (Altrocchi, Parsons, & Dickoff, 1960; Guerney & Burton, 1963; Leary, 1957; Lomont, 1966). Although he shows that Ideal scores are highly stereotyped, Leary (1957) does not discuss the relative contribution of the Ideal score to the 2-part [Self — Ideal] score.

Since the octant scores are intercorrelated, and the Dom, Lov, and total [Self — Ideal] scores are based on items which overlap each other and the octant scores, testing hypotheses with the use of each of these leads to uninterpretable t or F values (e.g., as in Leff & Lamb's, 1969, analyses).

Internal Analyses

Intercorrelations among scales and internal factor analyses are available, although all three of the latter are based on octant inter-correlations rather than on item intercorrelations.

Theoretically, the farther apart on the circle the interpersonal behavior characteristics are from one another, the lower should be their intercorrelation. This tended to be true empirically when intercharacteristic correlations were computed on several samples. The theory predicts that characteristics opposite each other on the circle will correlate negatively. Such negative correlations were not found, however. This lack of predicted negative correlations was partly due to contamination from the response set to check many or few items, regardless of their content. It is possible to remove this influence by dividing each of S's scores by his total number of checks. When this is done, negative correlations do appear between variables opposite one another on the circle (LaForge & Suczek, 1955).

The three factor analyses (Bentler, 1963; Briar & Bieri, 1963; LaForge, cited in Foa, 1961) suggest that the octant scores probably will not have discriminant validity and that a single self-regard factor is not represented in the total self-description (and hence would not be represented in [Self — Ideal] discrepancies). Although there is agreement that at least three factors are involved, two of which are labeled Dom and Lov by all investigators, the patterns of factor loadings on these two substantive factors are not the same from one study to another. The third factor differs considerably among studies, being a methods factor, number of words checked, in LaForge's unpublished factor analysis reported in Foa (1961).

We need to know more about the construct validity of the overall [Self — Ideal] scores as measures of self-regard and of the separate Dom and Lov scores, which are the most frequently used scores and which purport to measure discriminably different self-evaluative dimensions.

Leary's Work

Leary (1957) mentions that Level II (conscious self-description) and Level V (conscious description of ideal self) were *each* measured by three other indices besides the ICL; trained personnel rated diagnostic interviews, therapy interviews, and autobiographies according to the 16-variable scheme. Unfortunately, however, no correlations between Interpersonal Check List Level II and any of these other three Level-II measures are presented, however. Also, no correlations between Interpersonal Check List Level V and any of these other measures of Level V are presented. Thus, Leary presented none of the potential evidence for convergent or discriminant validities.

Some data are given showing the percentage of various diagnostic groups which are high on each of the octants (Leary, 1957, chapters 18 to 22). These, however, are not directly useful to us in estimating the construct validity of the instrument for inferring phenomenal self-regard.

Leary says that "self-acceptance" may be inferred from the discrepancy between Level II (conscious self-description) and Level V (conscious description of ideal self). He states that "this variable plays a most crucial role in arousing motivation for therapy [1957, p. 205]." No data are cited in support of this contention, however. In a personal communication (1959), Leary has stated that he has data relating Level II (conscious self-description) to motivation for therapy; but these data remain unpublished.

Total [Self − Ideal] Discrepancies

Convergent Validity. Virtually no data are available on the correlation between total [Self − Ideal] discrepancies from ICL and other scores also purporting to measure overall self-regard. However, Hamilton (1971) included ICL [Self − Ideal] discrepancies as one of five measures of self-esteem in a multitrait-multimethod matrix. The matrix involved three traits (self-esteem, dogmatism, dominance), most of which were purportedly measured by each of five methods. Hamilton (1971) gives rs between [Self − Ideal] scores from ICL and self-esteem scores from three other measures as follows: .26 with CPI; .20 (n. s.) with Janis-Field; and .12 (n. s.) with self-ratings. CPI self-esteem scores correlated .65 with ICL Dom scores; and ICL self-esteem scores correlated .36 with CPI Dom scores. All this gives no support to the convergent validity of [Self − Ideal] discrepancies from ICL as indicants of self-esteem, nor to the idea that [Self − Ideal] discrepancies have discriminant validity as a measure of self-esteem as opposed to, say, validity as a measure of Dom.

Studies Based on Assumed Validity. Only five other studies seem to have involved any type of total [Self − Ideal] score from ICL, and these give little or no support to either convergent or discriminant validity of this score as a measure of overall self-regard. Altrocchi, Parsons, and Dickoff (1960) found that MMPI-defined "repressors," as compared to "sensitizers," had significantly smaller total [Self − Ideal] discrepancy scores. This difference was determined by the more unfavorable self-descriptions of the sensitizers. No change was observed in [Self − Ideal] discrepancies of their counseled, student-nurse Ss. (No control group was used.) Although Kogan, Boe, and Valentine (1965) (using Kogan & Fordyce's, 1962, 64-item revision of ICL) found improvement in unwed mothers during their stay in a special home, these researchers also had no control group. Cooper, Adams, and Cohen (1965) report significant improvement in [Self — Ideal] scores among experimental Ss, psychiatric patients who underwent three hours of sensory deprivation. No such increase was observed among control Ss who underwent only the normal ward routine. A correlation of .46 with Taylor Manifest Anxiety scores was reported by Guerney and Burton (1963). "Adjustment," as measured by the Bell Inventory, correlated .09 (n. s.) for boys and .49 for girls, according to Lockwood and Guerney (1962).

There is every reason to think, therefore, that total [Self — Ideal] discrepancy scores of the ICL have nothing to recommend their continued use as a measure of overall self-regard.

Octant Scores

Studies involving separate scores for each octant, whether Self or [Self — Ideal] scores, offer slight support to the predictions made by their authors. Collier (1969) found no differences between normal and diabetic adolescent Ss. For seven out of eight octants, Armstrong and Wertheimer (1959) report larger [Self — Ideal] discrepancies for alcoholics as compared to normal Ss, but only three of these were significant. Luckey's (1960a) Ss, classed as more or less happily married according to Locke's and Terman's scales, showed some tendencies to differ on [Self — Ideal] discrepancies on four scores derived from the octant scales. For husbands' and wives' data separately considered, eight comparisons were available; all differences were in the expected direction, and five were significant.

Dom and Lov Scores

The validity picture is not noticeably better regarding Dom and Lov scores.

Hamilton (1971) reports rs between ICL Dom and other "dominance" scores as follows: CPI, $r = .78$; self-ratings, $r = .52$; peer ratings, $r = .41$. Goldstein, Neuringer, Reiff, and Shelly (1968) report a significant r of .51 between ICL Dom and GAMIN "ascendance" from the Guilford-Martin Inventory. Although these rs suggest that the Dom score has some convergent validity, we must note that Goldstein et al. failed to obtain significant rs between ICL Dom scores and several other measures they predicted would correlate with Dom.

There are few available studies in which ICL Dom or Lov have correlated as predicted with theoretically relevant other variables. MMPI-defined "sensitizers," as compared to "repressors," obtained more "negative self-concepts" on Dom and perhaps on Lov, according to Altrocchi (1961) and Altrocchi, Parsons, and Dickoff (1960). In a further analysis based on some of the same Ss plus additional Ss, Altrocchi and Perlitsch (1963) failed to support their prediction that sensitizers' Self scores on Lov would be significantly lower, that is, sensitizers would "attribute more hostility to self."

Lomont (1966) replicated the association between repression-sensitization and Dom scores; and he, too, failed to find a significant association between repression-sensitization and Lov scores. (Somewhat related to these studies is McDonald's 1965, finding that repressors as compared to sensitizers attained significantly higher scores on Octants 3 and 4. The latter loaded on both Dom and Love-[Hate] factors in two factor analyses) Bentler, 1963; Briar & Bieri, 1963).

Bentler (1963) found that Ss high on his Factor II scores (Love) or its highest-loading component (cooperative-overconventional) were more hypnotizable. However, scores on Factor I (Dominance-Submission) were unrelated to hypnotizability. Taylor Manifest Anxiety scores correlated $-.44$ with Dom [Self $-$ Ideal] discrepancies, and .12 (n. s.) with Lov [Self $-$ Ideal] discrepancies in Guerney and Burton's (1963) study. Neither Self, Ideal, nor [Self $-$ Ideal] discrepancies on Dom differentiated overachievers from underachievers; but overachievers' Self scores on Lov were significantly lower (Guerney & Burton, 1967). Contrary to prediction, no relation of Dom or Lov scores with drawing the opposite-sex person first in DAP was found by Armstrong and Hauck (1961). Boyd and Sisney (1967) report that a video tape "self-confrontation" (as opposed to comedy viewing) resulted in a significant change in deviance of Dom and Lov self-descriptions from the center of the coordinates. These results must be viewed with caution, N being seven in each group. Apparently failing to support their expectations, Gynther and Brilliant (1967) found hospitalized alcoholics' Dom scores comparale to the LaForge and Suczek (1955) norms. Also, failing to support their prediction, Goldstein, Neuringer, Reiff, and Shelly (1968) found no correlation between the Witkin Rod and Frame Test of "field dependency" and Dom or Lov scores on the ICL. Although they predicted that obese men would describe themselves as more dominant than would control Ss, Weinberg, Mendelson, and Stunkard (1961) obtained no difference between the groups in ICL Dom scores. Adams, Robertson, and Cooper (1966) report ambiguous findings concerning the effects of sensory deprivation on Dom and Lov scores of psychiatric patients. In yet another failure to support a hypothesis, Lawton (1965) found no relation between Dom and Lov Self, Ideal, or [Self — Ideal] discrepancies and nurses' evaluations of psychiatric aides' performance, while associations between these ICL variables and psychiatrists' ratings and rankings of psychiatric aide performance were, with one exception, null or contradictory to the hypothesis.

Thus, evidence for validity of either Dom or Lov scores is not encouraging, both because of the miscellaneous nature of the other variables which were studied by various Es and because of the tendency toward weak, null, and contradictory findings.

I have examined 39 studies, listed below, which used the ICL but which, for the following reasons, did not seem useful in the analysis of the construct validity of ICL scores: (a) Some researches were purely empirical; that is, they tested no theoretical prediction either because of uncertainty as to what to predict or because empirical exploration was their aim. (b) Many used a type of score other than those analyzed here, precluding mutual comparisons and syntheses. (c) A large proportion of these studies was methodologically poor. For example, many made unanalytical use of 2-part scores; and many made multiple t tests or multiple F tests using the same Ss and applying the significance test separately and successively to variables which correlate or even overlap with each other. Some compared "known groups" (e.g., socioeconomic groups) without attention to the probable lack of comparability of these groups on other variables than the alleged independent variable. Some generalized without presenting any significance test. Several had no control groups. (Quite a few of the studies cited in the validity section above had some of these flaws and they, too, must be viewed with caution.)

The 39 references which I have not included, but which the reader may wish to examine, are: Armstrong and Hauck (1961); Barber and Calverley (1964); Beard and Pishkin (1970); Bieri and Lobeck (1961); Brooks and Hillman (1965); Cairns and Lewis (1962); Cone (1971); Crandall (1969); Dinitz, Mangus, and Pasamanick (1959); Gibby, Gibby, and Hogan (1967); Gynther (1962); Gynther and Kempson (1962); Gynther, Miller, and Davis (1962);

Karp, Jackson, and Lester (1970) (they used only 54 adjectives from ICL); Kogan, Boe, Gocka, and Johnson (1966); Kogan and Jackson (1963) (they used masculinity-feminity scale values for ICL items); Kotlar (1962); Lantz (1965); Luckey (1960b, 1966); McDavid and Sistrunk (1964); McDonald (1962a, 1962b, 1963, 1968); McDonald and Gynther (1965a, 1965b); McKegney (1967); Meers and Neuringer (1967); Murstein and Glaudin (1966); Preston and Gudiksen (1966); Rawlinson (1965); Savage, Fadiman, Mogar, and Allen (1966); Seegars (1963); Simmons (1967); Spilka and Lewis (1959); Taylor (1967); Walhood and Klopfer (1971); and Zuckerman, Levitt, and Lubin (1961).

CONCLUSIONS AND RECOMMENDATIONS

The development of the ICL on rational grounds and its emphasis on interpersonal aspects of the self-concept may suggest that it has special promise as a measure of (a) overall self-regard and/or (b) self-evaluation along discriminable dimensions such as love-hate and dominance-submission.

Unfortunately, the accumulation of research gives virtually no information on appropriate reliabilities. Also, many problems of the invalidating influence of irrelevant response determiners remain untouched. Available studies suggest that the total [Self − Ideal] score has no convergent or discriminant validity as a measure of overall self-regard. Although the Dom and Lov score may be worth researching further, results involving these scores are not particularly encouraging so far.

The very unsatisfactory state of research on this instrument stems partly from scattered application of varying scoring techniques even for variables given the same name (e.g., dominance as defined by various Es); partly from an unusually high incidence of serious methodological flaws; and partly from the extremely miscellaneous, often atheoretical nature of the variables explored. It should be especially noted that a large proportion of the successfully predicted findings involve correlating two self-report scores, a method that is particularly vulnerable to artifactual influences.

For another opinion and additional bibliographic listings on ICL, the reader should see Bentler's review in Buros (1970). Robinson and Shaver (1969) give the items arranged according to octants and weights.

3. The Semantic-Differential Technique of Osgood, Suci, and Tannenbaum (1957) (SD)

In the semantic-differential technique, *S* is asked to rate each of several *concepts* on each of a number of bipolar adjective scales. A concept can refer to a specific person or object, for example, *Eisenhower* or *The Mona Lisa;* or its referent can be more inclusive, for example, *Republican, woman,* or *boulder;* or it can refer to more abstract ideas, such as *justice* or *idleness.* The adjectival bipolar scales which were used by Osgood and his associates were selected on various grounds indicated below. They include literally applicable adjectives, for example, large-small for *boulder;* and adjectives which are only metaphorically applicable if relevant at all, for example, sweet-sour for *boulder,* or yellow-blue for *me.* Among other concepts, the self-referent construct *me* was used by Osgood et al. (1957) in their first two factor analyses of scale intercorrelations. These analyses yielded factors such as evaluation, potency, and activity, interpreted by Osgood and his associates as basic dimensions of "connotative meaning" or "semantic space."

There are two reasons why one might at first think that the semantic differential, either in one of the specific forms presented by Osgood or as a general format for a measuring instrument, should be given a detailed critical review in such a book as this one. First, more than 80 studies have reportedly employed the semantic-differential method of measuring self-referent constructs such as *me, self,* or *ideal self.* Thus it appears that many investigators have accepted the opinion of Osgood et al. (1957, pp. 219–221) that the semantic-differential method is appropriately applicable to self-concept measurement. Moreover, it might at first appear that this technique offers some desirable definements of method as compared to other rating-scale approaches, and that the reliability studies and factor analytic work of Osgood and his associates might be used to support the reliability and construct validity of the instrument as a self-concept measure.

A more careful examination of both the empirical work and methodological considerations shows that such initial impressions are untenable, however, as I shall now explain. Although methodological considerations comprise the more important argument against the value of the semantic differential in self-concept measurement, the arguments based on the present state of empirical affairs will be discussed first.

When more than 80 semantic-differential self-concept studies are available, one might hope that there is enough in common among their measuring techniques that the studies could be organized into groups in such a way as to throw light on the construct validity of the self-concept measure used in all of them. Unfortunately, this is not the case. Only about 40% of the 81 publications I examined reported *both* that Osgood's semantic differential was used *and* that specified scales had been chosen for the investigation being reported. (An additional 20% of the publications apparently were based on some version of the Osgood semantic differential, but the reports did not indicate which scales were used; 24% reported using non-Osgood scales, chosen for various reasons, while 16% were so vague that the reader can learn nothing about the scales or the basis for their choice.) Directing our attention first to those studies which did use specified Osgood scales, we most frequently find that the scales were chosen because they represented the familiar Osgood factors of evaluation, potency, or activity. Usually, however, the investigator did not indicate which of Osgood's sets of scales and which factor-analytic results served as the basis for the particular scale choice. The amount of overlap from study to study in regard to actual scales employed was amazingly small. For example, so far as scales representing the evaluative factor are concerned, only one (good-bad) was used in as many as two-thirds of the studies, while only four other evaluative scales were used in as many as a quarter of the researches (clean-dirty; nice-awful; beautiful-ugly; happy-sad). Add to these disparities among the studies the fact that the chosen evaluative scales for self were embedded in a wide range of contexts of other scales, and it becomes apparent that the available studies cannot be used to appraise the construct validity of any particular Osgood scales, let alone to appraise either of the original total forms of the semantic-differential scales presented in Osgood, Suci, and Tannenbaum's (1957) book (that is, scales based on associations to Kent-Rosanoff word stimuli, or thesaurus-based scales).

One should note, too, that both variations in scale choice among studies and the failure to specify which scales were used imply that the investigators assume it to be relatively unimportant which scales are applied so long as the semantic-differential technique is used. This assumption, of course, cannot be defended on either logical grounds or on the basis of Osgood's empirical work.

Although self-concept studies thus far have not used comparable scales, thus vitiating their value in assaying the construct validity of the semantic-differential technique in self-concept measurement, it might be thought that this could be corrected by selection of a "standard" list of Osgood scales for future use and evaluating the results from future comparable studies as they might shed light on the construct validity of the "standard" list of adjective scales. Unfortunately, this cannot furnish a defensible solution, because the most basic trouble lies in the attempt to apply an instrument which is based on a rationale and procedure not ideally applicable to self-concept measurement. That contention may be explained as follows.

We have frequently stressed that indispensable first steps in developing a measure of a personality construct, in the present case a self-concept measure, are to formulate as precisely as possible a "literary" definition of the construct one desires to measure, and then to choose items which appear a priori to have possible construct validity for measuring the defined concept. The items, in this case the bipolar adjective scales, should appear to represent important, salient features of the concept; and their structure should be made as clear as possible so as to minimize inter-S variability in interpretation of the items. The Osgood scales fall short on both these points because the goal of Osgood et al. was not primarily self-concept measurement, and accordingly, the scales were not chosen to be primarily relevant to the self-concept. The reader will remember that the goal of the Osgood research was to see whether human beings' "connotative" meanings for a very wide variety of concepts might be construed as involving a limited number of dimensions. (The label *connotative meaning*, an ambiguous and misleading choice, as several critics such as Brown, 1958, and Weinrich, 1958, have pointed out, has come to be replaced by the label *affective* or *emotional* in more recent discussions, such as those of Kuusinen, 1969, and Osgood, 1969.) Consistent with their goal, Osgood, Suci, and Tannenbaum (1957, p. 186) say

> For an ideal semantic measuring instrument we would like to select a small set of scales having the following properties: (a) high loading on the factor they represent, (b) high correlation with the other scales representing the same factor, (c) low correlation with scales representing other factors (and hence low loading on other factors), and (d) *a high degree of stability across the various concepts judged* [emphasis added].

Their stated goal and their research relevant to it have several implications for the potential use of the semantic-differential technique as a valid self-concept measure. The choice of adjectival descriptions had to be made from a very broad range of possibilities, since the scales were to cover so many possible concepts. For example, in the first factor-analytic study, common associates to Kent-Rosanoff nouns were used as the source of adjectival scales, while in the second, adjective pairs were drawn from Roget's *Thesaurus* in a specified manner. Obviously, many adjectives of great relevance to self-description were excluded, while others inapplicable to self or applicable only metaphorically to self were included. The inclusion of scales which could be applied only metaphorically was defended by Osgood and his associates as providing subtle ways of getting Ss' affective reactions which they might otherwise presumably hide from the investigator or be unable to express. However, as I have repeatedly emphasized, there is no evidence that such subtle or "tricky" approaches increase the validity of Ss' replies as indicants of their phenomenal self-concepts; and in fact, there is considerable reason to think that many troublesome, ambiguous inter-S differences in interpreting the items are created by such an approach (Fiske, 1966).

In short, the aim of these investigators appropriately led them to create item sets which they did not even try to defend in terms of their being maximally useful in measuring self-concept. If anything uniquely relevant to self-concept measurement could be obtained from this particular approach, it might be to find out whether the self-concept can be "located" with reference to the same "dimensions of semantic space" ("dimensions of affective or emotional reactions") as may be used to "locate" other concepts. Common sense supports the plausibility that such dimensions as evaluativeness, activity, and potency might be important in self-appraisals as well as in reactions to other concepts. But it does not follow that those scales which load most highly on a factor in the Osgood studies which involved many concepts are the scales which also best represent that factorial dimension with reference to the concepts with which we are most concerned here, for example, the self-concept and the concept of the ideal self. That the latter assertion is true should be apparent when one thinks of the way in which the factors were derived in the Osgood work, that is, by intercorrelating scales after summing across both subjects and concepts. Thus, although the concept *me* was included in both of their first factor analyses, it does not follow that the scales which loaded highest and/or showed purest loadings on, say, the evaluative factor were the scales which would most validly index individual differences along a dimension of self-evaluation. In general, the possibility and the fact of concept-scale interaction have been acknowledged by both Osgood et al. (1957) and their critics (e.g., Gulliksen, 1958). Thus, when a separate factor analysis was performed on scale intercorrelations obtained respectively from each of a number of concepts, it was found that the particular scales contributing to the evaluative factor differed markedly from concept to concept. Particularly pertinent to problems of measuring the self-concept is the fact that two of the five scales which best represented the evaluative factor in the analysis of the scale intercorrelations involving the concept *me* did not appear as the best representatives of the evaluative dimension of "semantic space" for *all* the concepts they studied.

In summary, the implications of all this for self-concept researchers should by now be clear. First, we must remind ourselves that the general approach of Osgood et al. to selection of adjectival scales, while justifiable in terms of the major goals of their research, is bound to produce a less than optimal set of adjectives for use in describing the concept *self*. Beyond this limitation is the fact that one is not justified in choosing bipolar adjective scales for measuring, for example, self-evaluation from those scales which Osgood et al. found to be the best representatives of the evaluative dimension of "semantic space" for *all* the concepts they studied.

The reader may be convinced by the foregoing arguments that it would be inappropriate to try to use the present form of the Osgood Semantic Differential as a self-concept measuring instrument. But would the general semantic-differential format used with bipolar adjective scales specially selected for self-concept relevance have special merits for this measurement problem? Perhaps so, but several cautions must be noted. In general, the use of bipolar adjective sets may be commendable in that the explicit contrast presented within each scale could help to communicate to S the meaning of each adjective more clearly than is the case in an adjective check list or a unipolar adjective scale. The use of multi-step scales can decrease uninterpretable "remainder variance" and increase dependable, potentially valid inter-S differences (Fiske, 1966).

If one wished to capitalize on these potential advantages, a new semantic-differential instrument could be built by especially selecting adjective pairs for their apparent self-concept dimensions, factor analyzing adjective-scale intercorrelations, and choosing clusters of adjective scales which best represent the interpretable factors obtained. However, even with bipolar adjective pairs appropriately chosen for clarity and relevance to self-concept description, an optimal number of scale steps, and the appropriate application of factor-analytic techniques as a basis for weeding and grouping items, we still would not have answered the following old, familiar questions: Are Ss' metrics comparable between Ss and across adjectival scales? Is obtaining a total score by summing across scales justified in terms of each item's relevance to the self-concept dimension the total score is supposedly measuring? Only proper application of scaling techniques and internal factor analyses of scale intercorrelations could serve to answer these question for any new application of semantic-differential format in the area of measuring some specified aspect(s) of self-concept.

The semantic differential has been used by Osgood and many others as a means of comparing "profiles" of two or more concepts on the adjectival scales; and difference scores were suggested by Osgood, Suci, and Tannenbaum (1957) as meaningful indicants of the degree of similarity between S's meanings for two concepts, for example, me and my mother, or me and my ideal self. The problems of metrics and dimensional interpretations which we have just mentioned are, of course, present in such comparisons; in fact, such interpretational problems are compounded when one uses such two-part indices, as we have repeatedly emphasized.

For the possible interest and use of readers who might wish to check for themselves the studies which formed the basis for my analysis of the state of empirical affairs in applying the semantic-differential technique to self-concept measures, I list here the references: Aiken (1965); Babbitt (1962); Back and Guptill (1966); Bass and Fiedler (1961); W. C. Becker (1960); Berzon, Reisel, and Davis (1969); Bethlehem (1969); Block (1958); Borislow (1962); Carter (1968); Cole, Oetting, and Hinkle (1967); Cole, Oetting and Miskimins (1969); Crumpton, Wine, and Drenick (1966); Dolich (1969); Downing, Moed, and Wight (1961); Downing and Rickels

(1967); Eisenman (1970); Endler (1961); Epstein and Baron (1969); Feshbach and Beigel (1968); Fiedler, Hutchins, and Dodge (1959); Flippo and Lewinsohn (1971); Frisbie, Vanasek, and Dingman (1967); Goslin (1962); Grigg (1959a, 1959b); Guggenheim and Hoem (1967); Hall (1969); Hamid (1969); Harmatz (1967); Hartlage and Hale (1968); Hartman (1965); Hodgkins and Stakenas (1969); Hunt (1967); Jorgensen and Howell (1969); Kamano (1960, 1961); Kamano and Crawford (1966); Kelly and Baer (1969); Kingston and White (1967); Kubiniec (1970); Laxer (1964a, 1964b); Lazowick (1955); Lipsitt (1968); Loehlin (1961, 1967); Maddox, Back, and Liederman (1968); McCallon (1966b); McGlothlin, Cohen, and McGlothlin (1967); Morse (1964); Moss and Waters (1960); Musella (1969); Neale and Proshek (1967); Nichols and Berg (1970); Ogston, Altman, and Lane (1970); O'Leary and Hood (1969); Oskamp (1968); Pallone, Rickard, Hurley, and Tirman (1970); Pedersen (1969); Pervin and Lilly (1967); Peters (1970); Platt and Taylor (1966); Reitz and Thetford (1967); Salomon and McDonald (1970); Schuh (1966); Schwartz and Dubitsky (1968); K. H. Smith (1970); Solley and Stagner (1956); Stimpson and Pedersen (1970); Talbot, Miller, and White (1961); Thomas and Yamamoto (1971); Walberg (1967a, 1967b, 1968); Weaver, Kingston, Bickley, and White (1969); Weaver, White, and Kingston (1968); White and Richmond (1970); Wright and Tuska (1966); Yamamoto, Thomas, and Karns (1969); Zagona and Babor (1969); Zahran (1967); Zellner (1970).

4. The Tennessee Self Concept Scale (TSCS)

The Tennessee Self Concept Scale (TSCS) is one of the more frequently used self-regard instruments among those which have been published since the original edition of this book. Unfortunately, TSCS seems to have been employed, and its numerous scores computed and interpreted, with little or no regard to the dearth of methodologically adequate published research.

RATIONALE AND GENERAL DESCRIPTION

The self-regard items (which are published in the commercially available specimen set, Fitts, 1964), were drawn from a vaguely specified pool of three unpublished sources plus "written self descriptions of patients and nonpatients" (Fitts, 1965). No explicit definitions of the constructs which guided item choice are offered. Items are phrased half positively and half negatively to control acquiescence response set. *S* marks each item on a 5-step scale from "completely true" to "completely false." Frequency is sometimes a part of the item statement, sometimes not, making consistent application of the 5-point scale to each item almost impossible for *S*. The favorability of each item is either "positive" or "negative," as determined by clinician judges, so the scores are not as consistently phenomenological as self-minus-ideal discrepancy scores or self-ideal *r* scores.

Each of the 90 self-concept items was included only if seven clinical psychologists could agree perfectly on its location in one of three rows (*identity*, what I am; *self-satisfaction*, how I accept myself; and *behavior*, how I act); and also in one of five Self columns (physical, moral-ethical, personal, family, and social).

A total self-regard score is derived from the 90 items; and separate self-regard scores are computed and interpreted for each row and each column. That discriminant uses of these separate scores are unjustified until otherwise demonstrated is shown by the following facts: (a) row and column items overlap; (b) column intercorrelations (with no item overlap) run from .41 to .75; (c) row intercorrelations (with no item overlap) run from .80 to .91; (d) total self-regard scores correlate from .93 to .96 with rows (one-third of the items overlapping in each correlation); (e) total self-regard scores correlate from .75 to .90 with each column (with one-fifth of the items overlapping in each correlation). In a factor analysis of a matrix of intercorrelations of 12 TSCS scales, Rentz and White (1967a) found that all self scores (three row and five column scores) loaded highly on only the first ("evaluative") factor. However, the application of factor analysis is inappropriate, since row scores are redundant with column scores in this test.

Numerous other scores, recommended in the manual, will not be discussed here, although they are open to various methodological criticisms.

RELIABILITY

The manual (Fitts, 1965) reports the following 2-week test-retest reliability coefficients for 60 college students: total self-regard = .92; rows, from .88 to .91; columns, from .85 to .90. However, research offered in support of validity uses many other groups, such as neuropsychiatric patients, delinquents, and sixth-grade children; and appropriate reliability estimates for these groups are not available. The procedure which S has to follow in responding could easily open the way to clerical errors, especially in younger, disturbed, and less able groups; and no published information is available about the reading level which would be required for reliable responding.

It seems, therefore, a plausible and parsimonious hypothesis that some of the "known-group" differences one might cite in support of construct validity are actually due to differences in incidence of random responding between the groups being compared rather than to differences in their self-regard. This is so because, as we have fully explained above (p. 119f.), what is empirically a "low self-regard" score on this type of instrument on any particular occasion confounds random responding with S's intention to express a relatively unfavorable degree of self-regard.

CONSTRUCT VALIDITY

Convergent Validity

Information regarding convergent construct validity between self-regard scores from TSCS and other alleged measures of self-regard is not particularly encouraging. In an unpublished study by Wayne (1963), cited in Fitts (1965), a correlation of .68 was found between Izard's Self Rating Positive Affect Scale and TSCS. In Rentz and White's (1967b) factor-analytic study, using college Ss, the Osgood semantic-differential "good-bad" rating for actual self was the only one of 24 self and ideal semantic-differential scales which loaded significantly on the first factor on which all row and column scores from TSCS loaded highly. (We must note that factor analyzing five row scores, three column scores, and one total score from TSCS would lead to artifactual results in that numerous rerundancies among scores are involved.) Vincent (1968), using Self-Satisfaction and Personal Satisfaction scores, found insignificant correlations between TSCS scores and CPI Self-Acceptance and Self-Control scores; rs of .61 and .67 with Maslow's Security S-II scores; rs of .39 and .39 with 16 PF Emotional Stability scores; and rs of .44 and .43 with 16 PF Confident Adequacy scores. Her Ss were undergraduate students.

Discriminant Validity

So far as discriminant validity among rows or among columns is concerned, we have already shown that interrow rs and intercolumn rs make it seem unlikely that this kind of discriminant valid-ity can be established. It certainly has not been thus far. Suggestive negative evidence comes from Vacchiano and Strauss's (1968) factor analysis of the 90 self and 10 lie items which yielded 20 factors. These did not correspond to the three row and five column scales. (Additionally, we note that Factors II to XX accounted for only 6% to 2% of the variance each. Only 75 of the 90 self-regard items contributed at all to factor formation.) Although Fitts (1965) im-plicitly assumes discriminant validity in talking about profiles, no information is given as to how far apart two column scores (or two row scores) should be in order to be interpretable as anything other than chance differences, let alone as indicative of valid differences in specified aspects of self-regard. Meanwhile, many of the research uses and the recommended counseling uses of this instrument treat the separate scores as if they could be discriminantly interpreted, a serious violation of adequate standards of methodology. In research, Es present numerous significance tests involving scores based on overlapping items or scores which highly intercorrelate; and these are erroneously interpreted as if all "significant" comparisions war-ranted rejecting the null hypothesis, and with no regard for what would be expected by chance in multiple t tests.

Studies Based on Assumed Validity

As is common in self-concept scale development, it is theoretically predicted that certain "known-group" comparisons will be relevant to simultaneous evaluation of the construct validity of the instru-ment and the theoretically based hypotheses. Thus, most neuro-psychiatric patients, alcoholics, and delinquents (as compared to appropriate controls), Negroes (vs. whites), and Ss with low reading-comprehension scores or low "comprehension coping strength" in reading (as compared to Ss high on these variables) are expected to have lower self-regard. Five unpublished studies briefly cited in Fitts (1965) (his own and those by Congdon, 1958; Piety, 1958; and Wayne, 1963), have found the expected differences between self-regard scores of patients and normals. However, Havener and Izard (1962) predicted and found that paranoid schizophrenic Ss' Self-Acceptance scores (Row 1 minus Row 2) were significantly more favorable than normal control Ss. Among numerous t tests, Vander-pool (1969) and Gross and Alder (1970) report that self-regard scores of alcoholics were significantly lower than those of the normative group. Two unpublished studies cited by Fitts (1965) (Atchison, 1958, and Lefeber, 1964, report significant differences in self-regard between delinquents and normals and between repeating delinquents and first offenders. Hebert (1968) found lower reading comprehension scores associated with lower self-regard scores; and Hughes (1968) reports association between poor self-regard scores and poor "comprehension coping strength" (operationally measured by comprehension of paragraphs read under delayed auditory feedback). Williams and Cole (1968) found TSCS significantly associated with reading and mathematics achievement scores in sixth-grade children. Collins, Burger, and Doherty (1970) found relatively few significant differences in TSCS self-regard scores between educable mentally retarded and normal Ss.

Except for Havener and Izard's (1962) study, any of the significant positive results reported in the preceding list of known-group studies could be plausibly accounted for in terms of random responding as a determinant of "low self-regard" scores of the lower group, as explained above. Hence they offer highly questionable support to construct validity of self-regard scores from TSCS.

Five other relevant studies comparing known groups are available. Duncan (1966) compared college student Ss who received many nominations on a Personality Integration Reputation Test with a "contrast group" chosen without regard to their standing on the reputation test. Supporting his hypothesis, which was based on Rogerian theory, Ss in the contrast group received lower self-regard scores on TSCS.

Resnick, Fauble, and Osipow (1970) hypothesized, on the basis of Super's theory, that Ss with high self-esteem should show greater "vocational crystallization." This hypothesis was confirmed in terms of Ss' reported vocational certainty, but not in terms of another purported measure of vocational crystallization, number of high Kuder preference scores.

Contrary to their expectations, Williams and Byars (1968) report no significant association of self-regard and Negro-white status in sixth-grade southern students.

In a probability learning situation (Clark & Epstein, 1969), pictures of faces were presented with 70 : 30 proportions of angry : smiling (or, for some groups, 70 : 30 proportions of smiling : angry). Ss with high self-regard scores underestimated the 70% incidence of angry faces (or, in other groups, accurately estimated the 70% incidence of smiling faces). Ss with low self-regard scores, on the other hand, underestimated the 70% incidence of smiling faces (or, in other groups, accurately estimated the 70% incidence of angry faces). One can argue that this seems congruent with the theoretical expectation of different kinds of social reinforcements in the past experience of Ss respectively high and low in self-regard. The Ss were male homosexuals, limiting the generalizability of the study.

Schwab, Clemmons, and Marder (1966) found, in a group of patients with medical illnesses, that lower self-regard scores were associated with patients' feeling their illness had adversely affected their social life and accomplishment, and with patients' holding a less favorable outlook for their illness (despite the fact that these Ss were judged to be no sicker than those with more favorable self-concepts and other attitudes). This, of course, suggests some covariation between self-regard and more specific beliefs about oneself.

Several studies involving a manipulated variable and a theoretical prediction are available. Unfortunately, predictions were not always sustained, which means that these studies offer negligible support to the construct validity of self-regard scores of TSCS. For example, contrary to theoretical predictions, alcoholics (Vanderpool, 1969) decreased rather than increased their self-regard scores when drinking under experimental conditions. (This could be another example of confounding of low self-regard and random responding as determinants of so-called low self-regard scores.) Ss with low self-regard scores in Schalon's (1968) study suffered significant decrement in digit-symbol performance following failure, while high self-regard Ss did not. The findings for the low group followed his prediction; however, he had hypothesized that Ss with high self-regard scores would increase digit-symbol performance after stress, not just show an insignificant decrement. In Ashcraft and Fitts's (1964) report, among numerous significance tests, we find that total self-regard scores increased significantly in therapy patients, as opposed to no change in patients waiting for therapy.

CONCLUSIONS AND RECOMMENDATIONS

In a review of TSCS much more sanguine than this one, Crites (1965, p. 331) concludes, "What are the particular advantages of this instrument over its long line of precursors, e.g., the Bills *Index*

of Adjustment and Values, the various published *Q* sorts, etc.? It is
incumbent upon the author to demonstrate that his Scale is 'simpler
for the subject, more widely applicable, better standardized, etc.'
than other similar measuring devices." My conclusion is that no
justification can be offered, either from a priori analyses in terms
of acceptable methodological criteria or from a survey of empirical
results to justify using this scale rather than certain others which are
available or better ones to be devised in the future. Since preparing
this review I have had the opportunity to see Bentler's evaluation of
TSCS in Buros (1971). The reader may wish to consult his review
for another concurring opinion of TSCS.

Certain studies using TSCS self-regard scores were not included
in the above analysis of the reliability and validity of the scale
because they did not belong in any of the categories considered:
Cardillo (1971); Deutsch and Solomon (1959); Grant (1969); Greenberg and Frank (1965, 1967); Imboden, Canter, Cluff, and Trevor
(1959); Mabel and Rosenfeld (1966); Vacchiano, Strauss, and
Schiffman (1968); Williams (1971); Williams and Byars (1970).

5. Body Cathexis Scale (BC)

RATIONALE AND GENERAL DESCRIPTION

In its usual scoring, the Body Cathexis Scale is among those
which purport to index self-acceptance directly, as opposed to
measuring it through self-minus-ideal discrepancies or through self
scores compared to externally judged norms. The authors define
body cathexis as "the degree of feeling of satisfaction or dissatisfaction with various parts or processes of the body [Secord & Jourard, 1953, p. 343]." Accordingly, this scale is concerned with a more
limited aspect of self-regard than is the case with those instruments
discussed in Section C. It seems intuitively plausible that this particular aspect of self-regard is broad and salient to Ss and would
be expected to correlate with overall self-regard.

The Body Cathexis Scale (BC) has been used in two versions and
in only a small number of studies, few of them recent. Nevertheless,
it is the only scale of its kind which has been used more than once
or twice; and it offers researchers at least a takeoff point for further
scale development or exploration of this area.

Robinson and Shaver (1969) give the earlier 46-item version, but
most studies have employed a 40-item modification (Jourard &

Secord, 1954). In either case, S rates his feelings about each listed body part or function, using a 5-point scale from "strong positive" to "strong negative." The rationale for item selection is not explained, but the items appear to cover a wide range. Eleven of the items most negatively cathected by a standardization group comprise a "body anxiety" or "anxiety indicator" subscale, respectively different for male and female Ss. For the total scale or "anxiety indicator" subscale, item ratings are added to yield the S's score.

RELIABILITY

Corrected split-half reliability coefficients for the 46-item BC scores are given by Secord and Jourard (1953) as .78 (males) and .83 (females); and by Weinberg (1960) for the 40-item BC scale as .84 (males), and .75 (females). We must note that Secord and Jourard removed from their groups Ss whose records suggested the presence of response sets according to a predetermined degree of piling up at one end of the scale. Had these Ss been retained, reliability coefficients would have been higher. Jourard and Remy (1955) report split-half coefficients of "at least .91."

Body anxiety (anxiety indicator) scores yielded split-half reliabilities of .72 (males) and .73 (females) (Secord & Jourard, 1953).

For 52 male students, test-retest coefficients of .72 for BC and .76 for anxiety indicator scores were obtained by Johnson (1956) after a 6- to 8-week interval.

CONSTRUCT VALIDITY

We concern ourselves here with the construct validity of the BC scale as an indicant of an overall attitude toward body parts and functions. Additionally, we examine evidence of the discriminant validity of the scale for measuring body-relevant attitudes as differentiated from overall self-esteem or even from more general attitudes of satisfaction with others and the world in general.

Analysis of Irrelevant Response Determiners

Virtually nothing can be said about the influence of irrelevant response determiners upon the construct validity of this instrument. It is obviously open to faking or to more subtle social-desirability influences. In their research, Secord and Jourard allowed Ss to remain anonymous and they stressed the importance of honesty

and carefulness. Their method of scoring by summing across disparate items is open to the familiar criticism that this assumes
without warrant the equal salience and metric of each item. Although an internal factor analysis could at least suggest the degree
to which all items load on a common factor, none is available. That
some items seem particularly salient to Ss is brought out by Secord
and Jourard's (1953) success in selecting an 11-item subscale with
relatively high reliability, and by Rosen and Ross's (1968) finding
that Ss could choose body-relevant items which they felt were more
and less salient to them.

The fact that low BC scores run toward the lower end of the
rating-scale range suggests that a low score does *not* represent the
confounding of the influences of random responding and low regard
for body in the manner discussed on pages 119 to 121.

Convergent Validity

It is impossible to estimate convergent validity of the BC scale
because no other extant scale purports to measure the construct as
defined by Secord and Jourard. (Hunt & Feldman, 1960, found no
relationship between BC scores and Draw-a-Person Scores indicative
of disturbance. However, DAP does not purport to measure phenomenal attitudes toward the body, so this null correlation may be
considered irrelevant to the convergent validity of BC.)

Studies Based on Assumed Validity

A number of researchers predicted and obtained correlations
between BC scores and other theory-relevant variables as indicated
below. All rs are significant unless otherwise indicated.

Maslow's Security-Insecurity Inventory. Pearson rs range from
$-.21$ to $-.37$ (Jourard & Remy, 1955; Secord & Jourard, 1953; Weinberg, 1960).

Self Cathexis (a purported measure of self-esteem developed by
Jourard, 1957, in the same format as BC). Although White and
Gaier's (1965) AA members yielded an r of only $-.13$, Pearson rs
obtained from other Ss range from .31 to .84 (Jourard & Remy, 1955;
Secord & Jourard, 1953; Weinberg, 1960; White & Wash, 1965).
The latter rs are probably inflated by response sets related to the
common format of BC and SC. Unfortunately, BC scores seem never
to have been correlated with a measure of overall self-regard having a dissimilar format.

S's Perception of How His Parents Perceive His Body and Self. Pearson *r*s ranging from .56 to .74 were obtained between BC and parents' perceived acceptance of *S*'s body and self (Jourard & Remy, 1955). Again, of course, the inflating influence of response sets is particularly likely.

Bodily Concern (as measured by the number of times *S*s give body-referent responses to a list of homonyms which could arouse either bodily or nonbodily associations, for example, *colon, gag, system* [Secord, 1953]). Pearson *r*s are −.18 (n. s., males) and −.41 (females) (Secord & Jourard, 1953); and .36 (hospitalized *S*s) and −.01 (nonhospitalized *S*s) (Jaskar & Reed, 1963). (The split-half *r*s of the Homonyms Test were .81 and .73 in two groups [Secord, 1953].)

Scores from the Cornell Medical Index Health Questionnaire correlated with BC scores −.33 (males) and −.40 (females); and with anxiety indicator scores derived from BC −.42 (males) and −.54 (females), in Johnson's (1956) study.

Johnson (1956) also obtained *r*s between BC and Taylor's Manifest Anxiety Scale (containing many items referring to body functions). These *r*s were −.40 (males) and −.53 (females).

Sobriety Interval in Alcoholics. Concern with body appearance allegedly characterizes improvement stages in alcoholism. Thus, White and Gaier's (1965) curvilinear *r* between BC scores and length of sobriety interval only partially supported their expectations. Unfortunately, their data, gathered at a single AA meeting, were cross-sectional rather than involving test and retest; so they are entirely inconclusive.

Mental Illness. Schizophrenic *S*s yielded significantly lower BC scores than psychiatric aides (Cardone & Olson, 1969), as predicted. Also as predicted, hospitalized *S*s obtained significantly less favorable BC scores than did employment applicants (Jaskar & Reed, 1963).

Chlorpromazine. Although chlorpromazine was predicted to improve BC scores, it showed no effects when treated schizophrenic *S*s were compared to schizophrenic *S*s given a placebo or no drug (Cardone & Olson, 1969).

Nudist-Group Affiliation. Nudists were significantly higher on BC than were control *S*s, members of a private swim club (Blank, Sugerman, & Roosa, 1968).

Size of Body Parts. For a number of parts, BC ratings correlated significantly and in the expected direction with size of the part (Jourard & Secord, 1954 [males], and 1955 [females]).

Discriminant Validity

Although almost all of the above studies obtained associations in the theoretically predicted direction, thus offering some oblique support to the construct validity of the BC scale, crucial questions regarding discriminant validity remain unanswered. Multitrait-multimethod matrices (Campbell & Fiske, 1959) are indispensable to an evaluation of this problem. Such as it is, available information does not support discriminant validity of BC as a measure of body cathexis or body acceptance as different from self-acceptance. For example, BC correlations with Self Cathexis are greater than BC correlations with the Homonyms Test, which is called by its author a "body cathexis" measure. This is true even for those BC items selected as most likely to indicate body anxiety. Low reliability of the Homonyms Test cannot be the explanation, because its split-half reliability is approximately the same as that of the Self Cathexis questionnaire (Secord & Jourard, 1953).

The following articles also report results involving the BC, though they are not clearly pertinent to the question of its construct validity: Arkoff and Weaver (1966); Clifford (1971) (modified BC); Jourard and Remy (1957).

SUMMARY AND RECOMMENDATIONS

It seems intuitively obvious that attitudes toward the body are important aspects of self-regard. Accordingly, measurement techniques in this area are needed. Although BC (the only extant instrument) has fairly good reliability and has shown theoretically predicted correlations with a number of other variables, its convergent and discriminant validity have not as yet been adequately explored. Using the presently available information as suggestive, more research in the development and modification of this instrument might well prove worthwhile.

6. Who Am I? and Twenty Sentences Test (WAY and TST)

In 1950, Bugental and Zelen suggested a method in which S was asked to give three answers to the question, Who am I? the content of the responses to be analyzed to indicate aspects of S's self-concept. Shortly thereafter, Kuhn and McPartland (1954) proposed a version of this method in which S was asked to give 20 answers to the question. The shorter version is sometimes known as WAI or WAY (Who are you?), the longer as TST (Twenty Sentences Test).

RATIONALE FOR INCLUDING WAY AND TST AMONG EVALUATED INSTRUMENTS

If my decision to describe and evaluate this instrument had depended on the amount of firm information about it, the instrument would have been excluded here, despite the appearance of about 45 publications concerning it. In 1950, Bugental and Zelen remarked, "The further question as to whether what the subject says is in turn validly representative of important areas of his personality must await investigations much more searching than the present [1950, p. 492]." Unfortunately, in 1964, Bugental found it necessary to point out that WAY was still "in the exploratory stage, and such values as it may have are still largely undemonstrated [1964, p. 643]."

Nevertheless, a discussion of this method is given here because it represents a group of viewpoints and methods contrasting with those represented by other tests I am evaluating in detail, and because a greatly elaborated rationale and proposed scoring method for TST has recently been published by Gordon (1968), which may lead to further research and development.

CONTRASTS BETWEEN WAY-TST AND OTHER SELF-CONCEPT INSTRUMENTS

The purported merits of this test may be evaluated most clearly when the method is contrasted in several respects to the other tests discussed in this volume.

Influences of Sociological Theories

While the more usual thing is for self-concept tests to be developed by psychologists, and this was true for Bugental and Zelen's (1950) version, the main interest in the TST has come from sociologists. This has important implications, since the members of the respective disciplines differ somewhat regarding the theoretical goals and kinds of variables they find useful.

The first distinction I consider here turns out to be more apparent than real, as this paragraph explains. Self-concept psychologists explicitly assume that self-concept characteristics are largely determined by social interaction and that these self-conceptions are measurable, stable psychological predispositions which will predict behavior in a variety of test and nontest situations. In contrast, some sociologists of the symbolic-interaction school have asserted that psychologists underestimate the importance of the "specific interaction context" in determining respectively relevant aspects of self-concept and their expression. Thus Kuhn (in Hickman & Kuhn, 1956) argued that self-attitudes are meaningless without explication of their particular context, the testing context in the case of the TST. It seems, though, that sociologists are beginning to realize that this supposed distinction between their work and that of psychologists is not defensible. Tucker (1966), for example, points out that the vague, brief, and unsystematic exposition of Kuhn's theory (in Hickman and Kuhn, 1956), prevented recognition of intrinsic contradictions in the theory and inconsistencies between Kuhn's theoretical assumptions and the scoring and application of TST. Thus, although Kuhn argues that self-attitudes are meaningless without explication of the particular context, he also implicitly makes the contradictory assumption that TST responses will be indicative of S's reactions in a variety of situations (Tucker, 1966). This being the case, the actually applied assumptions of the sociologists on this point are essentially similar to those of the psychologists. Although the alleged distinction gave rise to an instrument which supposedly was basically different from those used by psychologists, the TST is now seen as capable in principle of yielding information about self-conceptions which either psychologists or sociologists may find useful.

A potentially important characteristic of the TST, and one which does differentiate it from the self-concept instruments developed by psychologists, is the broadening of self-descriptions to include "categories" in addition to "attributes." Gordon (1968), for example, points out that the usual Q sorts, check lists, questionnaires, and rating scales provide no opportunity for Ss to describe themselves in "noun forms" which refer to such things of special interest to sociologists as roles, group memberships, activities, and loyalties. Instead, these instruments have thus far been restricted to attributes represented by adjectives or adverbs. Gordon's criticism is well taken in that such things as S's roles and group-membership status quite possibly have important implications for his self-concept. In this vein, Kuhn and his followers have emphasized a "locus score" which is the number of "consensual references" S makes. Although the term *consensual reference* is vaguely defined, and its use seems to vary somewhat among researchers, Kuhn described it as "one which requires no further explanation in order to be understood by the analyst—or, for that matter, by anyone [Hickman & Kuhn, 1956, p. 244]." Examples are "I am a U.S. citizen," or "I am 22 years old." By contrast, "a subconsensual statement is one that refers to norms which may vary and into which the analyst must inquire if he is to grasp the denotation of the statement [Hickman & Kuhn, 1956, p. 244]." An example would be "I am very subject to changes in mood." The locus score is alleged to indicate the degree of "social anchorage," or the importance of role status in S's self-concept (Kuhn & McPartland, 1954). Of course, categories of interest to sociologists such as consensual references, demographic variables, roles, and group memberships are not psychologically meaningful. Therefore much remains to be done to form a defensible basis for inferring psychological aspects of self-conception and self-evaluation from observations of S's locus scores or his status in the noun categories of Gordon (1968).

Unstructured Format

Obviously, the opportunity to obtain locus scores and categorical responses is only one of the possibilities which follow from the unstructured format of the TST. Most generally, this format has a priori appeal to both self-concept psychologists and sociologists because it should give S the best possible chance to express his self-concept in his own way (Hickman & Kuhn, 1956; Gordon, 1969). Although there is no demonstration that this opportunity leads, in practice, to greater accuracy of self-concept representation, there is some information as to whether Ss believe that the TST gives them the best chance to communicate their self-concepts. The results of Spitzer, Stratton, Fitzgerald, and Mach (1966) show that most Ss do not feel that they can give a more accurate account of themselves with this instrument as compared, for example, to the ACL, IAV, and Fiedler's Semantic Differential Scales. While only 17.7% of Ss reported that the TST allowed them to represent their self-concepts most accurately (because, they said, it allowed expres-

sion of personal constructs and required no forced choices and artificial distinctions), 40% thought it provided the least good opportunity for accurate self-construct representation (because, they said,
of the indefiniteness of the task, its lack of structure, and the strain
it puts on the powers of introspection).

From E's viewpoint, a further hypothetical advantage of the
unstructured format of the TST is that the order in which S produces his chosen responses may provide E some clue about their
salience to him. Gordon (1968), for instance, has proposed that
salience to S is a decreasing function of the ordinal position of the
characteristic in S's list, while psychoanalytic theory would perhaps
propose the opposite function. In any event, E has an opportunity
to explore whether ordinal position of response is a basis for inferring salience. Gordon's (1968) preliminary research on this problem
has yielded varying results, depending on the group used. It seems
questionable, therefore, whether salience can be accurately inferred
from order; and this skepticism is suggestively supported by the
findings of Brown and Ferguson (1968). They showed that, among
Ss who reported on a structured attitude scale that religious beliefs
were strong and important for them, only 57% gave any responses
on the TST which were codable as related to religion.

Self-Regard Scores from TST

The fact that demographic or sociological scoring schemes are
possible and are those most commonly used does not, of course,
prevent researchers from making other types of content analysis; and
in fact, some of this has been tried. For example, TST can be coded
for self-favorability or self-unfavorability (e.g., Spitzer, Stratton,
Fitzgerald, & Mach, 1966; Gordon, 1968; Zelen, 1954a, 1954b); and
one would expect such a coded score to correlate with total scores
from the more familiar questionnaire, rating scales, and check-list
types of measures. This was the case in the study by Spitzer et al.
(1966), where rs about .3 to .4 were obtained with self-regard scores
from IAV, ACL, and Fiedler's Semantic Differential Scales; and
in Zelen's (1954a, 1954b) study involving an r of .73 between coded
self-acceptance on WAY and "feelings of personal worth" from the
California Test of Personality. In the case of many responses, the
"favorability" score assigned would, of course, have to depend on
E's opinions, since there would be no consistent opportunity to com-

pare S's self-description with his ideal self. Thus the score would, in principle, not be consistently phenomenological. A scheme of some interest to psychologists, and somewhat similar to self-favorability coding, is scoring for negative and positive affect, which has been used occasionally (Armstrong, Hambacher, & Overley, 1962; Brodsky, 1967; Zelen, Sheehan, & Bugental, 1954).

FURTHER PROBLEMS IN SCORING

Mention of the variations in types of content analysis and the lack of a consistently phenomenological approach brings us back to the matter of inconsistencies between Kuhn's theory and his (or any E's) approach to scoring the TST. Tucker (1966) has pointed out that Kuhn's theory stresses the necessity of using S's own perspective and "plan of action" as a focus of study; but in practice, the type of content analysis Kuhn recommended or which most Es use imposes E's categories and interpretive meanings upon Ss' responses. Although Kuhn intended to make an instrument which would be more consistently phenomenological than the ones psychologists had created, he did not actually accomplish this.

Aside from that point, there are several obvious questions about any of the scoring schemes for such an open-ended instrument. One is how to handle the fact that Ss differ greatly in the number of responses they give, despite the request to give a standard number. Variations in total output must be controlled in some defensible way when groups which supposedly differ with respect to particular scores are being compared. The common use of percentages does not provide an appropriate answer when the base for the percentage values is as small as four or five total answers per S, in the case of many Ss. For example, in Mulford and Salisbury's (1964) large sample of Iowa adults, the mean total number of responses was 4.4. Related to this is the problem of coding answers of such different length that, in effect, S may have given 30 instead of 20 responses because each one is compound or complex. It is common to code each "response" (i.e., whatever fills each of the 20 blanks provided to S) into only one of the categories E is using; but it seems that this is arbitrary and may lead to serious loss of information. Gordon (1968) recommends coding each "meaning element" for category, tense, evaluation, and importance as ranked by the respondent.

STATUS OF VALIDITY RESEARCH

If one wishes to develop support for the idea that the TST has construct validity for inferring one or more aspects of self-conception, one must first work out a scoring plan which will take care of the problems stated above and then use these types of scores in a sizable number of researches which explore convergent and discriminant validity and the relationships between TST scores and other theoretically relevant variables. Unfortunately, serious difficulties with various extant scoring schemes have not been overcome. Furthermore, very few studies have used the same or approximately the same scoring scheme, precluding comparisons among studies. Exploration of convergent and discriminant validity for any extant scoring scheme is virtually untouched. Moreover, the collection of available researches is miscellaneous with respect to the variables related to TST scores, rather than being directed toward a systematic exploration of theoretical predictions. Of great importance is the fact that researches involving this instrument very frequently contain many serious methodological flaws, such as improper statistical analyses; unanalytical use of discrepancy scores or 2-part scores; application of multiple-t tests on results from the same Ss, and involving correlated dependent variables; and use of comparison groups which vary in multiple, unspecified, and uninterpretable ways.

CONCLUSIONS

Obviously, nothing can be concluded regarding the construct validity of extant scoring schemes for inferring self-conceptions from TST responses.

As I have already said, the fairly elaborate scheme proposed by Gordon (1968) may cause an increase of interest in the TST, and valuable additions to self-concept measurement may yet be forthcoming. McLaughlin (1966) even describes a computer program for content analysis of the TST. However, the values of these proposals for developing the TST into an instrument with unique and quantitatively satisfactory reliability and construct validity for measurement of important aspects of self-conception remains to be demonstrated. The empirical yield will have to be substantial to warrant the extra time and energy which must necessarily be spent on content analyses (as opposed to scoring the more usual instruments), even if computer-based schemes are perfected.

SUPPLEMENTARY REFERENCES

For the use of readers who may wish to examine at first hand those sources which formed the basis for my description and evaluation of WAY and TST, the list of references below supplements those specifically cited in the text: Back and Paramesh (1969); Bigner (1971); Brim and Wood (1956); Brodsky and Owens (1969); Bugental and Gunning (1955); Couch (1962, 1966); Dorn (1968); Erickson, Crow, Zurcher, Connett, and Stillwell (1971); Garretson (1962); Gebel (1954); Grossack (1960); Gustav (1962); Insel, Reese, and Alexander (1968); Isenberger (1959a, 1959b); Jones and Strowig (1968); Kaplan and Meyerowitz (1970); Koenig (1969); Kuhn (1960); McPartland and Cumming (1958); McPartland, Cumming, and Garretson (1961); Mason (1954a); Mason, Adams, and Blood (1966, 1968); Mason and Blood (1966); Schmitt (1966); Schneider and Zurcher (1970); Schwirian (1964); Tolor (1957); Vernon (1962).

5

Operational Definitions of the Nonphenomenal Self

A. GENERAL PROBLEMS OF CONSTRUCT VALIDITY

As we stated at the outset, theorists who accord a prominent role to constructs concerning the self are not consistently or exclusively phenomenological. Typically, however, they are very vague and incomplete as to (a) what kinds of nonphenomenological constructs shall be admitted into their theories; (b) how these constructs shall be articulated into their system of "postulates"; and (c) how these nonphenomenological determinants shall be tied to observables. Nevertheless, some effort has been expended by empirical workers in attempts to measure such processes as unconscious aspects of the self-concept and other nonphenomenological variables which they believe to be pertinent to self theories. Researchers who do this seem to base their work implicitly and/or explicitly on two lines of reasoning: (a) It is obvious that the phenomenal self, at least as measured by currently used instruments, is far from providing a sufficient basis for accurate predictions of Ss' behaviors. This lack of predictive power may be presumed to stem in part from the fact that instruments which purport to measure the phenomenal field will provide an incomplete inventory of relevant variables, no matter how highly perfected they may eventually become for the purpose of measuring the phenomenal field. (b) Because of theoretical reasons one might expect that important characteristics of S and his relationships with his environment would be unavailable to his conscious awareness. For one thing, theorists point out that much important learning occurs preverbally, and the need to maintain self-esteem will lead to repression and denial. Moreover, Roger-

248

ians would expect that self-characteristics incongruent with the conscious self-concept might be excluded from awareness even if they were favorable characteristics.

With the measurement of such nonphenomenal determinants we are again presented with the question of construct validity. The specifications presented in chapter 3 for establishing such validity could and should be applied here as well. With few exceptions, however, these specifications have been almost entirely ignored by users of nonphenomenal indices, and such measures have remained largely unvalidated.

In particular there is a unique and difficult requirement of discriminant validity for this type of measure which has received little or no recognition: If one is to say that a certain projective response or score represents an *unconscious* attitude toward the self, one must prove not only that S holds this attitude but that he is at least to some extent unaware of it. At the very least, one should check to see whether the same attitude might be consciously present, as inferred from a self-report. If the inferences from the self-report and the projective measure differ, one may then have grounds for exploring the more complex assumption that the projective measure is revealing an unconscious self-attitude. Almost universally, however, this measurement problem has been overlooked by workers interested in the measurement of the so-called unconscious self-concept.

B. Survey of Specific Measures Used in This Area

There are relatively few measures purporting to index aspects of the unconscious self-concept, and the state of measurement in this area is underdeveloped and confused. Except for the Witkin's Sophistication-of-Body-Concept score for the Draw-a-Person Test, the Barrier and Penetration scores for inferring body-image (Fisher, 1970), and the Self-Social Esteem Test of Long, Henderson, and Ziller (1970), no validational work is available regarding alleged indices of unconscious self-concept, so far as I know. Moreover, with the exception of the three scores just mentioned, attempts to measure the nonphenomenal or unconscious self-concept appear to have become much less numerous in the last decade. Perhaps this decline is due to increasing recognition of the complex burden of conceptual clarification and empirical proof which must be assumed by anyone who wishes to defend a measure as a valid indicator of any aspect of unconscious self-concept. Perhaps the decline is part of the more general recognition that thousands of researchs have yielded meager or null results regarding the construct validity of any of the major projective techniques for inferring any unconscious determinants of behavior, let alone unconscious self-concept (e.g., see reviews of the Rorschach and the TAT in Buros, 1970, and previous Mental Measurements Yearbooks referred to in that volume).

With reference to all the purported indices of nonphenomenal self-concept, it must be said that the chain of assumptions under-lying the assertion that the score is indicative of *unconscious* self-concept is incompletely specified in published sources. It is not possible to be sure, even in the case of the most explored scores mentioned above, to what extent the self-referent construct allegedly measured by the score is assumed by its researchers to be uncon-scious (as opposed to being conscious or being unrelated to the conscious-unconscious dimension).

Since little or nothing is known about most of the proposed indices, they are mentioned only briefly in this chapter. Only the Draw-a-Person Test and the Fisher and Cleveland Barrier score are given detailed evaluations here. The Self-Social Esteem Test of Long, Henderson, and Ziller (1970) is evaluated in detail in chap-ter 4, for reasons explained there.

For convenience, the proposed indices of nonphenomenal self-concept are presented under the following categories in the order listed.

1. Thematic Apperception Test (TAT) and other pictures as a basis for story telling
2. Sentence completion and story completion
3. Rorschach scores (except Barrier and Penetration)
4. Judgments of S's own unrecognized image or forms of expression
5. Behavior Interpretation Inventory
6. Draw-a-Person
7. Barrier score from Rorschach or Holtzman Inkblot Test

1. TAT and Other Pictures as a Basis for Story Telling
TAT PICTURES

The TAT has been used by several workers for the purpose of inferring something about the self-concept. The implication seems to be that it indexes the nonphenomenal rather than the phenomenal self-concept. However, as the studies described below reveal, there is no satisfactory support for the idea that any TAT "score," including the attributes which S assigns to TAT figures, reflects S's unconscious picture of himself.

Friedman (1955) used, as a measure of "projected self," a Q sort made by E on the basis of his global appraisal of S's stories about Cards 1, 3BM, 6BM, 7BM, and 14 of the TAT. Friedman correlated this sort with S's self-sort of the same statements, which was supposed to index S's phenomenal self. It was assumed that lack of correlation between phenomenal self and TAT self indicates "a large portion of personal experience out of awareness." Therefore, it was predicted that correlations between phenomenal self and projected self would be higher for normals than for neurotics and paranoid schizophrenics. He found the expected rank order among the magnitudes of the correlations, but the difference between correlations for normal and neurotic Ss was small and not significant. (Those of the paranoid schizophrenics were significantly smaller than each of the other two groups.)

The findings are puzzling, however, because the self-ideal correlations of neurotics were near zero, while the correlations between their phenomenal self and projected self were as high as those of the normals. This implies, according to the author's interpretation, that the qualities they projected into the TAT were their own negative ones of which they were already aware (as indicated through their self-ideal correlations).

Child, Frank, and Storm (1956) could find no consistent or significant pattern of relationships between TAT scores for twenty Murray variables and the respective self-ratings. They used the group procedure of McClelland et al. to obtain stories for Cards 1, 18BM, 7BM, 13B, 6 BM, 12M, 14, and 10. In thus failing to find a correspondence between the TAT and an alleged measure of the phenomenal self, they of course did not prove that the low correlations were due to the fact that the TAT was revealing the unconscious self-concepts of their Ss (nor did they make such a claim).

Davids, Henry, McArthur, and McNamara (1955) gave the TAT to 20 male college students and used the stories they gave in response to Cards 3, 6, 7, 8, and 13 of the male series. Amount of aggression and direction of aggression were scored blindly. An experienced clinical psychologist who had known the Ss for about 18 months also rated each S as to amount and direction of aggression, and Ss rated themselves on amount of aggression. The investigators obtained no correlation between self-evaluations of aggression and TAT or clinician's ratings of Ss' aggressiveness.

At first glance this might seem to imply that the TAT was measuring an unconscious self-picture of aggression which differed from S's consciously avowed aggressiveness, and in this respect their findings may be compared to those of Child, Frank, and Storm (1956) regarding aggression. However, a highly significant relationship was found between the direction of aggression, as rated from TAT, and strength of aggression, as evaluated by self: Ss showing "anger out" on the TAT evaluated themselves high on aggression, while Ss showing "anger in" on the TAT evaluated themselves low on aggression. Since aggression was evidently not clearly defined for Ss on their self-rating scale, it is quite plausible, as the authors point out, that Ss assumed aggression meant outwardly directed hostility. If Ss did so interpret the self-rating scale, the findings offer no reason to suppose that the TAT was necessarily measuring a variable of which Ss were unaware. Had they been specifically instructed to rate themselves on strength of inwardly directed aggression, their self-ratings might have correlated with degree of "anger in" inferred from the TAT. This possibility was essentially unexplored by the method used.

Lindzey and Tejessy (1956) also attempted to correlate 10 TAT signs of aggression with Ss' self-ratings of aggression and with ratings of Ss' aggression by an observer and by a diagnostic council. Although only one correlation involving observer ratings, and no correlation involving diagnostic council ratings were significant, seven correlations between TAT signs and self-ratings were significant. This clearly does not support the idea that the TAT signs were indexing unconscious self-concepts of aggression.

Murstein (1968) used TAT cards of three levels of scaled pictorial hostility; two types of administration context ("impersonal" vs. "look your best"); two levels of peer-rated hostility-friendliness; and two levels of self-rated hostility-friendliness. He reported,

> The second most important determinant after cards in the overall analyses of scoring systems, ignoring the analyses of separate [TAT hostility] stimulus levels, was self-concept. . . . Despite the fact that the author had chosen either very hostile or very friendly persons, as

judged by their social stimulus values, on only one occasion [Internal Punishment–External Punishment score] did the group variable prove significant. [P. 363]

As with the Lindzey and Tejessy (1956) study, these data clearly do not support the idea that TAT signs were indexing *unconscious* self-concepts of aggression.

Kardiner and Ovesy (cited in Karon, 1958) used the TAT to infer self-hatred in their Negro Ss. Rorschachs, psychoanalytic interviews, and TATs agreed in indicating a large amount of self-hatred in the group. It is not clear, however, that the TAT was revealing nonphenomenal self-hatred.

Mussen and Jones (1957) found that "late-maturing boys" showed more "negative self-concepts" than "early-maturing boys." Negative self-concept is inferred if the TAT hero is described in negative terms such as *imbecile, weakling,* or *fanatic.* No empirical information on relevant construct validity is offered.

Mussen and Porter (1959) employed five TAT cards and three other pictures to index "negativity of self-concept" in their study of the self-concepts of college male leaders. Each story was given one point toward the negativity-of-self-concept score if the hero was pictured as a failure, disgusted, ashamed, angry with himself, or was described in unflattering terms. Each story was also given one point toward a feelings-of-adequacy score if the hero was described as self-confident, self-assured, satisfied with the way things are going, or capable of solving his own problems. (*N* Affiliation, *n* Achievement, *n* Aggression were also scored.) No provision was made for the possible influence of total verbal output upon the opportunity to accumulate points on any or all of these scales. Two judges reached 87% agreement on all scales combined, on 120 stories. Construct validity for inferring "basic self-concepts" was only assumed.

In the study of nondirective therapy reported in Rogers and Dymond (1954), 23 clients took the TAT three times: before therapy, after therapy, and at a follow-up point. Sixteen control Ss took the test at comparable points in time. By means of a specially prepared set of criteria, the TATs were scored on 23 scales, including self-concept, ideal self, and self and others (Grummon & John, 1954). Each scale was rated by at least five judges, and interjudge agreement was significant at the .01 level. Two judges rerated 23 protocols after 6 months to 1 year, and a *rho* for each scale was computed for each judge. An average *rho* of .77 was obtained for the first 18 scales (which included the 3 self scales). Apparently the TAT self scales were intended to tap the nonphenomenal self-concept, since they were devised by a psychoanalytically oriented researcher and they were obtained from a projective test. If correlations had been presented between the TAT self scales and self-ideal *r*s which were obtained from these *S*s, some light would have been thrown on the discriminant validity of the TAT scales as indicators of the nonphenomenal self. However, no such correlations are reported.

PICTURES OTHER THAN TAT

In a study using pictures not from the TAT, Alexander (1951) hypothesized that certain "structural characteristics of the self" (devaluation of self, dependency, anxiety, conflict) would prevent teachers from showing affection for children. Stories told by 25 teachers in response to child and child-adult pictures were coded on the four characteristics, and teachers were then classified as to the amount of affection they would show to children. Staff observers rated the actual behavior of each teacher on a 3-point scale of affection and warmth. The operations for arriving at both sets of ratings are incompletely specified, and no reliability or validity information is available in the 1951 reference (although some additional facts about the instrument are given in Alexander, 1950). The correspondence between the two sets of data is reported to exceed the .01 level, but the method of determining chance expectancy is not clearly specified and seems possibly inappropriate. Consequently there is doubt whether even R-R conclusions can be reached.

Mason (1954b), in a study of self-attitudes in aged persons, used the fifteen Caldwell Pictures. *S* told a story to each picture, and the stories were judged for "feeling tone" of the identification figure. In addition, *S* made a forced sort of the pictures themselves, according to the degree to which they were (a) "like me," and (b) "like an ideal person." No information on reliability or validity is given. In this study, Mason applied a number of other self-concept measures to the same *S*s. However, intercorrelations among the measures, which might have thrown some light on convergent and discriminant construct validity, are not presented.

SUMMARY REGARDING STORIES TOLD ABOUT TAT
AND OTHER PICTURES

Nine studies used Ss' stories which were given in response to
varying parts of the TAT, and two other studies employed Ss'
stories to non-TAT pictures to index some aspect of the unconscious self-concept. Each author wished to infer different things
about the unconscious self-concept, and these varied inferences
included: (a) aggression or self-hatred; (b) negativity of self-attitudes, devaluation of self, and feelings of adequacy; (c) overall self-
concept and overall ideal self.

Most or all of the scoring schemes were apparently devised for
the particular study in which they were used. Questions concerning
the construct validity of any of these scores for indexing the nonphenomenal self-concept remain unanswered. In only four researches
were TAT scores correlated with phenomenal self-concept measures; and in three of these the results suggest significant congruence
between the phenomenal and the supposedly nonphenomenal measures. This raises the question whether TAT scores have discriminant validity for indexing the nonphenomenal self-concept.

Since the studies are so disparate with regard to hypotheses,
types of Ss, pictures, and scoring schemes, no synthesized conclusions can be drawn.

2. Sentence-Completion and Story-Completion Techniques

Smith and Lebo (1956) had prepubescent and postpubescent
boys complete, in the third person, two stories involving, respectively, heterosexual development and emancipation from parents.
Six psychologists reached 87% agreement in assigning the heterosexual stories, and 75% agreement in assigning the emancipation
stories to one of five categories along a scale of maturity. Although
the Es presumed that the stories revealed self-attitudes of their
Ss without Ss' being "aware of the purpose of the task," no evidence
of such construct validity is presented. These Es applied to the
same Ss (a) a figure-drawing test which also purported to measure
the nonphenomenal self-concept, and (b) a Vineland Maturity
Scale purporting to measure the phenomenal self-concept. No intercorrelations among the measures are given to throw light on convergent or discriminant validity of the various measures. The
authors hypothesized that physiological development (as indexed

through pubic hair ratings) would be associated with self-concept differences. None of the nonphenomenal measures was significantly related to pubic hair ratings, however, when CA, with all that it implies psychologically, was held constant. The only positive findings, with CA controlled, involved the Vineland scale.

Walsh (1956) used the Driscoll Play Kit to have 40 Ss make up 10 stories from incomplete stems. Each verbatim story was judged globally on a 5-point scale in each of five categories, detailed directions for which are published. Exact scale agreement among three judges across all categories ranged from 68% to 93% on 40 randomly selected stories. S's self-concept was inferred from the behavior and attitudes he attributed to the boy doll. Twenty bright academic underachievers showed more "inadequate and crippling" self-concepts than did 20 matched, bright, normal achievers. This finding is interpreted in two ways: (a) as support for the validity of the instrument for inferring the self-concept; (b) as confirmation of the author's hypothesis in regard to the relationship between self-concept and underachievement.

Although this is a projective test, there is no demonstration of its discriminant validity in contrast to what would have been obtained by questioning the boys about their phenomenal self-concepts. Also, the fact that the E who administered the play test scored all the stories raises some question of contamination of findings. It seems possible that she might have remembered the source of some of the stories, even though identifying data had been removed from the protocols before scoring was begun.

3. Rorschach Scores (Other Than Barrier and Penetration)

The ways in which the Rorschach test has been used to infer unconscious self-attitudes have been very vaguely specified by most authors who employed this instrument, and the pattern of results from the studies in which it has been used is not conclusive.

Several investigators (e.g., Diller & Riklan, 1957; Linton & Graham, 1959; Sarbin & Farberow, 1952) have assumed that some aspect of M may be used to infer something about Ss' self-concepts.

Diller and Riklan (1957) assumed that high M on the Rorschach represented self-revealing tendencies. Apparently on the premise that what one would usually reveal or conceal are negative aspects of the self-concept, they predicted that number of M would correlate with number of negative self-statements on the Robinson-Freeman Self-Continuity Test. Although their hypothesis was supported, it seems to me that the possibilities of artifact were not adequately controlled. That is, since number of M correlated with total number of self-statements on the Robinson-Freeman test, no clear interpretation of the relation between number of M and negativity of conscious self-concept seems possible. The authors have considered the problem of total R on each instrument, but their means of ruling it out as the explanation of their correlation seems to me to be inadequate. Linton and Graham (1959) assumed that self-assertive or passive M responses to the Rorschach blots may be used to infer self-assertive or passive unconscious self-concept. High Hd on the Rorschach was alleged to indicate self-criticality and preoccupation with self and body. Sarbin and Farberow (1952) inferred the "organization of self percepts" from "structural features of the [Rorschach] protocols," for example, M, FM, C. It is not clear whether the phenomenal or nonphenomenal self is allegedly measured.

Two investigations (Haimowitz & Haimowitz, 1952; and Cohen, 1954) entailed using Rorschach characteristics to infer attitudes toward self, but the Rorschach bases for such inferences were not specified.

Murstein (1956) applied two hostility-scoring schemes to the Rorschach protocols of four groups of Ss selected so that their self-concept ratings and peer ratings showed the following self-peer combinations: (1) friendly-friendly; (2) hostile-friendly; (3) hostile-hostile; and (4) friendly-hostile. Group 3 (the hostile-hostile group) obtained higher Rorschach hostility scores than any of the other groups, which did not differ from one another. This finding gives no support to the contention that Rorschach hostility scores index Ss' hostility of which they are *unconscious*. Neither do the results clearly support the idea that the Rorschach scores are indicative of S's conscious self-concept of hostility, since the Rorschach hostility scores of Groups 1 and 4 (conceiving of themselves as friendly persons) did not differ from those of Group 2 (one of the groups of Ss who conceived of themselves as hostile persons).

4. Judgments of Own Unrecognized Image or Forms of Expression

Wolff (1943) suggested that Ss' unconscious self-esteem might be revealed in the evaluations they make of their own unrecognized profiles, photographs of hands unrecognized as their own, or unrecognized forms of their own expression, such as handwriting in mirror image or recorded voice. It may seem intuitively plausible to hypothesize that such evaluations of one's own physical characteristics or expressive behaviors might be more likely to represent "unconscious self-evaluation" than would such indicators as human figure drawings, stories told about hero figures in TAT cards, or responses to inkblots. However, the necessarily complex psychological and methodological assumptions behind the kinds of procedures suggested by Wolff have never been explicitly specified.

A small group of studies has concerned itself with this sort of approach. For several reasons, however, no conclusions can be drawn from these researches: no one technique has been used in more than a few studies; the very difficult problem of operationalizing degrees of awareness in this type of experiment has not been resolved; problems of convergent and discriminant validity of the purported measures for indexing *unconscious* self-evaluation have not been handled; and methodological flaws characterize many of the studies. It appears that this general line of approach has been used very infrequently in the last decade, possibly because researchers have come to recognize the many complexities and pitfalls in it. I cite only briefly the studies which I have used as a basis for my evaluation given above.

It appears that the use of the tachistoscope to present S with his own photograph or profile has been the most commonly used technique. The results of these tachistoscopic studies may not be synthesized because different tachistoscopic techniques and different types of materials were apparently used in each, except the two studies by A. Rogers and associates; and different variables were examined in relation to the alleged unconscious self-evaluations. Fisher and Mirin (1966) used shadow profiles and full-face pictures of Ss; Rogers and Walsh (1959) and Rogers and Paul (1959) presented Ss with four faces simultaneously, their own photographs supposedly being disguised by superimposing them on a neutral line-drawing of a face; Schlicht (1967) showed each S two separate photographs, one of which was his own.

Other methods of presenting Ss with their own supposedly unrecognized images include the presentation of two pictures in a stereoscope, S's own image being presented to the nondominant eye to increase nonrecognition of self (Beloff & Beloff, 1959); the presentation of nude photographs in which the head was blacked out with India ink (Arnhoff & Damianopolous, 1962); and the presentation of a full-length silhouette (Korner, Allison, Donoviel, & Boswell, 1963). In Fisher's (1962) study, Ss were asked to describe their appearances after briefly viewing their masked faces in a mirror. Although Ss were of course aware that they had been looking at themselves, Fisher assumed that their self-descriptions would be "projective."

Epstein (1955) inferred unconscious self-attitudes from three measures: (a) speed of recognition of own name in a tachistoscope; (b) liking for one's own unrecognized handwriting presented in a mirror upside down or right side up; (c) liking for one's own tape-recorded voice played backwards. Rothstein and Epstein (1963) presented Ss' own voices to them with varying degrees of distortion and played in both forward and backward directions. Diller (1954) presented S's own handwriting in a mirror, to be evaluated by S among three other samples. These evaluations supposedly indicated S's "covert," though not necessarily "unconscious," self-attitudes.

(Some of the pre-1960 studies cited above are more fully described and criticized in Wylie, 1961.)

5. Behavior Interpretation Inventory

Moeller and Applezweig (1957a, 1957b) developed a forced-choice Behavior Interpretation Inventory which was intended to measure motivations for Escape, Avoidance, Social Approval, and Self-Approval. The latter scale was also called "self-realization" or "consistency with the self picture." Forty-nine stems describe behavior modes from Murray, and each of the four possible completions for each stem ostensibly represents one of the four motives. Thus the scale necessarily suffers from the limitations of forced-choice instruments, discussed in chapter 3. The items were written by test constructors on a rational basis. Split-half and test-retest coefficients for each motive score on several samples are given in the manual (Moeller & Applezweig, 1957b). In a personal communication, Applezweig said that the profile of scores is intended to reflect the unconscious self-image. Zero correlations were obtained between BII scores and self-ratings of each of the four motives, which would be congruent with the hypothesis that the BII was measuring the nonphenomenal self-referent dimensions respectively parallel to the phenomenal ones revealed in the self-ratings. However, such null relationships could be interpreted in numerous other ways as well; and no other information seems to be available to support the contention that this inventory reveals the unconscious self-image.

6. Draw-a-Person (DAP)

Over a period of several decades, numerous clinicians and researchers have operated on implicit or explicit assumptions that characteristics of a human-figure drawing can be used to make valid inferences about aspects of the drawer's self-concept (Machover, 1949; Roback, 1968; Swensen, 1957, 1968). Unfortunately, despite the long time and considerable amount of effort involved, little or nothing can be said in scientific support of the defensibility of such assumptions. One reason for this disappointing state of affairs lies in the variation and nebulousness of the assumptions which have been stated or implied by various workers, as I now illustrate.

1. In one group of researches, it seems that the drawing is assumed to represent (among other things) some fairly literal or *perceptual-cognitive aspect of the drawer's body image.* Thus, Centers and Centers (1963), Schmidt and McGowan (1959), Silverstein and Robinson (1956), Wachs and Zaks (1960), and Wysocki and Whitney (1965) expected the figure drawings of physically disabled Ss to differ from those made by normal controls. Jernigan (1970) expected judges to be able to infer from Ss' drawings whether Ss were black or white. Maloney and Payne (1969) expected Goodenough-Harris scores for DAP to reflect changes in body image resulting from sensory-motor training; and they also expected these DAP scores to correlate with an Eye, Hand, and Ear Test and a Personal Orientation Test, the latter involving location of parts on one's own body corresponding to body parts indicated on pictures. Apfeldorf and Smith (1966) expected Ss' drawings to correspond in unspecified ways to Ss' photographs. Bailey, Shinedling, and Payne (1970) expected obese Ss to draw larger figures than would normal Ss; while Kotkov and Goodman (1953) assumed that, "if there is any real meaning to the concept of body image," drawings of obese women would differ "in some way" from those of control Ss of ideal weight. Silverstein and Robinson (1961) expected actual body measurements to correspond to the measured size of Ss' drawings.

Craddick (1963) expected S's size and sex to correspond to the size and sex of the figure drawn. McHugh (1965) expected Ss to conceive of their drawn figures as being the same ages as themselves. Witkin, Dyk, Faterson, Goodenough, and Karp (1962) based much of their research on the assumption that their Sophistication-of-Body-Concept score indicated "the extent to which the body is experienced as having definite limits or 'boundaries' and the 'parts' within those boundaries are experienced as discrete yet joined into a definite structure [p. 116]."

2. A second group of studies involves another class of assumptions, namely, that aspects of S's drawing indicate his *emotional-evaluative reactions to his body*. For example, Hunt and Feldman (1960) predicted that total body-dissatisfaction scores from a modification of the Jourard and Secord (1954) Body Cathexis Scale should correlate with "signs-of-disturbance" scores from 25 body parts on figure drawings. Fisher (1960) used 14 of Machover's signs of "lack of body confidence" to provide a Body Disturbance score, supposedly indicative of "body-image maturity." Marais and Struempfer (1965) expected the Fisher Body Disturbance score to be correlated with Rorschach Barrier and Penetration scores, two other purported measures of cognitive-emotional reactions to the body (see pp. 265–286 for a full discussion of the Barrier score). As explained above, Witkin et al. (1962, p. 116) seem at one point to wish to infer a cognitive body-articulation construct from their Sophistication score; but at another point, they assume that this same score (when high) may also reveal "a high level of interest in and respect for the body," or (when extremely high) "a high degree of narcissistic self-absorption." Low Sophistication scores may "reflect too little interest in and respect for the body [Witkin et al., 1962, p. 129]." Sugerman and Haronian (1964) and Blank, Sugerman, and Roosa (1968) also used the Sophistication score with the assumption that it indicated degrees of esteem for the body, while Young (1959) used a modification of the Witkin scoring to infer S's lack of trust in his own feelings and body experiences. Craddick and Leipold (1968) expected male alcoholics to draw male figures smaller than female figures "since more anxiety is attached to their own body image [p. 486]." Ludwig (1969) assumed that "physical self-esteem," whether it be a stable self-concept characteristic inferred from self-rating scales or a transient state manipulated by criticizing Ss' physical fitness, would be associated with the height

and athletic appearance of the figures Ss draw. Gottesfeld (1962) expected to find poor "body cathexis" manifested in the drawings of superobese patients.

3. In a third group of researches, it has been assumed that the drawn figure represents *aspects of S's self-concept or self-evaluation other than cognitions or feelings about his body per se.* Thus, Bodwin and Bruck (1960), and Bruck and Bodwin (1962) assumed that their scoring scheme for the DAP test was "a valid measure of self-concept defined as consisting of . . . (a) self-confidence, (b) freedom to express appropriate feelings, (c) liking for one's self, (d) satisfaction with one's attainments, and (e) feeling of personal appreciation of others [p. 427]." (Daniels and Stewart, 1970, also used the Bodwin and Bruck scoring scheme.) Kamano (1960) assumed that Ss' drawings represented their self-conceptions in terms of 15 semantic-differential scales representing three factors of Osgood, Suci, and Tannenbaum (1957). Tolor and Colbert (1961) assumed that "body image disturbance indicators" actually reflected "one aspect of ego strength." Korner, Allison, Donoviel, and Boswell (1963) assumed that a clinical psychologist's ratings of the degree of "adjustment" manifested in Ss' figure drawings would provide a nonverbal measure of self-acceptance. Bennett (1964b) predicted that the size of the figure drawn by children might indicate their degree of self-regard as inferred from a score from a specially devised Q sort. In a later publication, Bennett (1966) predicted that specified detailed measurements of the drawn figures might indicate self-regard inferred from her Q sort. Gray and Pepitone (1964) assumed that size of figure and several other DAP scores would reflect degree of self-esteem induced by false feedback given to male undergraduates from personality tests. Armstrong and Hauck (1961) assumed that drawing the opposite-sex figure first indicates a problem in sexual identification; while Fisher (1959d) assumed that differences in the size of the two sides of the figure drawn were indicative of differential size attributions Ss made to the sides of their own bodies which might indicate S's failure to discriminate appropriately between masculine and feminine roles.

One reason many of these widely varying assumptions can be called nebulous is that they typically are not clear as to whether the body-image or self-concept aspects to which they refer are supposedly conscious or unconscious. Of course an investigator may not wish to refer his construct to this dimension at all; but if so, he should explicitly say so. The fact that the DAP is often classed as a projective test obliquely implies that its scores are properly considered under the heading of measures of unconscious self-concept. However, Witkin et al. (1962, p. 117) seem to be saying that both conscious and unconscious body concepts are tapped by their Sophistication score. Moreover, the occasional use of phenomenological self-concept measures as alleged alternate indicators of E's construct obliquely suggests that these Es assume their DAP scores also indicate conscious aspects of body-concept or self-concept (e.g., Hunt & Feldman, 1960; Bennett, 1964b, 1966). In any event, if a measure is purported to be an index of a conscious or unconscious concept, the investigator must assume the burden of exploring its discriminant validity with respect to this dimension.

Obviously a wide range of assumptions is represented in the studies listed in the three groups above. However, if any one of the proposed scoring schemes and corresponding assumptions had been subjected to an appropriate *series* of studies, we might be able to say something about the reliability and the construct validity of that particular scoring scheme. Unfortunately, work has been widely and thinly scattered across assumptions and scoring schemes, as is evident when one realizes that the studies I mentioned represent a substantial proportion of those which could be appropriately cited. Some of these studies suffered from shortcomings of design, and a good many found few or no significant findings in support of their hypotheses, let alone any cross-validated findings.

There is one score mentioned above, Witkin's Sophistication-of-Body-Concept, which has been used in a series of studies. Therefore I consider it in a bit more detail here. As I indicated earlier, the literary definitions which served as a rationale for developing and interpreting this score seem somewhat vague, and they are probably contradictory inasmuch as they refer to both "articulation of body concept" and to "body esteem." In any event, it is obvious in principle that a single score cannot simultaneously or alternately be used to index two conceptually different constructs.

The interjudge reliability of the Sophistication score is high (e.g., .83 and .92 for 16 college male Ss; .84 for 30 boys reported in Witkin et al., 1962; .91 for 104 emotionally disturbed children studied by Fuller and Lunney, 1965). Eleven test-retest reliability coefficients reported in Faterson and Witkin (1970) run from .47 to .86 over intervals of 3 to 7 years.

No *convergent validity* studies relevant to the body-articulation interpretation of the score are available. Perhaps correlations with Fisher and Cleveland's (1958a) Barrier score might be appropriate; but none has been published, so far as I know. Concerning the body-esteem interpretation of the Sophistication score, Hunt and Feldman's (1960) correlations with Jourard's Body Cathexis scores may be relevant to convergent validity. In only one of four groups did the r reach the .05 level of significance.

In the light of the rs between Sophistication-of-Body-Concept scores and intelligence test scores, the *discriminant validity* of the Sophistication score as an indicant of either body articulation or body esteem must be seriously questioned. For example, Witkin et al. (1962) report that $r = .74$ with Goodenough Draw-a-Man intelligence scores; $r = .79$ with WISC "intellectual index scores," and $r = .55$ with WISC total IQ. Moreover, Solar, Bruehl, and Kovacs (1970) found a Pearson r of .76 between Sophistication scores and "artistic ability ratings" assigned by artist judges to Ss' drawings. Thus these results, too, clearly question the discriminant construct validity of the Sophistication score for inferring either body articulation or body esteem.

Regarding the body-articulation interpretation of the Sophistication scores, the *studies based on assumed validity* mostly show that there are substantial or at least significant rs between Sophistication scores and "perceptual index scores" from the rod-and-frame, body-adjustment, and/or embedded-figures tests (Dreyer, Hulac, & Rigler, 1971; Witkin et al., 1962; Silberman, 1961, cited in Witkin et al., 1962; Sugerman & Cancro, 1964). Reilly and Sugerman (1967) assumed that Sophistication scores should correlate with a verbal test purporting to measure cognitive complexity, Schroder and Streufert's Sentence Completion Test; but the obtained association was significant only on a one-tailed test. (In a study which did not make a theoretically based prediction, Fuller and Lunney, 1965, obtained low positive rs between Sophistication scores and scores from the Minnesota Percepto-Diagnostic Test, which is scored in terms of the degree to which Ss' drawn copies of geometrical figures are rotated away from their presented vertical or horizontal axes.) Contrary to expectations, Reitman and Cleveland (1964) found no differences in Sophistication score between schizophrenic and normal groups, and no changes as a function of sensory deprivation. Burton and Sjoberg (1964) also did not find a significant difference

in mean Sophistication score between schizophrenic and normal
Ss. Contrary to his hypothesis, Cancro (1971) found no relationship
between Sophistication scores and a measure of process-reactive
schizophrenia.

Obliquely relevant to the body-esteem interpretation of the Sophistication score are Sugerman and Haronian's (1964) findings of
r = .29 with mesomorphy and r = −.24 with endomorphy among
college males. Failing to support their theory and their body-
esteem interpretation of the Sophistication score, Blank, Sugerman,
and Roosa (1968) found no differences in Sophistication scores
between nudists and swim-club members.

One must conclude that the Witkin Sophistication-of-Body-
Concept score, though reliable, has no demonstrated convergent
validity for inferring either body articulation or body esteem; and
it apparently lacks discriminant validity for measuring either of
these concepts as opposed to measuring intellectual functioning of
the type measured by the Wechsler or Goodenough scales.

In summary, my review of all the above studies concerning the
use of figure drawings to infer aspects of body concept or self-
concept has led me to consider Swensen's (1968) and Roback's
(1968) conclusions to be too optimistic. For example, Swensen
(1968) says, "In any case, the results of the last 10 years' research
provides [sic] more evidence in support of the body image hypothesis than the previous 10 years had produced [p. 25]." Roback
(1968) states, "There appears to be some support for Machover's
[body-image and self-image] hypotheses [p. 3]."

I conclude that there is no scientific justification as yet for
asserting that any score based on DAP has construct validity
for making inferences regarding S's body concept or self-concept,
whether these concepts are assumed by E to be conscious, unconscious, or not necessarily related to the conscious-unconscious
dimension.

7. Barrier Scores

By far the most widely used body-image index is Fisher and
Cleveland's (1958a) Barrier score based on Rorschach or Holtzman
inkblots (Holtzman, Thorpe, Swartz, & Herron, 1961). Research
involving this score has been reported in four books (Fisher &
Cleveland, 1958a; Fisher & Cleveland, 1968; Fisher, 1970; Holtzman
et al., 1961), in about 100 published articles since 1955, and in

many unpublished studies which are briefly reported in one or more of the books. Fisher and Cleveland also use a Penetration score of body image, but since it has been involved in fewer researches and is subject to many of the same evaluative comments as the Barrier score, I do not consider it further in this book.

Briefly to anticipate the conclusions for which I argue below, the construct validity of the Barrier score remains assumed rather than adequately supported, despite the large volume of published and unpublished research which presents associations between the Barrier score and a wide range of other variables. My analysis of the status of the Barrier score applies the criteria for evaluating self-referent measures presented in chapter 3.

DEFINITION OF THE CONSTRUCTS

The conceptual or literary definitions of the construct(s) purportedly indexed by the Barrier score are complex, not rigorously stated, and apparently different from one statement to another. Thus, in 1958 Fisher and Cleveland assumed that persons differ "in the degree to which they experience their body boundaries as definite and firm versus inadequate and vague [Fisher & Cleveland, 1958a, p. 56]." In 1968, Fisher and Cleveland said that research has given "greater substance to the *equation* of the Barrier image with a specific dimension of body experience based upon the differential sensory vividness of boundary and nonboundary body sectors [Fisher & Cleveland, 1968, p. 370, emphasis added]." On the other hand, at the end of their first book, quoted above, they introduced quite a different assertion as to the probable type of construct indexed by their Barrier score. Thus:

> We have almost taken the "body" out of "body image" by postulating that the body-image boundary does not really mirror the actual properties of the body surface, but that it is rather a representation of attitudes and expectancy systems which have been projected onto the body periphery. . . . [Although] some of our best predictive studies (e.g., psychosomatic and physiological) grew out of our assumption that the Barrier score could be conceptualized as indicating the degree to which the individual assigned certain attributes to his body, . . . we regard the Barrier score as having little to do with the actual physical appearance of the individual's body; [but] . . . as a measure of important properties associated with the body as a social object, . . . this position of the body, intermediate between "outside" and "inside," . . .

makes it a unique projection screen for patterns of attitudes. . . . We have concluded that the body image is formed of these projected attitudes. [Fisher & Cleveland, 1958a, p. 367]

In their interpretations of most of the Barrier research up through 1970, this second sort of inference is involved alternately or simultaneously with the first-mentioned one. As illustrated above, then, they have not followed the recommendations of Fiske (1966) to formulate one's construct as clearly and precisely as possible before devising a purported measure of it. Accordingly, extremely difficult and unresolved problems of construct validation ensue from their diffuse and shifting definitions.

Their statements that body image involves "sensory vividness" might seem to imply that a conscious body-image dimension is the conceptual referent for Barrier scores. That this is evidently *not* their idea is shown by their statement (Fisher & Cleveland, 1958a), "It was immediately apparent that the individual had little conscious information about his attitudes toward his body boundaries and that such attitudes could only with difficulty be deduced from information obtained from a depth interview [p. 57]." That Fisher continued to view the Barrier index as *not* primarily a measure of conscious experience is indicated by his statement (Fisher, 1970), "Various body image measures . . . have been devised to tap in at different levels of awareness. . . . The Barrier index . . . [depends] upon response samples which are much less susceptible to conscious control and censorship. It would be quite surprising if body image measures based on such differing response samples were consistently correlated [p. 317]." Relevant to this issue, Fisher and Cleveland are pleased to report null associations between conscious self-concept measures and Barrier scores; and they expect no relationships between actual body characteristics and Barrier scores. It is because of these statements that I chose to consider the Barrier score among the measures of the *unconscious* self-concept. It must be noted, then, that all the problems of validating an *unconscious* self-concept measure must be faced with respect to this score, at least to the extent that the authors assume that unconscious dimensions are indexed by it.

CHACTERISTICS OF THE BARRIER SCORE

The Barrier score is based on content involving distinctive surface, enclosed openings, or containerlike properties. (The original hunch that such Rorschach content validly indexed the firmness of Ss' body-image boundaries came from inspection of the Rorschach protocols of arthritic patients who showed muscle stiffness. Fisher and Cleveland, 1958a, reasoned that both muscle stiffness and Rorschach boundaries were defenses against feelings with catastrophic implications.) A score of 1 is given to any response where Barrier content is present, 0 if Barrier is absent.

Presently there are two sources of Barrier scores: responses to Rorschach blots and responses to Holtzman blots (Holtzman et al., 1961). The scoring directions given in Fisher and Cleveland (1958a) were closely followed by Holtzman et al. (1961), where detailed examples are given. Holtzman et al. (1961) note that, at several points, the Fisher-Cleveland system seems "unduly arbitrary," especially with respect to "what aspects of a response to include as valid signs of the basic concept implied by Barrier [p. 74]." Barrier, they note, is a highly complex variable. Since correlations have evidently not been published between Rorschach and Holtzman Barrier scores obtained from the same Ss, a problem is posed in comparing and synthesizing studies involving this score.

Psychometric Properties

Holtzman et al. (1961) present extensive data regarding the properties of the Holtzman Barrier score, based on large samples varying in age, sex, health status, and educational status. Gorham, Moseley, and Holtzman (1968) present norms for computer-scored Holtzman Inkblot variables for over 5,000 Ss varying in age, educational status, health status, and nationality status. Fisher and Cleveland's (1958a) normative information on the Rorschach Barrier score is based mostly on 200 adult cases, the characteristics of this group being insufficiently specified. (Measures of central tendency and variability are given for many of the groups used in published researches involving the Rorschach score; but this information does not constitute a systematic presentation of normative data regarding the Rorschach Barrier score.)

Since Barrier scores are correlated .41 to .66 with response totals (Fisher & Cleveland, 1958a), some means of controlling for R total must be used. Fisher and Cleveland propose and alternately use one of three methods: ask S to give a fixed number of responses, reduce available records to a set number of responses, or show that the

groups to be compared in a particular study do not differ significantly regarding the total number of responses. The instrument
developed by Holtzman et al. (1961) automatically uses the first of
these methods, inasmuch as only one response per blot is obtained
in the Holtzman test. Since it remains to be directly demonstrated
that these methods of controlling R total are equivalent, a problem
in comparing and synthesizing research results is created when the
studies involve different ways of controlling response totals. Moreover, controlling the number of responses does not control response
length (RL); and RL has been shown to have highly significant
positive relationships with several Holtzman Inkblot scores, including the Barrier score (Megargee, 1966). As Megargee (1966) pointed
out, RL may be an important variable in the obtained relationship
between inkblot scores and other personality variables. Accordingly,
RL, too, probably needs to be controlled in studies involving the
Barrier score.

With few exceptions, distributions of Barrier scores "tend to be
normal in character" (Fisher & Cleveland, 1958a, p. 70) or "only
slightly skewed" (Holtzman et al., 1961).

RELIABILITY

Interscorer Reliability

Fisher and Cleveland (1958a) found interscorer reliability of
Rorschach Barrier scores to be "rather high when the scorers are
trained," namely, $rho = .82$ between the authors' scoring of 20
records and .97 on a second set of 20 records. Ramer (1963), Eigenbrode and Shipman (1960), and Daston and McConnell (1962) all
report interscorer rs between .80 and .90. Using Holtzman Barrier
scores, Allardice and Dole (1966) and Megargee (1965) obtained rs
in the high .80s. Fisher (1970, p. 158) tabulated interscorer reliability values from six unpublished sources, all rs being .85 or
higher.

Split-Half Reliabilities

There are evidently no published split-half reliabilities for Rorschach barrier scores, but Holtzman et al. (1961) give such values
for Holtzman Barrier scores for 15 groups varying widely in age,
health status, and educational status. They say, "Although indi-

cating satisfactory precision of measurement for some purposes, the reliability estimates are relatively low, ranging from .47 to .70 in the normal groups [p. 124]."

Test-Retest Reliabilities

Regarding the test-retest reliabilities of the Rorschach Barrier scores, Daston and McConnell (1962) report Pearson r values of about .9 for each of two raters' scorings of 20 records from hospitalized males, none of whom had a psychiatric disorder. The test-retest interval was 2 months. Fisher (1970) reports an r of .65 for a 5-day test-retest of 50 schizophrenic women, and an unpublished "pre- and post-surgery" r of .78 on 11 kidney transplant patients.

Since the Holtzman blots are divided into two forms, the test-retest correlations reported in Holtzman et al. (1961) are actually alternate-form reliabilities. Intraclass correlation values for four samples were: college Ss, 1-week interval, .38; college Ss, 1-year interval, .40; eleventh graders, 3-month interval, .51; elementary-school children, 1-year interval, .42. All these values are significant well beyond the .01 level. As Holtzman et al. (1961) point out, such intraclass correlations may be considered to be the lower bounds for intrasubject stability. Even so, they are not very encouraging regarding the test-retest reliability of the Barrier score. Fisher, however, reaches a different conclusion, namely, "Most of those [reliability coefficients] in the test-retest category . . . are of acceptable magnitude [Fisher, 1970, p. 161]." In support of this conclusion, he cites not only the Rorschach Barrier test-retest values mentioned above, but also three studies involving Holtzman blots: Fisher and Renik (1966) found a 15-minute test-retest r for 20 women equals .85, and for 20 men equals .86. Lerner, using odd versus even items from Holtzman Form A, and a 3-day test-retest interval, obtained $r = .87$ for 20 sleep-deprived Ss, and $r = .83$ for 20 placebo Ss.

It is impossible to know why such a range of test-retest values has been obtained for the Holtzman Barrier scores. In view of the unexplainable variety of values, the stability of the Barrier score cannot be assumed, but should be determined when appropriate to the problem, for groups of Ss used in each study.

If Rorschach and Holtzman Barrier scores are to be interpreted as being essentially equivalent, correlations between them are needed to support such an assumption. Although Holtzman et al.

(1961) did correlate eight types of scores obtained from both Rorschach and Holtzman blots, Barrier was not one of these; and to my knowledge, no correlations between Rorschach Barrier and Holtzman Barrier scores have been published. Accordingly, studies involving different Barrier scores should not be compared and synthesized without explicitly stated reservations regarding this difference.

VALIDITY

A priori arguments for the construct validity of the Barrier score are based on an analogy between the boundedness of S's inkblot percept (whether or not the percept involves a body) and the boundedness of S's body image. However, as I said earlier, S's inferred "body boundaries" are usually regarded by Fisher and Cleveland as being of a symbolic rather than literal nature. When one takes this view, the appropriateness of the analogy seems highly questionable. Certainly, what would constitute relevant construct-validity findings concerning the Barrier score is far from being clearly implied by the original analogy.

It seems apparent from examining their publications concerning the Barrier score that Fisher and Cleveland did not view their validational task as including the systematic exploration of the convergent and discriminant construct validity of that score. Rather, they assumed the construct validity of the Barrier score and proceeded directly to perform studies based on theoretical premises which were tested with the use of the assumedly valid Barrier score as one measure. As Cronbach and Meehl (1955) point out, this type of study, while of some value in exploring the construct validity of a score, is insufficient and necessarily ambiguous. I consider relevant research of this kind at the end of this section, but first I present what I have been able to glean about convergent and discriminant validity of the Barrier score.

Convergent Validity

Fisher and Cleveland (1958a) report two studies of possible relevance to the convergent validity of the Barrier score as an indicant of S's unconscious perception of his body boundedness. In one study, there was some tendency for high Barrier scores to be associated with "firm boundary dreams," when the latter were desig-

nated according to clinicians' ratings of intactness of physical boundaries in the dream and/or boundedness of "any behavior sequence
in the dream." In the other study, male Ss who were high Barrier
scorers drew more elaborate facades for houses. (Corresponding
results with female Ss were not significant.) Since neither the dream
nor the drawing index necessarily purports to measure the same
construct as the Barrier score allegedly measures, it is questionable
whether these studies should be considered to be relevant to the
convergent validity of the Barrier score. In any event, there is no
evidence for or against the construct validity of either the dream or
drawing index, making Barrier associations with either not clearly
interpretable. All in all, it seems that there are no direct studies
of convergent validity of the Barrier score as an index of body
image in any of the senses Fisher and Cleveland have in mind as
referents for their Barrier score. This is so because apparently there
are no extant instruments which purport to measure exactly the
same body-image construct(s) which Fisher and Cleveland wish to
measure with the Barrier score.

Discriminant Validity

Campbell and Fiske (1959) have suggested that any new measure
should be shown to be more than just another measure of intelligence. This discriminant-validity requirement has been met to a
considerable degree by the Barrier score. Fisher and Cleveland
(1958a) report that Rorschach Barrier scores are not significantly
related to Wonderlic, MAT, or Wechsler scores. Similarly, Holtzman et al. (1961) obtained no relationship of Barrier score to verbal
intelligence scores. Fisher (1970, p. 161) cites five other studies,
three of which found low but significant positive associations
between Barrier scores and an alleged intelligence measure. The
largest r given by Fisher was .35. In some instances it is unclear
from Fisher's report whether Rorschach or Holtzman Barrier scores
were involved.

Mednick (1959), Wylie (1961), Hirt and Kurtz (1969), and
Shontz (1971a) have pointed out the serious problem of discriminant
validity posted by correlations between Barrier scores and other
Rorschach variables which purport to measure constructs seemingly
different from body image in any of the meanings of that concept
suggested by Fisher and Cleveland. For example, Fisher and Cleveland (1958a) reported that the number of Whole responses is sig-

nificantly greater among high-Barrier Ss, while $F + \%$ is significantly greater among low-Barrier Ss. (Later, in their rejoinder to Hirt and Kurtz, 1969, Fisher and Cleveland, 1969a, said that $F + \%$ is not significantly associated with Barrier.) Holtzman et al. (1961) present 16 intercorrelation matrices of 23 variables scored on the Holtzman Inkblot Test. No N is given for Matrix D-8, so I could not determine the significance levels of r for that matrix. Of the remaining 15 matrices. Barrier scores correlated $\leq .05$ level of significance with other variables as follows: with Integration (organization of two or more adequately perceived blot elements into a larger whole), in all 15 matrices; with Movement responses, in all 15 matrices; with Human responses, in 14 matrices; with Form Definite responses, in 12 matrices. Holtzman et al. (1961) factor analyzed each of the 16 matrices, looking for factors which might reappear in most or all matrices. They concluded as follows:

> The matching of Factor I across all 16 samples shows remarkably good fit. With only minor exception, all the factor loadings for Movement, Integration and Human are high, the majority being above .70. Most of the loadings for Form Definiteness and Popular, the remaining two variables in the hypothesized pattern, are also high. . . . Together they imply that Factor I deals mainly with perceptual maturity, integrated ideational activity, and awareness of conventional percepts.
>
> Barrier also loads as highly on Factor I as the hypothesized pattern. [p. 151]

They also reported for each matrix the percentage of total variance not accounted for by the factor analysis and estimated to be specific nonerror variance for that score (Holtzman et al., 1961, p. 169).

In the 16 samples, these estimated percentages for the Barrier score varied from 0 to 32, with nine of the percentage values being 20 or less.

All of these findings pose serious questions about tht discriminant validity of the Barrier score for measuring Fisher and Cleveland's body-image construct(s), as opposed to measuring certain other apparently different constructs proposed by users of these inkblot scores which are consistently correlated with Barrier scores.

How did Fisher and Cleveland react to this line of argument and evidence? In their 1968 book they did not take account of the above-cited correlational findings reported by Holtzman et al. (1961). In his 1970 book, Fisher briefly alluded to the 16 factor analyses, but he did not mention their relevance to the problem of discriminant validity of the Barrier score. He did acknowledge (Fisher, 1970) consistent reports of significant positive rs (.30 to .45) between Barrier and Movement scores; but he argued that these possibly imply that both Barrier and Movement "reflect the impact of kinesthetic experience upon the perceptual-imaginative process involved in the production of ink blot responses [p. 164]." That is, these scores should overlap insofar as they are tapping the same construct. This argument pertains to one score, Movement; but in the light of all the above-mentioned correlational results given by Holtzman et al. (1961), it is difficult to understand how Fisher (1970) could say, "It should be emphasized that the Movement score is the only conventional ink blot index to be consistently related to Barrier [p. 164]." Perhaps he meant that some of the Holtzman scores which consistently correlate with Barrier scores are not literally "conventional" inkblot indexes (e.g., Holtzman's Integration, Human, Form Definite, Popular). But whether or not these Holtzman scores are considered to be conventional inkblot indexes, their correlations with Barrier scores still pose unsolved discriminant-validity problems for the Barrier score.

Fisher and Cleveland (1960) also made another sort of reply to Mednick's (1959) comment that correlations between Barrier and other Rorschach scores raise questions about the discriminant validity of the Barrier score. They asserted that such criticisms were inappropriate since, in a number of studies, conventional Rorschach measures had already proven themselves not to be related to the variables Fisher and Cleveland were studying, such as suggestibility, physiological reactivity to stress, and direction of expression of anger. One must note, however, that published studies of this kind are few in number, they cover relatively few of the variables which Fisher and Cleveland eventually wish to associate theoretically with their body-image constructs, and they are frequently open to some of the methodological criticisms discussed further on in this section.

In his critique of Fisher's 1970 book, Shontz (1971a) alluded to this continuing problem of discriminant validity. In reply, Fisher (1971a, p. 745) argued that Shontz was "pitting his intuitive doubt" about the Barrier score against a "number of carefully done experiments." However, in no publication does Fisher seem to realize that multiple confirmations of hypotheses involving use of a given score (in this case, Barrier) do not logically suffice to rule out alternate interpretations of results in terms of constructs which are allegedly measured by scores which are highly correlated with the given score (Barrier). He does not publicly agree in principle that a requirement for discriminant validation is to hold constant related inkblot variables while looking at association between Barrier scores and *each* of the other noninkblot variables hypothetically associated with Barrier scores. In practice there has been no effort made, to my knowledge, to control for all covariant inkblot scores in studies which purport to test associations between Fisher's body-image construct and other variables of theoretical relevance to the body-image construct.

Another question of discriminant validity is also important: Since Fisher and Cleveland indicate that their body-image construct refers at least to some extent to Ss' *unconscious* processes or states, they must assume the burden of showing that the referent processes or states for the Barrier score are indeed unconscious to some extent, as opposed to being conscious attitudes or experiences which S has in connection with his body or self.

First, let us consider Fisher and Cleveland's *unconscious* body-image construct with a more literal body meaning left in it. The situation regarding this question of discriminant validity is puzzling and possibly contradictory. As quoted above, Fisher and Cleveland (1958a) say that the individual has little conscious information about his body boundaries. However, they have not asserted, to my knowledge, that the determinants of the magnitude of the Barrier score are entirely unconscious.

In various places they predict associations between the Barrier score and the location of conscious body sensations at exterior or interior sites. What kinds of assumptions could underlie such predictions? One possibility is that they implicitly assume that some part of their body-image-boundary construct is conscious, and their prediction concerns this part. Alternately, they may have assumed that the body-image-boundary construct per se is entirely or mostly unconscious, and the conscious body sensations in question are only the conscious correlates of the unconscious body-image-boundary, rather than being conscious aspects of the body-image-boundary itself. If it turns out empirically that there is no association between Barrier score and the location of conscious body sensation in exterior or interior sites, this null finding could plausibly, though not necessarily, be interpreted as indicative of the discriminant validity of the Barrier score as an index of *unconscious* body-image-boundary vividness. On the other hand, if there *is* a significant association between Barrier score and the location of conscious body sensation, this could be interpreted in one or more of several ways: It may be evidence for the validity of the Barrier score for indexing the conscious aspects of body-image-boundary experiences, in which case the studies do not tell anything about the discriminant validity of the Barrier score for indexing *unconscious* body-image boundaries. Alternately, such significant associations may result from the influence of conscious body sensations on the unconscious body-image boundaries indexed by the Barrier score, in which case, again, the results do not tell anything about the discriminant validity of the Barrier score for indexing unconscious body-image boundaries.

Although the studies reported below sometimes gave null or weak associations, there seems to be a trend toward an association of high Barrier scores with relatively greater prominence of exterior sensations, and low Barrier scores with relatively greater prominence of interior sensations.

In one of the studies obtaining null associations, Fisher and Cleveland (1958a) failed to sustain predictions that high Barrier scores would be associated with (a) a higher number of skin, as opposed to body-interior, sensations checked in a 3-minute period; (b) a higher number of muscle, as opposed to interior, sensations checked in a 3-minute period. In 1964, Fisher and Fisher again predicted that the Barrier score would relate to the excess of exterior (skin, muscle) to interior (heart, stomach) body sensations in a 5-minute period. This time they confirmed their predictions significantly in two samples, but confirmed it only in a male sample in groups reporting sensations after swallowing a "harmless drug" (actually a placebo). In another phase of this study, they found that high-Barrier Ss tended significantly to recall past emotional states as involving a higher proportion of exterior than interior body sensations (Fisher & Fisher, 1964).

In research somewhat similar to that just described, Fisher and Renik (1966) and Renik and Fisher (1968) tested the hypothesis that Barrier scores would increase during periods when Ss were asked to focus their attention on exterior parts of their bodies (skin and muscles) and would decrease during periods when Ss were asked to focus their attention on the interior of their bodies. Control Ss were not asked to focus their attention on their bodies. Barrier-score differences for exterior focusers versus controls differed nonsignificantly for females and significantly only on a one-tail test for males. Barrier-score differences for exterior and interior focusers differed from each other at $< .02$ and $< .05$ level on one-tail tests for males and females, respectively.

In the more carefully controlled of two studies which applied the same procedure to schizophrenic Ss, the exterior focusers obtained higher Barrier scores than did the interior focusers ($p < .05$, one-tail test); but no other comparisons between pairs of groups were significant (Fisher, 1970, p. 187).

In the same vein, Van de Mark and Neuringer (1969) had their six groups of Ss participate in physical and cognitive activities intended to induce internal-focus arousal, external-focus arousal, or neutral-focus arousal. For example, listening to one's own heart beat for 1 minute or imagining this activity were two of the ways (one physical, one cognitive) by which Es hoped to arouse internal focusing in Ss. Postmanipulation checks showed that this procedure did induce appropriate directionality of conscious attention. The external somatic focus groups gave significantly more Barrier responses than did the internal and neutral somatic focus Ss.

In short, this group of studies seems to show a trend toward associations between the exterior or interior location of conscious body sensations and the Barrier score. For reasons already explained, however, the findings offer no support for the discriminant validity of the Barrier score for inferring *unconscious* body image; but neither do they offer a clear refutation of such discriminant validity.

There is another group of studies having plausible relevance to the discriminant validity of the Barrier score as an index of unconscious images concerning the body per se. In all of these researches, actual body characteristics of which Ss must be consciously aware seem not to be related to Barrier scores. Thus, null relationships have been obtained between Barrier scores and somatotype (Fisher & Cleveland, 1958a); and between Barrier scores and the advancement of the aging processes (in which decline in physique and appearance is obvious) (Fisher, 1959b). Moreover, Barrier scores did not change between late pregnancy and 3 days after parturition (McConnell & Daston, 1961); and Barrier scores have sometimes (though not always) been found to be unrelated to the extent of bodily disability (Mitchell, 1969, 1970; Ware, Fisher &

Cleveland, 1957). Also, Allardice and Dole (1966) found no relationships between Barrier scores and degree of observable disfigurement in Hansen's disease. In all these studies, the groups of Ss who did not differ with respect to Barrier score obviously had different conscious experiences in connection with their bodies.

Of course null findings are always ambiguous. Nevertheless, one possible interpretation of these null findings is that they are congruent with the assumption that Barrier scores are not a function of conscious body image and may be indexing unconscious body-image boundary.

Overall, it is unclear conceptually which conscious and/or unconscious dimensions of *body* experience the Barrier score purports to measure. Correspondingly, the empirical situation is also ambiguous regarding the question whether Barrier scores do index the conscious and/or unconscious aspects of *body* experience referred to in Fisher and Cleveland's theorizing.

Continuing our consideration of the conscious-unconscious dimention, the second kind of discriminant validity question about the Barrier score is this: To what extent does the score index the *unconscious* (as opposed to conscious) body image in the *widened, symbolic meanings* of this term that Fisher and Cleveland suggest?

In this connection they predicted and found null associations between Barrier scores and a self-report test which purportedly covers a wide range of attitudes toward the self, namely, Bills's IAV scores (Fisher & Cleveland, 1958a). Such findings would be most relevant if one assumes that the IAV purports to get reports regarding the complex pattern of *conscious* self-attitudes which would be conceptually parallel to the self-attitudes the Barrier score purportedly taps at the unconscious level. Given the varying and complex statements of Fisher and Cleveland regarding their body-image construct in its widened, symbolic sense, it is difficult or impossible to evaluate the degree to which the IAV and the Barrier score purport to have discriminant validity for measuring corresponding attitudes at the conscious and unconscious levels, respectively. Thus this second discriminant validity question is left essentially unexplored.

Studies Based on Assumed Validity

By far the greatest number of validity-relevant studies of the Barrier score involve tests of theoretical predictions, such tests being based on the assumed construct validity of the Barrier score. As is well known, and explained in detail in chapter 3, this approach to construct validation always offers the weakest line of support for the alleged construct validity of any score. No matter how many studies of this sort are accumulated, they cannot supplant the more basic approaches to exploring convergent and discriminant validity, approaches which have not been used sufficiently in the case of the Barrier score, as I have argued above. Moreover, the intrinsic limitations on the interpretability of "assumed-validity" research are magnified when the following conditions obtain, as is the case with the potentially validity-relevant studies of the Barrier score:

1. The theoretical speculations underlying hypotheses about Barrier scores are diffuse, complex, and sometimes apparently contradictory. This means that what one may legitimately hypothesize is not always clear. Moreover, ad hoc speculations are offered freely by Fisher and Cleveland in order to accommodate within the bounds of their theory unpredicted null or contradictory findings (not infrequently obtained by themselves or others).

For example, Fisher and Cleveland's exterior-interior model associates definiteness of body-image boundary (Barrier scores) with physiological reactivity and psychosomatic disorder. Ss with high Barrier scores are expected to show relatively more exterior physiological reactivity and exterior psychosomatic symptoms, while Ss with low Barrier scores are expected to show relatively more interior physiological reactivity and interior psychosomatic symptoms. Supposedly, the body-image boundary differences somehow lead to these reactivity and symptom differences. Along this line, Cleveland, Reitman, and Brewer (1965) reported a significant *chi* square for a table showing arthritis patients to have proportionately more high Barrier scores while asthmatic patients had proportionately more low Barrier scores. They concluded that these results were "in keeping with" earlier results associating exterior psychosomatic symptoms with high Barrier scores, interior ones with low Barrier scores. Moreover, in their 1968 book, Fisher and Cleveland cite this study among those which allegedly support their exterior-interior model and the construct validity of the Barrier score. However, when Hirt and Kurtz (1969) reported finding nonsignificantly *lower* Barrier scores in arthritics than in asthmatics, Fisher and Cleveland criticized them, saying that the asthmatic syndrome was never explicitly labeled by them (Fisher and Cleveland) as appropriate to assessing their exterior-interior model. According to Fisher and Cleveland (1969a), Hirt and Kurtz's null findings may be a "function of the fact that asthma may have a strong hereditary component [p. 146]." That is, asthma is not necessarily an interior psychosomatic disorder and so Hirt and Kurtz's hypothesis was not justified.

Similarly, several studies (e.g., Williams & Krasnoff, 1964; Fisher, 1959c; and A. D. Davis, 1960) yielded significant associations between high Barrier scores and slower heart rate under stress. These results seemed to be accepted by Fisher and Cleveland as relevant to the exterior-interior model and relevant to the construct validity of the Barrier score. However, when Hirt and Kurtz (1969) found that Ss with cardiac pathology had nonsignificantly *higher* Barrier scores than arthritis patients did, Fisher and Cleveland (1969a) criticized their hypothesis by saying that coronary pathology may not provide an appropriate test of the exterior-interior model because smoking or diet might play a role in determining such pathology. In reviewing such complications as these, Fisher (1970) says,

> The temptation arises, of course, to argue that any illness which does not conform to exterior-interior expectations does not have a sufficient psychosomatic component to make it a valid candidate for exterior-interior classification; and to urge the obverse for those that do conform well to the model. There is in this respect an ambiguity about the exterior-interior model which is unfortunate. One must acknowledge that this ambiguity limits one's ability to define its validity. However, the dilemma can only in part be attributed to deficiencies in the exterior-interior formulation. A significant part is simply due to our lack of knowledge concerning the causation of many major illnesses. [P. 217]

Another example of apparently unclear communication of theoretical expectations is found in Fisher and Cleveland's (1969b) criticism of Mitchell's (1969) work which attempted to test Fisher and Cleveland's views about the association of clear body boundaries and "self-steering behavior" under stress. As part of their discussion of the "self-steering syndrome," Fisher and Cleveland (1958a) stated that "our model of the high Barrier individual suggests that he would have particularly good facility for maintaining equilibrium in the midst of stress [p. 137]." Relevant to this argument they referred to two unpublished studies (cited in Fisher & Cleveland, 1968), and one published one (Ware, Fisher & Cleveland, 1957). These studies found that Barrier score was not associated with degree or duration of physical disability, but was associated with adjustment to disability as measured by ratings and sentence completions in the unpublished studies; and by ratings made by three physicians, a psychologist, and/or a social worker who knew the patients well in the Ware et al. (1957) study. Believing he was testing Fisher and Cleveland's theory and the assumed validity of the Barrier score, Mitchell (1969) separately classified his paraplegic Ss and his quadraplegic Ss into high and low adjustment groups only if they were high or low on all three of his alleged measures of adjustment: Eysenck's Neuroticism, Secord's Body-Disturbance score from his Homonyms Test, and an anxiety score from Cattell's 16 PF. When Mitchell failed to find within either the paraplegic or the quadraplegic group that better adjusted Ss had higher Barrier scores than did the poorly adjusted Ss, Fisher and Cleveland (1969b) criticized Mitchell's assumptions. Fisher and Cleveland argued that the Eysenck, Cattell, and Secord scales were not measuring the aspects of adjustment which would be appropriate for testing the Fisher-Cleveland hypotheses. It appears that the proper meaning of adjustment had not been communicated to or at least understood by Mitchell. (In a subsequent study [Mitchell, 1970], other groups of paraplegics and quadraplegics were each classed as high or low on adjustment on the basis of all three previously used pencil-and-paper measures plus a "rehabilitation rating on adjustment." Here, paraplegic groups high and low on adjustment differed with respect to Barrier scores $[p < .05]$; but quadraplegic groups high and low on adjustment still did not.)

Yet another example of unclear explication of theory which precludes relating one's results to clear hypotheses involves the theoretical relationship of "health," "adjustment," or "ego soundness" to Barrier scores. Arthritics, neurodermatitis patients, conversion hysterics with muscle disorder, and breast and skin cancer patients are all assumed to be unhealthy in the psychological sense inasmuch as these disorders are assumed by Fisher and Cleveland to be at least partly psychosomatic. Likewise, classical paranoids are considered to be malajusted or unhealthy. On theoretical grounds related to their *maladjustment,* all these groups are predicted to have high Barrier scores. But in other places, Fisher and Cleveland predict that high Barrier scores will characterize Ss whom they evidently consider to be in some sense "healthy," "adjusted," or high in "ego soundness." For example, it was predicted that higher Barrier scores would be found among normal or neurotic Ss, as opposed to schizophrenic Ss (but most studies did not support the prediction). It was predicted and found that higher Barrier scores would characterize Ss who resist laboratory or polio stresses better; Ss who show higher aspirations and are more realistic; Nisei women as opposed to Nisei men (who are presumably having the greater difficulty adjusting to cultural transition); and Ss showing psychiatric improvement or success in psychotherapy (Fisher & Cleveland, 1958a; Fisher, 1970).

The seeming inconsistencies in the theorizing about associations between Barrier scores and adjustment have not been satisfactorily clarified. Regarding the theoretical proposition that high boundedness of the body image is one influence in the development of external psychosomatic symptoms, it remains unclear why higher boundedness would be expected to occur in a group prone to psychological maladjustment. In 1970, Fisher stated,

> It has been necessary to give up previous formulations which equate degree of boundary definiteness with ego soundness. The new formulation with respect to this matter accepts the notion that the boundary can remain well delineated if a disorganizing or regressive process does not destroy an individual's sense of having meaningful worth or importance. But it remains difficult to accept that the boundary of a grandiose schizophrenic does not really differ from that of a person who is successfully testing and adjusting to reality. One would guess that the Barrier score is in this instance telling only part of a more complicated story that we have yet to learn. [P. 318]

Overall, the lack of clarity of the theory about the association of adjustment and Barrier score severely limits the usefulness of this line of research to the process of evaluating the construct validity of the Barrier score.

2. A second kind of characteristic which jeopardizes the interpretability of potentially validity-relevant studies involving the Barrier score is the presence of methodological flaws in many of the studies.

First, as I partially explained earlier, studies using various methods of deriving the Barrier score are cited, compared, and interpretatively synthesized without demonstration or consideration of the equivalence of the Barrier measures used. This is not only the case so far as the equivalence of Rorschach Barrier scores and Holtzman Barrier scores is concerned. In most of the studies cited in the Fisher and Cleveland (1958a) book and in some of the more recent research, the cited studies were originally designed and executed for another purpose and by other investigators. As a consequence of this fact, the researches differ among themselves in conditions of Rorschach administration and in the means of controlling response totals. This means that in different studies there may be various unidentified, irrelevant effects on the Barrier score.

Second, it is often impossible to know within any one study whether groups chosen so as to differ on a certain variable supposedly relevant to the Barrier score were adequately equated with respect to other variables which would plausibly be relevant to the Barrier score. This lack of proper matching of groups is especially possible when data from groups studied by an original investigator for one purpose are reanalyzed to explore associations between Barrier scores and theory-relevant variables. Even if the groups were appropriately formed by the original investigator for his own purposes, they may not have been comparable with respect to variables relevant to Fisher and Cleveland's Barrier scores.

Third, groups used from study to study were quite different, so one cannot clearly interpret contradictions which occur when an effect is found within one study but not within another, for example, when high Barrier score is found to be associated with "anger out" in Funkenstein and King's Ss, but with failure to be able to express anger outwardly in arthritics (Fisher & Cleveland, 1958a).

Fourth, in numerous validity-relevant studies of the Barrier score, the associations between Barrier scores and each of a number of theoretically relevant variables is tested. Insufficient attention is paid to the problems of determining which one(s) of multiple significance tests might be "significant" by chance alone and which merit psychological interpretation. This interpretive problem is particularly acute when the variables being related to the Barrier scores are themselves intercorrelated, as is surely or plausibly the case in many such studies, and when the relationships which turn out to be significant are particularly stressed in the interpretation, with relatively minor consideration being given to insignificant results within the same study.

A further statistical problem stems from the use of one-tailed tests of significance in some studies which are cited in support of the construct validity of the Barrier score. One-tailed tests are, of course, defensible if one is testing a directional hypothesis. By choosing a one-tailed test one increases the possibility of using a small obtained effect to support the assumptions of one's theory and the assumed validity of one's instruments. However, one also increases the probability of interpreting in psychological terms what are actually chance findings. Moreover, such an option is statistically legitimate only if one follows the logical consequences; that is, one must forego ad hoc theoretical explanations which bring statistically significant findings opposite to one's hypothesis into congruence with one's theory and the assumed validity of one's instruments. Not all Barrier researchers have accepted these logical consequences.

The interpretation of some Barrier studies is occasionally vitiated by the use of complex two-part indices without sufficient regard to the possible contributions of the separate parts of the index to the obtained findings or sufficient attention to the fact that equalsized changes or differences from different parts of a dimension are not necessarily comparable. Barrier-minus-Penetration scores and change scores in studying autonomic reactivity as related to Barrier scores are occasionally used in this way, for example.

3. A third class of conditions limiting the value of potentially validity-relevant Barrier studies includes the somewhat unsystematic or miscellaneous nature of a number of the studies and the relatively low occurrence of true cross-validational studies. Of course, it is true that Fisher and Cleveland believe their Barrier score to be theoretically related to a very wide range of other variables, for example, physiological reactivity, site of psychosomatic illness, selfsteering behavior under stress (which includes achievement striving, lack of suggestibility, anger-out reactions, perceptual-motor performance under stress, adjustment to physical illness, and perceptual stability); group behavior; and mental illness or adjustment. Accordingly, a wide range of studies is appropriate (Fisher & Cleveland, 1958a; Fisher, 1970), and a very large number of studies have been done, covering a wide range of variables. At the same time, if the researches are not systematically planned and ordered so as to mesh together, their quantity and variety do not offer increasingly

definitive information about the construct validity of the Barrier score as an index of any of the constructs Fisher and Cleveland wish to infer from it.

SUMMARY AND CONCLUSIONS

Although the Barrier score based on content of responses to inkblots has been used in many studies over a period of about two decades and is apparently correlated with a wide range of other variables, its construct validity for measuring body-image boundary in any of Fisher and Cleveland's senses of this term has not been systematically and rigorously explored. Most basic to this state of affairs is the complexity and lack of clarity of both the conceptual definitions of body image and the theorizing about relationships between body image and other variables.

Considerable information regarding the reliability of the Barrier score is at hand, but there is no information about its convergent validity.

A number of discriminant-validity questions need to be more rigorously defined and explored. One kind of discriminant-validity question is posed by correlations between Barrier scores and several other inkblot variables which purport to measure constructs other than body image (Holtzman et al., 1961). Fisher and Cleveland have not fully faced the kind of discriminant-validity question these correlations pose. Regarding a second kind of discriminant-validity question, namely, whether Barrier scores indicate *unconscious* body image as opposed to conscious body image, one may perhaps interpret some of the extant evidence as relevant to the matter. However, the state of the evidence on this type of discriminant validity merits no conclusion at this time.

One might imagine that the numerous available researches could serve to explore the construct validity of the Barrier score by means of testing theoretical hypotheses, using that score as one's measure while assuming its validity. In the case of the Barrier score studies, however, the intrinsic limitations of this approach to construct validation are magnified by factors such as unclear theorizing, methodological flaws in the studies, and lack of systematic planning and ordering of successive studies in a way conducive to increasingly definitive interpretations of patterns of results. I cannot agree with the conclusions of a recent reviewer of the Holtzman

Inkblot Technique (Gamble, 1972), who said, after citing seven studies, "Taken together, these studies reinforce the significance of the body-boundary construct in personality research, and they tend to support the construct validity of the HIT *Br* and *Pn* scores [p. 183]."

As a basis for preparing this evaluation, I have examined the following publications (in his most recent book, Fisher, 1970, briefly describes about 25 published studies in addition to those listed here): Allardice and Dole (1966); Armstrong (1968); Armstrong and Armstrong (1968); Cassell (1964, 1965, 1966); Cassell and Fisher (1963); Cassell and Hemingway (1970); Cauthen and Boardman (1971); Cleveland (1960); Cleveland and Fisher (1954, 1957, 1960); Cleveland and Johnson (1962); Cleveland and Morton (1962); Cleveland, Reitman, and Brewer (1965); Cleveland and Sikes (1966); Cleveland, Snyder, and Williams (1965); Daston and McConnell (1962); Davis (1960); Dosey and Meisels (1969); Eigenbrode and Shipman (1960); R. Fisher (1966a, 1966b, 1966c, 1968); S. Fisher (1959a, 1959b, 1959c, 1960, 1963a, 1963b, 1964a, 1964b, 1965, 1966, 1967, 1970, 1971a, 1971b); S. Fisher and Cleveland (1955, 1956a, 1956b, 1956c, 1957, 1958a, 1958b, 1960, 1961, 1965, 1968, 1969a, 1969b); S. Fisher and R. Fisher (1959, 1964); S. Fisher and Renik (1966); Frede, Gautney, and Baxter (1968); Gamble (1972); Gorham, Moseley, and Holtzman (1968); Hammerschlag, Fisher, DeCosse, and Kaplan (1964); Hartley (1967); Hartung, McKenna and Baxter (1970); Hirt and Kurtz (1969); Holtzman, Thorpe, Swartz, and Herron (1961); Jaskar and Reed (1963); Kernaleguen and Compton (1968); McConnell and Daston (1961); Malev (1967); Mednick (1959, 1960); Megargee (1965, 1966); Mitchell (1969, 1970); Mosher, Oliver, and Dolgan (1967); Nichols and Tursky (1967); Osofsky and Fisher (1967); Ramer (1963); Reitman and Cleveland (1964); Renik and Fisher (1968); Shipman (1965); Shipman, Oken, Goldstein, Grinker, and Heath (1964); Shontz (1969, 1971a, 1971b); Van de Mark and Neuringer (1969); Ware, Fisher, and Cleveland (1957); Williams and Krasnoff (1964); Zimny (1965).

C. Summary Comments on the Measurement of the Unconscious Self-Concept

Since constructs concerning the phenomenal self appear to be insufficient bases for predicting behavior, a number of psychologists have felt that constructs concerning the nonphenomenal self may

be worth introducing into hypotheses of personality theories emphasizing self-referent constructs. However, one cannot proceed fruitfully with investigations of such hypotheses until one has a defensible way of measuring the nonphenomenal self constructs involved.
Unfortunately, both the conceptual and methodological problems
of establishing construct validity of indices purporting to reveal
the unconscious self-concept have not been clearly recognized or
coped with, and consequently, no measure in use has been demonstrated to be adequate for this purpose.

6

Studies Concerned with the Insightfulness of the Self-Concept

A. INTRODUCTION

Next to researches involving self-regard, the most numerous studies relevant to self-concept theory are those which concern *insight*. This term has been used in the psychological literature with a number of literary and operational meanings, and most or all of the latter have involved evaluative traits. Thus this chapter is, in a sense, an extension or elaboration of chapters 3 and 4.

I shall not attempt a comparative review of the literary meanings of insight to various theorists, nor of the alternative roles it is assumed to play in their theories. When one considers only the lines of thought which underlie the empirical studies performed to date, one sees them falling mainly into two groups: In the classical Freudian and neo-Freudian view, lack of insight is alleged to be accompanied by defensiveness and/or maladjustment, when the latter is defined in terms of S's experience and/or an observer's diagnosis. So far as phenomenal theorists are concerned, it sometimes seems that they, too, espouse this view. On the other hand, they occasionally seem to be saying that the S will not become anxious (and hence defensive) unless and until he becomes at least dimly aware of the disparity between his phenomenal self and the views others hold of him (C. R. Rogers, 1951b, p. 321). Of course, such a disparity may render S more potentially vulnerable, in the sense of increasing the likelihood that a discomfort-producing discrepancy will come to his attention. But until that eventuality does occur (i.e., until at least a dim awareness of the inappropriateness or incompleteness of the self-concept develops) , lack of insight presumably would not lead to anxiety or defensiveness. (It may, of course, lead to maladjusted or inappropriate behavior, as judged by an external observer.)

Many workers have indicated that there is a great deal of surplus meaning to their concept of insight, or accuracy of self-perception, beyond that which their operational definitions cover.

B. Varieties of Operational Definitions

1. Self-Other Discrepancy Scores and Self-Other Correlations

Most of the studies which purport to study insight, or accuracy of self-perception, use comparisons of S's self-reports with a report of an O concerning S. Two means of making such comparisons are commonly used. In one, E obtains an insight score for each S by computing a difference between S and O reports. (Such difference scores are hereafter called [S-O] discrepancies.) Some Es who have computed [S-O] discrepancies are interested in associating individual differences in Ss' insight with individual differences in some other variable, such as adjustment; while some Es use groups differing in mean or median [S-O] discrepancies to study associations between [S-O] discrepancies and some other variable(s), such as adjustment. In either case, the use of [S-O] discrepancies is fraught with many methodological difficulties, some of them parallel to those discussed in chapter 3 in my earlier consideration of self-minus-ideal discrepancies.

In the second way of making S-O comparisons, E uses a correlation across Ss between S and O reports. This correlation may take the form of r, rho, or chi square for contingency tables. In contrast to the [S-O] discrepancy approach, this correlational approach is not intended to yield an insight score for each S which can then be associated with one or more other variables. Rather, E tries to see whether the across-S correlations between S and O reports are higher under one condition than another (e.g., in different age groups or for different characteristics).

It should be obvious that most of the influences which could lower the construct validity of [S-O] discrepancy scores as measures of individual differences in insight could also make the across-S correlation values inaccurate indicants of the overall degree of insight within a group of Ss.

In order to subclassify and criticize the extant operational definitions of insight in terms of [S-O] discrepancies or S-O correlations, it is important to note first the following possibilities on the parts of S and O.

INSTRUCTIONS TO S

So far as instructions to S are concerned, three types have occurred in the research literature.

Private-Self-Concept Instructions

S may be instructed to report how he privately sees himself with respect to stated characteristics, as distinguished from trying to say how generalized or particular Os would characterize him. (I shall call such a report a private-self-concept report.) This approach leads to a completely inappropriate basis for defining insight or accuracy of self-perception, either in terms of the size of an [S-O] discrepancy or in terms of an S-O correlation. This is so because, if S is following instructions, he presumably has not been trying systematically to report on his self-concept regarding how he impresses the Os whose reports will be used to define his [S-O] discrepancy score of insight, or used to compute an S-O correlation supposedly indicative of the degree of insight in his group. (The use of this inappropriate type of self-report would be expected to lead to an underestimation of the degree of insight or self-perception accuracy of which Ss are capable; and that expectation is substantiated, as I show below.) Examples of this type of score occur in the following studies: Beer, Buckhout, Horowitz, and Levy (1959); Brownfain (1952); Flyer, Barron, and Bigbee (1953); Gaier (1961); Goldings (1954); Israel (1958); Webb (1952).

Social-Self-Concept Instructions

S may be instructed to report on what I shall call his social self-concept; that is, regardless of his own private view of himself, he is instructed to tell how he thinks generalized or particular Os would characterize him. This is a potentially defensible way to approach the problem of getting S-O correlations or [S-O] discrepancies which might, under certain conditions, conceivably indicate degrees of insight or accuracy of self-perception in a group of Ss or in individual Ss, respectively. However, such [S-O] discrepancies or *S-O* correlations will possibly index degrees of insight only if *S*s are clearly instructed to report their social self-concepts with reference to the *O*(s) whose reports will be used in the [*S-O*] discrepancies or *S-O* correlations. Examples of social-self-concept reports include those listed below. In some of these studies the social-self-concept reports are not directed to the appropriate reference *O*s: Ausubel and Schiff (1955); Ausubel, Schiff, and Gasser (1952); Bowers (1963); Brownfain (1952); deJung and Gardner (1962); Dymond (1950) ("empathy" score); Elliott (1960); Flyer, Barron, and Bigbee (1953); Kay, French, and Meyer (1962); Miyamoto and Dornbusch (1956); Rawlinson (1965); Reeder, Donohue, and Biblarz (1960); Rodgers (1957); G. M. Smith (1958); Soares and Soares (1970); Wylie (1957).

Instructions Vague or Vaguely Reported

The instructions given to *S* may be so vague (or at least the published information *E* gives his readers about instructions to *S* is so vague) that *S*s' self-reports are not definitely interpretable as indicative of either private or social self-concept. Of course, research reports in which these conditions obtain cannot be clearly interpreted as relevant to insight or accuracy of self-perception, regardless of the authors' interpretative statements. Examples of these kinds of lack of specificity may be found in the following: Amatora (1956); Bartlett (1959); Burke (1969); Calvin and Holtzman (1953); Cogan, Conklin, and Hollingworth (1915); Eisenman and Robinson (1968); Friedsam and Martin (1963); Gough and Heilbrun (1965); Green (1948); Kay, French, and Meyer (1962); Kelman and Parloff (1957); Lomont (1966); Mahone (1960); Mann and Mann (1959); Mayo and Manning (1961); G. McConnell (1959); Mueller (1963); Murstein (1956); R. D. Norman (1953); W. T. Norman (1967); Parsons, Fulgenzi, and Edelberg (1969); Phillips (1963); Purkey (1966); Rawlinson (1965); Reeder, Donohue, and Biblarz (1960); Ringness (1961); Rodgers (1957); Rokeach (1945); Sears (1936); E. E. Smith (1959); G. M. Smith (1958); Tschechtelin (1945); Walhood and Klopfer (1971); Winthrop (1959). In some studies two sets of instructions were used, one of which asked *S*s to estimate ratings or rankings they would receive from *O*s and one of which asked *S*s to rate or rank themselves. Use of these two sets of instructions seems to imply that the self-ratings or self-rankings were supposed to be of Ss' private self-concepts. However, the published reports do not always make explicitly clear that this distinction was unequivocally conveyed to Ss in the instructions, as is necessary if the self-ratings or self-rankings may be appropriately interpreted as indicative of private self-concept. Thus, interpretability of the findings is impaired. Examples of such studies are: Brownfain (1952); Dymond (1950); Flyer, Barron, and Bigbee (1953); Goldings (1954); Israel (1958); Miyamoto and Dornbusch (1956); W. T. Norman (1969); Rawlinson (1965); Reed and Cuadra (1957); Reeder, Donohue, and Biblarz (1960); Walhood and Klopfer (1971).

Obviously, S's private self-concept and his social self-concept may overlap considerably, so one can expect that instructions of the first two types described above should yield correlated self-concept reports. On these grounds, one might try to argue that private-self-concept reports, while not directly appropriate for use in [S-O] insight scores or S-O correlations purporting to index within-group insight, have at least some indirect validity for inferring individual or group standings with respect to insight. However, empirical evidence suggests that self-reports or [S-O] discrepancies taken under private and social instructions, although significantly correlated, are far from identical, for example, Dymond (1950); Flyer, Barron, and Bigbee (1953); Israel (1958); W. T. Norman (1969); Rawlinson (1965); Reeder, Donohue, and Biblarz (1960); and Walhood and Klopfer (1971). I say that the results from these studies suggest rather than demonstrate a certain amount of correspondence between private-self ratings and social-self ratings, since, as I indicated above, the information about instructions for making the private-self-concept ratings is often ambiguous or unpublished. In any event, so far as the evidence goes, the occurrence of imperfect correspondence between private-self-concept ratings and social-self-concept ratings vitiates the above argument for the indirect validity of the private-self-concept ratings as a basis for either [S-O] insight scores for individuals or S-O correlations purporting to index within-group insight.

When one is trying to evaluate the degree of accuracy of self-perception or insight of which Ss are capable, it is of considerable interest to note that higher correlations are found between social-self-concept reports and actually obtained O reports than between self-reports (assumedly more indicative of the private self-concept) and actually obtained O reports, for example, Flyer, Barron, and Bigbee (1953); W. T. Norman (1969); Walhood and Klopfer (1971). *Thus the use of unqualified "self" reports or of clearly specified "private-self-concept" reports underestimates the accuracy which Ss are capable of demonstrating under appropriate instructions.* As I mentioned earlier, this is what one would expect when inappropriate instructions are given to Ss.

SOURCES OF O's INFORMATION

So far as O is concerned, the report concerning S made by "another informed person," which Hilgard (1949) has called the "inferred self," has several possible variants. In regard to the source of O's information, we may identify two basic kinds of sources.

Informal Interaction

In many studies O's information is based on informal interaction with S in work, military, social, or school settings (e.g., Amatora, 1956; Ausubel & Schiff, 1955, Ausubel, Schiff, & Gasser, 1952; Bartlett, 1959; Beer et al., 1959; Bowers, 1963; Brownfain, 1952; Calvin & Holtzman, 1953; Cogan, Conklin, & Hollingworth, 1915; deJung & Gardner, 1962; Elliott, 1960; Eisenman & Robinson, 1968; Flyer, Barron, & Bigbee, 1953; Green, 1948; Israel, 1958; Kay, French, & Meyer, 1962; Lomont, 1966; Mann & Mann, 1959; Mayo & Manning, 1961; Miyamoto & Dornbusch, 1956; Mueller, 1963; Murstein, 1956; R. D. Norman, 1953; W. T. Norman, 1969; Phillips, 1963; Powell, 1948; Rawlinson, 1965; Reeder et al., 1960; Ringness, 1961; Rokeach, 1945; Sears, 1936; Tschechtelin, 1945; Webb, 1955; Wylie, 1957).

Special Observational Procedures

In some studies O's information is based on special observational procedures such as standardized observational techniques, interviews, or the application of tests and diagnostic tools (e.g., Arsenian, 1942; Barrett, 1968; Bidwell, 1969; Brandt, 1958; Brown & Pool, 1966; Eisenman & Robinson, 1968; Froehlich & Moser, 1954; Keefer, 1969; Kelman & Parloff, 1957; Kemp, 1964; Klein, 1948; Rychlak, 1959; G. M. Smith, 1958; Sumner, 1932; Torrance, 1954a; Touhey, 1971).

In the latter case, but not the former, the informed person is usually more or less expert by training.

INSTRUCTIONS TO *O*s

What *O* is instructed to report about *S* may vary in the following ways.

O's Personal Impressions

O may be told to report on the impression *S* makes on him personally as to overt behavior and/or covert inferred character-istics such as feelings or abilities, for example, "I like *S*," or "*S* seems to me to be intelligent." Examples of this occur in Ausubel, Schiff, and Gasser (1952); Beer et al. (1959); Beilin (1957); Bowers (1963); Cogan, Conklin, and Hollingworth (1915); deJung and Gardner (1962).

O's Impressions of Others' Impressions of S

O may be told to try to report on the impression *S* makes on a more or less specified group of others, perhaps including *O*, in regard to overt and/or covert characteristics, for example, "*S* is well liked by the boys in this fraternity," or "*S* maintains rapport with patients to whom he gives therapy."

O's Inferences about S's Self-Concept

O may be told to try to report his inferences concerning *S*'s self-concept, including those aspects of which *S* is conscious and those of which he is not (e.g., Beilin, 1957).

Most research reports tell the reader so little about the instruc-tions given to *O*s or report such vague instructions given to *O*s that one cannot tell whether the *O* reports are defensible, appropriate components of an [*S-O*] discrepancy score or an *S-O* correlation purporting to measure insight or accuracy of self-perception.

It seems likely that reports of *O*s under the varying frames of reference listed above will be far from identical, but there is no systematic empirical information as to how much they differ. In any event, it is clear that the only procedure defensible in principle is for instructions to *O*s to correspond to instructions given to *S*s, so that the *S* and *O* components of the [*S-O*] discrepancy scores or *S-O* correlations may reasonably be expected to refer to the same dimension.

COMBINATIONS OF Ss' AND Os' REPORTS

Because the research operations and/or the reports about them have been so imprecise and vague, it is not possible to classify most of the available studies according to which types of S and O reports have been used to define insight. Obviously, then, it is not even possible to determine how many of the possible combinations of S and O reports have been used. I list below those which seem to be fairly common types of discrepancy scores used to infer insight.

1. S reports his personal view of himself (his private self-concept); and this is compared to O's report on S's actual characteristics. O's report is based on informal peer interaction and includes in unknown amounts O's idea of the group's impression of S, and O's own impression of S. Examples include Beer, et al. (1959); Brownfain's Insight II (1952); and Flyer, Barron and Bigbee (1953).

2. S reports on himself as he thinks specified Os will view him; that is, he reports on his social-self-concept, and this is compared to O's actual statements about S. Each O's statements are based on informal interaction and they include unknown amounts of O's own impression of S and O's idea of the group's impression of S. Examples include Brownfain's Insight I (1952); deJung and Gardner (1962); Elliott (1960); Flyer, Barron, and Bigbee (1953); and Wylie (1957).

While this approach is more acceptable than that in paragraph 1 above, it could be improved by more stringent instructions to each O to give his *own* opinion of S.

3. S reports on what he expects to score or rank on a specified standard or objective test, personality inventory, or grade-point scale; and this is compared to his actual score or standing. Examples include Barrett (1968); Brown and Pool (1966); Keefer (1969); Kemp (1964); Klein (1948); Preiss (1968); Rychlak (1959); Sumner (1932); Torrance (1954a, 1954b); Touhey (1971).

4. S makes his self-report apparently without knowledge that this report will be compared to a report by O(s); and the O reports have such bases as a standard test, a personality inventory, a projective test, or O's "expert" observations. Examples of this include Beilin (1957); Bidwell (1969); Child, Frank, and Storm (1956); Cogan, Conklin, and Hollingworth (1915); Friedman (1955); Friedsam and Martin (1963); Kelman and Parloff (1957); Ringness (1961); and G. M. Smith (1958).

Clearly, the approaches described in paragraphs 1 and 4 above are indefensible in principle as ways of obtaining [S-O] discrepancy scores or S-O correlations validly indicative of Ss' insight. The approach described in paragraph 2, while defensible in principle, could be improved in practice in the ways indicated above; and its value also depends on other methodological considerations discussed more fully below. The value of the approach described in paragraph 3 depends on the particular information S has and is able to understand about the test's substantive and psychometric characteristics, as discussed more fully below.[1]

2. Insightfulness of S Directly Inferred by O

A second general type of insight measurement has employed direct inferences of this characteristic itself by O. That is, O rates S as to how insightful S is concerning specified or general characteristics. Such a procedure requires O to infer both what S thinks about himself *and* whether those thoughts are accurate in terms of O's other impressions or sources of information about S. Two assumptions, completely without empirical check, are common to all the examples of this type of measure: (a) O's ideas about S's self-picture and S's actual characteristics are more accurate than S's; (b) O can intuitively synthesize his impressions of S's self-concept and S's actual characteristics with optimum weighting assigned to the variables involved.

---

[1] Gough and Heilbrun's Insight I and Insight II scores for their Adjective Check List are not [S-O] discrepancy scores, but instead are ratio scores: The numerator for each S's score is the number of adjectives checked by both S and "composite Os" as characterizing S (a value called a). The denominator for Insight I is a plus the number of adjectives checked by "self" only; and the denominator for Insight II is a plus the number of adjectives checked by "composite Os" only. These scores per se are uninterpretable because of many weaknesses, including those already discussed in connection with [S-O] discrepancy scores, namely, questionable construct validity of the S and O reports which enter the ratio, possible incomparability of S's and O's reference frames when responding, and summation across many items with quite disparate content. In addition, these scores are subject to other methodological criticisms which are not always applicable to [S-O] discrepancies, for example, lack of control for number of adjectives checked by either S or "composite Os." It is clear that Gough and Heilbrun (1965) have not held self-concept constant across Ss when correlating, for example, Insight I with Likeability (the latter being a ratio score based on Os' reports). Accordingly, the correlational findings which they interpret as associations between insight and other traits of Ss may most parsimoniously be interpreted as correlations between Self-reports and the measures in question.

The examples cited below show that, in addition to the above-mentioned common assumptions, the various researchers have made additional quite varied assumptions about what should be included in the "literary" definition of insight. The rationale for these variations is not obvious or compelling; and in any case it seems clear that studies using such differing instructions to Os cannot meaningfully be synthesized in order to draw a general conclusion, even though all Es have claimed to measure insight. None of these approaches has been subjected to any serious methodological research which might give a basis for its being designated the preferred index of insight.

The earliest use of this type of approach is cited in Rogers, Kell, and McNeil (1948), where ratings on "self-insight" were made directly from filed case materials on delinquents. O's instructions were as follows:

Consider in relation to the norm for his age, the degree to which the child has or lacks understanding of his own situation and problems; consider such things as defensiveness; inability to admit faults, or tendency to depreciate self and exaggerate faults. Consider not only intellectual understanding of problem but emotional acceptance of the reality situation. Consider child's planfulness and willingness to take responsibility for self; ability to be objectively self-critical. Consider stability of attitudes—whether erratic and changeable or cautious and settled. [P. 178]

About the same time, Weingarten (1949) also attempted to have Os rate Ss' insight on the basis of written materials rather than personal interaction; but in this case, on the basis of autobiographies written by Ss. By implication, Weingarten defined insight as

a person's capacity to understand the dynamics of his behavioral patterns and emotional reactions and the extent to which he represses, falsely emphasizes, or misunderstands his own motivation [which] can be estimated from the psychological congruence of the various aspects of the total picture he presents. [P. 378]

Reed and Cuadra (1957) gave the following instructions to their student-nurse Ss who were to rate their peers' degrees of insightfulness:

An insightful person has the ability to recognize and understand the motives underlying her behavior and is aware of the effects of her behavior on other persons. She is alert to what other people think of her as a person. (In making judgments do not be influenced by intelligence, likeability, etc., which are not necessarily related to insight. An unpleasant person for example could still be an insightful person). [P. 388]

Thayer (1971) asked each member of a small club

to make ratings of another member who was a close friend on various dimensions related to self-insight. Subjects ranked girlfriends, whom they judged among all girls in the participating groups, on the following statements: (a) likes to understand her own behavior; (b) understands herself; (c) judges others accurately; (d) seems to be aware of the impression she makes on others; (e) understands how friends feel about the various problems they face. [P. 60]

3. Insightfulness of S Inferred from Test Results

The most indefensible purported measures of insight are those based on test scores. For example, although he thought it "questionable . . . whether these scores . . . are indeed valid measures of self-understanding or self-insight," Tarwater (1953, p. 126) operationally defined *self-understanding* in terms of scores on the Bell Adjustment Inventory. In three other studies, Ss' self-insight was defined in terms of discrepancies between T scores made on scales from a standard personality inventory and T scores from self-rating or self-ranking scales allegedly corresponding respectively to the trait dimensions measured in the inventory. Bugental and Lehner (1958) used the Guilford-Zimmerman Temperament Survey; Renzaglia, Henry, and Rybolt (1962) used Edwards's EPPS; and Purkey (1966) used the California Psychological Inventory in this fashion. It is never made clear why one of these self-report measures should be considered the "accurate" measure of S's "actual" characteristics, while the other should be considered indicative of his self-concept concerning these characteristics (which may or may not "insightfully" correspond to his "actual" characteristics). Moreover, no grounds are given for expecting S to have the psychometric knowledge necessary to make his T scores on two instruments the same even if his "actual" and "self-concept" standings on the respectively corresponding dimensions do coincide.

Gross (1948a) based his Self-Insight Scale on the following nonoperational definition of insight:

Self-insight is the acceptance and admission of both the presence and absence of personality traits within oneself when this acceptance runs counter to a system of emotionally toned ideas or when the admission of the presence or absence of these traits clashes with one's feelings of self-esteem. [P. 223]

Sixty-four psychologists judged a large group of items, and items were retained in the final form of the scale only if they fell in one of the following two combinations: (a) judged to be true of most persons in our society, but "disesteemed"; (b) judged to be false of most persons in our society, but "esteemed." This procedure of item selection necessarily implies that "insight" is equivalent to derogating one's self, whether or not such a derogation is objectively warranted. Such a definition seems theoretically inappropriate and the operations do not permit the establishment of discriminant validity of the instrument as a measure of insight per se. Two of the four validating studies for which formal statistics are reported consist, in effect, of correlations between the Self-Insight Scale and some other self-report on which S has the opportunity to admit undersirable characteristics. In a third study there was no relation between the Self-Insight Scale and professors' ratings of the self-insight of social-work students, even though the ratings were based largely on socially undesirable characteristics. A low but significant *rho* with Chapin's Social Insight Scale was obtained. Gross (1948b) and Costin (1959) have used the Self-Insight Scale as a dependent-variable measure in attempts to evaluate the effects of teaching methods, but such studies cannot really clarify the construct-validity status of this instrument. We must conclude that this scale is not and cannot become a satisfactory measure of "self-insight."

C. Construct Validity Problems in [Self-Other] Discrepancy Measures of Insight and Self-Other Correlations

As already indicated, the most commonly used measurements of individual or group differences in insight involve combinations of two classes of variables (S's reports and O's reports). It is evident that the problem of construct validity of such insight measurements is even more complicated and confused than was the question of construct validity of some of the measures of self-regard discussed in chapters 3 and 4.

If an [S-O] discrepancy is to be taken as indicative of an individual S's degree of insight, or an S-O correlation is to be taken as indicative of a group's degree of insight, we must try to assure ourselves that irrelevant response determiners are not influencing either component of the discrepancy score or the correlation.

1. Construct Validity of O's Reports on S

There are many questions one must raise about the construct validity of O's reports on S's characteristics. First, consider the simplest case, in which O has been clearly instructed to give his *own* impressions of S's characteristics and O is sincerely trying to follow these instructions. Even under these conditions, one must still evaluate the possibility that the construct validity of O's reports has been diminished by one or more of the same influences which were discussed in chapter 3 as possible deleterious influences on self-reports. These influences include acquiescence and extreme-response sets; carelessness; faking; lack of understanding of E's instructions (because of their ambiguity, or because of O's limitations, or because of other reasons); use of forced-choice techniques which do not permit O to express his opinion of S in what seems to him to be the most accurate way; or (conversely) use of open-ended techniques which do not yield the maximum amount of ratee discrimination of which O is capable; and items which include ambiguous terms or are instrinsically confusing in structure so that O can legitimately construe their meaning in various idiosyncratic ways (and, of particular relevance here, in ways different from the S whose [S-O] insight score is being computed). Also, it seems clear from the work of Passini and Norman (1966) that O's ratings are not only subject to simple "halo" effects, but also that these ratings are determined by O's "implicit personality theory" as to what variables "go together." When this tendency is operating in the case of a particular O, it may or may not be a factor lowering the construct validity of that O's report of *his personal impressions of S* (which is what S should be trying to predict). This is so because, to the extent that O's implicit personality theory actually influences his view or evaluation of S's characteristics in a particular way, his implicit personality theory does not invalidate his report on S as an index of his view. But to the extent that O's implicit personality theory leads O to be hasty and nondiscriminating when responding to E's items or scales regarding S, O's reports will not then represent his best efforts to give his personal impressions of S as an individual. Norman and Goldberg (1966) have suggested methods whereby one can infer whether raters' responses have been to some degree systematically influenced by ratees' characteristics (though not necessarily by the ratee characteristics supposedly under study). However, neither their approach nor any other developed so far can determine the relative degree to which O's implicit personality theory (a) actually influences O's views of S, and (b) lowers the construct validity of O's reports as indicative of his actual views of that S.

Of course, when O presumes to report not just his own opinion of S but what others think of S, the validity of O's report is potentially able to be influenced not only by all of the above response determiners which may lower construct validity, but by additional possible distorting factors as well. This is so because O's opinions of others' opinions of S may be biased through insufficient knowledge, motivational distortions, etc.

When O relies on tests, especially projective tests, he is making many assumptions concerning the validity of these tests for inferring anything about S's actual characteristics, and/or for inferring anything about S's self-concept, conscious or unconscious. Most of these assumptions are poorly supported or completely unsupported, rendering research findings obtained by this method of determining [S-O] discrepancies or S-O correlations essentially uninterpretable.

2. Construct Validity of S's Reports

Turning now to the self-report side of the [S-O] discrepancy scores or S-O correlations, one finds that many of the problems of construct validity here are the same as those already examined in detail in chapter 3 and reviewed immediately above as applicable to the construct validity of O's reports about S. For example, numerous potentially irrelevant response determiners may lower the construct validity of S's report as an indicant of his self-concept: acquiescence or extreme-response sets; carelessness or faking; lack of understanding of E's instructions (because of their ambiguity, or because of S's limitations, or because of other reasons); use of forced-choice techniques which do not permit S to express his self-concept in what seems to him to be an accurate manner; or (conversely) use of open-ended techniques which may not yield maximally precise and full self-reports; and items which include ambiguous terms or are intrinsically confusing in structure so that S can legitimately construe the item meaning in an idiosyncratic way (and, of particular relevance here, in a way different from the O(s) whose report will comprise one part of the [S-O] discrepancy scores or S-O correlations used to define S's insight.

Of particular pertinence to the construct validity of [S-O] discrepancy scores or the interpretability of S-O correlations is the point already stressed earlier concerning the need to instruct S clearly to report his *social* self-concept, the only type of self-report one can legitimately use as a basis for the [S-O] discrepancy scores or S-O correlations purportedly indicative of insight. As I have already emphasized, Ss can scarcely be said to lack insight if they have not even been told to try to direct their self-reports toward the O reports which will be used to compute individual [S-O] discrepancies or S-O correlations.

Let us suppose for the moment that instructions to S have appropriately told him definitely to report about his social self-concept, regarding the particular O or class of Os whose reports will be used to determine the [S-O] discrepancy score purportedly indexing S's insight. Let us further suppose that E has done everything he can to minimize the above-mentioned possibly irrelevant influences on S's self-report responses, that is, to maximize the construct validity of S's self-reports as indicants of his social self-concept. Even under these conditions, S's task in an insight study is more complicated than it is in some of the simpler self-regard studies. This is true because S, if he is to receive a valid insight score or contribute to a valid S-O correlation, must have some knowledge of the psychometric characteristics of the O scores to which his S score (social-self-concept report) is to be compared. For example, if E uses objective tests as the basis for O scores from which to derive [S-O] discrepancies or S-O correlations, S needs to know something about the psychological characteristics to which the test purportedly refers, the norm group to which he is to compare himself, and the way the scores of the reference group distribute themselves. If S does not know these things, a "good insight" score could be largely or entirely a matter of chance coincidence of S and O scores; or a "poor insight" score could stem primarily from S's making the wrong assumptions about the characteristics of E's instrument for obtaining O scores. Similarly, lack of coincidence of S and O scores across Ss within a group (yielding a low S-O correlation, supposedly indicative of poor insight within the group) could actually represent Ss' lack of knowledge about the above-mentioned characteristics of Os' instrument (e.g., Amatora,

1956; Eisenman & Robinson, 1968; and Powell, 1948). In the case in which *E* uses ratings by *O* as a basis for [*S-O*] discrepancies, *S* must, if he is to achieve a valid insight score, know something about the general rating behavior of *O*(s) whose reports will enter into the [*S-O*] insight score. For example, he needs to know what score or scale location is "average" for *O*(s) and how widely *O*(s)' ratings of *S*s are dispersed. This is, of course, a version of the problem of stereotype and individual accuracy discussed by Cronbach (1955), Gage and Cronbach (1955), and Brofenbrenner, Harding, and Gallwey (1958). Again, if correlations between *S* and *O* ratings are computed as a basis for inferring a *group's* insight, low *r*s (rather than being indicative of poor insight) may actually stem from *S*s' lack of knowledge about general characteristics of *O*s' rating behavior (e.g., Amatora, 1956; and Webb, 1952, 1955).

This problem can be surmounted to a certain extent by having *S* rank himself in a specified group. Of course, *O*s' reports should then be taken also in terms of ranking *S* within the specified group, in order to render the comparison of *S* and *O* reports even approximately appropriate. This procedure rules out one possible source of irrelevant determiners of insight scores, namely, the possibility that *O*s will vary from *S*s in elevation of all their ratings, as can happen with the use of rating scales (e.g., Bandura, 1956; Brownfain's Insight I, 1952). This procedure also minimizes, although it does not eliminate, the irrelevant effects upon insight scores of intra-*S* and inter-*S* differences in knowledge of the characteristics of *O*-score distributions on various dimensions.

Even with the use of ranking procedures, problems remain in that, if several *O*s are used for each *S*, the *O* score for that *S* will necessarily be a mean or median rank; and therefore, the size of [*S-O*] differences will necessarily be determined in part by the fact that mean or median ranks will have a smaller dispersion than the ranks to which each *S* is referring his self-report (i.e., smaller than the total number of *S*s comprising the reference group in which *S* is to rank himself).

3. Validity of [S-O] Discrepancy Scores as Indicants of Individual Differences in Insight

Thus far I have considered influences on the construct validity of [*S-O*] insight scores and *S-O* correlations across *S*s which stem from (a) construct validity of *O*s' reports on *S*; (b) construct validity of S's self-report; and (c) methodological factors which might artifactually preclude S's report from corresponding to O's report in a way validly indicative of S's degree of accuracy in estimating O's report. However, one must also consider the problem of the validity of the two-part [S-O] score per se.

I consider first some aspects of the simplest situation involving only a single psychological dimension, for example, a single trait scale. Later the complications introduced by summing across trait scales to get an overall score are discussed.

COMPLEXITIES IN THE INSIGHT CONSTRUCT

The most basic question concerning the [S-O] score per se is whether a discrepancy between an S and an O report can be used to define a psychological construct of the sort Es have in mind when they use the word *insight*, that is, a construct involving an inferred state of S. As I discussed in detail in chapter 3, the alleged theoretical status of such a construct as insight is much different from that of an experienced self-ideal discrepancy, another self-referent construct for which a subtractive score is often used. In the case of the self-ideal discrepancy, the referents for both components of the discrepancy score are presumably within S's phenomenal field, as is the discrepancy itself. Insight, by contrast, is operationally defined in terms of a discrepancy between a report of S about his phenomenal self and a report by an O about S. This discrepancy score, if it defines any construct, certainly does not define one having direct meaning in terms of S's experience and consequent behavior, in the way a self-ideal discrepancy may be conceived to have such meaning. In the case of insight, it is only because E thinks of the [S-O] gap as indicating indirectly a significant within-S state of affairs that the [S-O] discrepancy score is assumed to have implications for understanding S's behavior. Often, for example, an implicit assumption is made that noncorrespondence between S and O reports indicates repression or active avoidance on S's part; that is, S has unconscious recognition, though not conscious awareness, of the characteristics which O attributes to him. In other words, the presence of a discrepancy *within* S between his conscious social self-concept and his unconscious social self-concept is often apparently assumed to be the conceptual meaning of the [S-O] discrepancy score. Alternately, the [S-O] discrepancy score may be construed by

E to be indicative only of *S*'s potential vulnerability to eventual feedback information from others which will be disturbingly incongruent with his self-concept and which, by this route, will affect *S*'s behavior. According to either interpretation, however, *E*'s inferences regarding the psychological meaning to *S* of the [*S-O*] discrepancy go far beyond the construct which could possibly be defined by an [*S-O*] discrepancy.

It should be quite clear that neither of these complicated inferences can be justified simply in terms of an [*S-O*] discrepancy. This is true no matter how valid and reliable each component of the discrepancy is or how careful *E* has been to rule out influences which artifactually preclude *S*'s report from corresponding to *O*'s report in a way validly indicative of *S*'s degree of accuracy. In the sense of these complicated chains of constructs, we do not know whether any [*S-O*] score has any construct validity.

Assume for the moment, however, that we wish to use an [*S-O*] discrepancy score initially as a definition of a much more "neutral" or "empty" construct called "insight," so that we can eventually use this score in research designed to clarify the meaning of the construct and its relation to other variables within a theory. If proper care has been taken to minimize irrelevant response determiners, as described above, this limited kind of inference seems plausible. But can we say that [*S-O*] discrepancies of a given size taken from anywhere in the scale range are indicative of equal degrees of even this restricted concept of insight? We cannot. One reason for this is that difference scores tend to be associated systematically with random errors of measurement, so that "raw" difference scores of a given size taken from one part of the range may be more likely to be inflated by chance factors than are the same-size raw differences taken from another part of the range. The use of estimated true X and estimated true Y values should help us here (Cronbach & Furby, 1970); but such a "correction" has not been commonly used.

DISCRIMINANT VALIDITY PROBLEMS IN [*S-O*] SCORES

Usually *E*s have been interested in relating varying sizes of [*S-O*] discrepancy to variations in a dependent variable. If these *E*s wish to show that the dependent variable is a function of the *discrepancy* (that is, a function of "insight"), they must, of course, show that the differences among their Ss in [S-O] scores represent differences with respect to a construct dimension discriminably different from a self-concept dimension. In other words, a kind of discriminant-validity problem is involved. For example, suppose that the "defensiveness" of insightful Ss is compared to the defensiveness of noninsightful Ss when insight is measured in terms of a discrepancy between Ss' and Os' reports about Ss. Suppose further that Ss' self-ratings are not equated between so-called insightful and noninsightful groups formed for the purposes of a particular study or that [S-O] scores are simply correlated with the alleged measure of defensiveness. This would mean that differences in insight are confounded with differences in self-concept. In other words, in terms of the requirements for discriminant validity, the discrepancy score for insight has not been shown to differentiate among Ss in any way discriminably different from the way in which self-concept reports differentiate among these Ss. If associations between insight and defensiveness, for example, are obtained in studies having this confounding, the findings might be parsimoniously interpreted as meaning that defensiveness is associated with differences in self-concept rather than with level of insight.

The research literature contains numerous instances of the confounding of insight and self-concept (especially self-regard) in studies attempting to relate insight to a dependent variable. See, for example, Arsenian (1942); Bandura (1956); Beer, Buckhout, Horowitz, and Levy (1959); Bidwell (1969); probably, Brandt (1958); Brown and Pool (1966); Brownfain (1952); Calvin and Holtzman (1953); probably, Chodorkoff (1954a); deJung and Gardner (1962); Dymond (1950); Goslin (1962); Gough and Heilbrun (1965, pp. 17–18); Holt (1951); Kates and Jordan (1955); Lomont (1966); G. McConnell (1959); R. D. Norman (1953); Parsons, Fulgenzi, and Edelberg (1969); Reed and Cuadra (1957); Reeder, Donohue, and Biblarz (1960); Rokeach (1945); Sears (1936); E. E. Smith (1959); G. M. Smith (1958); Torrance (1954a); Trent (1957, 1959).

COMPLEXITIES INTRODUCED BY SUMMATION OF [S-O] DISCREPANCIES

The conceptual discussion thus far has considered the problems of valid inferences from [S-O] discrepancies on a single dimension. But many Es have apparently assumed that there is a potentially meaningful construct, "overall degree of insight," which can be measured by summing an S's [S-O] discrepancies obtained from each of a number of different trait scales. This practice raises two kinds of serious questions:

1. Is a discrepancy of a given size on one trait-scale dimension equal, in terms of the construct *insight*, to a discrepancy of the same size on another trait-scale dimension, as the summation procedure implies? For many reasons, the assumption of such equivalences seems questionable, in the same ways that simple summing across items in a self-regard measure is questionable or simple summing of self-ideal discrepancies across trait scales is questionable, as discussed in chapter 3.

2. When evaluative dimensions are used in which +, for example, could be assigned to an [S-O] discrepancy in which S's report is more favorable than O's and − could be assigned to an [S-O] discrepancy in which S's report is less favorable than O's, does it make psychological sense to sum absolutely rather than algebraically, as is sometimes done, for example, by Bidwell (1969); Brownfain (1952); Calvin and Holtzman (1953); Dymond (1950); Holt (1951); R. D. Norman (1953); E. E. Smith (1959); and G. M. Smith (1958). That is, absolute summation implies the psychological equivalence, in terms of the construct *insight*, of (a) a discrepancy in which S's self-report is more favorable than O's report to (b) a discrepancy in which S's self-report is less favorable than O's report. To me, this equivalence is not intuitively plausible. On the other hand, algebraic summation (as in Parsons, Fulgenzi, & Edelberg, 1969) could conceivably lead to a low or zero [S-O] score (supposedly indicative of good insight), when in fact S has seriously deviated from O, in one direction on some trait scales and in the other direction on other trait scales. These problems have not been satisfactorily conceptualized or empirically handled by insight researchers, with consequent uninterpretability of their findings; and in general, insight scores summated across traits should be avoided.

VALIDATION STUDIES BASED ON ASSUMED VALIDITY OF [S-O] INSIGHT SCORES

Thus far I have considered some of the unsolved conceptual and methodological problems of the construct validity of insight scores, namely, problems of irrelevant score determiners and of the discriminant validity of these scores. I have not considered that approach to construct validation in which E simultaneously tests a theoretically derived hypothesis and an unvalidated instrument used to measure one variable in that hypothesis. As I have repeatedly stressed, this approach, even when well planned and executed, is the most equivocal line of research germane to the construct validation of an index. And in the case of [S-O] insight scores, the extant research is neither well planned nor well executed. For one thing, no one [S-O] insight score has been used in a series of studies, let alone in a systematic program of studies which might collectively throw light on the construct validity of the insight score. For another thing, even those studies which have related one or another insight score to a dependent variable have been seriously flawed methodologically in ways additional to those already mentioned.

The most common error involves artifactual associations between the independent and dependent variables. For example, many investigators have used some measure of "adjustment" as their dependent variable, and many have used self-reports of S as their index of adjustment. Now we know from many studies that evaluative self-reports tend to intercorrelate positively. I have also said immediately above that self-reports have not usually been held constant across groups which differed in insight. These facts imply that positive findings from such studies may simply be artifacts of the well-known tendency for two evaluative self-reports to correlate positively, for example, Calvin and Holtzman (1953); Holt (1951); and Reed and Cuadra (1957).

Another version of the same kind of artifact may be seen in studies where insight has been related to "projection," and projection has been measured partly through Ss' ratings of others. We know from a number of studies that Ss' evaluative self-ratings tend to correlate positively with the evaluative ratings which those Ss assign to others. If the groups that differ in insight also differ in self-rating, there is a possibility that the supposed relationship between insight and projection may simply be attributed to the tendency for Ss' ratings of self and of others to correlate positively, for example, Rokeach (1945); and Sears (1936).

Occasionally other sources of contamination between dependent and independent variables crop up, as when the same instrument, or items from the same instrument, are involved in some way in both the independent variable and the dependent variable, for example, Gough and Heilbrun (1965); Holt (1951); and Rokeach (1945).

And finally, it seems to me that some investigators have assigned psychological significance to findings which might have occurred by chance alone. I say this because there has been frequent use of one-tailed tests, multiple t tests based on correlated measures obtained from the same Ss, and lack of replication of "significant" findings.

In short, no one insight score has been used often enough and systematically enough to enable one to evaluate the relevance of a pattern of studies to the construct validity of the score. Even the relatively isolated studies involving respectively different [S-O] discrepancies are typically so methodologically limited or flawed that they cannot be used as even a beginning of an accumulation of studies regarding the construct validity of whatever [S-O] score is in question.

4. Appropriateness of [S-O] Discrepancy Scores and Other Methods in Insight Research

There is a serious question whether discrepancy scores purporting to measure individual differences in insight or accuracy of self-perception will ever be useful, necessary, or even interpretable. Cronbach and Furby's (1970) general analysis of problems of interpreting all kinds of difference scores, including insight scores, is relevant to this question.

Their major argument is that individual discrepancy scores introduce many methodological problems of a very serious nature and that, furthermore, it is *not* necessary or useful to compute these troublesome difference scores for individuals as a way of operationalizing individual differences with respect to a construct dimension in order to do research concerning the construct. In the paragraphs immediately below, I identify various classes of research questions concerning insight, and attempt to evaluate whether [S-O] scores would be a useful or even preferred method, or whether alternate methods might be equally, or more, appropriate.

ANTECEDENTS OF INSIGHT

Consider first the case in which one wishes to see whether certain antecedents lead to greater insight or accuracy of self-perception. It would not be necessary to use individual [S-O] discrepancy scores to answer this type of question. Instead, S-O correlations within each of several differently treated groups could appropriately be compared between groups, providing that the study was properly designed and that irrelevant determiners of S-O correlations, such as S-score variability and O-score variability, could be ruled out as explanations of any obtained differences between rs obtained from the respective groups. Whether or not rs were equal between groups, it would also be important in such studies to see whether antecedent conditions had apparently created (a) between-group differences in S-report means; (b) between-group differences in O-report means; and (c) between-group differences in mean S minus mean O. Such findings could be of considerable potential theoretical interest. The third type of finding would have to be evaluated in the light of the first two types; and the third type would be subject to many of the same interpretational hazards as are individual [S-O] scores.

CORRELATES AND CONSEQUENTS OF INSIGHT

Consider next whether [S-O] discrepancy scores would be necessary or appropriate for answering another class of questions, those concerning the association of insight with either contemporary or consequent behavior variables. I argue below that such discrepancy scores are not appropriate or necessary to research bearing on these queries.

It is enlightening to view this class of questions in a wider context, that is, to see that they actually form a subclass of the following more inclusive questions of crucial theoretical and empirical importance: To what extent will self-concept measures suffice to predict behavior? In what manner, and in what respective degrees, will it be necessary to introduce various non-self-concept measures into one's predictions in order to maximize predictive accuracy? Here I am speaking of predictive accuracy not merely for the sake of empirical prediction, but in the context of theory.

The above-mentioned more inclusive questions obviously assume that, no matter how valid one's self-concept measures may be, they will probably be insufficient to make as reliable predictions of behavior as one would like, and that self-concept measures will, therefore, need to be supplemented by non-self-concept measures of Ss' characteristics. For theory-relevant research, the choice of likely non-self-concept measures should be made on the basis of theoretical statements, of course. However, as I have pointed out before, self-concept theorists have not addressed themselves systematically to the issue of how such variables are to be incorporated into their theories; and it will be necessary for them to do so in order to form a theoretical basis for choice of all the relevant non-self-concept measures to be explored. Even with the present primitive theory, however, it appears that Os' evaluations of S, based on a variety of sources, should be among the non-self-concept measures to be introduced along with the self-concept measures. Studies may be said to be pertinent to insight when they involve supplementing self-concept reports with this particular kind of non-self-concept measure. One can see whether non-self-concept measures (including those O reports relevant to "insight") increase the accuracy of prediction of various contemporary or consequent behavior variables. Thus studies relevant to the role of insight in behavior prediction need not involve the questionable [S-O] discrepancy scores.

One way to see whether an O report helps to predict S's behavior is to hold self-report constant while varying O reports. One method of doing this might be to select and compare groups equated on S reports, but different with respect to O reports, as in studies by Murstein (1956) and Wylie (1957). If groups so formed differ with respect to a theoretically associated behavior variable, one might most parsimoniously conclude that O reports do help to predict S's behavior. One might also wish to assume that the amounts of discrepancy between S and O reports is somehow involved in the obtained behavioral differences between groups. However, since mean between-group differences in O reports are completely confounded with between-group differences in "mean S minus mean O," one could not safely conclude that degree of insight within S had any connection with the associated behavioral variable. In any case, it would not be necessary or desirable to compute and use individual [S-O] discrepancy scores for this type of study. Moreover, in interpreting results from this method, one needs to consider carefully whether Ss equated with respect to self-reports are comparable in regard to the inferred self-concept variable presumably indexed by self-report; or whether some kind of bias has made the observed self-reports equal, when in fact the groups have unequal standing with respect to the inferred self-concept variable.

Another way to approach the question about the relative contributions of self-concept and non-self-concept variables in behavior prediction would be to see whether multiple rs which involve non-self-concept measures of S's characteristics are higher than rs obtained between self-concept measures alone and other behavior variables. As I have stressed, the correlations relevant to insight are only a special case of this type of multiple-r exploration. That is, one could compute a multiple r by adding any number of non-self-concept measures to the correlation between self-concept reports and the behavior measures to be predicted; but only one sort of non-self-concept measure would be pertinent to the study of insight. This non-self-concept measure must purport to index the same dimension as that to which S is attempting to direct his self-report. Again, use of individual [S-O] discrepancies is not necessary or desirable for this type of exploration.

An interesting point to note is that the multiple-r technique does not make the arbitrary assumption that the most valid [S-O] discrepancy is that obtained from simple subtraction of O from S, or even from the subtraction of an estimated true O score from an estimated true S score. In the multiple regression equation, S and O variables are entered with weights which will maximize predictive accuracy. Moreover, one can consider data from more than one type of information, since one is not dealing with a subtraction of a single type of O report from an allegedly corresponding S report.

D. Summary and Recommendations

Insight into self (accuracy in self-perception) continues to be an important construct in many personality theories; but the theoretical definitions of this construct are still quite varied, broad, and imprecise. Despite the lack of attention to refinement of the theoretical definitions, many researchers have attempted to operationalize the construct. These attempts seem to fall into three main groups: (a) indexing of individual differences among Ss in [S-O] discrepancies, that is, in discrepancies between self-reports and others' reports about S; (b) indexing of individual differences in insight by direct judges' ratings of this characteristic in Ss; and (c) indexing the degree of insight within a group by means of across-S correlations between S and O reports.

I have examined about 90 studies which either explicitly purported to measure insight (accuracy of self-perception) or which used operations classifiable in one of the above three groups. This examination clearly shows that the very complex measurement problems in this field have not as yet been satisfactorily conceptualized or empirically handled.

Over one-third of the studies I examined appeared between 1955 and 1959, the peak 5-year period for this type of research. Since that time there has been a marked decline in such publications. This decrease may be due to personality researchers' growing realization of the forbidding methodological difficulties in the study of insight, with resulting abandonment of the field. Unfortunately, the decrease in quantity of research has not been accompanied by appreciable improvements in methodology in those studies which have appeared, as is shown by an examination of the 15 cited articles with publication dates between 1965 and 1971. For example, 6 of these studies purported to measure insight by [S-O] discrepancy scores with completely unsupported construct validity, and they related these discrepancy scores to other variables without any control for the confounding of self-concept (especially self-regard) and insight in their alleged measures of insight.

It seems to me that researchers should abandon attempts to index Ss' degrees of insight or self-perceptive accuracy by means of direct judges' ratings of this characteristic in Ss. The measures of this type that have already been introduced into the literature do not even provide an adequate theoretical definition of insight or accuracy of self-perception, as distinct from numerous other characteristics such as self-regard or acceptance of others. Even considering a more appropriately restricted theoretical idea of Ss' insight as judged by others, I find it implausible that judges could possess the many complex abilities implicitly attributed to them by the use of such judging operations. Moreover, the possibility of empirically testing the construct validity of this type of measure seems remote, perhaps even impossible in principle.

Should Es continue to try to study insight or accuracy of self-perception by using measures of correspondence between S and O reports? Certainly not without drastic improvements in method. It seems to me that researchers who continue to be interested in the area of insight or accuracy of self-perception must first concern themselves with all the conceptual and methodological problems of self-concept measurement, and with the establishment of more organized and complete empirical knowledge about the construct validity of their self-measures as indices of the phenomenal self-concept. No matter what question researchers may eventually wish to ask about antecedents, correlates, or consequents of accuracy of self-perception, the construct validity of the self-concept measure is crucially involved. Since we are obviously so far from handling competently these problems of construct validity of self-concept measurement, it seems appropriate to postpone studies of insight or accuracy of self-perception until better self-concept measurement techniques are developed. Only then would one be ready to tackle the many difficult problems in developing an interpretable index of discrepancy or correspondence between self-concept reports and other non-self-report measures *purporting to index the same dimension as that to which the self-concept reports are directed.*

Regarding such studies of [S-O] correspondence, two major methodological points merit reemphasis. First, the degree of [S-O] correspondence or discrepancy per se is insufficient to define insight in any of the complex senses of that term which interest personality theorists, for example, in terms of active repression or avoidance of recognition of one's own characteristics with a concomitant discrepancy between S's conscious and unconscious self-concept. Second, the use of [S-O] discrepancy scores purporting to index individual difference in insight in even a limited or theoretically "empty" sense is both inappropriate and unnecessary in research which attempts to answer questions self-concept theorists are asking. These individual [S-O] discrepancy scores should therefore be supplanted by other methods of indexing [S-O] correspondences and relating such correspondences to other theory-relevant variables. Third, the study of how S-O correlations should be used brings out the fact that O reports are just one of several kinds of non-self-concept variables which self-concept theorists may wish to introduce into the multiple-r studies which attempt to predict behavior more accurately by means of introducing non-self-concept prediction to supplement self-concept predictors.

E. SUPPLEMENTARY REFERENCES

In addition to the publications cited earlier in this chapter, the following were used as a basis for my stated evaluations and recommendations: Arbuckle (1958); Crook (1937); Dinitz, Mangus, and Pasamanick (1959); Mueller (1963); Reed (1953); Rubenstein and Lorr (1957); Russell (1953); Weiner (1964).

7

Summary, Conclusions, and Recommendations

This chapter contains a summary and evaluation of the recent history and present status of theory and research methods in the study of self-referent constructs. Consideration of all the materials in this volume leads inevitably to the conclusion that the present state of affairs leaves much to be desired, differing all too little from the situation described in the 1961 edition of this book.

I argue in this chapter that there are only two defensible alternatives: abandon theorizing and research involving self-referent constructs, or make whatever theoretical and methodological improvements are necessary in order to put such work on a more respectable scientific base. My own predilection today, as in 1961, is toward the second alternative. This choice must be based largely on faith in the ultimate scientific usefulness of self-referent constructs, because nothing has been published since 1961 to enable me to substantiate the choice unequivocally by pointing to sufficient recent progress in theory or methods. However, in my view, the second alternative has not yet been given a fair chance to prove its scientific fruitfulness.

The brief overview of the theory situation, given below, points out that the persisting primitive state of theory undoubtedly is a factor in determining the continuing methodological limitations. I believe this situation is remediable and I suggest ways in which theorizing might be made more fruitful scientifically. Some have argued that even greatly refined trait and state inferences will prove fruitless in scientific personality study, but their argument is seriously questioned.

Faults in measurement and research design pertinent to self-referent constructs stem from causes in addition to theoretical shortcomings. The sections below on measurement and other aspects of method suggest some of these other possible determinants. It will become clear to the reader why those who would choose to retain self-referent constructs in the science of personality can be justified in doing so only if they are willing to undertake a long, difficult series of methodological tasks. I believe these tasks can be accomplished and that their probable contribution to the science of personality is worth the strenuous effort required.

A. Brief Overview of the Status of Theorizing

Beginning in the 1940s, there was a widespread resurgence of interest in the self-concept in psychology and related disciplines; and this interest was reflected in part in a wide variety of personality theories. The last decade has seen no important refinements or elaborations of any of these early theories, but there have been two main "new" influences in the area of personality study: existentialism and Skinnerian behaviorism (Hall & Lindzey, 1970). As it happens, neither of these has been concerned with contributing to a scientific psychology of personality which makes use of self-referent constructs. That is, existentialists have employed self-referent constructs, but they have deliberately avoided scientifically useful clarification of terms and propositions. In fact, they have taken considerable pains to derogate the potential applicability of the scientific attitude and method to the study of personality. By contrast, Skinnerians have stressed the importance of the scientific approach, but they have argued vigorously against the scientific utility of introducing any constructs, including, of course, self-referent constructs. As I discuss below, the continuing primitive state of formal theories involving self-referent constructs has much to do with the degree of adequacy of methodology in researches relevant to the self-concept.

Despite the relative lack of refinement and elaboration of purportedly scientific personality theories invoking self-referent constructs, it has recently become widely fashionable and acceptable to write about such hypothetical constructs as the self-concept and self-esteem without seriously attempting to define terms and without referring the assertions to any particular theory. In such writings many behavior-influencing properties are attributed to the self-concept. Moreover, these authors have gratuitously assumed that many of the factors with which socially conscious citizens and professionals are concerned (for example, parental treatment, socio-economic status, race, and traditional, as opposed to progressive or humanistic, educational practices) influence the self-concept. It is unfortunately true that an appreciable number of professional persons in psychology, psychiatry, education, and sociology are willing to make sweeping assertions along these lines without hinting that such statements require the backing of research evidence and that such evidence is often missing, uninterpretable, or controversial. Naturally this trend in "theorizing" has unfortunate implications for the status of measurement methodology and research-design methodology in the area of self-concept.

B. Brief Overview of the Status of Methodological Practices

While relevant formal theorizing has been relatively stagnant during the last decade, the rate of research output has been very high. The interpretability of these researches depends, of course, upon their methodological adequacy; and it is on methodological considerations that this volume is focused.

Publications relevant to methodology have burgeoned since the appearance of the 1961 edition of this work, and the large output seemed to justify dividing the original work into two volumes: the first offering methodological criticisms and recommendations, and the second critically reviewing substantive studies in the light of methodological criteria developed in the first. I hoped that this division would not only make my task more manageable, but that the earlier appearance of the methodological critiques and standards would enable them to be of immediate use to self-concept researchers.

As I have shown, methodologically relevant publications involve (a) methodological critiques, arguments, and guidelines; and (b) several hundred researches of relevance to methodology, especially to the state of self-concept measurement. So far as the apparent impact of these publications on the methodological adequacy of substantive research on the self-concept is concerned, there are some encouraging improvements, especially in certain journals. On the whole, however, methodology in self-concept research has not shown the improvements in the last decade which one might, with reasonable optimism, have hoped for. Even the most prestigious laboratories and journals are occasionally publishing studies based on completely unvalidated instruments and flawed research designs. Accordingly, the contributions of substantive self-concept studies cannot "add up to" as much as their total number might imply.

C. Characteristics of Theory Especially Relevant to Methodology

Before elaborating concretely on the above evaluative assertions concerning the state of methodology, I turn to a brief analysis of the scientific shortcomings of all those personality theories which emphasize constructs concerning the self. I do this because some understanding of these shortcomings offers a partial answer to the ultimately important questions: How can we explain various particular aspects of the disappointing methodological state of affairs? What recommendations for methodological improvements can be made?

The first issue is whether self-referent constructs, as presently formulated, are adequate analytical and predictive categories. Let us examine the scientific utility of these constructs.

We may begin by asking why some persons have felt the need to postulate such inferred variables referring to the self. It is obvious that, on a nonscientific level, self-referent cognitions and feelings have subjective validity. But of course, this is no necessary justification for putting constructs concerning the self into a theory which purports to be scientific. To some, however, these constructs have seemed to be necessary in order to give a complete, scientific account of human behavior.

What sorts of observations are theorists trying to account for by introducing constructs referring to the self? For one thing, psychologists of a number of schools of thought have noted that antecedent conditions, defined in terms of interexperimenter agreement, are not sufficient to predict either group trends or individual differences in human behavior. They have suggested that one could increase the accuracy of predictions of behavior if one found out what the subject perceives, knows, or feels about the "objective" situation, including his own characteristics. At the time that personality theorists first began stressing the importance of self-referent constructs, they were able to point out that general behavior theorists, for purposes of their own, had thus far delimited their theories in such a way that they were unable to account for some of the behavior one can observe in the clinic, in school, and in other "everyday-life" situations. For example, early general behavior theories in the area of motivation had been mostly concerned with organic drives and physically painful aversive stimuli. To theorists interested in the self, these did not seem to be adequate motivational constructs to account for all the kinds of behavior they wished to explain. In fact, the general experimental psychologist himself had recognized this limitation, as evidenced, for example, by the increasing attention being paid to "ego-involvement" as an independent variable, or as a variable which must be controlled in experiments on basic learning and perceptual processes. Likewise, various more recently developed social-learning theories springing from earlier general behavior theories recognized the need to try to account for some of the phenomena which interested the personality theorists. In other words, there is increasing agreement that those personality theorists who emphasized self-referent constructs were correct in pointing out the restricted potential of early behavior theories.

In addition, many personality theorists have felt that the organizational or configurational properties of human functioning are not subsumed by the constructs of most present-day general behavior theories, even by the social-learning theories developed recently. It was partly to account for the apparent interrelatedness of observed behavior sequences that Gestalt characteristics were attributed to the phenomenal and nonphenomenal self, and the centrality of self-regarding attitudes was postulated.

While constructs concerning the self may seem to be needed for the above reasons, the way they have been used poses a dilemma. That is, as I pointed out in 1961, these constructs have been stretched to cover so many inferred cognitive and motivational processes that their utility for analytic and predictive purposes has been greatly diminished. At that time I suggested that one possible implication of this dilemma is that theories which depend heavily on overgeneralized self-referent constructs should be abandoned as potentially fruitful scientific tools. Certainly, if the construct system cannot be more precisely reformulated, this alternative seems the correct one.

As an alternate possible way out of the dilemma, I suggested that perhaps the constructs and hypotheses could be improved. For example, it appeared in 1961, and it still seems plausibly the case, that more molecular inferred variables may have greater research utility. That is, such characteristics as self-actualization, self-differentiation, and self-consistency have not led to enlightening research. By contrast, constructs such as self-acceptance or self-esteem, especially when referring to specified attributes, have yielded somewhat more manageable and fruitful research procedures. There is a basic question as to why it has been so difficult to try to conceptualize and measure such broad constructs as "global" self-esteem and to relate these broad constructs to theoretically relevant behavior: Have we proposed constructs too inclusive for manageable verbal and empirical definition? Or, more fundamentally, are people in fact not characterized by such broad-range behavior-determining inferred states as, for example, "global" self-esteem? That is, is it possible that a larger number of more restricted inferred states play a part in determining behavior? It seems plausible that the more delimited self-evaluative aspects may be theoretically appropriate and easier to define verbally and operationally.

In 1961 I suggested that an additional possible alternative to abandoning self theories might be to improve their predictiveness by the addition of more variables. The question is whether, in introducing and emphasizing constructs of certain kinds, some personality theorists have also restricted their conceptual systems to such an extent that they have limited the predictiveness of the theories. In other words, they may be simply failing to take into account the role of some important determinants of behavior. A possible example of this kind of restrictiveness is the emphasis of self-concept theory upon the subject's conscious processes.

For instance, certain psychologists have thought that self-concept research yields weak or equivocal results because the theory does not systematically include the unconscious self-concept or other unconscious cognitive and dynamic processes. With reference to the unconscious self-concept, for example, some theorists believe that one should be able to predict behavior more accurately from a knowledge of S's unconscious self-concept than one can from a knowledge of his conscious self-concept. And of course it follows that valid unconscious self-concept measures, if added to conscious self-concept measures, should improve the predictiveness of the theory.

In 1961 I suggested that, quite possibly, the omission of unconscious self-concept variables from self-concept theories could be one of the reasons why these theories have had limited success in predicting important behaviors. However, there was then and still is no proof that one can predict behavior as well, let alone better, with unconscious self-concept measures than with conscious self-concept measures. In 1961, the state of validation of unconscious self-concept measures was even more parlous than was the state of validation of conscious self-concept measures; and this disparity is still greater today. Therefore, the burden of proof is presently on the person favoring the addition of the unconscious self-concept to the variables from which we try to predict behavior. Although it seems plausible that phenomenological theories could become more predictive by the addition of constructs concerning the nonphenomenal self, my point here is that this has not been demonstrated with the indices we now have.

A similar argument applies to any of the currently available indices of other unconscious processes, such as the unconscious motivations postulated by Freudian theorists. Although valid measures are not at hand to test unequivocally the value of adding such constructs to phenomenal theory, these nonphenomenal constructs may someday prove to be of equal or greater predictive value than phenomenal constructs.

One must remember, too, that we cannot say how much the obtained associations between conscious self-concept measures and behavior would be strengthened if the conscious self-concept measures themselves could be made more reliable and valid.

There is another important limitation of self-concept theory which also stems from the theory's emphasis on the subject's conscious processes. In stressing the importance of S's view, objectively measurable variables have been slighted. It has been suggested that predictions of behavior could be made more accurate by the inclusion of objectively specifiable antecedent factors, including facts about S's previous experiences, S's objective characteristics, and objectively defined current stimuli. In this connection, it might prove profitable to effect more connections with the general experimental psychology of learning, motivation, and perception. There are many pertinent facts, already established through experiment, to which theorists stressing the self have not referred. And some of the constructs of these theorists, for example, in regard to learning, might also have utility in making predictions of interest to personality theorists who emphasize the self. All these possible improvements in theorizing have important implications for measurement methodology and other aspects of research methodology, of course.

Again, it remains to be demonstrated whether behavior can be predicted more efficiently by objective measures than by indices of the phenomenal self, or whether adding objective measures to self-concept measures improves the predictions one could make from either type of measure alone.

Not all theories which emphasize self-referent constructs are phenomenological. But in the case of self-concept theory, the objection may be raised that the addition of objective measures and measures of unconscious processes is inconsistent with the phenomenal premises of the theory. However, this cannot be taken too seriously since, for one thing, self-concept theory is already internally inconsistent, as I have pointed out in chapter 2. Besides, empirical improvements in predictiveness should be the test of the worth of any suggestion about broadening self-concept theory.

I have just mentioned the internal inconsistency in self-concept theory. In fact, internal inconsistency apparently characterizes all personality theories which emphasize constructs concerning the self, although the vagueness of their statements often makes it impossible to identify inconsistencies with certainty. On this score alone, none of these theories, as presently formulated, can be called wholly scientific. Probably these inconsistencies are partly responsible for the poor state of measurement and research design in this area. Regarding both the possibly improved phenomenological constructs and any other sorts of constructs theorists might decide to introduce, ideas about interactions should be stated in the theory's propositions in order to imply particular research procedures and to furnish some plausible, a priori rational basis for synthesizing results of studies which might otherwise seem contradictory or not supportive of one another.

Not only are delimited constructs and internal consistency among postulates necessary, but "lower-order" hypotheses are required as well, if personality theories which stress the self are to become scientifically useful. Some personality psychologists have argued that general behavior theorists have been too molecular and that they have failed to attack really significant aspects of human development and functioning. Even if one were to accept this allegation, it does not follow that stating vague, overarching, unverifiable generalizations will remedy the situation. As Morison (1960) reminds us, it may be satisfying to psychologists' needs to have a comprehensive theory, but it is probably more scientifically productive in the long run to begin one's work with limited but testable hypotheses.

If, as was suggested above, self theorists were to seek connections with general behavior theories, the "tough-minded" approach could be helpful in making the needed reformulations in hypotheses involving the self.[1]

In short: It is true that personality theories which stress the self have addressed themselves to important, unanswered questions concerning human behavior.

When we examine the history of scientific thought we find that prescientific speculations seem to be a necessary way of beginning to understand any phenomenon one is trying to explain. From some of these kinds of prescientific efforts, hypotheses of a scientific sort have come, when proper steps were taken. Those who have presented personality theories which stress self-referent constructs have performed a useful pioneering function, and their work may point to a scientific metamorphosis with regard to the psychology of personality.

However, as time has passed and a considerable body of research has accumulated, it seems that the crisis situation mentioned in my 1961 book is still at hand with regard to personality theories and research which emphasize the self. For one thing, the usefulness of these theories is called into question by the state of the empirical evidence, and the latter depends on methodological quality which, in turn, is partly a function of ambiguities in the theories.

If personality theories stressing self-referent constructs are going to be counted among scientifically useful theories, they must move in the directions I have outlined above. If the theoretical difficulties cannot eventually be overcome, both the theoretical and related empirical efforts might just as well be abandoned, so far as their probable contribution to scientific psychology is concerned. On the other hand, these theories are concerned with important issues.

---

[1] I have not, of course, attempted an exhaustive appraisal of self theories in the light of criteria for a good scientific theory, nor have I attempted a detailed comparison of the scientific usefulness of various personality and general behavior theories. Such an undertaking is beyond the scope of this book.

Therefore, a serious attempt to develop lower-order hypotheses concerning more molecular and carefully defined constructs and dealing with these important issues in a more precise, manageable way might be worthwhile.

D. THE CURRENT MEASUREMENT SITUATION

I turn now to a descriptive elaboration of the brief evaluative statements made above about the status of methodology, focusing first on the improvements and remaining shortcomings in the measurement situation.

1. Evaluative Summary

1. One notable improvement is that there is more widespread verbal recognition of the need for (a) using instruments with acceptable levels of reliability and construct validity; (b) doing more construct-validation work; and (c) qualifying one's conclusions in the light of limitations on the measuring instruments used. However, despite this increasing recognition of what is needed, most studies still seem to be carried out with instruments which have been used only once or a few times and are completely unvalidated for their purpose. This practice may reflect in part the fact that theoretical statements have not been clear enough to lead researchers to agree on any particular operational definition or class of operations for a given construct.

2. A second improvement is that work in measurement areas which have proved to be "blind alleys" has definitely declined, for example, use of (a) discrepancy and other indefensible purported measures of "insight," (b) undefended and unexplored alleged measures of "unconscious self-concept," and (c) alleged measures of "configurational" properties of the self-concept. It seems probable that many researchers have begun to realize the formidable methodological requirements and pitfalls involved in trying to establish valid indices of such constructs. The decline in the creation and use of uninterpretable measures is all to the good. However, the constructs which they attempted to index are still of importance to theorists, so the eventual testing of theoretical propositions would seem to demand a return to the conceptual and methodological problems of their measurement. No doubt the fuzziness of the theories has contributed to the failures to operationalize the

constructs appropriately, and to the discouragement with even attempting to measure constructs in these areas. As I said, there have been no constructive attempts in the last decade to improve the theories in ways which could promote more appropriate operationalizing of these constructs.

3. Although a great many instruments have been used only once or twice, the last decade has seen considerable validity-relevant work on a few instruments. Some of this work has commendably applied certain relevant technologies such as item analysis, factor analysis, and controls for response set. But no one instrument intended to measure self-concept variables has been developed by the process of beginning with close attention to stating rigorous conceptual definitions; followed by item building or item selection relevant to the conceptual definitions; and followed, finally, by the application of all appropriate modern procedures for refining a purported index of a construct and establishing its construct validity. Two especially noteworthy shortcomings characterize even the most thoroughly studied instruments: lack of clarity in the establishment of the basic construct definitions, and failure to apply multitrait-multimethod analyses and other techniques for establishing discriminant validity. Part of the difficulty stems from inadequate delineation of the constructs by personality theorists.

The majority of those instruments which have received the most empirical attention have attempted to measure some sort of global self-regard, such as overall self-esteem or overall self-acceptance. As I said above, it may be the questionable features of such global constructs which cause difficulties in establishing the construct validity of these instruments and in demonstrating the relationships of such scores to other theoretically associated variables. Perhaps more molecular and carefully conceptualized constructs might have more scientific utility.

In any event, after a thorough overview of publications on these more fully studied instruments, I have had to conclude, in the light of modern methodological standards and such evidence as is available, that use of a number of these instruments should be abandoned. Others may prove useful for research in their present form, pending the kind of work that is really indispensable, namely, starting from scratch to develop new instruments, using all available conceptual and methodological refinements in instrument development. As I indicated in my discussion of theory, we need much more careful thought about the constructs we are aiming to index, and more thought about the sorts of behaviors which would be appropriate to the respective constructs, for example, the relationship of verbal behaviors to phenomenal constructs, the proper behavioral grounds for inferring nonphenomenal constructs, and the behavior areas respectively relevant to more molecular construct dimensions.

Those instruments which have received the greatest amount of empirical attention are probably best used as springboards for creation of new instruments or drastic revisions of present ones. The instruments which have been very little used may also serve some purpose in this connection, in that they may be mined for ideas about items.

2. Reasons for the Current State of Measurement

One may well wonder why, after more than 20 years of research on the self-concept, no new instrument has been developed and validated using *all* of the relevant published conceptual and practical methodological guidelines. Several plausible reasons for this may be suggested:

1. In some quarters there has been apparently little or no appreciation of (a) the reason why adequate instrumentation is indispensable for progress in substantive research; (b) the reason why ready-made instruments usually will not answer the purpose of the researcher; and (c) the fact that, if adequate measurement of a variable proves impossible to attain, the research enterprise involving the alleged variable should be abandoned.

2. Perhaps, as psychologists and others have developed a fuller recognition of the great conceptual, methodological, and practical difficulties, they have been thereby discouraged from beginning on what is bound to be a tedious, formidable task. In large part the conceptual difficulties and ensuing discouragement may stem from the continuing poor state of self-concept theories, already outlined earlier in this chapter. Another reason why the area has been recognized as discouragingly difficult is that much of the methodological literature is concerned with warning the reader about important difficulties for which, in many cases, no ready remedies can be given at this time, such as problems concerning the possible influence upon measurement of social desirability or the possible

influence upon measurement of social interaction between E and S. In other words, researchers have been forced to recognize many potentially invalidating influences which must be considered, but they have not been provided with answers about how to take care of these possible influences in actual measurement procedures. This situation can understandably cause many a potential researcher to abandon an area rather than try to work out needed procedures.

3. Further, I suspect that some of the lag in proper instrument development stems from the fact that relatively little prestige is attached (especially by personality theorists) to the activity of building and refining a valid instrument for measuring a personality construct.

4. One might also guess that the lag in proper instrument development stems in part from the fact that most persons interested in self-concept theory (or, for that matter, in many different personality theories) are insufficiently versed in conceptual and technical principles of measurement of personality constructs. For their part, sophisticated methodologists are not well enough versed in substantive and conceptual problems of personality theories to become directly involved in personality research. One can only speculate why this is so. There are perhaps temperamental differences between those who find their intellectual rewards in theorizing about personality and those who like to think about and apply rigorous methodologies. Then, too, perhaps the training of personality theorists is not what it should be, beginning at the undergraduate level, where texts make sweeping generalizations about personality without seriously attempting to orient the student to the need for research based on sophisticated methodologies. Finally, the needed sources of guides to methodological improvements are widely scattered; and even when the advanced student of personality theory finds and reads them, it is not always obvious how to apply them to the problem at hand.

5. Moreover, it is entirely possible that part of the lag in instrument development is due to the fact that the work on the most studied instruments is widely scattered and is thus not easily available to researchers wishing to evaluate one of these instruments or to mine it for ideas for new instruments.

6. It is apparent that proper instrument development implies that nothing less systematic than a *program* of research must be carried out. This means long-continued application of a consider-

able number of resources—more than are available to many persons interested in self-concept research. I have the impression that many researchers (especially doctoral candidates) who use self-concept variables in their studies are doing what will remain "one-shot" investigations. This situation multiplies research output but does not yield the needed programmatic approach to instrument development.

7. It is also unfortunately true that most researchers who use self-concept variables seem to be interested in getting on with substantive research, even when they recognize that suitable measuring instruments are not at hand. Therefore, rather than carrying out a program of research for measuring the construct, they proceed with their substantive study, offering a disclaimer and a warning "let the reader beware." In effect, then, there is a refusal in some quarters to admit that there are no shortcuts or fast roads to substantive conclusions when there are no adequate instruments for measuring the constructs to which the conclusions refer.

8. Finally, note should be taken of another possible reason why a really well-developed instrument has not appeared in the self-concept area. Disturbing questions about the potential value of the entire enterprise of trying to measure inferred "traits" or "states" (including self-concept variables) are raised by the generally quite limited success in using trait or state measures to predict behavior within any situation or across situations. Are these disappointing results a function of inadequacies in the measuring process or in the research procedures by which we have thus far attempted to relate the measured constructs to behavior? Or are these disappointing results perhaps due to the fact that individual differences in Ss' inferred characteristics (here, their self-concept characteristics) really have a negligible influence on individual differences in behavior? If the latter is the case, the approach to personality study via measurement of inferred characteristics should be abandoned, because it involves an erroneous set of assumptions about behavior-influencing variables, as Mischel (1968) has suggested. Those who are persuaded by Mischel's viewpoint naturally could not be expected to try to develop an adequate instrument, because to make such an attempt would be to engage in what, for them, would be an absurd activity. Others (e.g., Fiske, 1971) have offered the counterargument that the enterprise of conceptualizing and attempting to measure constructs of personality is not necessarily

misguided and should not be abandoned. Instead, problems of measuring the constructs of personality should be completely rethought, and procedures should be started from the ground up. However, like their opponents, thinkers who agree with Fiske can offer only informed guesses as to the likelihood that their approach will eventually succeed in improving the science of personality. And as is abundantly clear, the approach recommended by the proponents of Fiske's viewpoint is an exceedingly difficult one.[2] Thus, those who wish to agree with Fiske may nevertheless find that this uncertainty about the ultimate scientific significance of their work discourages them from undertaking the arduous task of instrument development. (Self-concept students who are interested in the argument described above and suggestions as to fruitful future approaches should examine recent articles by Alker, 1972, and Bem, 1972.)

E. EVALUATION OF NONMEASUREMENT ASPECTS OF THE CURRENT METHODOLOGICAL SITUATION

I turn now to a consideration of the situation regarding methodological problems other than measurement. Repeatedly I have argued that planning adequate research procedures for studies relevant to self-concept theories is hampered because the theories as presented often imply no precise hypotheses concerning the mode of functional relationship of allegedly important variables. Especially noteworthy is the lack of theoretical guidance for stating testable multivariate hypotheses which predict interactions between construct variables and between these variables and situation variables.

I have also argued that, contrary to the opinion of some, phenomenological and self-concept theories imply no unique methodological requirements in principle; but that, for various reasons, suitable designs are much more difficult to plan and execute in practice than is the case in many areas of psychology. In many instances, adequate tests of hypotheses would require longitudinal research; multivariate studies; and, of course, the use of many Ss. All such requirements increase E's practical difficulties. (A fuller consideration of the adequacy of research designs for testing stated substantive hypotheses will be given in volume 2.)

---

[2] This is not to imply that there are any fewer methodological complications in the approach recommended by Mischel (1968).

The defensibility of using deception techniques has come seriously into question on both ethical and methodological grounds,
creating the need for new techniques to test a number of important
hypotheses, and especially to test them under controlled laboratory
conditions.

Granting the many practical difficulties, and granting that there
are no easy guides to creative thinking about hypotheses and ways
to test them, still, many inexcusable and avoidable flaws occur in
current research. These were briefly outlined in chapter 2.

Why is there such a high incidence of avoidable flaws in published research relevant to the self-concept? Many of the same
reasons may be suggested that were proposed to explain the undeveloped state of measurement in this area. For example, self-concept
researchers are not adequately trained in methodology; there is a
wide scattering of relevant methodological guides; it is not always
made explicit in the references how the presented guidelines would
be concretely applicable in the case of self-concept research; and
most researchers seem anxious to state a substantive generalization
even if they have to "push things," for example, by ignoring the
weaknesses in their research designs, or by inappropriately choosing,
applying, or interpreting statistical tests. Perhaps editors deserve
some of the blame for perpetuation of these avoidable flaws, since
they evidently have not set up and maintained proper standards.

In many ways, *avoidable* flaws in research design and execution
seem less defensible than do shortcomings in measurement techniques. This is so because rectifying the latter would be a very
long, difficult process, while improving the rigorousness in planning
other aspects of research and interpreting one's statistical results
could, in many instances, be accomplished with relatively less additional time and effort.

F. Implications for the Future

The import of all the above discussion is that scientific personality psychologists have only two alternatives regarding self-
referent constructs. As I have already mentioned, there is the
possibility being promulgated today that the entire enterprise of
attempting to predict behavior from theoretical inferred traits and
states (including self-concept variables) is founded on an empirically
mistaken assumption that individual differences in inferred vari-

ables have a substantial influence in creating individual differences in behavior, especially in behavior consistencies across situations. If it is true that this assumption is erroneous, theorizing and methodological work on trait and state variables, including the self-concept, should be abandoned (whether or not one would agree with the proposed substitute suggested by Mischel, 1968).

On the other hand, those theorists and researchers who reject this view may logically choose to be interested in theory and research on self-referent constructs. However, if they do decide that the present crisis in predictability cannot be attributed to basic misconceptions in their theoretical assumptions, and if they also decide to continue the task of trying to demonstrate the importance of self-concept variables in explaining and predicting behavior, they must do what is necessary to put their work on a more solid footing so that the viability of their basic assumptions will be more scientifically tested. The process will be arduous and time-consuming. In this respect these workers will be in the same position as any other psychologist, or any other scientist, for that matter. That is, the required procedures are not peculiar to these theories. Morison (1960) has represented very well my final thoughts on this matter: Although interpreting the facts thoughtfully and going beyond them are the most important things, gradualness, drudgery, and patience are the price of attaining those significant increments in factual knowledge from which valid psychological laws may be formed. We still have as great a need to pay attention to this in the 1970s as we did in 1960.

As for my own opinion, I believe that abandoning research on self-referent constructs is not the more justifiable alternative. Of course, I can offer no assurances as to the ultimate usefulness of pursuing further study of such constructs. I do believe that continuing to spawn and subsequently publish numerous researches with avoidable conceptual and methodological flaws would be a most unfortunate waste of professional time and energy and would harm the development of scientific personality study. However, it seems plausible that choosing the alternative of continuing the empirical study of self-referent constructs could lead to significant increments in our scientific knowledge of personality, provided that there is a much more widespread and serious commitment to the conceptual and methodological rigors necessarily involved in scientific work.

Bibliography

Adams, H. B.; Robertson, M.H.; & Cooper, G. D. Sensory deprivation and personality change. *Journal of Nervous and Mental Disease*, 1966, 143, 256–265.

Aiken, E. G. Alternate forms of semantic differential for measurement of changes in self-description. *Psychological Reports,* 1965, 16, 177–178.

Akeret, R. U. Interrelationships among various dimensions of the self concept. *Journal of Counseling Psychology*, 1959, 6, 199–201.

Alexander, T. The prediction of teacher-pupil interaction with a projective test. *Journal of Clinical Psychology*, 1950, 6, 273–276.

Alexander, T. Certain characteristics of the self as related to affection. *Child Development,* 1951, 22, 285–290.

Alker, H. A. Is personality situationally specific or intrapsychically consistent? *Journal of Personality,* 1972, 40, 1–16.

Allardice, B. S., & Dole, A. A. Body image in Hansen's disease patients. *Journal of Projective Techniques and Personality Assessment,* 1966, 30, 356–358.

Allport, G. W. *Pattern and growth in personality.* New York: Holt, Rinehart & Winston, 1961.

Altrocchi, J. Interpersonal perceptions of repressors and sensitizers and component analysis of assumed dissimilarity scores. *Journal of Abnormal and Social Psychology,* 1961, 62, 528–534.

Altrocchi, J.; Parsons, O. A.; & Dickoff, H. Changes in self-ideal discrepancy in repressors and sensitizers. *Journal of Abnormal and Social Psychology,* 1960, 61, 67–72.

Altrocchi, J., & Perlitsch, H. Ego control patterns and attribution of hostility. *Psychological Reports,* 1963, 12, 811–818.

Amatora, Sister M. Validity in self-evaluation. *Educational and Psychological Measurement,* 1956, 16, 119–126.

American Psychological Association. *Technical recommendations for psychological tests and diagnostic techniques.* Washington, D.C.: APA, 1954.

American Psychological Association. *Standards for educational and psychological tests and manuals.* Washington, D.C.: APA, 1966.

Anderson, T. B., & Olsen, L. C. Congruence of self and ideal-self and occupational choices. *Personnel and Guidance Journal,* 1965, 44, 171–176.

Angyal, A. *Foundations for a science of personality*. New York: Commonwealth Fund, 1941.

Ansbacher, H. L., & Ansbacher, R. R. (Eds.). *The individual psychology of Alfred Adler*. New York: Basic Books, 1956.

Apfeldorf, M., & Smith, W. J. The representation of the body self in human figure drawings. *Journal of Protective Techniques and Personality Assessment*, 1966, 30, 283–289.

Arbuckle, D. S. Self-ratings and test scores on two standardized personality inventories. *Personnel and Guidance Journal*, 1958, 37, 292–293.

Archibald, W. P. Self-esteem and balance with impersonal attitude objects. *Psychonomic Science*, 1970, 21, 363–364.

Argyris, C. Some unintended consequences of rigorous research. *Psychological Bulletin*, 1968, 70, 185–197.

Arkoff, A., & Weaver, H. B. Body image and body dissatisfaction in Japanese-Americans. *Journal of Social Psychology*, 1966, 68, 323–330.

Armstrong, H. E., Jr. Relationship between a dimension of body image and two measures of conditioning. *Journal of Consulting and Clinical Psychology*, 1968, 32, 696–700.

Armstrong, H. E., Jr., & Armstrong, D. C. Relation of physical fitness to a dimension of body image. *Perceptual and Motor Skills*, 1968, 26, 1,173–1,174.

Armstrong, R. G. The Leary Interpersonal Check List: A reliability study. *Journal of Clinical Psychology*, 1958, 14, 393–394.

Armstrong, R. G.; Hambacher, W. O.; & Overley, J. F. Self concepts of psychiatric and normal subjects as revealed by the WAY test. *Journal of Clinical Psychology*, 1962, 18, 271–276.

Armstrong, R. G., & Hauck, P. A. Sexual identification and the first figure drawn. *Journal of Consulting Psychology*, 1961, 25, 51–54.

Armstrong, R. G., & Wertheimer, M. Personality structure in alcoholism. *Psychological Newsletter*, 1959, 10, 341–349.

Arnhoff, F. N., & Damianopoulos, E. N. Self-body recognition: An empirical approach to the body image. *Merrill-Palmer Quarterly*, 1962, 8, 143–148.

Arnold, F. C., & Walter, V. A. The relationship between a self- and other-reference sentence completion test. *Journal of Counseling Psychology*, 1957, 4, 65–70.

Aronson, E., & Carlsmith, J. M. Experimentation in social psychology. In G. Lindzey & E. Aronson (Eds.), *The handbook of social psychology*. (2nd ed.) Vol. 2. Reading, Mass.: Addison-Wesley, 1968. Pp. 1–79.

Arsenian, S. Own estimate and objective measurement. *Journal of Educational Psychology*, 1942, 33, 291–302.

Ashcraft, C., & Fitts, W. H. Self-concept change in psychotherapy. *Psychotherapy: Theory, Research and Practice*, 1964, 1, 115–118.

Ausubel, D. P., & Schiff, H. M. Some intrapersonal and interpersonal determinants of individual differences in socioempathic ability among adolescents. *Journal of Social Psychology*, 1955, 41, 39–56.

Ausubel, D. P.; Schiff, H. M.; & Gasser, E. B. A preliminary study of developmental trends in socioempathy: Accuracy of perception of own and others' sociometric status. *Child Development*, 1952, 23, 111–128.

Babbitt, H. G. An attempt to produce changes in attitudes toward the self by means of verbal conditioning. *Journal of Verbal Learning and Verbal Behavior*, 1962, 1, 168–172.

Bachman, J. G. *Youth in transition.* Vol. 2. *The impact of family background and intelligence on tenth-grade boys.* Ann Arbor, Mich.: Survey Research Center, Institute for Social Research, 1970.

Back, K. W., & Guptill, C. S. Retirement and self-ratings. In I. H. Simpson & J. C. McKinney (Eds.), *Social aspects of aging.* Durham: Duke University Press, 1966. Pp. 120–129.

Back, K. W., & Paramesh, C. R. Self-image, information exchange, and social character. *International Journal of Psychology*, 1969, 4, 109–117.

Bailey, W. L.; Shinedling, M. M.; & Payne, I. R. Obese individuals' perception of body image. *Perceptual and Motor Skills*, 1970, 31, 617–618.

Baker, F. Measures of ego identity: A multitrait-multimethod validation. *Educational and Psychological Measurement*, 1971, 31, 165–174.

Baker, S. R. Factor analytic study of self perception of graduate and undergraduate students. *Perceptual and Motor Skills*, 1968, 26, 1,073–1,074.

Bandura, A. Psychotherapist's anxiety level, self-insight, and psychotherapeutic competence. *Journal of Abnormal and Social Psychology*, 1956, 52, 333–337.

Bannister, D., & Mair, J. M. M. *The evaluation of personal constructs.* New York: Academic Press, 1968.

Barber, T. X., & Calverley, D. S. Hypnotizability, suggestibility, and personality: IV. A study with the Leary Interpersonal Check List. *British Journal of Social and Clinical Psychology*, 1964, 3, 149–150.

Barrett, R. L. Changes in accuracy of self-estimates. *Personnel and Guidance Journal*, 1968, 47, 353–357.

Bartlett, C. J. The relationships between self-ratings and peer ratings on a leadership behavior scale. *Personnel Psychology*, 1959, 12, 237–246.

Bass, A. R., & Fiedler, F. E. Interpersonal perception scores and their components as predictors of personal adjustment. *Journal of Abnormal and Social Psychology*, 1961, 62, 442–445.

Baumrind, D. Some thoughts on ethics of research: After reading Milgram's "Behavioral study of obedience." *American Psychologist*, 1964, 19, 421–423.

Baymurr, F. B., & Patterson, C. H. A comparison of three methods of assisting underachieving high school students. *Journal of Counseling Psychology*, 1960, 7, 83–89.

Beard, B. H., & Pishkin, V. Self-concept changes in training medical and nursing students. *Diseases of the Nervous System*, 1970, 3, 616–623.

Becker, G. Sex-role identification and the needs for self and social approval. *Journal of Social Psychology*, 1968, 69, 11–15.

Becker, G., & Dileo, D. T. Scores on Rokeach's Dogmatism Scale and the response set to present a positive social and personal image. *Journal of Social Psychology*, 1967, 71, 287–293.

Becker, W. C. Relationship of factors in parental ratings of self and each other to the behavior of kindergarten children as rated by mothers, fathers, and teachers. *Journal of Consulting Psychology*, 1960, 24, 507–527.

Becker, W. C. A comparison of the factor structure and other properties of the 16 PF and the Guilford-Martin Personality Inventories. *Educational and Psychological Measurement*, 1961, 21, 393–404.

Beer, M.; Buckhout, R.; Horowitz, M. W.; Levy, S. Some perceived properties of the differences between leaders and non-leaders. *Journal of Psychology*, 1959, 47, 49–56.

Beilin, H. The prediction of adjustment over a four year interval. *Journal of Clinical Psychology*, 1957, 13, 270–274.

Beloff, H., & Beloff, J. Unconscious self-evaluation using a stereoscope. *Journal of Abnormal and Social Psychology*, 1959, 59, 275–278.

Bem, D. J. An experimental analysis of self-persuasion. *Journal of Experimental Social Psychology*, 1965, 1, 199–218.

Bem, D. J. The epistemological status of interpersonal simulations: A reply to Jones, Linder, Kiesler, Zanna, and Brehm. *Journal of Experimental Social Psychology*, 1968, 4, 270–274.

Bem, D. J. Constructing cross-situational consistencies in behavior: Some thoughts on Alker's critique of Mischel. *Journal of Personality*, 1972, 40, 17–26.

Bendig, A. W., & Hoffman, J. L. Bills' Index of Adjustment and the Maudsley Personality Inventory. *Psychological Reports*, 1957, 3, 507.

Bennett, V. D. C. Development of a self concept Q sort for use with elementary age school children. *Journal of School Psychology*, 1964, 3, 19–25. (a)

Bennett, V. D. C. Does size of figure drawing reflect self-concept? *Journal of Consulting Psychology*, 1964, 28, 285–286. (b)

Bennett, V. D. C. Combinations of figure drawing characteristics related to the drawer's self concept. *Journal of Projective Techniques and Personality Assessment*, 1966, 30, 192–196.

Bentler, P. J. Interpersonal orientation in relation to hypnotic suscepti-bility. *Journal of Consulting Psychology*, 1963, 27, 426–431.

Berger, C. R. Sex differences related to self-esteem factor structure. *Journal of Consulting and Clinical Psychology*, 1968, 32, 442–446.

Berger, E. M. The relation between expressed acceptance of self and the expressed acceptance of others. *Journal of Abnormal and Social Psychology*, 1952, 47, 778–782.

Berzon, B.; Reisel, J.; & Davis, D. P. Peer: An audio tape program for self-directed small groups. *Journal of Humanistic Psychology*, 1969, 9, 71–86.

Bethlehem, D. W. Guilt, self-ideal discrepancy, the approval motive, and recollections of socialization: Some interrelationships. *British Journal of Social and Clinical Psychology*, 1969, 8, 323–332.

Bidwell, G. P. Ego strength, self-knowledge, and vocational planning of schizophrenics. *Journal of Counseling Psychology*, 1969, 16, 45–49.

Bieri, J., & Lobeck, R. Self-concept differences in relation to identification, religion, and social class. *Journal of Abnormal and Social Psychology*, 1961, 62, 94–98.

Bigner, J. J. Sibling position and definition of self. *Journal of Social Psychology*, 1971, 84, 307–308.

Bills, R. E. Index of Adjustment and Values. Manual. University, Ala-bama: Mimeographed, n.d.

Bills, R. E. Index of Adjustment and Values. Forms: Elementary, Junior High School and High School. Manual. University, Alabama: Mimeo-graphed, n.d.

Bills, R. E. Rorschach characteristics of persons scoring high and low in acceptance of self. *Journal of Consulting Psychology*, 1953, 17, 36–38. (a)

Bills, R. E. A validation of changes in scores on the Index of Adjustment and Values as measures of changes in emotionality. *Journal of Con-sulting Psychology*, 1953, 17, 135–138. (b)

Bills, R. E. A comparison of scores on the Index of Adjustment and Values with behavior in level-of-aspiration tasks. *Journal of Consulting Psychology*, 1953, 17, 206–212. (c)

Bills, R. E. Acceptance of self as measured by interviews and the Index of Adjustment and Values. *Journal of Consulting Psychology*, 1954, 18, 22. (a)

Bills, R. E. Self-concepts and Rorschach signs of depression. *Journal of Consulting Psychology*, 1954, 18, 135–137. (b)

Bills, R. E.; Vance, E. L.; & McLean, O. S. An index of adjustment and values. *Journal of Consulting Psychology*, 1951, 15, 257–261.

Blank, L.; Sugerman, A. A.; & Roosa, L. Body concern, body image, and nudity. *Psychological Reports*, 1968, 23, 963–968.

Bledsoe, J. C. Self concepts of children and their intelligence, achievement, interests, and anxiety. *Journal of Individual Psychology*, 1964, 20, 55–58.

Block, J. An unprofitable application of the semantic differential. *Journal of Consulting Psychology*, 1958, 22, 235–236.

Block, J. Ego identity, role variability, and adjustment. *Journal of Consulting Psychology*, 1961, 25, 392–397. (a)

Block, J. *The Q-sort method in personality assessment and psychiatric research.* Springfield, Illinois: Charles C. Thomas, 1961. (b)

Block, J. *Challenge of response sets: Unconfounding meaning, acquiescence, and social desirability in the MMPI.* New York: Appleton-Century-Crofts, 1965.

Block, J., & Thomas, H. Is satisfaction with self a measure of adjustment? *Journal of Abnormal and Social Psychology*, 1955, 51, 254–259.

Block, J., & Turula, E. Identification, ego control, and adjustment. *Child Development*, 1963, 34, 945–953.

Bodwin, R. F., & Bruck, M. The adaptation and validation of the Draw-a-Person Test as a measure of self concept. *Journal of Clinical Psychology*, 1960, 26, 427–429.

Boe, E. E., & Kogan, W. S. An analysis of various methods for deriving the Social Desirability score. *Psychological Reports*, 1964, 14, 23–29.

Boe, E. E., & Kogan, W. S. Social desirability in individual performance on thirteen MMPI scales. *British Journal of Psychology*, 1966, 57, 161–170.

Bohn, M. J., & Stephenson, R. R. Vocational interests and self concept. *Newsletter for Research in Psychology*, 1963, 5, 21–22.

Borgatta, E. F. The stability of interpersonal judgments in independent situations. *Journal of Abnormal and Social Psychology*, 1960, 60, 188–194. (a)

Borgatta, E. F. Rankings and self-assessments: Some behavioral characteristics replication studies. *Journal of Social Psychology*, 1960, 52, 279–307. (b)

Borgatta, E. F. The structure of personality characteristics. *Behavior Science*, 1964, 8, 8–17.

Borislow, B. The Edwards Personal Preference Schedule (EPPS) and fakability. *Journal of Applied Psychology*, 1958, 42, 22–27.

Borislow, B. Self-evaluation and academic achievement. *Journal of Counseling Psychology*, 1962, 9, 246–254.

Boruch, R. F. Extensions of a multitrait-multimethod model to experimental psychology. *Multivariate Behavioral Research*, 1970, 5, 351–368.

Boruch, R. F.; Larkin, J. D.; Wolins, L.; & MacKinney, A. C. Alternative methods of analysis: Multitrait-multimethod data. *Educational and Psychological Measurement*, 1970, 30, 833–853.

Boruch, R. F., & Wolins, L. A procedure for estimation of trait, method, and error variance attributable to a measure. *Educational and Psychological Measurement,* 1970, 30, 547–574.

Boshier, R. Self esteem and first names in children. *Psychological Reports,* 1968, 22, 762. (a)

Boshier, R. Attitudes toward self and one's proper name. *Journal of Individual Psychology,* 1968, 24, 63–66. (b)

Boshier, R. A study of the relationship between self-concept and conservatism. *Journal of Social Psychology,* 1969, 77, 139–140.

Boshier, R. W., & Hamid, P. N. Academic success and self concept. *Psychological Reports,* 1968, 22, 1,191–1,192.

Bower, E. M., & Tashnovian, P. J. Q methodology: An application in investigating changes in self and ideal self in a mental health workshop. *California Journal of Educational Research,* 1955, 6, 200–205.

Bowers, D. G. Self-esteem and the diffusion of leadership style. *Journal of Applied Psychology,* 1963, 47, 135–140.

Bown, O. H.; Fuller, F. F.; & Richek, H. G. A comparison of self-perceptions of prospective elementary and secondary school teachers. *Psychology in the Schools,* 1967, 4, 21–24.

Boyd, H. S., & Sisney, V. V. Immediate self-image confrontation and changes in self-concept. *Journal of Consulting Psychology,* 1967, 31, 291–294.

Brandt, R. M. The accuracy of self estimate: A measure of self-concept reality. *Genetic Psychology Monographs,* 1958, 58, 55–99.

Braun, J. R., & Tinley, J. J. Comment on Fricke's approach to controlling social desirability in the forced-choice format. *Psychological Reports,* 1969, 25, 93–94.

Briar, S., & Bieri, J. A factor analytic and trait inference study of the Leary Interpersonal Check List. *Journal of Clinical Psychology,* 1963, 19, 193–198.

Brim, O. G., Jr., & Wood, N. Self and other conceptions in courtship and marriage pairs. *Marriage and Family Living,* 1956, 18, 243–248.

Brodsky, S. L. The WAYTE method for investigating self-perceptions. *Journal of Projective Techniques and Personality Assessment,* 1967, 31, 60–64.

Brodsky, S. L., & Owens, S. Reliability of the WAYTE method of investigating self-perceptions. *Psychological Reports,* 1969, 25, 389–390.

Bronfenbrenner, U.; Harding, J.; & Gallwey, M. The measurement of skill in social perception. In D. C. McClelland; A. L. Baldwin; U. Bronfenbrenner; & F. L. Strodtbeck (Eds.), *Talent and society.* New York: Van Nostrand, 1958. Pp. 29–111.

Brookover, W. B.; Erickson, E. L.; & Joiner, L. M. *Self-concept of ability and school achievement, relationship of self-concept to achievement in high school.* U.S. Office of Education, Cooperative Research Project No. 2831, Michigan State University, 1967.

Brooks, M., & Hillman, C. Parent-daughter relationship as factors in nonmarriage studied in identical twins. *Journal of Marriage and the Family,* 1965, 27, 383–385.

Brophy, A. L. Self, role, and satisfaction. *Genetic Psychology Monographs,* 1959, 59, 263–308.

Brown, C. M., & Ferguson, L. W. Self-concept and religious belief. *Psychological Reports,* 1968, 22, 266.

Brown, R. A., & Pool, D. A. Psychological needs and self-awareness. *Journal of Counseling Psychology,* 1966, 13, 85–88.

Brown, R. W. Is a boulder sweet or sour? *Contemporary Psychology,* 1958, 3, 113–115.

Brown, R. W. Models of attitude change. In T. M. Newcomb (Ed.), *New directions in psychology.* New York: Holt, Rinehart & Winston, 1962. Pp. 1–85.

Brown, R. W. *Social psychology.* New York: Free Press, 1965.

Brownfain, J. J. Stability of the self-concept as a dimension of personality. *Journal of Abnormal and Social Psychology,* 1952, 47, 597–606.

Bruck, M., & Bodwin, R. F. The relationship between self concept and the presence and absence of scholastic underachievement. *Journal of Clinical Psychology,* 1962, 18, 181–182.

Brunkan, R. J., & Shen, F. Personality characteristics of ineffective, effective, and efficient readers. *Personnel and Guidance Journal,* 1966, 44, 837–843.

Brunswik, E. *Perception and the representative design of psychological experiments.* Berkeley: University of California Press, 1956.

Bugental, D. E., & Lehner, G. F. J. Accuracy of self-perception and group perception as related to two leadership roles. *Journal of Abnormal and Social Psychology,* 1958, 56, 396–398.

Bugental, J. F. T. Investigations into the self-concept: III. Instructions for the W-A-Y method. *Psychological Reports,* 1964, 15, 643–650.

Bugental, J. F. T., & Gunning, E. C. Investigations into self concepts: II. Stability of reported self-identifications. *Journal of Clinical Psychology,* 1955, 11, 41–46.

Bugental, J. F. T., & Zelen, S. L. Investigations into the "self-concept": I. The W-A-Y technique. *Journal of Personality,* 1950, 18, 483–498.

Burke, R. J. Some preliminary data on the use of self-evaluations and peer ratings in assigning university course grades. *Journal of Educational Research,* 1969, 62, 444–448.

Burke, R. L., & Bennis, W. G. Changes in perception of self and others during human relations training. *Human Relations,* 1961, 14, 165–182.

Buros, O. K. (Ed.). *Personality tests and reviews.* Highland Park, N.J.: Gryphon Press, 1970.

Buros, O. K. (Ed.). *Seventh mental measurements yearbook.* Highland Park, N.J.: Gryphon Press, 1971.

Burton, A., & Sjoberg, B., Jr. The diagnostic validity of human figure drawings in schizophrenia. *Journal of Psychology,* 1964, 57, 3–18.

Buss, A. H., & Gerjuoy, H. The scaling of terms used to describe personality. *Journal of Consulting Psychology,* 1957, 21, 361–369.

Butler, J. M. Self-ideal congruence in psychotherapy. *Psychotherapy: Theory, Research, and Practice,* 1968, 5, 13–17.

Butler, J. M., & Haigh, G. V. Changes in the relation between self-concepts and ideal concepts consequent upon client-centered counseling. In C. R. Rogers & R. F. Dymond (Eds.), *Psychotherapy and personality change.* Chicago: University of Chicago Press, 1954. Pp. 55–75.

Byrne, D.; Barry, J.; & Nelson, D. Relation of the revised Repression-Sensitization Scale to measures of self-description. *Psychological Reports,* 1963, 13, 323–334.

Cairns, R. B., & Lewis, M. Dependency and the reinforcement value of a verbal stimulus. *Journal of Consulting Psychology,* 1962, 26, 1–8.

Calkins, M. W. Mary Whiton Calkins. In C. Murchison (Ed.), *A history of psychology in autobiography.* Vol. 1. Worcester, Mass.: Clark University Press, 1930. Pp. 31–62.

Calvin, A. D., & Holtzman, W. H. Adjustment and the discrepancy between self concept and inferred self. *Journal of Consulting Psychology,* 1953, 17, 39–44.

Campbell, D. Another attempt at configural scoring. *Educational and Psychological Measurement,* 1963, 23, 721–727.

Campbell, D. T. Factors relevant to the validity of experiments in social settings. *Psychological Bulletin,* 1957, 54, 297–312.

Campbell, D. T. A phenomenology of the other one: Corrigible, hypothetical, and critical. In T. Mischel (Ed.), *Human action: Conceptual and empirical issues.* New York: Academic Press, 1969. Pp. 41–69. (a)

Campbell, D. T. Prospective: Artifact and control. In R. Rosenthal & R. L. Rosnow (Eds.), *Artifact in behavioral research.* New York: Academic Press, 1969. Pp. 351–382. (b)

Campbell, D. T., & Fiske, D. W. Convergent and discriminant validation by the multitrait-multimethod matrix. *Psychological Bulletin,* 1959, 56, 81–105.

Campbell, D. T., & O'Connell, E. J. Method factors in multitrait-multimethod matrices: Multiplicative rather than additive? *Multivariate Behavioral Research,* 1967, 2, 409–426.

Campbell, D. T.; Siegman, C. R.; & Rees, M. B. Direction-of-wording effects in the relationship between scales. *Psychological Bulletin,* 1967, 68, 293–303.

Campbell, D. T., & Stanley, J. C. Experimental and quasi-experimental designs for research. In N. L. Gage (Ed.), *Handbook of research on teaching.* Chicago: Rand McNally, 1963. Pp. 171–246.

Campbell, P. B. School and self concept. *Educational Leadership,* 1967, 24, 510–515.

Cancro, R. Sophistication of body concept in process-reactive schizophrenia. *Perceptual and Motor Skills,* 1971, 32, 567–570.

Cangemi, J. P. The effects of organized camp experiences on the perception of self and society among a group of potential school dropouts. *Archivos Panamenõs de Psicologia,* 1966, 30–36.

Caplan, S. W. The effect of group counseling in junior high school boys' concepts of themselves in school. *Journal of Counseling Psychology,* 1957, 4, 124–128.

Cardillo, J. P. The effects of teaching communication roles on interpersonal perception and self-concept in disturbed marriages. *Proceedings of the Annual Convention of the American Psychological Association,* 1971, 6, 441–442.

Cardone, S. S., & Olson, R. E. Chlorpromazine and body image: Effects on chronic schizophrenics. *Archives of General Psychiatry,* 1969, 20, 576–582.

Carlson, R. On the structure of self-esteem: Comments on Ziller's formulation. *Journal of Consulting and Clinical Psychology,* 1970, 2, 264–268.

Carroll, J. L., & Fuller, G. B. The self and ideal-self concept of the alcoholic as influenced by length of sobriety and/or participation in Alcoholics Anonymous. *Journal of Clinical Psychology,* 1969, 25, 363–364.

Carson, G. L. The self-concept of welfare recipients. *Personnel and Guidance Journal,* 1967, 45, 424–428.

Carter, T. P. The negative self-concept of Mexican-American students. *School and Society,* 1968, 96, 217–219.

Cartwright, D. S.; Kirtner, W. L.; & Fiske, D. W. Method factors in changes associated with psychotherapy. *Journal of Abnormal and Social Psychology,* 1963, 66, 164–175.

Cartwright, D. S., & Roth, I. Success and satisfaction in psychotherapy. *Journal of Clinical Psychology,* 1957, 13, 20–26.

Cartwright, R. D. Self-conception patterns of college students, and adjustment to college life. *Journal of Counseling Psychology,* 1963, 101, 47–52.

Cartwright, R. D., & Vogel, J. L. A comparison of changes in psychoneurotic patients during matched periods of therapy and no therapy. *Journal of Consulting Psychology,* 1960, 24, 121–127.

Cassel, R. N., & Harriman, B. L. A comparative analysis of personality and ego strength test scores for in-prison, neuro-psychiatric and typical individuals. *Journal of Educational Research,* 1959, 53, 43–52.

Cassell, W. A. A projective index of body-interior awareness. *Psychosomatic Medicine,* 1964, 26, 172–177.

Cassell, W. A. Body perception and symptom localization. *Psychosomatic Medicine,* 1965, 27, 171–176.

Cassell, W. A. A tachistoscopic index of body perception: I. Body boundary and body interior awareness. *Journal of Projective Techniques and Personality Assessment,* 1966, 30, 31–36.

Cassell, W. A., & Fisher, S. Body-image boundaries and histamine flare reaction. *Psychosomatic Medicine,* 1963, 25, 344–350.

Cassell, W. A., & Hemingway, P. Body consciousness in states of pharmacological depression and arousal. *Neuropharmacology,* 1970, 9, 169–173.

Casteneda, A.; McCandless, B. R.; & Palermo, D. S. The children's form of the manifest anxiety scale. *Child Development,* 1956, 27, 317–326.

Catron, D. W. Educational-vocational group counseling: The effects on perception of self and others. *Journal of Counseling Psychology,* 1966, 13, 202–207.

Cattell, R. B. The three basic factor-analytic research designs: Their interrelations and derivatives. *Psychological Bulletin,* 1952, 49, 499–520.

Cattell, R. B. *Scientific analysis of personality.* Chicago: Aldine, 1966.

Cattell, R. B.; Wagner, A.; & Cattell, M. D. Adolescent personality structure, in Q-data, checked in the high school personality questionnaire. *British Journal of Psychology,* 1970, 61, 39–54.

Cauthen, N. R., & Boardman, W. K. Body boundary and stimulus enhancement. *Perceptual and Motor Skills,* 1971, 32, 559–563.

Centers, L., & Centers, R. A comparison of the body images of amputee and non-amputee children as revealed in figure drawings. *Journal of Projective Techniques and Personality Assessment,* 1963, 27, 158–165.

Chase, P. H. Self concepts in adjusted and maladjusted hospital patients. *Journal of Consulting Psychology,* 1957, 21, 495–497.

Chein, I. The awareness of self and the structure of the ego. *Psychological Review,* 1944, 51, 304–314.

Child, I. L.; Frank, K. F.; & Storm, T. Self-ratings and TAT: Their relations to each other and to childhood background. *Journal of Personality,* 1956, 25, 96–114.

Chittick, E. V., & Himelstein, P. The manipulation of self-disclosure. *Journal of Psychology,* 1967, 65, 117–121.

Chodorkoff, B. Self-perception, perceptual defense, and adjustment. *Journal of Abnormal and Social Psychology,* 1954, 49, 508–512. (a)

Chodorkoff, B. Adjustment and the discrepancy between the perceived and ideal self. *Journal of Clinical Psychology,* 1954, 10, 266–268. (b)

Chodorkoff, B. Anxiety, threat, and defensive reactions. *Journal of General Psychology,* 1956, 54, 191–196.

Clark, T. R., & Epstein, R. Self-concept and expectancy for social reinforcement in non-institutionalized male homosexuals. *Proceedings of the 77th Annual Convention of the American Psychological Association,* 1969, 4, 575–576.

Cleveland, S. E. Body image changes associated with personality reorganization. *Journal of Consulting Psychology,* 1960, 24, 256–261.

Cleveland, S. E., & Fisher, S. Behavior and unconscious fantasies of patients with rheumatoid arthritis. *Psychosomatic Medicine,* 1954, 16, 327–333.

Cleveland, S. E., & Fisher, S. Body image and small group behavior. *Human Relations,* 1957, 10, 223–233.

Cleveland, S. E., & Fisher, S. A comparison of psychological characteristics and physiological reactivity in ulcer and rheumatoid arthritis groups: I. Psychological measures. *Psychosomatic Medicine,* 1960, 22, 283–289.

Cleveland, S. E., & Johnson, D. L. Personality patterns in young males with coronary diseases. *Psychosomatic Medicine,* 1962, 24, 600–610.

Cleveland, S. E., & Morton, R. B. Group behavior and body-image: A follow-up study. *Human Relations,* 1962, 15, 77–85.

Cleveland, S. E.; Reitman, E. E.; & Brewer, E. J., Jr. Psychological factors in juvenile rheumatoid arthritis. *Arthritis and Rheumatism,* 1965, 8, 1,152–1,158.

Cleveland, S. E., & Sikes, M. P. Body image in chronic alcoholics and non-alcoholic psychiatric patients. *Journal of Projective Techniques and Personality Assessment,* 1966, 30, 265–269.

Cleveland, S. E.; Snyder, R.; & Williams, R. L. Body image and site of psychosomatic symptoms. *Psychological Reports,* 1965, 16, 851–852.

Cliff, N. Adverbs as multipliers. *Psychological Review,* 1959, 66, 27–44.

Clifford, E. Body satisfaction in adolescence. *Perceptual and Motor Skills,* 1971, 33, 119–125.

Coan, R. W. Facts, factors, and artifacts: The quest for psychological meaning. *Psychological Review,* 1964, 71, 123–140.

Coan, R. W., & Cattell, R. B. The development of the Early School Personality Questionnaire. *Journal of Experimental Education,* 1959, 28, 143–152.

Cogan, L. C.; Conklin, A. M.; & Hollingworth, H. L. An experimental study of self-analyses, estimates of associates, and the results of tests. *School and Society,* 1915, 2, 171–179.

Cohen, A. R. Some implications of self-esteem for social influence. In C. I. Hovland & I. L. Janis (Eds.), *Personality and persuasibility.* New Haven: Yale University Press, 1959. Pp. 102–120.

Cohen, L. D. Level of aspiration behavior and feelings of adequacy and self-acceptance. *Journal of Abnormal and Social Psychology,* 1954, 49, 84–86.

Cole, C. W.; Oetting, E. R.; & Hinkle, J. Non-linearity of self-concept discrepancy: The value dimension. *Psychological Reports,* 1967, 21, 58–60.

Cole, C. W.; Oetting, E. R.; & Miskimins, R. W. Self-concept therapy for adolescent females. *Journal of Abnormal Psychology,* 1969, 74, 642–645.

Collier, B. N., Jr. Comparisons between adolescents with and without diabetes. *Personnel and Guidance Journal,* 1969, 47, 679–684.

Collins, H. A.; Burger, G. K.; & Doherty, D. Self-concept of EMR and nonretarded adolescents. *American Journal of Mental Deficiency,* 1970, 75, 285–289.

Combs, A. W., & Soper, D. W. The self, its derivative terms, and research. *Journal of Individual Psychology,* 1957, 13, 134–145.

Combs, A. W.; Soper, D. W.; & Courson, C. C. The measurement of self concept and self report. *Educational and Psychological Measurement,* 1963, 23, 493–500.

Cone, J. D. Social desirability, marital satisfaction, and concomitant perceptions of self and spouse. *Psychological Reports,* 1971, 28, 173–174.

Conger, A. J. An evaluation of multimethod factor analysis. *Psychological Bulletin,* 1971, 75, 416–420.

Connell, D. M., & Johnson, J. E. Relationship between sex-role identification and self-esteem in early adolescents. *Developmental Psychology,* 1970, 3, 268.

Constantinople, A. An Eriksonian measure of personality development in college students. *Developmental Psychology,* 1969, 1, 357–372.

Cooper, A., & Cowen, E. L. The social desirability of trait descriptive terms: A study of feeling reactions to adjective descriptions. *Journal of Social Psychology,* 1962, 56, 207–215.

Cooper, G. D.; Adams, H. B.; & Cohen, L. D. Personality changes after sensory deprivation. *Journal of Nervous and Mental Disease,* 1965, 140, 103–118.

Coopersmith, S. A method for determining types of self-esteem. *Journal of Abnormal and Social Psychology,* 1959, 59, 87–94.

Coopersmith, S. Self-esteem and need achievement as determinants of selective recall and repetition. *Journal of Abnormal and Social Psychology,* 1960, 60, 310–317.

Coopersmith, S. Relationship between self-esteem and sensory (perceptual) constancy. *Journal of Abnormal and Social Psychology,* 1964, 68, 217–222.

Coopersmith, S. *The antecedents of self-esteem.* San Francisco: Freeman, 1967.

Corah, N. L.; Feldman, M. J.; Cohen, I. S.; Gruen, W.; Meadow, A.; & Ringwall, E. A. Social desirability as a variable in the Edwards Personal Preference Schedule. *Journal of Consulting Psychology*, 1958, 22, 70–72.

Corfield, V. The role of arousal and cognitive complexity in susceptibility to social influence. *Journal of Personality*, 1969, 37, 554–566.

Corsini, R. J. *Standard adjective Q sort*. Chicago: Psychometric Affiliates, 1956.

Costin, F. The effect of an introductory psychology course on self-insight. *Journal of Educational Psychology*, 1959, 50, 83–87.

Couch, A., & Keniston, K. Yeasayers and naysayers: Agreeing response set as a personality variable. *Journal of Abnormal and Social Psychology*, 1960, 60, 151–174.

Couch, C. J. Family role specialization and self-attitudes in children. *Sociological Quarterly*, 1962, 3, 115–121.

Couch, C. J. Self-identification and alienation. *Sociological Quarterly*, 1966, 7, 255–264.

Cowen, E. L. The "negative self concept" as a personality measure. *Journal of Consulting Psychology*, 1954, 18, 138–142.

Cowen, E. L. An investigation of the relationship between two measures of self-regarding attitudes. *Journal of Clinical Psychology*, 1956, 12, 156–160.

Cowen, E. L. The social desirability of trait descriptive terms: Preliminary norms and sex differences. *Journal of Social Psychology*, 1961, 53, 225–233.

Cowen, E. L.; Budin, W.; & Budin, F. A. The social desirability of trait descriptive terms: A variation in instructional set. *Journal of Social Psychology*, 1961, 53, 317–323.

Cowen, E. L.; Budin, W.; Wolitzky, D. L.; & Stiller, A. The social desirability of trait descriptive terms: A factor in the prediction of Q sort. *Journal of Personality*, 1960, 28, 530–544.

Cowen, E. L.; Davol, S. H.; Reimanis, G.; & Stiller, A. The social desirability of trait descriptive terms: Two geriatric samples. *Journal of Social Psychology*, 1962, 56, 217–225.

Cowen, E. L.; Heilizer, F.; & Axelrod, H. S. Self-concept conflict indicators and learning. *Journal of Abnormal and Social Psychology*, 1955, 51, 242–245.

Cowen, E. L.; Heilizer, F.; Axelrod, H. S.; & Alexander, S. The correlates of manifest anxiety in perceptual reactivity, rigidity, and self concept. *Journal of Consulting Psychology*, 1957, 21, 405–411.

Cowen, E. L.; Staiman, M. G.; & Wolitzky, D. L. The social desirability of trait descriptive terms: Applications to a schizophrenic sample. *Journal of Social Psychology*, 1961, 54, 37–45.

Cowen, E. L., & Stricker, G. The social desirability of trait descriptive terms: A sample of sexual offenders. *Journal of Social Psychology,* 1963, 59, 307–315.

Cowen, E. L., & Tongas, P. N. The social desirability of trait descriptive terms: Applications to a self-concept inventory. *Journal of Consulting Psychology,* 1959, 23, 361–365.

Craddick, R. A. The self image in the Draw-A-Person Test and self portrait drawings. *Journal of Projective Techniques and Personality Assessment,* 1963, 27, 288–291.

Craddick, R. A., & Leipold, W. D. Note on the height of Draw-A-Person figures by male alcoholics. *Journal of Projective Techniques and Personality Assessment,* 1968, 32, 486.

Crandall, J. E. Self-perception and interpersonal attraction as related to tolerance-intolerance of ambiguity. *Journal of Personality,* 1969, 37, 127–140.

Crandall, V.; Crandall, V. J.; & Katkovsky, W. A children's social desirability questionnaire. *Journal of Consulting Psychology,* 1965, 29, 27–36.

Crandall, V. J., & Bellugi, U. Some relationships of interpersonal and intrapersonal conceptualizations to personal-social adjustment. *Journal of Personality,* 1954, 23, 224–232.

Crites, J. O. Test reviews: Tennessee Self Concept Scale. *Journal of Counseling Psychology,* 1965, 12, 330–331.

Crites, J. O.; Bechtoldt, H. P.; Goodstein, L. D.; & Heilbrun, A. B., Jr. A factor analysis of the California Psychological Inventory. *Journal of Applied Psychology,* 1961, 45, 408–414.

Cronbach, L. J. Response sets and test validity. *Educational and Psychological Measurement,* 1946, 6, 475-494.

Cronbach, L. J. Processes affecting scores on "understanding of others" and "assumed similarity." *Psychological Bulletin,* 1955, 52, 177–193.

Cronbach, L. J. Test validation. In R. L. Thorndike (Ed.), *Educational measurement.* (2nd ed.) Washington, D.C.: American Council on Education, 1971. Pp. 443–507.

Cronbach, L. J., & Furby, L. How we should measure "change"—or should we? *Psychological Bulletin,* 1970, 74, 68–80.

Cronbach, L. J., & Gleser, G. C. Assessing similarity between profiles. *Psychological Bulletin,* 1953, 50, 456–473.

Cronbach, L. J., & Meehl, P. E. Construct validity in psychological tests. *Psychological Bulletin,* 1955, 52, 281–302.

Cronbach, L. J.; Rajaratnam, N.; & Gleser, G. C. Theory of generalizability: A liberalization of reliability theory. *British Journal of Statistical Psychology,* 1963, 16, 137–163.

Crook, M. N. The constancy of neuroticism scores and self-judgments of constancy. *Journal of Psychology,* 1937, 4, 27–34.

Crowne, D. P., & Marlowe, D. *The approval motive: Studies in evaluative dependence.* New York: Wiley, 1964.

Crowne, D. P., & Stephens, M. W. Self-acceptance and self-evaluative behavior: A critique of methodology. *Psychological Bulletin,* 1961, 58, 104–121.

Crowne, D. P.; Stephens, M. W.; & Kelly, R. The validity and equivalence of tests of self-acceptance. *Journal of Psychology,* 1961, 51, 101–112.

Crumpton, E.; Wine, D. B.; & Drenick, E. J. Starvation: Stress or satisfaction? *Journal of the American Medical Association,* 1966, 196, 394–396.

Cruse, D. B. Social desirability scale values of personal concepts. *Journal of Applied Psychology,* 1965, 49, 342–344.

Cureton, E. E. Reliability and validity: Basic assumptions and experimental designs. *Educational and Psychological Measurement,* 1965, 25, 327–336.

Dahlstrom, W. G., & Welsh, G. S. *An MMPI handbook.* Minneapolis: University of Minnesota Press, 1960.

Daniels, L. K., & Stewart, J. A. Mentally retarded adults' perceptions of self and parent related to their vocational adjustment. *American Institute for Mental Studies, Training School Bulletin,* 1970, 66, 164–171.

Daston, P. G., & McConnell, O. L. Stability of Rorschach penetration and barrier scores over time. *Journal of Consulting Psychology,* 1962, 26, 104.

David, K. H. Ego-strength, sex differences, and description of self, ideal, and parents. *Journal of General Psychology,* 1968, 79, 79–81.

Davids, A. Comparison of three methods of personality assessment: Direct, indirect, and projective. *Journal of Personality,* 1955, 23, 423–440.

Davids, A.; Henry, A. F.; McArthur, C. C.; & McNamara, L. F. Projection, self-evaluation, and clinical evaluation of aggression. *Journal of Consulting Psychology,* 1955, 19, 437–440.

Davis, A. D. Some physiological correlates of Rorschach body image productions. *Journal of Abnormal and Social Psychology,* 1960, 60, 432–436.

Davis, A. J. Self-concept, occupational role expectations, and occupational choice in nursing and social work. *Nursing Research,* 1969, 18, 55–59.

deJung, J. E., & Gardner, E. F. The accuracy of self-role perception: A developmental study. *Journal of Experimental Education,* 1962, 31, 27–41.

DeSoto, C. B.; Kuethe, J. L.; & Bosley, J. J. A redefinition of social desirability. *Journal of Abnormal and Social Psychology,* 1959, 58, 273–275.

Deutsch, M., & Solomon, L. Reactions to evaluations by others as influenced by self-evaluations. *Sociometry,* 1959, 22, 93–112.

Dicken, C. F. Simulated patterns on the Edwards Personal Preference Schedule. *Journal of Applied Psychology*, 1959, 43, 372–378.

Dicken, C. F. Convergent and discriminant validity of the California Psychological Inventory. *Educational and Psychological Measurement*, 1963, 23, 449–459.

Dielman, T. E., & Wilson, W. R. Convergent and discriminant validity of three measures of ability, aspiration-level, achievement, adjustment, and dominance. *Journal of Educational Measurement*, 1970, 7, 185–190.

Diggory, J. C. *Self-evaluation: Concepts and studies.* New York: Wiley, 1966.

Diller, L. Conscious and unconscious self-attitudes after success and failure. *Journal of Personality*, 1954, 23, 1–12.

Diller, L., & Riklan, M. Rorschach correlates in Parkinson's disease: *M*, motor inhibition, perceived cause of illness, and self-attitudes. *Psychosomatic Medicine*, 1957, 19, 120–126.

Dinitz, S.; Mangus, A. R.; & Pasamanick, B. Integration and conflict in self-other conceptions as factors in mental illness. *Sociometry*, 1959, 22, 44–55.

Dolich, I. J. Congruence relationships between self images and product brands. *Journal of Marketing Research*, 1969, 6, 80–84.

Dorn, D. S. Self-concept, alienation, and anxiety in a contraculture and subculture: A research report. *Journal of Criminal Law, Criminology, and Police Science*, 1968, 59, 531–535.

Dosey, M. A., & Meisels, M. Personal space and self-protection. *Journal of Personality and Social Psychology*, 1969, 11, 93–97.

Downing, R. W.; Moed, G.; & Wight, B. W. Studies of disability: A technique for measurement of psychological effects. *Child Development*, 1961, 32, 561–575.

Downing, R. W., & Rickels, K. Pre-treatment self estimates and clinical improvements with tranquilizer therapy. *Diseases of the Nervous System*, 1967, 28, 671–674.

Dreyer, A. S.; Hulac, V.; & Rigler, D. Differential adjustment to pubescence and cognitive style patterns. *Developmental Pychology*, 1971, 4, 456–462.

Dudek, F. J. Concerning "reliability" of tests. *Educational and Psychological Measurement*, 1952, 12, 293–299.

Dudek, F. J. A comparison of scale values for adverbs determined by the constant-sum method and a successive intervals procedure. *Educational and Psychological Measurement*, 1959, 19, 539–548.

Duncan, C. B. A reputation test of personality integration. *Journal of Personality and Social Psychology*, 1966, 3, 516–524.

Dunnette, M. D.; McCartney, J.; Carlson, H. C.; & Kirchner, W. K. A study of faking behavior on a forced-choice self-description checklist. *Personnel Psychology*, 1962, 15, 13–24.

Dykstra, P. Some methods for measuring changes in the behaviour of depressive patients. *Psychiatria, Neurologia, Neurochirurgia*, 1969, 72, 219–224.

Dymond, R. F. Personality and empathy. *Journal of Consulting Psychology*, 1950, 14, 343–350.

Dymond, R. F. An adjustment score for Q sorts. *Journal of Consulting Psychology*, 1953, 17, 339–342.

Dyson, E. A study of ability grouping and the self-concept. *Journal of Educational Research*, 1967, 60, 403–405.

Edelson, M., & Jones, A. E. Operational explorations of the conceptual self system and of the interaction between frames of reference. *Genetic Psychology Monographs*, 1954, 50, 43–139.

Edwards, A. L. *The social desirability variable in personality assessment and research.* New York: Holt, 1957. (a)

Edwards, A. L. Social desirability and probability of endorsement of items in the Interpersonal Check List. *Journal of Abnormal and Social Psychology*, 1957, 55, 394–396. (b)

Edwards, A. L. The social desirability variable: A broad statement. In I. A. Berg (Ed.), *Response set in personality assessment.* Chicago: Aldine, 1967. Pp. 32–47. (a)

Edwards, A. L. The social desirability variable: A review of the evidence. In I. A. Berg (Ed.), *Response set in personality assessment.* Chicago: Aldine, 1967. Pp. 48–70. (b)

Edwards, A. L. *The measurement of personality traits by scales and inventories.* New York: Holt, Rinehart & Winston, 1970.

Edwards, A. L.; Diers, C. J.; & Walker, J. N. Response sets and factor loadings on sixty-one personality scales. *Journal of Applied Psychology*, 1962, 46, 220–225.

Edwards, A. L.; Wright, C. E.; & Lunneborg, C. E. A note on "Social Desirability as a variable in the Edwards Personal Preference Schedule." *Journal of Consulting Psychology*, 1959, 23, 558.

Eigenbrode, C. R., & Shipman, W. G. The body-image barrier concept. *Journal of Abnormal and Social Psychology*, 1960, 60, 450–452.

Eisenman, R. Birth order, sex, self-esteem, and prejudice against the physically disabled. *Journal of Psychology*, 1970, 75, 147–155.

Eisenman, R., & Robinson, N. Peer-, self-, and test-ratings of creativity. *Psychological Reports*, 1968, 23, 471–474.

Eisenman, R., & Townsend, T. D. Studies in acquiescence: I. Social Desirability; II. Self-Esteem; III. Creativity; and IV. Prejudice. *Journal of Projective Techniques and Personality Assessment*, 1970, 34, 45–54.

Elliott, L. L. Factorial structure of airman self-ratings and their relationship to peer nominations. USAF WADD Technical Note, 1960, No. 60–141.

Endler, N. S. Changes in meaning during psychotherapy as measured by the semantic differential. *Journal of Counseling Psychology*, 1961, 8, 105–111.

Ends, E. J., & Page, C. W. A study of three types of group psychotherapy with hospitalized male inebriates. *Quarterly Journal of Studies on Alcohol*, 1957, 18, 263–277.

Engel, M. The stability of the self-concept in adolescence. *Journal of Abnormal and Social Psychology*, 1959, 58, 211–215.

Engel, M., & Raine, W. J. A method for the measurement of the self-concept of children in the third grade. *Journal of Genetic Psychology*, 1963, 102, 125–137.

Englander, M. E. Influencing vocational choice: A pilot study. *Vocational Guidance Quarterly*, 1965–66, 14, 136–140.

English, H. B., & English, A. C. *A comprehensive dictionary of psychological and psychoanalytical terms*. New York: Longmans, Green, 1958.

Epstein, R., & Baron, R. M. Cognitive dissonance and projected hostility toward outgroups. *Journal of Social Psychology*, 1969, 79, 171–182.

Epstein, S. Unconscious self-evaluation in a normal and a schizophrenic group. *Journal of Abnormal and Social Psychology*, 1955, 50, 65–70.

Erickson, R. J.; Crow, W. J.; Zurcher, L. A.; Connett, A. V.; & Stillwell, W. D. *The offender looks at his own needs*. LaJolla, California: Western Behavioral Sciences Institute, 1971.

Eriksen, C. W. Subception: Fact or artifact? *Psychological Review*, 1956, 63, 74–80.

Eriksen, C. W. Unconscious processes. In M. R. Jones (Ed.), *Nebraska symposium on motivation, 1958*. Lincoln: University of Nebraska Press, 1958. Pp. 169–228.

Erikson, E. H. *Childhood and society*. New York: Norton, 1950.

Erikson, E. H. Identity and the life cycle: Selected papers. *Psychological Issues*, 1959, 1, 1–171.

Eysenck, H. J. *The structure of human personality*. (3rd ed.) London: Methuen, 1970.

Fagan, J., & Guthrie, G. M. Perception of self and of normality in schizophrenics. *Journal of Clinical Psychology*, 1959, 15, 203–207.

Fairweather, G. W.; Simon, R.; Gebhard, M. E.; Weingarten, E.; Holland, J. L.; Sanders, R.; Stone, G. B.; & Reahl, J. E. Relative effectiveness of psychotherapeutic programs: A multicriteria comparison of four programs for three different patient groups. *Psychological Monographs*, 1960, 74 (5, Whole No. 492).

Farley, F. H. Global self-ratings, the independence of questionnaire drive and anxiety, and social desirability variance. *Acta Psychologica,* 1968, 28, 387–397.

Farson, R. E. Introjection in the psychotherapeutic relationship. *Journal of Counseling Psychology,* 1961, 8, 337–342.

Faterson, H. F., & Witkin, H. A. Longitudinal study of development of the body concept. *Developmental Psychology,* 1970, 2, 429–438.

Feldman, M. J., & Corah, N. L. Social desirability and the forced choice method. *Journal of Consulting Psychology,* 1960, 24, 480–482.

Feldman, M. J., & Siegel, S. M. The effect on self description of combining anxiety and hostility items on a single scale. *Journal of Clinical Psychology,* 1958, 14, 74–77.

Ferullo, R. J. The self-concept in communication. *Journal of Communication,* 1963, 13, 77–86.

Feshbach, N. D., & Beigel, A. A note on the use of the semantic differential in measuring teacher personality and values. *Educational and Psychological Measurement,* 1968, 28, 923–929.

Fiedler, F. E.; Hutchins, E. B.; & Dodge, J. S. Quasi-therapeutic relations in small college and military groups. *Psychological Monographs,* 1959, 73, 1–28.

Fiedler, F. E.; Warrington, W. G.; & Blaisdell, F. J. Unconscious attitudes as correlates of sociometric choice in a social group. *Journal of Abnormal and Social Psychology,* 1952, 47, 790–791.

Fiedler, F. E., & Wepman, J. M. An exploratory investigation of the self-concept of stutterers. *Journal of Speech and Hearing Disorders,* 1951, 16, 110–114.

Fink, M. B. Self concept as it relates to academic underachievement. *California Journal of Educational Research,* 1962, 13, 57–62.

Fisher, R. L. Body boundary and achievement behavior. *Journal of Projective Techniques and Personality Assessment,* 1966, 30, 435–438. (a)

Fisher, R. L. Failure of the conceptual styles test to discriminate normal and highly impulsive children. *Journal of Abnormal Psychology,* 1966, 71, 429–431. (b)

Fisher, R. L. Mother's hostility and changes in child's classroom behavior. *Perceptual and Motor Skills,* 1966, 23, 153–154. (c)

Fisher, R. L. Classroom behavior and the body image boundary. *Journal of Projective Techniques and Personality Assessment,* 1968, 32, 450–452.

Fisher, S. Extensions of theory concerning body image and body reactivity. *Psychosomatic Medicine,* 1959, 21, 142–149. (a)

Fisher, S. Body image boundaries in the aged. *Journal of Psychology,* 1959, 48, 315–318. (b)

Fisher, S. Prediction of body exterior vs. body interior reactivity from a body image schema. *Journal of Personality,* 1959, 27, 56–62. (c)

Fisher, S. Body reactivity gradients and figure drawing variables. *Journal of Consulting Psychology*, 1959, 23, 54–59. (d)

Fisher, S. Right-left gradients in body image, body reactivity, and perception. *Genetic Psychology Monographs*, 1960, 61, 197–228.

Fisher, S. Relationship of Rorschach human percepts to projective descriptions with self reference. *Journal of Projective Techniques*, 1962, 26, 231–233.

Fisher, S. A further appraisal of the body boundary concept. *Journal of Consulting Psychology*, 1963, 27, 62–74. (a)

Fisher S. Body image and hypnotic response. *International Journal of Clinical and Experimental Hypnosis*, 1963, 11, 152–162. (b)

Fisher, S. Sex differences in body perception. *Psychological Monographs*, 1964, 78 (14), 1–22. (a)

Fisher, S. The body boundary and judged behavioral patterns in an interview situation. *Journal of Projective Techniques and Personality Assessment*, 1964, 28, 181–184. (b)

Fisher, S. The body image as a source of selective cognitive sets. *Journal of Personality*, 1965, 33, 536–552.

Fisher, S. Body image in neurotic and schizophrenic patients: Further studies. *Archives of General Psychiatry*, 1966, 15, 90–101.

Fisher, S. Motivation for patient delay. *Archives of General Psychiatry*, 1967, 16, 676–678.

Fisher, S. *Body experience in fantasy and behavior.* New York: Appleton-Century-Crofts, 1970.

Fisher, S. Complexity reflected. *Contemporary Psychology*, 1971, 16, 744–745. (a)

Fisher, S. Boundary effects of persistent inputs and messages. *Journal of Abnormal Psychology*, 1971, 77, 290–295. (b)

Fisher, S., & Cleveland, S. E. The role of body image in psychosomatic symptom choice. *Psychological Monographs*, 1955, 69 (17), 1–15.

Fisher, S., & Cleveland, S. E. Relationship of body image boundaries to memory for completed and uncompleted tasks. *Journal of Psychology*, 1956, 42, 35–41. (a)

Fisher, S., & Cleveland, S. E. Body-image boundaries and style of life. *Journal of Abnormal and Social Psychology*, 1956, 52, 373–379. (b)

Fisher, S., & Cleveland, S. E. Relationship of body image to site of cancer. *Psychosomatic Medicine*, 1956, 18, 304–309. (c)

Fisher, S., & Cleveland, S. E. An approach to physiological reactivity in terms of a body-image schema. *Psychological Review*, 1957, 64, 26–37.

Fisher, S., & Cleveland, S. E. *Body image and personality.* Princeton, N.J.: Van Nostrand, 1958. (a)

Fisher, S., & Cleveland, S. E. Body image boundaries and sexual behavior. *Journal of Psychology*, 1958, 45, 207–211. (b)

Fisher, S., & Cleveland, S. E. Body image and personality. *Contemporary Psychology,* 1960, 5, 109.

Fisher, S., & Cleveland, S. E. Body image and personality. *Contemporary Psychology,* 1961, 6, 28–30.

Fisher, S., & Cleveland, S. E. Personality, body perception, and body image boundary. In S. Wapner & H. Werner (Eds.), *The body percept.* New York: Random, 1965. Pp. 48–67.

Fisher, S., & Cleveland, S. E. *Body image and personality.* (Rev. ed.) New York: Dover Publications, 1968.

Fisher, S., & Cleveland, S. E. Rejoinder to Hirt and Kurtz's "A reexamination of the relationship between body boundary and site of disease." *Journal of Abnormal Psychology,* 1969, 74, 144–147. (a)

Fisher, S., & Cleveland, S. E. Rejoinder to Mitchell's "The body image boundary construct: A study of the self-steering behavior syndrome." *Journal of Projective Techniques and Personality Assessment,* 1969, 33, 318–321. (b)

Fisher, S., & Fisher, R. L. A developmental analysis of some body image and body reactivity dimensions. *Child Development,* 1959, 30, 389–402.

Fisher, S., & Fisher, R. L. Body image boundaries and patterns of body perception. *Journal of Abnormal and Social Psychology,* 1964, 68, 255–262.

Fisher, S., & Mirin, S. Further validation of the special favorable response occurring during unconscious self-evaluation. *Perceptual and Motor Skills,* 1966, 23, 1,097–1,098.

Fisher, S., & Renik, O. D. Induction of body image boundary changes. *Journal of Projective Techniques and Personality Assessment,* 1966, 30, 429–434.

Fiske, D. W. Some hypotheses concerning test adequacy. *Educational and Psychological Measurement,* 1966, 26, 69–88.

Fiske, D. W. *Measuring the concepts of personality.* Chicago: Aldine, 1971.

Fitts, W. H. *Tennessee Self Concept Scale: Test Booklet.* Nashville, Tenn.: Counselor Recordings and Tests, Department of Mental Health, 1964.

Fitts, W. H. *Tennessee Self Concept Scale: Manual.* Nashville, Tenn.: Counselor Recordings and Tests, Department of Mental Health, 1965.

Flippo, J. R., & Lewinsohn, P. M. Effects of failure on the self-esteem of depressed and nondepressed subjects. *Journal of Consulting and Clinical Psychology,* 1971, 36, 151.

Flyer, E. S.; Barron, E.; & Bigbee, L. Discrepancies between self-descriptions and group ratings as measures of lack of insight. *USAF Human Resources Research Center Research Bulletin,* 1953, No. 53–33, III.

Flynn, J. T. The Adjective Check List, a device to assess perceived self. *Journal of Teacher Education,* 1966, 17, 247–248.

Foa, U. G. Convergences in the analysis of the structure of interpersonal behavior. *Psychological Review,* 1961, 68, 341–353.

Folds, J. H., & Gazda, G. M. A comparison of the effectiveness and efficiency of three methods of test interpretation. *Journal of Counseling Psychology,* 1966, 13, 318–324.

Forsyth, R. P., & Fairweather, F. W. Psychotherapeutic and other hospital treatment criteria: The dilemma. *Journal of Abnormal and Social Psychology,* 1961, 62, 598–604.

Foulkes, D., & Heaxt, S. Concept attainment and self concept. *Psychological Reports,* 1962, 11, 399–402.

Frank, G. H. Note on the reliability of Q-sort data. *Psychological Reports,* 1956, 2, 182.

Frede, M. C.; Gautney, D. B.; & Baxter, J. C. Relationships between body image boundary and interaction patterns on the MAPS test. *Journal of Consulting and Clinical Psychology,* 1968, 32, 575–578.

Freedman, J. Role playing: Psychology by consensus. *Journal of Personality and Social Psychology,* 1969, 13, 107–114.

Freud, S. *The ego and the id.* New York: W. W. Norton, 1962.

Friedman, I. Phenomenal, ideal, and projected conceptions of self. *Journal of Abnormal and Social Psychology,* 1955, 51, 611–615.

Friedman, I. Objectifying the subjective: A methodological approach to the TAT. *Journal of Projective Techniques,* 1957, 21, 243–247.

Friedman, N. *The social nature of psychological research: The psychological experiment as a social inter-action.* New York: Basic Books, 1967.

Friedsam, H. J., & Martin, H. W. A comparison of self and physicians' health ratings in an older population. *Journal of Health and Human Behavior,* 1963, 4, 179–183.

Frisbie, L. V.; Vanasek, F. J.; & Dingman, H. F. The self and the ideal self: Methodological study of pedophiles. *Psychological Reports,* 1967, 20, 699–706.

Frisch, P., & Cranston, R. Q-technique applied to a patient and the therapist in a child guidance setting. *Journal of Clinical Psychology,* 1956, 12, 178–182.

Froehle, T. C., & Zerface, J. P. Social self-esteem: A further look. *Journal of Consulting and Clinical Psychology,* 1971, 37, 73–74.

Froehlich, C. P., & Moser, W. E. Do counselees remember test scores? *Journal of Counseling Psychology,* 1954, 1, 149–152.

Fromm, E. Selfishness and self-love. *Psychiatry,* 1939, 2, 507–523.

Fuller, G. B., & Lunney, G. H. Relationship between perception and body image among emotionally disturbed children. *Perceptual and Motor Skills,* 1965, 21, 530.

Fuster, J. M. The self-concept approach to personal adjustment. *Journal of Social Psychology,* 1963, 59, 239–246.

Gage, N. L., & Cronbach, L. J. Conceptual and methodological problems in interpersonal perception. *Psychological Review,* 1955, 62, 411–422.

Gaier, E. L. Student self estimates of final course grades. *Journal of Genetic Psychology,* 1961, 98, 63–67.

Gamble, K. R. The Holtzman Inkblot Technique: A review. *Psychological Bulletin,* 1972, 77, 172–194.

Gardiner, H. W. Self-discrepancy and frequency of daydreams: Replication with female Ss. *Perceptual and Motor Skills,* 1970, 30, 970.

Garner, W. R.; Hake, H. W.; & Eriksen, C. W. Operationism and the concept of perception. *Psychological Review,* 1956, 63, 149–159.

Garretson, W. S. The consensual definition of social objects. *Sociological Quarterly,* 1962, 3, 107–113.

Gebel, A. S. Self-perception and leaderless group discussion status. *Journal of Social Psychology,* 1954, 40, 309–318.

Gergen, K. J., & Wishnov, B. Others' self-evaluations and interaction anticipation as determinants of self-presentation. *Journal of Personality and Social Psychology,* 1965, 2, 348–358.

Gibby, R. G., Jr.; Gibby, R. G., Sr.; & Hogan, T. P. Relationships between dominance needs and decision-making ability. *Journal of Clinical Psychology,* 1967, 23, 450–452.

Gibson, R. L.; Snyder, W. U.; & Ray, W. S. A factor analysis of measures of change following client-centered therapy. *Journal of Counseling Psychology,* 1955, 2, 83–90.

Gildston, P. Stutterers' self-acceptance and perceived parental acceptance. *Journal of Abnormal Psychology,* 1967, 72, 59–64.

Gocka, E. F., & Marks, J. B. Second-order factors in the 16 PF test and MMPI inventory. *Journal of Clinical Psychology,* 1961, 17, 32–35.

Golding, S. L., & Lichtenstein, E. Confession of awareness and prior knowledge of deception as a function of interview set and approval motivation. *Journal of Personality and Social Psychology,* 1970, 14, 213–223.

Goldings, H. J. On the avowal and projection of happiness. *Journal of Personality,* 1954, 23, 30–47.

Goldman, B. A. Effect of classroom experience and video tape self observation upon undergraduate attitudes toward self and toward teaching. *Proceedings of the 77th Annual Convention of the American Psychological Association,* 1969, 4, 647–648.

Goldstein, A. P. Therapist and client expectation of personality change in psychotherapy. *Journal of Counseling Psychology,* 1960, 7, 180–184.

Goldstein, G.; Neuringer, C.; Reiff, C.; & Shelly, C. H. Generalizability of field dependency in alcoholics. *Journal of Consulting and Clinical Psychology,* 1968, 32, 560–564.

Gordon, C. Self-conceptions: Configurations of content. In C. Gordon & K. J. Gergen (Eds.), *The self in social interaction*. Vol. 1. *Classic and contemporary perspectives*. New York: Wiley, 1968. Pp. 115–136.

Gordon, C. Self-conceptions methodologies. *Journal of Nervous and Mental Disease*, 1969, 148, 328–364.

Gorham, D. R.; Moseley, E. C.; & Holtzman, W. H. Norms for the computer-scored Holtzman Inkblot Technique. *Perceptual and Motor Skills*, 1968, 26, 1,279–1,305.

Gorlow, L.; Simonson, N. R.; & Krauss, H. An empirical investigation of the Jungian typology. *British Journal of Social and Clinical Psychology*, 1966, 5, 108–117.

Gorsuch, R. L.; Henighan, R. P.; & Barnard, C. Locus of control: An example of dangers in using children's scales with children. *Child Development*, 1972, 43, 579–590.

Goslin, D. A. Accuracy of self perception and social acceptance. *Sociometry*, 1962, 25, 283–296.

Gottesfeld, H. Body and self cathexis of super-obese patients. *Journal of Psychosomatic Research*, 1962, 6, 177–183.

Gough, H. G. The Adjective Check List as a personality assessment research technique. *Psychological Reports*, 1960, 6, 107–122.

Gough, H. G., & Heilbrun, A. B. *The Adjective Check List Manual*. Palo Alto, Calif.: Consulting Psychologists Press, 1965.

Gough, H. G., & Woodworth, D. G. Stylistic variations among professional research scientists. *Journal of Psychology*, 1960, 49, 87–98.

Graham, J. R., & Barr, K. G. Q-sort study of the relationship between students' self-acceptance and acceptance of their college. *Psychological Reports*, 1967, 21, 779–780.

Grande, P. P. The use of self and peer ratings in a Peace Corps training program. *Vocational Guidance Quarterly*, 1966, 14, 244–246.

Grant, C. H. Age differences in self-concept from early adulthood through old age. *Proceedings of the 77th Annual Convention of the American Psychological Association*, 1969, 4, 717–718.

Grater, H. Changes in self and other attitudes in a leadership training group. *Personnel and Guidance Journal*, 1959, 37, 493–496.

Graves, W. H., & Shearer, R. A. Use of the Adjective Check List to elicit description of self-ideal discrepancy. *Perceptual and Motor Skills*, 1971, 32, 781–782.

Gray, D. M., & Pepitone, A. Effect of self-esteem on drawings of the human figure. *Journal of Consulting Psychology*, 1964, 28, 452–455.

Green, G. H. Insight and group adjustment. *Journal of Abnormal and Social Psychology*, 1948, 43, 49–61.

Greenberg, G. U., & Frank, G. H. Response set in the Tennessee Department of Mental Health Self Concept Scale. *Journal of Clinical Psychology,* 1965, 21, 287–288.

Greenberg, G. U., & Frank, G. H. Personality correlates of attitude change: The tendency to alter attitudes toward self in other directed and inner directed people. *Journal of General Psychology,* 1967, 76, 85–90.

Greenberg, M. S. Role playing: An alternative to deception? *Journal of Personality and Social Psychology,* 1967, 7, 152–157.

Griffitt, W. B. Interpersonal attraction as a function of self-concept and personality similarity-dissimilarity. *Journal of Personality and Social Psychology,* 1966, 4, 581–584.

Griffitt, W. B. Personality similarity and self-concept as determinants of interpersonal attraction. *Journal of Social Psychology,* 1969, 78, 137–146.

Grigg, A. E. A validity study of the semantic differential technique. *Journal of Clinical Psychology,* 1959, 15, 179–181. (a)

Grigg, A. E. A validity test of self-ideal discrepancy. *Journal of Clinical Psychology,* 1959, 15, 311–313. (b)

Grigg, A. E., & Thorpe, J. S. Deviant responses in college adjustment clients: A test of Berg's deviation hypothesis. *Journal of Consulting Psychology,* 1960, 24, 92–94.

Gross, L. The construction and partial standardization of a scale for measuring self-insight. *Journal of Social Psychology,* 1948, 28, 219–236. (a)

Gross, L. An experimental study of the validity of the non-directive method of teaching. *Journal of Psychology,* 1948, 26, 243–248. (b)

Gross, W. F., & Alder, L. O. Aspects of alcoholics' self-concepts as measured by the Tennessee Self Concept Scale. *Psychological Reports,* 1970, 27, 431–434.

Grossack, M. M. The "Who Am I Test." *Journal of Social Psychology,* 1960, 51, 399–402.

Gruen, W. Rejection of false information about oneself as an indication of ego identity. *Journal of Consulting Psychology,* 1960, 24, 231–233.

Grummon, D. L., & John, E. S. Changes over client-centered therapy evaluated on psychoanalytically based Thematic Apperception Test Scales. In C. R. Rogers & R. F. Dymond (Eds.), *Psychotherapy and personality change.* Chicago: University of Chicago Press, 1954. Pp. 121–144.

Guardo, C. Sociometric status and self-concept in sixth graders. *Journal of Educational Research,* 1969, 62, 319–322.

Guerney, B. Jr., & Burton, J. L. Relationships among anxiety and self, typical peer, and ideal percepts in college women. *Journal of Social Psychology,* 1963, 61, 335–344.

Guerney, B. Jr., & Burton, J. L. Comparison of typical peer, self, and ideal percepts related to college achievement. *Journal of Social Psychology,* 1967, 73, 253–259.

Guertin, W. H., & Jourard, S. M. Characteristics of real-self-ideal-self discrepancy scores revealed by factor analysis. *Journal of Consulting Psychology,* 1962, 26, 241–245.

Guggenheim, F., & Hoem, A. Cross-cultural and intracultural attitudes of Lapp and Norwegian children. *Journal of Social Psychology,* 1967, 73, 23–36.

Guilford, J. P. *Psychometric methods.* (2nd ed.) New York: McGraw-Hill, 1954.

Gulliksen, H. *Theory of mental tests.* New York: Wiley, 1950.

Gulliksen, H. How to make meaning more meaningful. *Contemporary Psychology,* 1958, 3, 115–119.

Gunderson, E. K. E., & Johnson, L. C. Past experience, self-evaluation, and present adjustment. *Journal of Social Psychology,* 1965, 66, 311–321.

Gustav, A. Comparison of college grades and self-concept. *Psychological Reports,* 1962, 11, 601–602.

Guthrie, G. M.; Butler, A.; & Gorlow, L. Patterns of self-attitudes of retardates. *American Journal of Mental Deficiency,* 1961, 66, 222–229.

Guthrie, G. M.; Butler, A.; Gorlow, L.; & White, G. N. Non-verbal expression of self-attitudes of retardates. *American Journal of Mental Deficiency,* 1964, 69, 42–49.

Guttman, L. The basis for scalogram analysis. In S. A. Stouffer; L. Guttman; E. A. Suchman; P. F. Lazarsfeld; S. Star; & J. A. Clausen. *Studies in social psychology in World War II.* Vol. 4. *Measurement and prediction.* Princeton, N.J.: Princeton University Press, 1950. Pp. 60–90.

Gynther, M. D. Degree of agreement among three "interpersonal system" measures. *Journal of Consulting Psychology,* 1962, 26, 107.

Gynther, M. D., & Brilliant, P. J. Marital status, readmission to hospital, and intrapersonal and interpersonal perceptions of alcoholics. *Quarterly Journal of Studies on Alcohol,* 1967, 28, 52–58.

Gynther, M. D., & Kempson, J. O. Seminarians and clinical pastoral training: A follow-up study. *Journal of Social Psychology,* 1962, 56, 9–14.

Gynther, M. D.; Miller, F. T.; & Davis, H. T. Relations between needs and behavior as measured by the Edwards PPS and Interpersonal Check List. *Journal of Social Psychology,* 1962, 57, 445–451.

Haertzen, C. A., & Hooks, N. T., Jr. Effects of adaptation level, context, and face validity on responses to self-report psychological inventories. *Psychological Record,* 1968, 18, 339–349.

Haimowitz, N. R., & Haimowitz, M. L. Personality changes in client-centered therapy. In W. W. Wolff & J. A. Precker (Eds.), *Success in psychotherapy.* New York: Grune & Stratton, 1952.

Haley, G. A. Item-analysis procedures for enhancing validity of existing personality scales. *Psychological Reports,* 1970, 27, 847–853.

Hall, C. S., & Lindzey, G. *Theories of personality.* (2nd ed.) New York: Wiley, 1970.

Hall, D. T. The impact of peer interaction during an academic role transition. *Sociology of Education,* 1969, 42, 118–140.

Hamid, P. N. Word meanings and self descriptions. *Journal of Social Psychology,* 1969, 79, 51–54.

Hamilton, D. L. A comparative study of five methods of assessing self-esteem, dominance, and dogmatism. *Educational and Psychological Measurement,* 1971, 31, 441–452.

Hammerschlag, C. A.; Fisher, S.; DeCrosse, J.; & Kaplan, E. Breast symptoms and patient delay: Psychological variables involved. *Cancer,* 1964, 17, 1,480–1,485.

Hanlon, T. E.; Hofstaetter, P.; & O'Connor, J. Congruence of self and ideal self in relation to personality adjustment. *Journal of Consulting Psychology,* 1954, 18, 215–218.

Hansen, J. C.; Moore, G. D.; & Carkhuff, R. R. The differential relationships of objective and client perceptions of counseling. *Journal of Clinical Psychology,* 1968, 24, 244–246.

Harmatz, M. G. Verbal conditioning and change on personality measures. *Journal of Personality and Social Psychology,* 1967, 5, 175–185.

Harris, S., & Braun, J. R. Self-esteem and racial preference in black children. *Proceedings of the 79th Annual Convention of the American Psychological Association,* 1971, 6, 259–260.

Harrow, M.; Fox, D. A.; & Detre, T. Self-concept of the married psychiatric patient and his mate's perception of him. *Journal of Consulting and Clinical Psychology,* 1969, 33, 235–239.

Harrow, M.; Fox, D. A.; Markhus, K. L.; Stillman, R.; & Hallowell, C. B. Changes in adolescents' self-concepts and their parents' perceptions during psychiatric hospitalization. *Journal of Nervous and Mental Disease,* 1968, 147, 252–259.

Hartlage, L. C., & Hale, P. Self-concept decline from psychiatric hospitalization. *Journal of Individual Psychology,* 1968, 24, 174–176.

Hartley, R. B. The Barrier variable as measured by homonyms. *Journal of Clinical Psychology,* 1967, 23, 196–203.

Hartman, B. J. An investigation of hypnotic susceptibility as a function of selected attitudinal variables. *American Journal of Clinical Hypnosis,* 1965, 8, 44–46.

Hartung, J. R.; McKenna, S. A.; & Baxter, J. C. Body image and defensiveness in an LSD-taking subculture. *Journal of Projective Techniques and Personality Assessment,* 1970, 34, 316–323.

Hatfield, A. B. An experimental study of the self-concept of student teachers. *Journal of Educational Research,* 1961, 55, 87–89.

Havener, P. H., & Izard, C. E. Unrealistic self-enhancement in paranoid schizophrenics. *Journal of Consulting Psychology,* 1962, 26, 65–68.

Hebert, D. J. Reading comprehension as a function of self-concept. *Perceptual and Motor Skills,* 1968, 27, 78.

Heider, F. On Lewin's methods and theory. *Journal of Social Issues,* 1959, Suppl. Series No. 13.

Heilbrun, A. B., Jr. Male and female personality correlates of early termination in counseling. *Journal of Counseling Psychology,* 1961, 8, 31–36.

Heilbrun, A. B., Jr. Prediction of first year college drop-out using ACL need scales. *Journal of Counseling Psychology,* 1962, 9, 58–63.

Heilbrun, A. B., Jr. Social-learning theory, social desirability, and the MMPI. *Psychological Bulletin,* 1964, 61, 377–387.

Heilbrun, A. B., Jr. The social desirability variable: Implications for test reliability and validity. *Educational and Psychological Measurement,* 1965, 25, 745–756.

Heilbrun, A. B., Jr. Adjective Check List correlates of social conflict problems in college students. *Measurement and Evaluation in Guidance,* 1970, 3, 158–163.

Heilbrun, A. B., Jr., & Goodstein, L. D. Social desirability response set: Error or predictor variable? *Journal of Psychology,* 1961, 51, 321–329. (a)

Heilbrun, A. B., Jr., & Goodstein, L. D. The relationships between individually defined and group defined social desirability and performance on the Edwards Personal Preference Schedule. *Journal of Consulting Psychology,* 1961, 25, 200–204. (b)

Helson, H. *Adaptation-level theory.* New York: Harper & Row, 1964.

Helson, R., & Crutchfield, R. S. Creative types in mathematics. *Journal of Personality,* 1970, 38, 177–197.

Henderson, E. H.; Long, B. H.; & Ziller, R. C. Self-social constructs of achieving and nonachieving readers. *Reading Teacher,* 1965, 19, 114–118.

Henderson, E. H., & Long, B. H. Self-social concepts in relation to reading and arithmetic. In J. A. Figurel (Ed.), *Vistas in reading.* Vol. 2, Part 1. *Proceedings of the 11th Annual Convention, International Reading Association, 1967.* Pp. 576–581.

Hendrick, C., & Page, H. A. Self-esteem, attitude similarity, and attraction. *Journal of Personality,* 1970, 38, 588–601.

Herbert, E. W.; Gelfand, D. M.; & Hartmann, D. P. Imitation and self-esteem as determinants of self-critical behavior. *Child Development,* 1969, 40, 421–430.

Herman, M.; Sadofsky, S.; Bensman, J.; Lilienfeld, R.; & Manos, C. *Study of the meaning, experience, and effects of the neighborhood youth corps on Negro youth who are seeking work.* New York: New York University Graduate School of Social Work, 1967.

Hess, A. L., & Bradshaw, H. L. Positiveness of self-concept and ideal self as a function of age. *Journal of Genetic Psychology,* 1970, 117, 57–67.

Hickman, C. A., & Kuhn, M. H. *Individuals, groups, and economic behavior.* New York: Dryden Press, 1956.

Hilden, A. H. Q-sort correlation: Stability and random choice of statements. *Journal of Consulting Psychology,* 1958, 22, 45–50.

Hilgard, E. R. Human motives and the concept of the self. *American Psychologist,* 1949, 4, 374–382.

Hills, D. A., & Williams, J. E. Effects of test information upon self-evaluation in brief educational-vocational counseling. *Journal of Counseling Psychology,* 1965, 12, 275–281.

Hillson, J. S., & Worchel, P. Self concept and defensive behavior in the maladjusted. *Journal of Consulting Psychology,* 1957, 21, 83–88.

Himelstein, P., & Kimbrough, W. W., Jr. A study of self-disclosure in the classroom. *Journal of Psychology,* 1963, 55, 437–440.

Himelstein, P., & Lubin, B. Attempted validation of the self-disclosure inventory by the peer-nomination technique. *Journal of Psychology,* 1965, 61, 13–16.

Hirt, M., & Kurtz, R. A reexamination of the relationship between body boundary and site of disease. *Journal of Abnormal Psychology,* 1969, 74, 67–70.

Hodgkins, B. J., & Stakenas, R. G. A study of self-concepts of Negro and white youths in segregated environments. *The Journal of Negro Education,* 1969, 38, 370–377.

Hollon, T. H., & Zolik, E. S. Self-esteem and symptomatic complaints in the initial phase of psychoanalytically oriented psychotherapy. *American Journal of Psychotherapy,* 1962, 16, 83–93.

Holt, R. R. The accuracy of self-evaluation: Its measurement and some of its personalogical correlates. *Journal of Consulting Psychology,* 1951, 15, 95–101.

Holtzman, W. H.; Thorpe, J. S.; Swartz, J. D.; & Herron, E. W. *Inkblot perception and personality.* Austin: University of Texas Press, 1961.

Horney, K. *The neurotic personality of our times.* New York: W. W. Norton, 1937.

Horney, K. *Neurosis and human growth.* New York: Norton, 1950.

Horowitz, E. Reported embarassment memories of elementary school, high school, and college students. *Journal of Social Psychology,* 1962, 56, 317–325.

Horowitz, F. D. The relationship of anxiety, self-concept, and sociometric status among fourth, fifth, and sixth grade children. *Journal of Abnormal and Social Psychology,* 1962, 65, 212–214.

Howe, E. S. Probabilistic adverbial qualifications of adjectives. *Journal of Verbal Learning and Verbal Behavior,* 1962, 1, 225–242.

Hoyt, C. Test reliability estimated by analysis of variance. *Psychometrika,* 1941, 6, 153–160.

Hughes, T. M. The relationship of coping strength to self-concept, school achievement, and general anxiety level in sixth grade pupils. *Journal of Experimental Education,* 1968, 37, 59–64.

Hull, C. L. *Essentials of behavior.* New Haven: Yale University Press, 1951.

Humes, C. W., Jr.; Adamczyk, J. S.; & Myco, R. W. A school study of group counseling with educable retarded adolescents. *American Journal of Mental Deficiency,* 1969, 74, 191–195.

Humphreys, L. G. Note on the multitrait-multimethod matrix. *Psychological Bulletin,* 1960, 57, 86–88.

Hunt, D. E., & Hardt, R. H. The effect of Upward Bound programs on the attitudes, motivation, and academic achievement of Negro students. *Journal of Social Issues,* 1969, 25, 117–129.

Hunt, J. McV. Traditional personality theory in the light of recent evidence. *American Scientist,* 1965, 53, 80–96.

Hunt, R. A. Self and other semantic concepts in relation to choice of a vocation. *Journal of Applied Psychology,* 1967, 51, 242–246.

Hunt, R. G., & Feldman, M. J. Body image and ratings of adjustment on human figure drawings. *Journal of Clinical Psychology,* 1960, 16, 35–38.

Imboden, J. B.; Canter, A; Cluff, L. E.; & Trever, R. W. Brucellosis: III. Psychological aspects of delayed convalescence. *American Medical Association Archives of Internal Medicine,* 1959, 103, 406–414.

Insel, S. A.; Reese, C. S.; & Alexander, B. B. Self-presentations in relation to internal and external referents. *Journal of Consulting and Clinical Psychology,* 1968, 32, 389–395.

Isaacson, G. S., & Landfield, A. W. Meaningfulness of personal versus common constructs. *Journal of Individual Psychology,* 1965, 21, 160–166.

Isabell, L. A., & Dick, W. Clarity of self-concepts in the vocational development of male liberal arts students: An abstract. *Canadian Psychologist,* 1969, 10, 20–31.

Isenberger, W. Self-attitudes of women physical education major students and of women physical education teachers. *Research Quarterly of the American Association of Health, Physical Education, and Recreation,* 1959, 30, 44–53. (a)

Isenberger, W. Self-attitude of women physical education major students as related to measures of interest and success. *Research Quarterly of the American Association of Health, Physical Education, and Recreation,* 1959, 30, 167–177. (b)

Israel, J. Self-evaluation in groups. *Acta Sociologica,* 1958, 3, 29–47.

Ivanoff, J. M.; Layman, J. A.; & von Singer, R. Changes in ACL scales corresponding to changes in educational levels. *Psychological Reports,* 1970, 27, 359–363.

Jackson, D. N. Acquiescence response styles: Problems of identification and control. In I. A. Berg (Ed.), *Response set in personality assessment.* Chicago: Aldine, 1967. Pp. 71–114. (a)

Jackson, D. N. *Personality Research Form Manual.* Goshen, N.Y.: Research Psychologists Press, 1967. (b)

Jackson, D. N. Multimethod factor analysis in the evaluation of convergent and discriminant validity. *Psychological Bulletin,* 1969, 72, 30–49.

Jackson, D. N. Some perspectives on the analysis of multitrait-multimethod matrices. *University of Western Ontario Research Bulletin,* 1970, No. 159.

Jackson, D. N. Comments on "Evaluation of multimethod factor analysis." *Psychological Bulletin,* 1971, 75, 421–423.

Jackson, D. N., & Guthrie, G. M. Multitrait-multimethod evaluation of the Personality Research Form. *Proceedings of the 76th Annual Convention of the American Psychological Association,* 1968, 3, 177–178.

Jackson, D. N., & Messick, S. Content and style in personality assessment. *Psychological Bulletin,* 1958, 55, 243–252.

Jackson, D. N., & Messick, S. J. Acquiescence and desirability as response determinants on the MMPI. *Educational and Psychological Measurement,* 1961, 21, 771–792.

Jacob, T., & Levine, D. *A-B* distinction and prediction of interviewee self descriptions based on a quasi-therapeutic interaction. *Journal of Consulting and Clinical Psychology,* 1968, 32, 613–615.

James, W. *Principles of psychology.* New York: Holt, 1890, 2 vols.

Jaskar, R. O., & Reed, M. R. Assessment of body image organization of hospitalized and nonhospitalized subjects. *Journal of Projective Techniques and Personality Assessment,* 1963, 27, 185–190.

Jernigan, A. J. Judging whether a patient is white or black by his Draw-A-Person Test. *Journal of Projective Techniques and Personality Assessment,* 1970, 34, 503–506.

Jersild, A. T. *In search of self: An exploration of the role of the school in promoting self-understanding.* New York: Teachers College, 1952.

Jessor, R. Phenomenological personality theories and the data language of psychology. *Psychological Review,* 1956, 63, 173–180.

Joesting, J., & Joesting, R. Differences among self-descriptions of gifted black college students and their less intelligent counterparts. *Gifted Child Quarterly,* 1969, 13, 175–180.

Johnson, L. C. Body-cathexis as a factor in somatic complaints. *Journal of Consulting Psychology,* 1956, 20, 145–149.

Jones, A. Distribution of traits in current Q-sort methodology. *Journal of Abnormal and Social Psychology,* 1956, 53, 90–95.

Jones, E. E. *Ingratiation.* New York: Appleton-Century-Crofts, 1964.

Jones, E. E.; Gergen, K. J.; & Davis, D. E. Some determinants of reactions to being approved or disapproved as a person. *Psychological Monographs,* 1962, 76 (2, Whole No. 521).

Jones, J. G., & Strowig, R. W. Adolescent identity and self-perception as predictors of scholastic achievement. *Journal of Educational Research,* 1968, 62, 78–82.

Jones, R. A.; Lindner, D. E.; Kiesler, C. A.; Zanna, M.; & Brehm, J. W. Internal states or external stimuli: Observers' attitude judgments and the dissonance-theory-self-persuasion controversy. *Journal of Experimental Social Psychology,* 1968, 4, 247–269.

Jorgensen, E. C., & Howell, R. J. Changes in self, ideal-self correlations from ages 8 through 18. *Journal of Social Psychology,* 1969, 79, 63–67.

Jourard, S. M. Identification, parent-cathexis, and self-esteem. *Journal of Consulting Psychology,* 1957, 21, 375–380.

Jourard, S. M. A study of self-disclosure. *Scientific American,* 1958, 198, 77–82.

Jourard, S. M. Self-disclosure patterns in British and American college females. *Journal of Social Psychology,* 1961, 54, 315–320.

Jourard, S. M. The effects of experimenters' self-disclosure on subjects' behavior. In C. Spielberger (Ed.) , *Current topics in clinical and community psychology.* Vol. 1. New York: Academic Press, 1969. Pp. 109–150.

Jourard, S., & Friedman, R. Experimenter-subject "distance" and self-disclosure. *Journal of Personality and Social Psychology,* 1970, 15, 278–282.

Jourard, S. M., & Jaffe, P. E. Influence of an interviewer's disclosure on the self-disclosing behavior of interviewees. *Journal of Counseling Psychology,* 1970, 17, 252–257.

Jourard, S. M., & Kormann, L. A. Getting to know the experimenter, and its effects on psychological test performance. *Journal of Humanistic Psychology,* 1968, 8, 155–159.

Jourard, S. M., & Lasakow, P. Some factors in self-disclosure. *Journal of Abnormal and Social Psychology*, 1958, 56, 91–98.

Jourard, S. M., & Remy, R. M. Perceived parental attitudes, the self, and security. *Journal of Consulting Psychology*, 1955, 19, 364–366.

Jourard., S. M., & Remy, R. M. Individual variance scores: An index of the degree of differentiation of the self and the body image. *Journal of Clinical Psychology*, 1957, 13, 62–63.

Jourard, S. M., & Secord, P. F. Body size and body cathexis. *Journal of Consulting Psychology*, 1954, 18, 184.

Jourard, S. M., & Secord, P. F. Body-cathexis and the ideal female figure. *Journal of Abnormal and Social Psychology*, 1955, 50, 243–246.

Kamano, D. K. An investigation on the meaning of human figure drawing. *Journal of Clinical Psychology*, 1960, 16, 429–430.

Kamano, D. K. Self-satisfaction and psychological adjustment in schizophrenics. *Journal of Consulting Psychology*, 1961, 25, 492–496.

Kamano, D. K., & Crawford, C. S. Self-evaluations of suicidal mental hospital patients. *Journal of Clinical Psychology*, 1966, 22, 278–279.

Kania, W. Healthy defensiveness in theological students. *Ministry Studies*, 1967, 1, 3–20.

Kaplan, H. B. Self-derogation and childhood family structure. *Journal of Nervous and Mental Disease*, 1970, 151, 13–23. (a)

Kaplan, H. B. Self-derogation and adjustment to recent life experiences. *Archives of General Psychiatry*, 1970, 22, 324–331. (b)

Kaplan, H. B. Social class and self-derogation: A conditional relationship. *Sociometry*, 1971, 34, 41–64.

Kaplan, H. B., & Meyerowitz, J. H. Social and psychological correlates of drug abuse: A comparison of addict and nonaddict populations from the perspective of self-theory. *Social Science and Medicine*, 1970, 4, 203–225.

Kaplan, H. B., & Pokorny, A. D. Self-derogation and psychosocial adjustment. *Journal of Nervous and Mental Disease*, 1969, 149, 421–434.

Kaplan, H. B., & Pokorny, A. D. Age-related correlates of self-derogation: Report of childhood experiences. *British Journal of Psychiatry*, 1970, 117, 533–534. (a)

Kaplan, H. B., & Pokorny, A. D. Aging and self-attitude: A conditional relationship. *Aging and Human Development*, 1970, 1, 241–250. (b)

Kaplan, H. B., & Pokorny, A. D. Self-derogation and childhood broken home. *Journal of Marriage and the Family*, 1971, 33, 328–337.

Karon, P. B. *The Negro personality*. New York: Springer, 1958.

Karp, E. S.; Jackson, J. H.; & Lester, D. Ideal-self fulfillment in mate selection: A corollary to the complementary need theory of mate selection. *Journal of Marriage and the Family*, 1970, 32, 269–272.

Kassebaum, G. G.; Couch, A. S.; & Slater, P. E. The factorial dimensions of the MMPI. *Journal of Consulting Psychology*, 1959, 23, 226–236.

Kates, S. L., & Jordan, R. M. The social stimulus self and the self-image related to personality and psychotherapy. *Journal of Social Psychology*, 1955, 42, 137–146.

Katz, P., & Zigler, E. Self-image disparity: A developmental approach. *Journal of Personality and Social Psychology*, 1967, 5, 186–195.

Kavanagh, M. J.; MacKinney, A. C.; & Wolins, L. Issues in managerial performance: Multitrait-multimethod analyses of ratings. *Psychological Bulletin*, 1971, 75, 34–49.

Kay, E.; French, J. R. P., Jr.; & Meyer, H. H. *A study of the performance appraisal interview.* New York: Behavior Research Service, General Electric Company, 1962.

Keefer, K. E. Self-prediction of academic achievement by college students. *Journal of Educational Research,* 1969, 63, 53–56.

Kelly, F. J., & Baer, D. J. Jesness Inventory and self-concept measures for delinquents before and after participation in Outward Bound. *Psychological Reports,* 1969, 25, 719–724.

Kelman, H. C. Human use of human subjects: The problem of deception in social psychological experiments. *Psychological Bulletin,* 1967, 67, 1–11.

Kelman, H. C., & Parloff, M. B. Interrelations among three criteria of improvement in group therapy: Comfort, effectiveness, and self-awareness. *Journal of Abnormal and Social Psychology,* 1957, 54, 281–288.

Kemp, C. G. Self-perception in relation to open-closed belief systems. *Journal of Genetic Psychology,* 1964, 70, 341–344.

Kenny, D. T. The influence of social desirability on discrepancy measures between real self and ideal self. *Journal of Consulting Psychology,* 1956, 20, 315–318.

Kernaleguen, A. P., & Compton, N. H. Body-field perceptual differentiation related to peer perception of attitudes toward clothing. *Perceptual and Motor Skills,* 1968, 27, 195–198.

Kingston, A. J., & White, W. F. The relationship of reader's self concepts and personality components to semantic meanings perceived in the protagonist of a reading selection. *Reading Research Quarterly,* 1967, 2, 107–116.

Klausner, S. Z. Social class and self concept. *Journal of Social Psychology,* 1953, 38, 201–205.

Klein, G. S. Self-appraisal of test performance as a vocational selection device. *Educational and Psychological Measurement,* 1948, 8, 69–84.

Klein, H. P., & Parsons, O. A. Self-descriptions of patients with coronary disease. *Perceptual and Motor Skills,* 1968, 26, 1,099–1,107.

Klett, C. J. The stability of the social desirability scale values in the Edwards Personal Preference Schedule. *Journal of Consulting Psychology*, 1957, 21, 183–185. (a)

Klett, C. J. The social desirability stereotype in a hospital population. *Journal of Consulting Psychology*, 1957, 21, 419–421. (b)

Klett, C. J., & Yaukey, D. W. A cross-cultural comparison of judgments of social desirability. *Journal of Social Psychology*, 1959, 49, 19–26.

Knapp, R. H. A study of the metaphor. *Journal of Projective Techniques*, 1960, 24, 389–395.

Kniss, J. T.; Butler, A.; Gorlow, L.; & Guthrie, G. M. Ideal self patterns of female retardates. *American Journal of Mental Deficiency*, 1962, 67, 245–249.

Koenig, F. Definitions of self and ordinal position of birth. *Journal of Social Psychology*, 1969, 78, 287–288.

Kogan, K. L., & Jackson, J. K. Conventional sex role stereotypes and actual perceptions. *Psychological Reports*, 1963, 13, 27–30.

Kogan, W. S.; Boe, E. E.; Gocka, E. F.; & Johnson, M. H. Personality changes in psychiatric residents during training. *Journal of Psychology*, 1966, 62, 229–240.

Kogan, W. S.; Boe, E. E.; & Valentine, B. L. Changes in the self concept of unwed mothers. *Journal of Psychology*, 1965, 59, 3–10.

Kogan, W. S., & Fordyce, W. E. The control of social desirability: A comparison of three different Q sorts and a check list, all composed of the same items. *Journal of Consulting Psychology*, 1962, 26, 26–30.

Kogan, W. S.; Quinn, R.; Ax, A. F.; & Ripley, H. S. Some methodological problems in the quantification of clinical assessment by Q array. *Journal of Consulting Psychology*, 1957, 21, 57–62.

Kohn, M. L. *Class and conformity: A study in values.* Homewood, Ill.: Dorsey, 1969.

Korman, A. K. Self-esteem as a moderator in vocational choice: Replications and extensions. *Journal of Applied Psychology*, 1969, 53, 188–192.

Korner, I. N.; Allison, R. B., Jr.; Donoviel, S. J.; & Boswell, J. D. Some measures of self-acceptance. *Journal of Clinical Psychology*, 1963, 19, 131–132.

Kornreich, L. B.; Straka, J.; & Kane, A. Meaning of self-image disparity as measured by the Q sort. *Journal of Consulting and Clinical Psychology*, 1968, 32, 728–730.

Kotkov, B., & Goodman, M. The Draw-A-Person tests of obese women. *Journal of Clinical Psychology*, 1953, 9, 362–364.

Kotlar, S. L. Instrumental and expressive marital roles. *Sociology and Social Research*, 1962, 46, 186–194.

Krieger, M. H., & Worchel, P. A test of the psychoanalytic theory of identification. *Journal of Individual Psychology*, 1960, 16, 56–63.

Kubiniec, C. M. The relative efficacy of various dimensions of the self-concept in predicting academic achievement. *American Educational Research Journal,* 1970, 7, 321–336.

Kuhn, M. H. Self-attitudes by age, sex, and professional training. *Sociological Quarterly,* 1960, 9, 39–55.

Kuhn, M. H., & McPartland, T. S. An empirical investigation of self-attitudes. *American Sociological Review,* 1954, 19, 68–76.

Kulik, J. A.; Stein, K. B.; & Sarbin, T. R. Disclosure of delinquent behavior under conditions of anonymity and nonanonymity. *Journal of Consulting and Clinical Psychology,* 1968, 32, 506–509.

Kuncel, R. B. Response processes and relative location of subject and item. *Educational and Psychological Measurement,* in press.

Kurtz, R. M. Body attitude and self-esteem. *Proceedings of the 79th Annual Convention of the American Psychological Association,* 1971, 6, 467–468.

Kusyszyn, I., & Jackson, D. N. A multimethod factor analytic appraisal of endorsement and judgment methods in personality assessment. *Educational and Psychological Measurement,* 1968, 28, 1,047–1,061.

Kuusinen, J. Affective and denotative structures of personality ratings. *Journal of Personality and Social Psychology,* 1969, 12, 181–188.

LaForge, R. Research use of the ICL. *Oregon Research Institute Technical Report,* 1963, 3, No. 4.

LaForge, R., & Suczek, R. The interpersonal dimension of personality: III. An interpersonal check list. *Journal of Personality,* 1955, 24, 94–112.

Langer, P. Sex differences in response set. *Journal of Psychology,* 1962, 54, 203–207.

Lantz, D. L. Relationship between classroom emotional climate and concepts of self, others, and ideal among elementary student teachers. *Journal of Educational Research,* 1965, 59, 80–83.

Larsen, K. S., & Schwendiman, G. Authoritarianism, self esteem, and insecurity. *Psychological Reports,* 1969, 25, 229–230.

Lawler, E. E., III. The multitrait-multirater approach to measuring job performance. *Journal of Applied Psychology,* 1967, 51, 369–381.

Lawton, M. P. Personality and attitudinal correlates of psychiatric-aid performance. *Journal of Social Psychology,* 1965, 66, 215–226.

Laxer, R. M. Self-concept changes of depressive patients in general hospital treatment. *Journal of Consulting Psychology,* 1964, 28, 214–219. (a)

Laxer, R. M. Relation of real self-rating to mood and blame and their interaction in depression. *Journal of Consulting Psychology,* 1964, 28, 538–546. (b)

Lazowick, L. M. On the nature of identification. *Journal of Abnormal and Social Psychology,* 1955, 51, 175–183.

Leary, T. F. *Multilevel measurement of interpersonal behavior.* Berkeley, Calif.: Psychological Consultation Service, 1956.

Leary, T. F. *Interpersonal diagnosis of personality.* New York: Ronald, 1957.

Lecky, P. *Self consistency: A theory of personality.* New York: Island Press, 1945.

Leff, S., & Lamb, N. Experimental approach to defining the role of social desirability in personality assessment: Is there one process or two? *Journal of Consulting and Clinical Psychology,* 1969, 33, 287–291.

Lefkowitz, J. Self-esteem of industrial workers. *Journal of Applied Psychology,* 1967, 51, 521–528.

Lekarczyk, D. T., & Hill, K. T. Self-esteem, test anxiety, stress, and verbal learning. *Developmental Psychology,* 1969, 1, 147–154.

Lepine, L. T., & Chodorkoff, B. Goal setting behavior, expressed feelings of adequacy, and the correspondence between the perceived and ideal self. *Journal of Clinical Psychology,* 1955, 11, 395–397.

Lesser, M. The relationship between counseling progress and empathic understanding. *Journal of Counseling Psychology,* 1961, 8, 330–336.

Levinger, G. Social desirability in the ratings of involved and neutral judges. *Journal of Consulting Psychology,* 1961, 25, 554.

Levonian, E. Personality measurement with items selected from the 16 PF questionnaire. *Educational and Psychological Measurement,* 1961, 21, 937–946. (a)

Levonian, E. A statistical analysis of the 16 Personality Factor Questionnaire. *Educational and Psychological Measurement,* 1961, 21, 589–596. (b)

Levonian, E.; Comrey, A.; Levy, W.; & Procter, D. A statistical evaluation of Edwards Personal Preference Schedule. *Journal of Applied Psychology,* 1959, 43, 355–359.

Levy, L. H. The meaning and generality of perceived actual-ideal discrepancies. *Journal of Consulting Psychology,* 1956, 20, 396–398.

Lieberman, M. A.; Stock, D.; & Whitman, R. M. Self-perceptual patterns among ulcer patients. *American Medical Association Archives of General Psychiatry,* 1959, 1, 167–176.

Lindzey, G., & Tejessy, C. Thematic Apperception Test: Indices of aggression in relation to overt and covert behavior. *American Journal of Orthopsychiatry,* 1956, 26, 567–576.

Linton, H., & Graham, E. Personality correlates of persuasibility. In C. I. Hovland & I. L. Janis (Eds.), *Personality and persuasibility.* New Haven: Yale University Press, 1959. Pp. 69–101.

Lipsitt, L. P. A self-concept scale for children and its relationship to the children's form of the Manifest Anxiety Scale. *Child Development,* 1958, 29, 463–472.

Lipsitt, P. D. The juvenile offender's perceptions. *Crime and Delinquency,* 1968, 14, 49–62.

Livson, N. H., & Nichols, T. F. Discrimination and reliability in Q-sort personality descriptions. *Journal of Abnormal and Social Psychology,* 1956, 52, 159–165.

Lockwood, D. H., & Guerney, B., Jr. Identification and empathy in relation to self-dissatisfaction and adjustment. *Journal of Abnormal and Social Psychology,* 1962, 65, 343–347.

Loehlin, J. C. Word meanings and self-descriptions. *Journal of Abnormal and Social Psychology,* 1961, 62, 28–34.

Loehlin, J. C. Word meanings and self-descriptions: A replication and extension. *Journal of Personality and Social Psychology,* 1967, 5, 107–110.

Loevinger, J. Person and population as psychometric concepts. *Psychological Review,* 1965, 72, 143–155.

Lomont, J. F. Repressors and sensitizers as described by themselves and their peers. *Journal of Personality,* 1966, 34, 224–240.

Long, B. H., & Henderson, E. H. Self-social concepts of disadvantaged school beginners. *Journal of Genetic Psychology,* 1968, 113, 41–51.

Long, B. H., & Henderson, E. H. Social schemata of school beginners: Some demographic correlates. *Merrill-Palmer Quarterly,* 1970, 16, 305–324.

Long, B. H., & Henderson, E. H. Measuring esteem across cultures. *Proceedings of the 79th Annual Convention of the American Psychological Association,* 1971, 6, 255–256.

Long, B. H.; Henderson, E. H.; & Ziller, R. C. Developmental changes in the self-concept during middle childhood. *Merrill-Palmer Quarterly,* 1967, 13, 201–215. (a)

Long, B. H.; Henderson, E. H.; & Ziller, R. C. Self-social correlates of originality in children. *Journal of Genetic Psychology,* 1967, 111, 47–57. (b)

Long, B. H.; Henderson, E. H.; & Ziller, R. C. *Manual for the Self-Social Symbols Tasks and the Children's Self-Social Constructs Tests.* Mimeographed. Baltimore, Md.; Goucher College, 1970.

Long, B. H.; Ziller, R. C.; & Bankes, J. Self-other orientations of institutionalized behavior-problem adolescents. *Proceedings of the 76th Annual Convention of the American Psychological Association,* 1968, 3, 483–484.

Long, B. H.; Ziller, R. C.; & Bankes, J. Self-other orientations of institutionalized behavior-problem adolescents. *Journal of Counseling and Clinical Psychology,* 1970, 34, 43–47.

Long, B. H.; Ziller, R. C.; & Henderson, E. H. Developmental changes in the self-concept during adolescence. *School Review,* 1968, 76, 210–230.

Lorr, M., & Rubenstein, E. A. Personality patterns of neurotic adults in psychotherapy. *Journal of Consulting Psychology,* 1956, 20, 257–263.

Lövaas, O. I. Social desirability ratings of personality variables by Norwegian and American college students. *Journal of Abnormal and Social Psychology,* 1958, 57, 124–125.

Lubin, B., & Harrison, R. L. Predicting small group behavior with the self-disclosure inventory. *Psychological Reports,* 1964, 15, 77–78.

Luckey, E. B. Implications for marriage counseling of self perceptions and spouse perceptions. *Journal of Counseling Psychology,* 1960, 1, 3–9. (a)

Luckey, E. B. Marital satisfaction and parent concepts. *Journal of Consulting Psychology,* 1960, 24, 195–204. (b)

Luckey, E. B. Number of years married as related to personality perception and marital satisfaction. *Journal of Marriage and the Family,* 1966, 28, 44–48.

Ludwig, D. J. Self perception and the Draw-a-Person Test. *Journal of Projective Techniques and Personality Assessment,* 1969, 33, 257–261.

Lumsden, J. The construction of unidimensional tests. *Psychological Bulletin,* 1961, 58, 122–131.

Lynd, H. M. *On shame and the sense of identity.* New York: Harcourt Brace, 1958.

Mabel, S., & Rosenfeld, H. M. Relationship of self-concept to the experience of imbalance in p-o-x situations. *Human Relations,* 1966, 19, 381–389.

Machover, K. *Personality projection in the drawing of the human figure: A method of personality investigation.* Springfield, Ill.: Charles C. Thomas, 1949.

MacKinnon, D. W. Creativity and images of the self. In R. W. White (Ed.), *The study of lives.* New York: Atherton Press, 1963. Pp. 251–278.

Maddox, G. L.; Back, K. W.; & Liederman, V. R. Overweight as social deviance and disability. *Journal of Health and Social Behavior,* 1968, 9, 287–298.

Mahone, C. H. Fear of failure and unrealistic vocational aspiration. *Journal of Abnormal and Social Psychology,* 1960, 60, 253–261.

Malev, J. S. Body image, body symptoms, and body reactivity in children. *Journal of Psychosomatic Research,* 1967, 10, 281–289.

Maloney, M. P., & Payne, L. E. Validity of the Draw-A-Person Test as a measure of body image. *Perceptual and Motor Skills,* 1969, 29, 119–122.

Manasse, G. Self-regard as a function of environmental demands in chronic schizophrenics. *Journal of Abnormal Psychology,* 1965, 70, 210–213.

Mann, J. H., & Mann, C. H. Insight as a measure of adjustment in three kinds of group experience. *Journal of Consulting Psychology,* 1959, 23, 91.

Mann, P. H. Modifying the behavior of Negro educable mentally retarded boys through group counseling procedures. *Journal of Negro Education,* 1969, 38, 135–142.

Mann, P. H.; Beaber, J. D.; & Jacobson, M. D. The effect of group counseling on educable mentally retarded boys' self concepts. *Exceptional Children,* 1969, 35, 359–366.

Marais, H. C., & Struempfer, D. J. DAP body-image disturbance scale and quality of drawing. *Perceptual and Motor Skills,* 1965, 21, 196.

Markwell, E. D. Alterations in self-concept under hypnosis. *Journal of Personality and Social Psychology,* 1965, 1, 154–161.

Martin, D. G. Consistency of self-descriptions under different role sets in neurotic and normal adolescents and adults. *Journal of Abnormal Psychology,* 1969, 74, 173–176.

Martire, J. G., & Hornberger, R. H. Self congruence, by sex and between the sexes in a "normal" population. *Journal of Clinical Psychology,* 1957, 13, 288–291.

Maslow, A. H. *Motivation and personality.* New York: Harper, 1954.

Mason, E. P. Some factors in self judgments. *Journal of Clinical Psychology,* 1954, 10, 336–340. (a)

Mason, E. P. Some correlates of self-judgment of the aged. *Journal of Gerontology,* 1954, 9, 324–337. (b)

Mason, E. P.; Adams, H. L.; & Blood, D. F. Personality characteristics of gifted college freshmen. *Psychology in the Schools,* 1966, 3, 360–365.

Mason, E. P.; Adams, H. L.; & Blood, D. F. Further study of personality characteristics of bright college freshmen. *Psychological Reports,* 1968, 23, 395–400.

Mason, E. P., & Blood, D. F. Cross-validation study of personality characteristics of gifted college freshmen. *Proceedings of the 74th Annual Convention of the American Psychological Association,* 1966, 1, 283–284.

May, R. I. The origins and significance of the existential movement in psychology. II. Contributions of existential psychotherapy. In R. May; E. Angel; & H. F. Ellenberger, *Existence: A new dimension in psychiatry and psychology.* New York: Basic Books, 1958. Pp. 3–91.

May, R. (Ed.) *Existential psychology* (2nd ed.) New York: Random House, 1969.

Mayer, C. L. The relationship of early special class placement and the self-concepts of mentally handicapped children. *Exceptional Children,* 1966, 33, 77–81.

Mayer, C. L. Relationships of self-concepts and social variables in retarded children. *American Journal of Mental Deficiency,* 1967, 72, 267–271.

Mayo, G. D., & Manning, W. H. Motivation measurement. *Educational and Psychological Measurement,* 1961, 21, 73–83.

McAffee, R. O., & Cleland, C. C. The discrepancy between self-concept and ideal-self as a measure of psychological adjustment in educable mentally retarded males. *American Journal of Mental Deficiency,* 1965, 70, 63–68.

McCallon, E. L. Teacher characteristics and their relationship to change in the congruency of children's perception of self and ideal-self. *Journal of Experimental Education,* 1966, 34, 84–88. (a)

McCallon, E. L. Interpersonal perception characteristics of teachers. *Journal of Experimental Education,* 1966, 34, 97–100. (b)

McCarthy, B. W., & Brodsky, S. L. The effects of Marlowe-Crowne and instructional social desirability sets on the Self-Concept Scale. *Journal of Psychology,* 1970, 74, 237–238.

McClelland, D. C. *Personality.* New York: William Sloane, 1951.

McConnell, G. Questions about you. *Education,* 1959, 80, 1–3.

McConnell, O. L., & Daston, P. G. Body image changes in pregnancy. *Journal of Projective Techniques,* 1961, 25, 451–456.

McDavid, J. W., & Sistrunk, F. Personality correlates of two kinds of conforming behavior. *Journal of Personality,* 1964, 32, 420–435.

McDonald, R. L. Personality characteristics of freshman medical students as depicted by the Leary system. *Journal of Genetic Psychology,* 1962, 100, 313–323. (a)

McDonald, R. L. Intrafamilial conflict and emotional disturbance. *Journal of Genetic Psychology,* 1962, 101, 201–208. (b)

McDonald, R. L. Nonintellectual factors associated with performance in medical school. *Journal of Genetic Psychology,* 1963, 103, 185–194.

McDonald, R. L. Ego-control patterns and attribution of hostility to self and others. *Journal of Personality and Social Psychology,* 1965, 2, 273–277.

McDonald, R. L. Effects of sex, race, and class on self, ideal-self, and parental ratings in southern adolescents. *Perceptual and Motor Skills,* 1968, 27, 15–25.

McDonald, R. L., & Gynther, M. D. Relationship of self and ideal-self descriptions with sex, race, and class in Southern adolescents. *Journal of Personality and Social Psychology,* 1965, 1, 85–88. (a)

McDonald, R. L., & Gynther, M. D. Relations between self and parental perceptions of unwed mothers and obstetric complications. *Psychosomatic Medicine*, 1965, 27, 31–38. (b)

McGee, R. K. Response set in relation to personality: An orientation. In I. A. Berg (Ed.), *Response set in personality assessment*. New York: Aldine, 1967. Pp. 1–31.

McGlothlin, W.; Cohen, S.; & McGlothlin, M. S. Long lasting effects of LSD on normals. *Archives of General Psychiatry*, 1967, 17, 521–532.

McGuire, W. J. Suspiciousness of experimenter's intent. In R. Rosenthal & R. L. Rosnow (Eds.), *Artifact in behavioral research*. New York: Academic Press, 1969. Pp. 13–57.

McHugh, A. F. Age associations in children's figure drawings. *Journal of Clinical Psychology*, 1965, 21, 429–431.

McKegney, F. P. Psychological correlates of behavior in seriously delinquent juveniles. *British Journal of Psychiatry*, 1967, 113, 781–792.

McKenna, H. V.; Hofstaetter, P. R.; & O'Connor, J. P. The concepts of the ideal self and of the friend. *Journal of Personality*, 1956, 24, 262–271.

McLaughlin, B. The WAI dictionary and self-perceived identity in college students. In P. J. Stone; D. C. Dunphy; M. S. Smith; & D. M. Ogilvie (Eds.), *The general inquirer: A computer approach to content analysis*. Cambridge, Mass.: M.I.T. Press, 1966. Pp. 548–566.

McPartland, T. S., & Cumming, J. H. Self-conception, social class, and mental health. *Human Organization*, 1958, 17, 24–29.

McPartland, T. S.; Cumming, J. H.; & Garretson, W. S. Self-conception and ward behavior in two psychiatric hospitals. *Sociometry*, 1961, 24, 111–124.

Mead, G. H. *Mind, self, and society: From the standpoint of a social behaviorist*. Chicago: University of Chicago Press, 1934.

Medinnus, G. R., & Curtis, F. J. The relation between maternal self-acceptance and child acceptance. *Journal of Consulting Psychology*, 1963, 27, 542–544.

Mednick, S. A. The body's barriers go Rorschach. *Contemporary Psychology*, 1959, 4, 276–277.

Mednick, S. A. Body image, personality, and chi square. *Contemporary Psychology*, 1960, 5, 316–317.

Meers, M., & Neuringer, C. A validation of self-concept measures of the Leary Interpersonal Checklist. *Journal of General Psychology*, 1967, 77, 237–242.

Mees, H. L.; Gocka, E. F.; & Holloway, H. Social desirability values for California Psychological Inventory items. *Psychological Reports, Monograph Supplement*, 1964, 15, 147–158.

Megargee, E. I. Relation between barrier scores and aggressive behavior. *Journal of Abnormal Psychology*, 1965, 70, 307–311.

Megargee, E. I. The relation of response length to the Holtzman Inkblot Technique. *Journal of Consulting Psychology*, 1966, 30, 415–419.

Megargee, E. I., & Parker, G. V. An exploration of the equivalence of Murrayan needs as assessed by the Adjective Check List and Edwards Personal Preference Schedule. *Journal of Clinical Psychology*, 1968, 24, 47–51.

Meissner, A. L.; Thoreson, R. W.; & Butler, A. J. Relation of self-concept to impact and obviousness of disability among male and female adolescents. *Perceptual and Motor Skills*, 1967, 24, 1,099–1,105.

Merenda, P. F., & Clarke, W. V. Factor analysis of a measure of "social self." *Psychological Reports*, 1959, 5, 597–605.

Merenda, P. F., & Clarke, W. V. Relationships among AVA and ACL scales as measured on a sample of college students. *Journal of Clinical Psychology*, 1968, 24, 52–60.

Messick, S. Dimensions of social desirability. *Journal of Consulting Psychology*, 1960, 24, 279–287.

Messick, S. J. The psychology of acquiescense: An interpretation of research evidence. In I. A. Berg (Ed.), *Response set in personality assessment*. Chicago: Aldine, 1967. Pp. 115–145.

Messick, S., & Jackson, D. N. Desirability scale values and dispersions for MMPI items. *Psychological Reports*, 1961, 8, 409–414.

Meyerowitz, J. H. Self-derogations in young retardates and special class placement. *Child Development*, 1962, 33, 443–451.

Mikesell, R. H.; Calhoun, L. G.; & Lottman, T. J. Instructional set and the Coopersmith Self-Esteem Inventory. *Psychological Reports*, 1970, 26, 317–318.

Milgram, N. A., & Helper, M. M. The social desirability set in individual and grouped self-ratings. *Journal of Consulting Psychology*, 1961, 25, 91.

Milgram, S. Issues in the study of obedience: A reply to Baumrind. *American Psychologist*, 1964, 19, 848–852.

Miller, A. G. Role playing: An alternative to deception? *American Psychologist*, 1972, 27, 623–636.

Miller, K. S., & Worchel, P. The effects of need-achievement and self-ideal discrepancy on performance under stress. *Journal of Personality*, 1956, 25, 176–190.

Milton, G. A., & Lipetz, M. E. The factor structure of needs as measured by the EPPS. *Multivariate Behavior Research*, 1968, 3, 37–46.

Mischel, W. *Personality and assessment*. New York: Wiley, 1968.

Mitchell, J. V., Jr. An analysis of the factorial dimensions of the Bills' Index of Adjustment and Values. *Journal of Social Psychology*, 1962, 58, 331–337.

Mitchell, J. V., Jr. A comparison of the first and second order dimensions of the 16 PF and CPI Inventories. *Journal of Social Psychology,* 1963, 61, 151–166. (a)

Mitchell, J. V., Jr. Self-family perceptions related to self-acceptance, manifest anxiety, and neuroticism. *Journal of Educational Research,* 1963, 56, 236–240. (b)

Mitchell, J. V., Jr., & Pierce-Jones, J. A factor analysis of Gough's California Psychological Inventory. *Journal of Consulting Psychology,* 1960, 24, 453–456.

Mitchell, K. R. The body image boundary construct: A study of the self-steering behaviour syndrome. *Journal of Projective Techniques and Personality Assessment,* 1969, 33, 311–317.

Mitchell, K. R. The body image Barrier variable and level of adjustment to stress induced by severe physical disability. *Journal of Clinical Psychology,* 1970, 26, 49–52.

Miyamoto, S. F., & Dornbusch, S. M. A test of interactionist hypotheses of self-conception. *American Journal of Sociology,* 1956, 61, 399–403.

Moeller, G., & Applezweig, M. H. A motivational factor in conformity. *Journal of Abnormal and Social Psychology,* 1957, 55, 114–120. (a)

Moeller, G., & Applezweig, M. H. Manual for the Behavior Interpretation Inventory Form 59R. *Technical Report* No. 2, Project NR 172-228. New London: Connecticut College, 1957. (b)

Mohanty, G. S. Dimension of social desirability in Q-sort measure of self-ideal congruence in university students of Patna. *Journal of Psychological Researches,* 1965, 9, 136–140.

Morison, R. S. "Gradualness, gradualness, gradualness." *American Psychologist,* 1960, 15, 187–197.

Morrison, R. L. Self-concept implementation in occupational choices. *Journal of Counseling Psychology,* 1962, 9, 255–260.

Morse, R. N., & Piers, E. V. Variables affecting self-concept in black, disadvantaged boys. Mimeographed. University Park: Pennsylvania State University, n.d.

Morse, W. C. Self-concept in the school setting. *Childhood Education,* 1964, 41, 195–198.

Mosher, D. L.; Oliver, W. A.; & Dolgan, J. Body image in tatooed prisoners. *Journal of Clinical Psychology,* 1967, 23, 31–32.

Moss, C. S., & Waters, T. J. Intensive longitudinal investigation of anxiety in hospitalized juvenile patients. *Psychological Reports,* 1960, 7, 379–380.

Mossman, B. M., & Ziller, R. C. Self-esteem and consistency of social behavior. *Journal of Abnormal Psychology,* 1968, 73, 363–367.

Mowrer, O. H. (Ed.) *Psychotherapy; Theory and research.* New York: Ronald Press, 1953. (a)

Mowrer, O. H. "Q Technique": description, history and critique. In O. H. Mowrer (Ed.), *Psychotherapy: Theory and research*. New York: Ronald Press, 1953. Pp. 316–375. (b)

Mueller, W. J. The influence of self insight on social perception scores. *Journal of Counseling Psychology*, 1963, 10, 185–191.

Mulford, H. A., & Salisbury, W. W., II. Self-conceptions in a general population. *Sociological Quarterly*, 1964, 5, 35–46.

Murstein, B. I. The projection of hostility on the Rorschach and as a result of ego-threat. *Journal of Projective Techniques*, 1956, 20, 418–428.

Murstein, B. I. Effect of stimulus, background, personality, and scoring system on the manifestation of hostility on the TAT. *Journal of Consulting and Clinical Psychology*, 1968, 32, 355–365.

Murstein, B. I., & Glaudin, V. The relationship of marital adjustment to personality: A factor analysis of the Interpersonal Check List. *Journal of Marriage and the Family*, 1966, 28, 37–43.

Musella, D. Perceptual-cognitive style as related to self-evaluation and supervisor rating by student teachers. *Journal of Experimental Education*, 1969, 37, 51–55.

Mussen, P. H., & Jones, M. C. Self-conceptions, motivations, and interpersonal attitudes of late- and early-maturing boys. *Child Development*, 1957, 28, 243–256.

Mussen, P. H., & Porter, L. W. Personal motivations and self-conceptions associated with effectiveness and ineffectiveness in emergent groups. *Journal of Abnormal and Social Psychology*, 1959, 59, 23–27.

Nahinsky, I. D. The relationship between the self concept and the ideal-self concept as a measure of adjustment. *Journal of Clinical Psychology*, 1958, 14, 360–364.

Nakamura, C. Y. Salience of norms and order of questionnaire items: Their effect on responses to the items. *Journal of Abnormal and Social Psychology*, 1959, 59, 139–142.

Neale, D. C., & Proshek, J. M. School-related attitudes of culturally disadvantaged elementary school children. *Journal of Educational Psychology*, 1967, 58, 238–244.

Nebergall, N. S.; Angelino, H.; & Young, H. H. A validation study of the Self-Activity Inventory as a predictor of adjustment. *Journal of Consulting Psychology*, 1959, 23, 21–24.

Neff, W. S., & Cohen, J. A method for the analysis of the structure and internal consistency of Q-sort arrays. *Psychological Bulletin*, 1967, 68, 361–368.

Nefzger, M. D., & Drasgow, J. The needless assumption of normality in Pearson's r. *American Psychologist*, 1957, 12, 623–625.

Neisser, U. *Cognitive psychology.* New York: Appleton-Century-Crofts, 1967.

Neuringer, C., & Wandke, L. W. Interpersonal conflicts in persons of high self-concept and low self-concept. *Journal of Social Psychology,* 1966, 68, 313–322.

Nichols, D. C., & Tursky, B. Body image, anxiety, and tolerance for experimental pain. *Psychosomatic Medicine,* 1967, 29, 103–110.

Nichols, K. A., & Berg, I. School phobia and self-evaluation. *Journal of Child Psychology and Psychiatry and Allied Disciplines,* 1970, 11, 133–141.

Nichols, R. C., & Schnell, R. R. Factor scales for the California Psychological Inventory. *Journal of Consulting Psychology,* 1963, 27, 228–235.

Nidorf, L. J. Variables influencing the cognitive organization of the self. *Journal of Projective Techniques and Personality Assessment,* 1966, 30, 460–466.

Nocks, J. J., & Bradley, D. L. Self-esteem in an alcoholic population. *Diseases of the Nervous System,* 1969, 30, 611–617.

Norfleet, M. W. Personality characteristics of achieving and under-achieving high ability senior women. *Personnel and Guidance Journal,* 1968, 46, 976–980.

Norman, R. D. The interrelationships among acceptance-rejection, self-other identity, insight into self, and realistic perception of others. *Journal of Social Psychology,* 1953, 37, 205–235.

Norman, W. T. On estimating psychological relationships: Social desirability and self-report. *Psychological Bulletin,* 1967, 67, 273–293.

Norman, W. T. "To see oursels as ithers see us!": Relations among self-perceptions, peer-perceptions, and expected peer-perceptions of personality attributes. *Multivariate Behavioral Research,* 1969, 4, 417–443.

Norman, W. T., & Goldberg, L. R. Raters, ratees, and randomness in personality structure. *Journal of Personality and Social Psychology,* 1966, 4, 681–691.

Nunnally, J. C. An investigation of some propositions of self-conception: The case of Miss Sun. *Journal of Abnormal and Social Psychology,* 1955, 50, 87–92.

O'Connor, E. F., Jr. Extending classical test theory to the measurement of change. *Review of Educational Research,* 1972, 42, 73–97. (a)

O'Connor, E. F., Jr. Response to Cronbach and Furby's "How we should measure 'change'—or should we?" *Psychological Bulletin,* 1972, 78, 159–160. (b)

Ogston, D.; Altman, H. A.; & Lane, A. M. Meaning: A study of personality. *Western Psychologist,* 1970, 1, 106–110.

Ohnmacht, F. W., & Muro, J. J. Self-acceptance: Some anxiety and cognitive style relationships. *Journal of Psychology,* 1967, 67, 235–239.

O'Leary, V. E., & Hood, W. R. Latitudes of acceptance, rejection, and noncommitment, and attitudes towards self: A factor analytic study. *Journal of Social Psychology*, 1969, 79, 283–284.

Omwake, K. The relation between acceptance of self and acceptance of others shown by three personality inventories. *Journal of Consulting Psychology*, 1954, 18, 443–446.

Orne, M. T. On the social psychology of the psychological experiment: With particular reference to demand characteristics and their implications. *American Psychologist*, 1962, 17, 776–783.

Orne, M. T. Demand characteristics and the concept of quasi-controls. In R. Rosenthal & R. L. Rosnow (Eds.), *Artifact in behavioral research*. New York: Academic Press, 1969. Pp. 143–179.

Osgood, C. E. On the whys and wherefores of E, P, and A. *Journal of Personality and Social Psychology*, 1969, 12, 194–199.

Osgood, C. E.; Suci, G. J.; & Tannenbaum, P. H. *The measurement of meaning*. Urbana: University of Illinois Press, 1957.

Oskamp, S. Relationship of self-concepts to international attitudes. *Journal of Social Psychology*, 1968, 76, 31–36.

Osofsky, H. J., & Fisher, S. Psychological correlates of the development of amenorrhea in a stress situation. *Psychosomatic Medicine*, 1967, 29, 15–23.

Palermo, D. S., & Martire, J. G. The influence of order of administration on self-concept measures. *Journal of Consulting Psychology*, 1960, 24, 372.

Pallone, N. J., & Hosinski, M. Reality-testing a vocational choice: Congruence between self-ideal and occupational percepts among student nurses. *Personnel and Guidance Journal*, 1967, 45, 666–670.

Pallone, N. J.; Rickard, F. S.; Hurley, R. B.; & Tirman, R. J. Work values and self-meaning. *Journal of Counseling Psychology*, 1970, 17, 376–377.

Pannes, E. D. The relationship between self-acceptance and dogmatism in junior-senior high school students. *Journal of Educational Sociology*, 1963, 36, 419–426.

Parker, G. V. C., & Megargee, E. I. Factor analytic studies of the Adjective Check List. *Proceedings of the 75th Annual Convention of the American Psychological Association*, 1967, 2, 211–212.

Parker, G. V. C., & Veldman, D. J. Item factor structure of the Adjective Check List. *Educational and Psychological Measurement*, 1969, 29, 605–613.

Parker, J. The relationship of self report to inferred self concept. *Educational and Psychological Measurement*, 1966, 26, 691–700.

Parloff, M. B. Therapist-patient relationships and outcome of psychotherapy. *Journal of Consulting Psychology*, 1961, 25, 29–38.

Parsons, O. A.; Fulgenzi, L. B.; & Edelberg, R. Aggressiveness and psycho-physiological responsivity in groups of repressors and sensitizers. *Journal of Personality and Social Psychology*, 1969, 12, 235–244.

Passini, F. T., & Norman, W. T. A universal conception of personality structure? *Journal of Personality and Social Psychology*, 1966, 4, 44–49.

Payne, D. A., & Farquhar, W. W. The dimensions of an objective measure of academic self-concept. *Journal of Educational Psychology*, 1962, 53, 187–192.

Pearl, D. Ethnocentrism and the self concept. *Journal of Social Psychology*, 1954, 40, 137–147.

Pedersen, D. M. Evaluation of self and others and some personality correlates. *Journal of Psychology*, 1969, 71, 225–244.

Pedersen, D. M., & Breglio, V. J. The correlation of two self-disclosure inventories with actual self-disclosure: A validity study. *Journal of Psychology*, 1968, 68, 291–298.

Pedersen, D. M., & Higbee, K. L. An evaluation of the equivalence and construct validity of various measures of self-disclosure. *Educational and Psychological Measurement*, 1968, 28, 511–523.

Perkins, C. W., & Shannon, D. T. Three techniques for obtaining self-perceptions in preadolescent boys. *Journal of Personality and Social Psychology*, 1965, 2, 443–447.

Perkins, H. V. Teachers' and peers' perceptions of children's self-concepts. *Child Development*, 1958, 29, 203–220. (a)

Perkins, H. V. Factors influencing change in children's self-concepts. *Child Development*, 1958, 29, 221–230. (b)

Pervin, L. A., & Lilly, R. S. Social desirability and self–ideal self ratings on the semantic differential. *Educational and Psychological Measurement*, 1967, 27, 845–853.

Peters, D. R. Self-ideal congruence as a function of human relations training. *Journal of Psychology*, 1970, 76, 199–207.

Peterson, D. R. Scope and generality of verbally defined personality factors. *Psychological Review*, 1965, 72, 48–59.

Phillips, B. N. Age changes in accuracy of self-perceptions. *Child Development*, 1963, 34, 1,041–1,046.

Phillips, E. L. Attitudes toward self and others: A brief questionnaire report. *Journal of Consulting Psychology*, 1951, 15, 79–81.

Phillips, E. L.; Raiford, A.; & El-Batrawi, S. The Q-sort reevaluated. *Journal of Consulting Psychology*, 1965, 29, 422–425.

Pierce-Jones, J.; Mitchell, J. V., Jr.; & King, F. J. Configurational invariance in the California Psychological Inventory. *Journal of Experimental Education*, 1962, 31, 65–71.

Piers, E. V. *Manual for the Piers-Harris Children's Self-Concept Scale (The Way I Feel About Myself)*. Nashville, Tenn.: Counselor Recordings and Tests, 1969.

Piers, E. V. Parent prediction of children's self-concepts. *Journal of Consulting and Clinical Psychology*, 1972, 38, 428–433.

Piers, E. V., & Harris, D. B. Age and other correlates of self-concept in children. *Journal of Educational Psychology*, 1964, 55, 91–95.

Pishkin, V., & Thorne, F. C. A factorial study of ideological composition in institutionalized psychiatric patients. *Journal of Clinical Psychology*, 1968, 25, 273–277.

Platt, J. J., Eisenman, R., & Darbes, A. Self-esteem and internal-external control: A validation study. *Psychological Reports*, 1970, 26, 162.

Platt, J. J., & Taylor, R. E. Homesickness, future time perspective, and the self-concept. *Proceedings of the 74th Annual Convention of the American Psychological Association*, 1966, 2, 295–296.

Powell, M. G. Comparisons of self-ratings, peer-ratings, and expert's ratings of personality adjustment. *Educational and Psychological Measurement*, 1948, 8, 225–234.

Preiss, J. J. Self and role in medical education. In C. Gordon & K. J. Gergen (Eds.), *The self in social interaction*. New York: Wiley, 1968. Pp. 207–218.

Preston, C. E., & Gudiksen, K. S. A measure of self perception among older people. *Journal of Gerontology*, 1966, 21, 63–71.

Progoff, I. *Jung's psychology and its social meaning*. New York: Julian Press, 1953.

Purkey, W. W. Measured and professed personality characteristics of gifted high school students and an analysis of their congruence. *Journal of Educational Research*, 1966, 60, 99–104.

Purkey, W. W.; Graves, W.; & Zellner, M. Self-perceptions of pupils in an experimental elementary school. *Elementary School Journal*, 1970, 71, 166–171.

Pyron, B., & Kafer, J., Jr. Recall of nonsense sentences and self-reliance. *Psychological Reports*, 1967, 20, 331–334.

Quarter, J.; Kennedy, D. R.; & Laxer, R. M. Effect of order and form in the Q-sort. *Psychological Reports*, 1967, 20, 893–894.

Quimby, V. Differences in the self-ideal relationship of an achiever group and an underachiever group. *California Journal of Educational Research*, 1967, 18, 23–31.

Rabinowitz, M. The relationship of self regard to the effectiveness of life experiences. *Journal of Counseling Psychology*, 1966, 13, 139–143.

Ramer, J. The Rorschach barrier score and social behavior. *Journal of Consulting Psychology*, 1963, 27, 525–531.

Rawlinson, M. E. Projection in relation to interpersonal perception. *Nursing Research*, 1965, 14, 114–118.

Reece, M. M. Masculinity and femininity: A factor analytic study. *Psychological Reports*, 1964, 14, 123–139.

Reed, C. F., & Cuadra, C. A. The role-taking hypothesis in delinquency. *Journal of Consulting Psychology*, 1957, 21, 386–390.

Reed, H. J. An investigation of the relationship between teaching effectiveness and the teacher's attitude of acceptance. *Journal of Experimental Education*, 1953, 21, 277–325.

Reeder, L. G.; Donohue, G. A.; & Biblarz, A. Conceptions of self and others. *American Journal of Sociology*, 1960, 66, 153–159.

Reese, H. W. Relationships between self-acceptance and sociometric choices. *Journal of Abnormal and Social Psychology*, 1961, 62, 472–474.

Rehm, L. P., & Marston, A. R. Reduction of social anxiety through modification of self-reinforcement: An instigation therapy technique. *Journal of Consulting and Clinical Psychology*, 1968, 32, 565–574.

Reilly, D. H., & Sugerman, A. A. Conceptual complexity and psychological differentiation in alcoholics. *Journal of Nervous and Mental Disease*, 1967, 144, 14–17.

Reitman, E. E., & Cleveland, S. E. Changes in body image following sensory deprivation in schizophrenic and control groups. *Journal of Abnormal and Social Psychology*, 1964, 68, 168–176.

Reitz, W. E., & Thetford, P. E. Skin potential correlates and rating assessments of self-evaluation under different degrees of awareness. *Perceptual and Motor Skills*, 1967, 24, 631–638.

Renik, O. D., & Fisher, S. Induction of body image boundary changes in male subjects. *Journal of Projective Techniques and Personality Assessment*, 1968, 32, 45–48.

Rentz, R. R., & White, W. F. Factors of self perception in the Tennessee Self Concept Scale. *Perceptual and Motor Skills*, 1967, 24, 118. (a)

Rentz, R. R., & White, W. F. Congruence of the dimensions of self-as-object and self-as-process. *Journal of Psychology*, 1967, 67, 277–285. (b)

Renzaglia, G. A.; Henry, D. R.; & Rybolt, G. A., Jr. Estimation and measurement of personality characteristics and correlates of their congruence. *Journal of Counseling Psychology*, 1962, 9, 71–78.

Resnick, H.; Fauble, M. L.; & Osipow, S. H. Vocational crystallization and self-esteem in college students. *Journal of Counseling Psychology*, 1970, 17, 465–467.

Richards, J. M., Jr. A factor analytic study of the self-ratings of college freshmen. *Educational and Psychological Measurement*, 1966, 26, 861–870.

Riecken, H. W. A program for research on experiments in social psychology. In N. F. Washburne (Ed.), *Decisions, values, and groups.* Vol. 2. New York: Pergamon, 1962. Pp. 25–41.

Ring, K. Experimental social psychology: Some sober questions about some frivolous values. *Journal of Experimental Social Psychology,* 1967, 3, 113–123.

Ringness, T. A. Self concept of children of low, average, and high intelligence. *American Journal of Mental Deficiency,* 1961, 65, 453–461.

Rivlin, L. G. Creativity and the self-attitudes and sociability of high school students. *Journal of Educational Psychology,* 1959, 50, 147–152.

Roback, H. B. Human figure drawings: Their utility in the clinical psychologist's armamentarium for personality assessment. *Psychological Bulletin,* 1968, 70, 1–19.

Roberts, G. E. A study of the validity of the Index of Adjustment and Values. *Journal of Consulting Psychology,* 1952, 16, 302–304.

Robinson, J. P., & Shaver, P. R. *Measures of social psychological attitudes.* Ann Arbor: University of Michigan, Institute for Social Research, 1969.

Rodgers, D. A. Personality of the route salesman in a basic food industry. *Journal of Applied Psychology,* 1959, 43, 235–239.

Rodgers, D. A. Personality correlates of successful role behavior. *Journal of Social Psychology,* 1957, 46, 111–117.

Rogers, A. H. The self concept in paranoid schizophrenia. *Journal of Clinical Psychology,* 1958, 14, 365–366.

Rogers, A. H., & Paul C. Impunitiveness and unwitting self-evaluation. *Journal of Projective Techniques,* 1959, 23, 459–461.

Rogers, A. H., & Walsh, T. M. Defensiveness and unwitting self-evaluation. *Journal of Clinical Psychology,* 1959, 15, 302–304.

Rogers, C. R. *Client-centered therapy.* Boston: Houghton Mifflin, 1951. (a)

Rogers, C. R. Perceptual reorganization in client-centered therapy. In R. R. Blake & G. V. Ramsey (Eds.), *Perception: An approach to personality.* New York: Ronald Press, 1951. Pp. 307–327. (b)

Rogers, C. R. The case of Mrs. Oak: A research analysis. In C. R. Rogers & R. F. Dymond (Eds.), *Psychotherapy and personality change.* Chicago: University of Chicago Press, 1954. Pp. 259–348. (a)

Rogers, C. R. The case of Mr. Bebb: The analysis of a failure case. In C. R. Rogers & R. F. Dymond (Eds.), *Psychotherapy and personality change.* Chicago: University of Chicago Press, 1954. Pp. 349–409. (b)

Rogers, C. R. A theory of therapy, personality, and interpersonal relationships, as developed in the client-centered framework. In S. Koch (Ed.), *Psychology: A study of a science.* Vol. 3. New York: McGraw-Hill, 1959. Pp. 184–256.

Rogers. C. R. (Ed.) *The therapeutic relationship and its impact: A study of psychotherapy and schizophrenics.* Madison: University of Wisconsin Press, 1967.

Rogers, C. R., & Dymond, R. F. (Eds.) *Psychotherapy and personality change.* Chicago: University of Chicago Press, 1954.

Rogers, C. R.; Kell, B. L.; & McNeil, H. The role of self-understanding in the prediction of behavior. *Journal of Consulting Psychology,* 1948, 12, 174–186.

Rogers, J. M. Operant conditioning in a quasi-therapy setting. *Journal of Abnormal and Social Psychology,* 1960, 60, 247–252.

Rokeach, M. Studies in beauty: II. Some determiners of the perception of beauty in women. *Journal of Social Psychology,* 1945, 22, 155–169.

Rokeach, M., & Fruchter, B. A factorial study of dogmatism and related concepts. *Journal of Abnormal and Social Psychology,* 1956, 53, 356–360.

Rorer, L. G. The great response style myth. *Psychological Bulletin,* 1965, 63, 129–156.

Rosen, A. C. Some differences in self perceptions between alcoholics and non-alcoholics. *Perceptual and Motor Skills,* 1966, 23, 1,279–1,286.

Rosen, E. Self-appraisal and perceived desirability of MMPI personality traits. *Journal of Counseling Psychology,* 1956, 3, 44–51. (a)

Rosen, E. Self-appraisal, personal desirability and perceived social desirability of personality traits. *Journal of Abnormal and Social Psychology,* 1956, 52, 151–158. (b)

Rosen, E., & Mink, S. H. Desirability of personality traits as perceived by prisoners. *Journal of Clinical Psychology,* 1961, 17, 147–151.

Rosen, G. M., & Ross, A. O. Relationship of body image to self-concept. *Journal of Consulting and Clinical Psychology,* 1968, 32, 100.

Rosenberg, M. *Society and the adolescent self image.* Princeton, N.J.: Princeton University Press, 1965.

Rosenberg, M. J. The conditions and consequences of evaluation apprehension. In R. Rosenthal & R. L. Rosnow (Eds.), *Artifact in behavioral research.* New York: Academic Press, 1969. Pp. 279–349.

Rosenthal, R., & Rosnow, R. L. (Eds.) *Artifact in behavioral research.* New York: Academic Press, 1969.

Roth, R. M. The role of self-concept in achievement. *Journal of Experimental Education,* 1959, 27, 265–281.

Rothaus, P., & Worchel, P. The inhibition of aggression under nonarbitrary frustration. *Journal of Personality,* 1960, 28, 108–117.

Rothstein, R., & Epstein, S. Unconscious self-evaluation as a function of availability of cues. *Journal of Consulting Psychology,* 1963, 27, 480–485.

Rotter, J. B. Generalized expectancies for internal versus external control of reinforcement. *Psychological Monographs: General and Applied,* 1966, 80 (1, Whole No. 609).

Rubinstein, E. A., & Lorr, M. Self and peer personality ratings of psychotherapists. *Journal of Clinical Psychology,* 1957, 13, 295–298.

Rudikoff, E. C. A comparative study of the changes in the concept of the self, the ordinary person, and the ideal in eight cases. In C. R. Rogers & R. F. Dymond (Eds.), *Psychotherapy and personality change.* Chicago: University of Chicago Press, 1954. Pp. 85–98.

Russell, D. H. What does research say about self-evaluation? *Journal of Educational Research,* 1953, 46, 561–571.

Rychlak, J. F. Self-confidence, ability, and the interest-value of tasks. *Journal of Genetic Psychology,* 1959, 94, 153–159.

Salomon, G., & McDonald, F. J. Pretest and posttest reactions to self-viewing one's teaching performance on video tape. *Journal of Educational Psychology,* 1970, 61, 280–286.

Sappenfield, B. R. Perceived similarity to self as related to the stereotypically perceived "ideal personality." *Journal of Experimental Research in Personality,* 1970, 4, 297–302. (a)

Sappenfield, B. R. Perception of self as related to perception of the "ideal personality." *Perceptual and Motor Skills,* 1970, 31, 975–978. (b)

Sarason, I. G., & Winkel, G. H. Individual differences among subjects and experimenters and subjects' self-descriptions. *Journal of Personality and Social Psychology,* 1966, 3, 448–457.

Sarbin, T. R., & Farberow, N. L. Contributions to role-taking theory: A clinical study of self and role. *Journal of Abnormal and Social Psychology,* 1952, 47, 117–125.

Sarbin, T. R., & Rosenberg, B. G. Contributions to role-taking theory: IV. A method for obtaining a qualitative estimate of the self. *Journal of Social Psychology,* 1955, 42, 71–81.

Savage, C.; Fadiman, J.; Mogar, R.; & Allen, M. H. The effects of psychedelic (LSD) therapy on values, personality, and behavior. *International Journal of Neuropsychiatry,* 1966, 2, 241–254.

Schaefer, C. E. The self-concept of creative adolescents. *Journal of Psychology,* 1969, 72, 233–242.

Schalon, C. L. Effect of self-esteem upon performance following failure stress. *Journal of Consulting and Clinical Psychology,* 1968, 32, 497.

Schlicht, W. J. Discrepancies between self-images with and without awareness and their relationship to adjustment. *Journal of Clinical Psychology,* 1967, 23, 470–472.

Schlicht, W. J., Jr.; Carlson, H. J.; Skeen, D. R.; & Skurdal, M. A. Screening procedures: A comparison of self-report and projective measures. *Educational and Psychological Measurement,* 1968, 28, 525–528.

Schlicht, W. J., Jr.; Carlson, H. J.; Skeen, D. R.; & Skurdal, M. A. Self-images without awareness and projective methods of personality assessment. *Journal of Projective Techniques and Personality Assessment,* 1969, 33, 419–423.

Schludermann, S., & Schludermann, E. A methodological note on a "self-concept inventory." *Journal of Psychology,* 1969, 71, 259–260. (a)

Schludermann, S., & Schludermann, E. A note on the use of discrepancy scores in a self-concept inventory. *Journal of Psychology,* 1969, 72, 33–34. (b)

Schludermann, S., & Schludermann, E. Generalizability of California Personality Inventory factors. *Journal of Psychology,* 1970, 74, 43–50. (a)

Schludermann, S., & Schludermann, E. Personality correlates of adolescent self-concepts and security-insecurity. *Journal of Psychology,* 1970, 74, 85–90. (b)

Schmidt, L. D., & McGowan, J. F. The differentiation of human figure drawings. *Journal of Consulting Psychology,* 1959, 23, 129–133.

Schmitt, R. L. Major role change and self change. *Sociological Quarterly,* 1966, 7, 311–322.

Schneider, D. J. Tactical self-presentation after success and failure. *Journal of Personality and Social Psychology,* 1969, 13, 262–268.

Schneider, L., & Zurcher, L. Toward understanding the Catholic crisis: Observations on dissident priests in Texas. *Scientific Study of Religion,* 1970, 9, 197–207.

Schooler, C., & Tecce, J. J. Verbal paired-associates learning in chronic schizophrenics as a function of positive and negative evaluation. *Journal of Abnormal Psychology,* 1967, 72, 151–156.

Schuh, A. J. Use of the semantic differential in a test of Super's Vocational Adjustment Theory. *Journal of Applied Psychology,* 1966, 50, 516–522,

Schwab, J. J.; Clemmons, R. S.; & Marder, L. The self concept: Psychosomatic applications. *Psychosomatics,* 1966, 7, 1–5.

Schwartz, J. L., & Dubitsky, M. Changes in anxiety, mood, and self-esteem resulting from an attempt to stop smoking. *American Journal of Psychiatry,* 1968, 124, 1,580–1,584.

Schwirian, K. P. Variation in structure of the Kuhn-McPartland Twenty Statements Test and related response differences. *Sociological Quarterly,* 1964, 5, 47–59.

Sciortino, R. Factorial study of motivational self-ratings by male subjects. *Psychological Reports,* 1967, 21, 453–458. (a)

Sciortino, R. Factorial study of motivational self-ratings by female subjects. *Psychological Reports,* 1967, 21, 565–570. (b)

Sciortino, R. Factorial analysis of motivational self-ratings from a combined sample of male and female subjects. *Psychological Reports,* 1967, 21, 573–576. (c)

Sciortino, R. Analysis of factor variance of motivational self-ratings by male and female subjects. *Journal of Psychology,* 1968, 69, 169–174.

Sciortino, R. Factorial study and analysis of factor variance of intellective self-ratings from a combined sample of male and female subjects. *Journal of Psychology,* 1969, 71, 261–269. (a)

Sciortino, R. Factorial study of general adaptibility self-ratings by male and female subjects. *Journal of Psychology,* 1969, 71, 271–279. (b)

Scott, W. A. Social desirability and individual conceptions of the desirable. *Journal of Abnormal and Social Psychology,* 1963, 67, 574–585.

Scott, W. A. Comparative validities of forced-choice and single-stimulus tests. *Psychological Bulletin,* 1968, 70, 231–244.

Sears, R. R. Experimental studies in projection: I. Attribution of traits. *Journal of Social Psychology,* 1936, 7, 151–163.

Sears, R. R. Relation of early socialization experiences to self-concepts and gender role in middle childhood. *Child Development,* 1970, 41, 267–289.

Secord, P. F. Objectification of word-association procedures by the use of homonyms: A measure of body-cathexis. *Journal of Personality,* 1953, 21, 479–495.

Secord, P. F., & Jourard, S. M. The appraisal of body-cathexis: Body-cathexis and the self. *Journal of Consulting Psychology,* 1953, 17, 343–347.

Seegars, J. E., Jr., & McDonald, R. L. The role of interaction groups in counselor education. *Journal of Counseling Psychology,* 1963, 10, 156–162.

Shaw, M. C., & Alves, G. J. The self-concept of bright academic underachievers: Continued. *Personnel and Guidance,* 1963, 42, 401–403.

Shipman, W. G. Personality traits associated with body-image boundary concern. *Proceedings of the 73rd Annual Convention of the American Psychological Association,* 1965, 73, 271–272.

Shipman, W. G.; Oken, D.; Goldstein, I. B.; Grinker, R. R.; & Heath, H. A. Study in psychophysiology of muscle tension. II. Personality factors. *Archives of General Psychiatry,* 1964, 11, 330–345.

Shlien, J. M. Toward what level of abstraction in criteria? *University of Chicago Counseling Center Discussion Papers,* 1961, 6, No. 16.

Shlien, J. M.; Mosak, H. H.; & Dreikurs, R. Effect of time limits: A comparison of two psychotherapies. *Journal of Counseling Psychology,* 1962, 9, 31–34.

Shontz, F. C. *Perceptual and cognitive aspects of body experience.* New York: Academic Press, 1969.

Shontz, F. C. Body image: Data galore. *Contemporary Psychology,* 1971, 16, 362–364. (a)

Shontz, F. C. Reply to Fisher. *Contemporary Psychology,* 1971, 16, 745. (b)

Shure, G. H., & Rogers, M. S. Personality factor stability for three ability levels. *Journal of Psychology*, 1963, 55, 445–456.

Siegel, S. M., & Feldman, M. J. A note on the effect on self description of combining anxiety and hostility items on a single scale. *Journal of Clinical Psychology*, 1958, 14, 389–390.

Silber, E., & Tippett, J. S. Self-esteem: Clinical assessment and measurement validation. *Psychological Reports*, 1965, 16, 1,017–1,071.

Silverman, I.; Shulman, A. D.; & Wisenthal, D. L. Effects of deceiving and debriefing psychological subjects on performance in later experiments. *Journal of Personality and Social Psychology*, 1970, 14, 203–212.

Silverstein, A. B., & Robinson, H. A. The representation of orthopedic disability in children's figure drawings. *Journal of Consulting Psychology*, 1956, 20, 333–341.

Silverstein, A. B., & Robinson, H. A. The representation of physique in children's figure drawings. *Journal of Consulting Psychology*, 1961, 25, 146–148.

Simmons, D. D. Self-concept, occupational stereotype, and engineering career plans. *Psychological Reports*, 1967, 20, 514.

Simmons, R. K., & Lamberth, E. L. Q-sort technique as a means of determining the relation of family structure to self-concept. *Marriage and Family Living*, 1961, 23, 183–184.

Singer, S. Factors related to participants' memory of a conversation. *Journal of Personality*, 1969, 37, 93–110.

Smith, B. D., & Teevan, R. C. The relationship of the hostile press measure of fear of failure to self-ideal congruence and adjustment. Technical Report No. 11, 1964, Contract Nonr 3591 (01) NR 171-803, Office of Naval Research.

Smith, E. E. Defensiveness, insight, and the *K* scale. *Journal of Consulting Psychology*, 1959, 23, 275–277.

Smith, G. M. Six measures of self-concept discrepancy and instability: Their interrelations, reliability, and relations to other personality measures. *Journal of Consulting Psychology*, 1958, 22, 101–112.

Smith, K. H. Conformity as related to masculinity, self, and other descriptions, suspicion, and artistic preference by sex groups. *Journal of Social Psychology*, 1970, 80, 79–88.

Smith, M. B. The phenomenological approach in personality theory: Some critical remarks. *Journal of Abnormal and Social Psychology*, 1950, 45, 516–522.

Smith, P. A. A factor analytic study of the self-concept. *Journal of Consulting Psychology*, 1960, 24, 191.

Smith, P. A. A comparison of three sets of rotated factor analytic solutions of self-concept data. *Journal of Abnormal and Social Psychology*, 1962, 64, 326–333.

Smith, W. D., & Lebo, D. Some changing aspects of the self-concept of pubescent males. *Journal of Genetic Psychology,* 1956, 88, 61–75.

Snygg, D., & Combs, A. W. *Individual behavior: A new frame of reference for psychology.* New York: Harper, 1949.

Snygg, D., & Combs, A. W. The phenomenological approach and the problem of "unconscious" behavior: A reply to Dr. Smith. *Journal of Abnormal and Social Psychology,* 1950, 45, 523–528.

Soares, A. T., & Soares, L. M. Interpersonal and self perceptions of disadvantaged and advantaged high school students. *Proceedings of the 78th Annual Convention of the American Psychological Association,* 1970, 5, 457–458.

Solar, D.; Bruehl, D.; & Kovacs, J. The Draw-A-Person Test: Social conformity or artistic ability? *Journal of Clinical Psychology,* 1970, 26, 524–525.

Solley, C. M., & Stagner, R. Effects of magnitude of temporal barriers, type of goal, and perception of self. *Journal of Experimental Psychology,* 1956, 51, 62–70.

Spence, K. W. The nature of theory construction in contemporary psychology. *Psychological Review,* 1944, 51, 47–68.

Sperber, Z., & Spanner, M. Social desirability, psychopathology, and item endorsement. *Journal of General Psychology,* 1962, 67, 105–112.

Spilka, B. Social desirability: A problem of operational definition. *Psychological Reports,* 1961, 8, 149–150.

Spilka, B., & Lewis, M. Empathy, assimilative projection, and disowning projection. *Psychological Record,* 1959, 9, 99–102.

Spitzer, S. P.; Stratton, J. R.; Fitzgerald, J. D.; & Mach, B. K. The self concept: Test equivalence and perceived validity. *Sociological Quarterly,* 1966, 7, 265–280.

Springob, H. K., & Struening, E. L. A factor analysis of the California Psychological Inventory on a high school population. *Journal of Counseling Psychology,* 1964, 2, 173–179.

Stanley, J. C. Analysis of unreplicated three-way classifications, with applications to rate bias and trait independence. *Psychometrika,* 1961, 26, 205–219.

Stanley, J. C. Reliability. In R. L. Thorndike (Ed.), *Educational measurement.* (2nd ed.) Washington, D.C.: American Council on Education, 1971. Pp. 356–442.

Stephenson, W. Some observations on Q-technique. *Psychological Bulletin,* 1952, 49, 483–498.

Stephenson, W. *The study of behavior.* Chicago: University of Chicago Press, 1953.

Stevens, S. S. On the psychophysical law. *Psychological Review,* 1957, 64, 153–181.

Stevens, S. S., & Galanter, E. H. Ratio scales and category scales for a dozen perceptual continua. *Journal of Experimental Psychology*, 1957, 54, 377–411.

Stewart, L. H. Mother-son identification and vocational interest. *Genetic Psychology Monographs*, 1959, 60, 31–63.

Stewart, L. H. Relationship of two indices of interest stability to self-satisfaction and to mother-son identification. *California Journal of Educational Research*, 1962, 13, 51–56.

Stimpson, D. V., & Pedersen, D. M. Effects of a survival training experience upon evaluation of self and others for underachieving high school students. *Perceptual and Motor Skills*, 1970, 31, 337–338.

Stimson, R. C. Factor analytic approach to the structural differentiation of description. *Journal of Counseling Psychology*, 1968, 15, 301–307.

Stollak, G. E. EPPS performance under social desirability instructions: College females. *Psychological Reports*, 1965, 16, 119–122. (a)

Stollak, G. E. EPPS performance under social desirability instructions. *Journal of Personality and Social Psychology*, 1965, 2, 430–432. (b)

Stollak, G. E. Obedience and deception research. *American Psychologist*, 1967, 22, 678.

Stone, L. A., & Winkler, R. C. Utility for risk behavior as a function of selected self-acceptance and response-set measures. *Journal of General Psychology*, 1964, 71, 65–69.

Storm, T.; Rosenwald, G. C.; & Child, I. L. A factor analysis of self-ratings on social behavior. *Journal of Social Psychology*, 1958, 48, 45–49.

Stotland, E. Motivation for security, certainty, and self-esteem. *Journal of General Psychology*, 1961, 65, 75–87.

Stotland, E., & Cottrell, N. B. Self-esteem, group interaction, and group influence on performance. *Journal of Personality*, 1961, 29, 273–284.

Stotland, E., & Cottrell, N. B. Similarity of performance as influenced by interaction, self-esteem, and birth order. *Journal of Abnormal and Social Psychology*, 1962, 64, 183–191.

Stotland, E., & Dunn, R. E. Empathy, self-esteem, and birth order. *Journal of Abnormal and Social Psychology*, 1963, 66, 532–540.

Stotland, E.; Thorley, S.; Thomas, E.; Cohen, A. R.; & Zander, A. The effects of group expectations and self-esteem upon self-evaluation. *Journal of Abnormal and Social Psychology*, 1957, 54, 55–63.

Stouffer, S. A.; Borgatta, E. F.; Hays, D. G.; & Henry, A. F. A technique for improving cumulative scales. *Public Opinion Quarterly*, 1952, 16, 273–291.

Stricker, L. J. A review of the Edwards Personal Preference Schedule. In O. K. Buros (Ed.), *The sixth mental measurements yearbook*. Highland Park, N.J.: Gryphon Press, 1965. Pp. 200–207.

Stricker, L. J. The true deceiver. *Psychological Bulletin*, 1967, 68, 13–20.

Stricker, L. J.; Messick, S.; & Jackson, D. N. Suspicion of deception: Implications for conformity research. *Journal of Personality and Social Psychology*, 1967, 5, 379–389.

Stricker, L. J.; Messick, S.; & Jackson, D. N. Evaluating deception in psychological research. *Psychological Bulletin*, 1969, 71, 343–351.

Stricker, L. J. & Ross, J. An assessment of some structural properties of the Jungian personality typology. *Journal of Abnormal and Social Psychology*, 1964, 68, 62–71.

Strong, D. J. A factor analytic study of several measures of self concept. *Journal of Counseling Psychology*, 1962, 9, 64–70.

Suchman, E. A. The utility of scalogram analysis. In S. A. Stouffer; L. Guttman; E. A. Suchman; P. F. Lazarsfeld; S. A. Star; & J. A. Clausen, *Studies in social psychology in World War II*. Vol. 4. *Measurement and prediction*. Princeton, N.J.: Princeton University Press, 1950. Pp. 122–171.

Sugerman, A. A., & Cancro, R. Field dependence and sophistication of body concept in schizophrenics. *Journal of Nervous and Mental Disease*, 1964, 138, 119–123.

Sugerman, A. A., & Haronian, F. Body type and sophistication of body concept. *Journal of Personality*, 1964, 32, 380–394.

Suinn, R. M.; Osborne, D.; & Winfree, P. The self-concept and accuracy of recall of inconsistent self-related information. *Journal of Clinical Psychology*, 1962, 18, 473–474.

Sullivan, H. S. *The interpersonal theory of psychiatry*. New York: Norton, 1953.

Sumner, F. C. Marks as estimated by students. *Education*, 1932, 52, 429.

Sweetland, A., & Frank, G. A study of ideal psychological adjustment. *Journal of Clinical Psychology*, 1955, 11, 391–394.

Swensen, C. H., Jr. Empirical evaluations of human figure drawings. *Psychological Bulletin*, 1957, 54, 431–466.

Swensen, C. H., Jr. Empirical evaluation of human figure drawings. *Psychological Bulletin*, 1968, 70, 20–44.

Symonds, P. M. *The ego and the self*. New York: Appleton, 1951.

Talbot, E.; Miller, S. C.; & White, R. B. Some aspects of self-conceptions and role demands in a therapeutic community. *Journal of Abnormal and Social Psychology*, 1961, 63, 338–345.

Tarwater, J. W. Self-understanding and the ability to predict another's response. *Marriage and Family Living*, 1953, 15, 126–128.

Taylor, A. B. Role perception, empathy, and marriage adjustment. *Sociology and Social Research*, 1967, 52, 22–34.

Taylor, D. A. The development of interpersonal relationships: Social penetration processes. *Journal of Social Psychology*, 1968, 75, 79–90.

Taylor, D. A., & Altman, I. Intimacy-scaled stimuli for use in studies of interpersonal relations. *Psychological Reports,* 1966, 19, 729–730. (a)

Taylor, D. A., & Altman, I. Intimacy-scaled stimuli for use in studies of interpersonal relationships. Report No. 9, 1966, Research Report MF 022,01,03–1002, Naval Medical Research Institute, Bethesda, Maryland. (b)

Taylor, D. M. Changes in the self concept without psychotherapy. *Journal of Consulting Psychology,* 1955, 19, 205–209.

Taylor, J. B. Social desirability and MMPI performance: The individual case. *Journal of Consulting Psychology,* 1959, 23, 514–517.

Thayer, R. E. Personality and discrepancies between verbal reports and physiological measures of private emotional experiences. *Journal of Personality,* 1971, 39, 57–69.

Thomas, E. C., & Yamamoto, K. School-related perceptions in handicapped children. *Journal of Psychology,* 1971, 77, 101–117.

Thompson, W. R., & Nishimura, R. Some determinants of friendship. *Journal of Personality,* 1952, 20, 305–314.

Thorne, F. C., & Pishkin, V. A factorial study of ideological composition in vocationally successful adults. *Journal of Clinical Psychology,* 1968, 24, 269–273.

Tippett, J. S., & Silber, E. Self-image stability: The problem of validation. *Psychological Reports,* 1965, 17, 323–329.

Tolor, A. Self-perceptions of neuropsychiatric patients on the W-A-Y Test. *Journal of Clinical Psychology,* 1957, 13, 403–406.

Tolor, A., & Colbert, J. Relationship of body image to social desirability. *Journal of Mental Science,* 1961, 107, 1,060–1,061.

Torgerson, W. S. *Theory and methods of scaling.* New York: Wiley, 1958.

Torrance, E. P. Rationalization about test performance as a function of self-concepts. *Journal of Social Psychology,* 1954, 39, 211–217. (a)

Torrance, E. P. Some practical uses of a knowledge of self-concepts in counseling and guidance. *Educational and Psychological Measurement,* 1954, 14, 120–127. (b)

Touhey, J. C. A symbolic interactionist approach to self-referent behavior. *Psychological Reports,* 1971, 29, 87–90.

Trent, R. D. Socioempathic ability in a group of institutionalized delinquent boys. *Journal of Genetic Psychology,* 1957, 91, 99–108.

Trent, R. D. Anxiety and accuracy of perception of sociometric status among institutionalized delinquent boys. *Journal of Genetic Psychology,* 1959, 94, 85–91.

Trowbridge, N. Effects of socio-economic class on self-concept of children. *Psychology in the Schools,* 1970, 7, 304–306.

Truax, C. B.; Schuldt, W. J.; & Wargo, D. G. Self-ideal concept congruence and improvement in group psychotherapy. *Journal of Consulting and Clinical Psychology,* 1968, 32, 47–53.

Truax, C. B.; Wargo, D. G.; Carkhuff, R. R.; Kodman, F., Jr.; & Moles, E. A. Changes in self-concepts during group psychotherapy as a function of alternate sessions and vicarious therapy pretraining in institutionalized mental patients and juvenile delinquents. *Journal of Consulting Psychology,* 1966, 30, 309–314.

Tschechtelin, Sister M. A. Self appraisal of children. *Journal of Educational Research,* 1945, 39, 25–32.

Tucker, C. W. Some methodological problems of Kuhn's self theory. *Sociological Quarterly,* 1966, 7, 345–358.

Underwood, B. J. *Psychological research.* New York: Appleton-Century-Crofts, 1957.

Vacchiano, R. B.; Lieberman, L. R.; Adrian, R. J.; & Schiffman, D. C. A factor analytic comparison of TAT, self-description, and reputation assessment techniques. *Journal of Clinical Psychology,* 1967, 23, 416–419.

Vacchiano, R. B., & Strauss, P. S. The construct validity of the Tennessee Self Concept Scale. *Journal of Clinical Psychology,* 1968, 24, 323–326.

Vacchiano, R. B.; Strauss, P. S.; & Schiffman, D. C. Personality correlates of dogmatism. *Journal of Consulting and Clinical Psychology,* 1968, 32, 83–85.

Van de Mark, S. N., & Neuringer, C. Effect of physical and cognitive somatic arousal on Rorschach responses: An experimental test of the assumption that body image influences the perceptual organization of unstructured stimuli. *Journal of Consulting and Clinical Psychology,* 1969, 33, 458–465.

Vanderpool, J. A. Alcoholism and the self-concept. *Quarterly Journal of Studies on Alcohol,* 1969, 30, 59–77.

Veldman, D. J., & Parker, G. V. C. Adjective rating scales for self description. *Multivariate Behavioral Research,* 1970, 5, 295–302.

Veldman, D. J., & Pierce-Jones, J. Sex differences in factor structure for the California Psychological Inventory. *Journal of Consulting Psychology,* 1964, 28, 93.

Veldman, D. J., & Worchel, P. Defensiveness and self-acceptance in the management of hostility. *Journal of Abnormal and Social Psychology,* 1961, 63, 319–325.

Vernon, G. M. Religious self-identifications. *Pacific Sociological Review,* 1962, 5, 40–43.

Verplanck, W. S. & Burrhus F. Skinner. In W. K. Estes; S. Koch; K. Mac-Corquodale; P. E. Meehl; C. G. Mueller; W. N. Schoenfeld; & W. S. Verplanck. *Modern learning theory: A critical analysis of five examples.* New York: Appleton-Century-Crofts, 1954. Pp. 267–316.

Vincent, J. An exploratory factor analysis relating to the construct validity of self-concept labels. *Educational and Psychological Measurement,* 1968, 28, 915–921.

Viney, L. L. Congruence of measures of self-regard. *Psychological Record,* 1966, 16, 487–493.

Vroom, V. H. Projection, negation, and the self concept. *Human Relations,* 1959, 12, 335–344.

Wachs, H., & Zaks, M. S. Studies of body image in men with spinal cord injury. *Journal of Nervous and Mental Disease,* 1960, 130, 121–127.

Wahler, H. J. Social desirability and self-ratings of intakes, patients in treatment, and controls. *Journal of Consulting Psychology,* 1958, 22, 357–363.

Walberg, H. J. Religious differences in cognitive associations and self-concept in prospective teachers. *Journal of Social Psychology,* 1967, 73, 89–96. (a)

Walberg, H. J. The structure of self-concept in prospective teachers. *Journal of Educational Research,* 1967, 61, 84–86. (b)

Walberg, H. J. Personality: Role conflict and self-conception in urban practice teachers. *School Review,* 1968, 76, 41–49.

Walhood, D. S., & Klopfer, W. G. Congruence between self-concept and public image. *Journal of Consulting and Clinical Psychology,* 1971, 37, 148–150.

Walker, C. E., & Linden, J. D. Response formats and measurement qualities of an objective test. *Psychological Reports,* 1969, 24, 620.

Wallen, V. Background characteristics, attitudes, and self-concepts of Air Force psychiatric casualties from Southeast Asia. In P. G. Bourne (Ed.), *The psychology and physiology of stress: With reference to special studies of the Viet Nam war.* New York: Academic Press, 1969. Pp. 167–196.

Walsh, A. M. *Self-concepts of bright boys with learning difficulties.* New York: Bureau of Publications, Teachers College, Columbia University, 1956.

Walster, E.; Berscheid, E.; Abrahams, D.; & Aronson, V. Effectiveness of debriefing following deception experiments. *Journal of Personality and Social Psychology,* 1967, 6, 371–380.

Ware, K. E.; Fisher, S.; & Cleveland, S. Body-image boundaries and adjustment to poliomyelitis. *Journal of Abnormal and Social Psychology,* 1957, 55, 88–93.

Warr, P. B., & Knapper, C. Negative responses and serial position effects on the Adjective Check List. *Journal of Social Psychology*, 1967, 73, 191–197.

Washburn, W. C. Patterns of self-conceptualization in high school and college students. *Journal of Educational Psychology*, 1961, 52, 123–131.

Waters, L. K. Effect of instructions and item tone on reactions to forced-choice pairs. *Personnel Psychology*, 1966, 19, 297–300.

Waters, L. K., & Wherry, R. J., Jr. Evaluation of two forced-choiced formats. *Personnel Psychology*, 1961, 14, 285–289.

Weaver, W. W.; Kingston, A. J.; Bickley, A. C.; & White, W. F. Information-flow difficulty in relation to reading comprehension. *Journal of Reading Behavior*, 1969, 1, no page numbers.

Weaver, W. W.; White, W. F.; & Kingston, A. J., Jr. Affective correlates of reading comprehension. *Journal of Psychology*, 1968, 68, 87–95.

Webb, W. B. Self-evaluation compared with group evaluations. *Journal of Consulting Psychology*, 1952, 16, 305–307.

Webb, W. B. Self-evaluations, group evaluations, and objective measures. *Journal of Consulting Psychology*, 1955, 19, 210–212.

Weinberg, J. R. A further investigation of body-cathexis and the self. *Journal of Consulting Psychology*, 1960, 24, 277.

Weinberg, N.; Mendelson, M.; & Stunkard, A. A failure to find distinctive personality features in a group of obese men. *American Journal of Psychiatry*, 1961, 117, 1,035–1,037.

Weiner, P. S. Personality correlates of self-appraisal in four-year-old children. *Gentic Psychology Monographs*, 1964, 70, 329–365.

Weingarten, E. M. A study of selective perception in clinical judgment. *Journal of Personality*, 1949, 17, 369–406.

Weinreich, U. Travel through semantic space. *Word*, 1958, 14, 346–366.

Welsh, G. S. Factor dimensions A and R. In G. S. Welsh and W. G. Dahlstrom (Eds.), *Basic readings on the MMPI in psychology and medicine*. Minneapolis: University of Minnesota Press, 1956. Pp. 264–281.

Wessman, A. E., & Ricks, D. F. *Mood and personality*. New York: Holt, Rinehart & Winston, 1966.

Wessman, A. E.; Ricks, D. F.; & Tyl, M. M. Characteristics and concomitants of mood fluctuation in college women. *Journal of Abnormal and Social Psychology*, 1960, 60, 117–126.

White, B. J. The relationship of self concept and parental identification to women's vocational interests. *Journal of Counseling Psychology*, 1959, 6, 202–206.

White, W. F., & Gaier, E. L. Assessment of body image and self-concept among alcoholics with different intervals of sobriety. *Journal of Clinical Psychology*, 1965, 21, 374–377.

White, W. F., & Richmond, B. O. Perception of self and of peers by economically deprived black and advantaged white fifth graders. *Perceptual and Motor Skills,* 1970, 30, 533–534.

White, W. F., & Wash, J. A., Jr. Prediction of successful college academic performance from measures of body cathexis, self-cathexis, and anxiety. *Perceptual and Motor Skills,* 1965, 20, 431–432.

Wiener, M.; Blumberg, A.; Segman, S.; & Cooper, A. Judgment of adjustment by psychologists, psychiatric social workers, and college students, and its relationship to social desirability. *Journal of Abnormal and Social Psychology,* 1959, 59, 315–321.

Wiest, W. M. A quantitative extension of Heider's theory of cognitive balance applied to interpersonal perception and self-esteem. *Psychological Monographs,* 1965, 79, 1–20.

Wiggins, N. Individual viewpoints of social desirability. *Psychological Bulletin,* 1966, 66, 68–77.

Wilkinson, A. E. Relationship between measures of intellectual functioning and extreme reponse style. *Journal of Social Psychology,* 1970, 81, 271–272.

Wilkinson, A. E., & Worchel, P. Self-consistency as a function of the parental self. *Psychological Reports,* 1959, 5, 503.

Williams, A. F. Self-concepts of college problem drinkers: I. A comparison with alcoholics. *Quarterly Journal of Studies on Alcohol,* 1965, 26, 586–594.

Williams, A. F. Self-concepts of college problem drinkers: II. Heilbrun need scales. *Quarterly Journal of Studies on Alcohol,* 1967, 28, 267–276.

Williams, J. E. Changes in self and other perceptions following brief educational-vocational counseling. *Journal of Counseling Psychology,* 1962, 9, 18–30.

Williams, J. E. Order, sequence, and retest effects with the S-I-O procedure. *Perceptual and Motor Skills,* 1963, 17, 3–11.

Williams, R. L. Relationship of class participation to personality, ability, and achievement variables. *Journal of Social Psychology,* 1971, 83, 193–198.

Williams, R. L., & Byars, H. Negro self-esteem in a transitional society. *Personnel and Guidance Journal,* 1968, 47, 120–125.

Williams, R. L., & Byars, H. The effect of academic integration on the self-esteem of southern Negro students. *Journal of Social Psychology,* 1970, 80, 183–188.

Williams, R. L., & Cole, S. Self-concept and school adjustment. *Personnel and Guidance Journal,* 1968, 46, 478–481.

Williams, R. L., & Krasnoff, A. G. Body image and physiological patterns in patients with peptic ulcer and rheumatoid arthritis. *Psychosomatic Medicine,* 1964, 26, 701–709.

Windholz, G. Discrepancy of self and ideal-self and frequency of daydreams reported by male subjects. *Psychological Reports,* 1968, 23, 1,121–1,122.

Windholz, G. Discrepancy of self and ideal-self and frequency of hero, sexual, and hostile daydreams reported by males. *Psychological Reports,* 1969, 25, 136–138.

Winkler, R. C., & Myers, R. A. Some concomitants of self-ideal discrepancy measures of self-acceptance. *Journal of Counseling Psychology,* 1963, 10, 83–86.

Winthrop, H. Self-images of personal adjustment vs. the estimates of friends. *Journal of Social Psychology,* 1959, 50, 87–99.

Witkin, H. A.; Dyk, R. B.; Faterson, D. R.; Goodenough, D. R.; & Karp, S. A. *Psychological differentiation.* New York: Wiley, 1962.

Wittenborn, J. R. Contributions and current status of Q methodology. *Psychological Bulletin,* 1961, 58, 132–142.

Wolff, W. *The expression of a personality: Experimental depth psychology.* New York: Harper, 1943.

Woolington, J. M., & Markwell, E. D. The influence of hypnosis on self attitudes. *International Journal of Clinical and Experimental Hypnosis,* 1962, 10, 109–113.

Worchel, P. Adaptability screening of flying personnel: Development of a self-concept inventory for predicting maladjustment. USAF Report No. 56–62, 1957, School of Aviation Medicine.

Worchel, P. Personality factors in the readiness to express aggression. *Journal of Clinical Psychology,* 1958, 14, 355–359.

Worchel, P. Displacement and the summation of frustration. *Journal of Experimental Research in Personality,* 1966, 1, 256–261.

Worchel, P., & Hillson, J. S. The self-concept in the criminal: An exploration of Adlerian theory. *Journal of Individual Psychology,* 1958, 14, 173–181.

Worchel, P., & McCormick, B. L. Self-concept and dissonance reduction. *Journal of Personality,* 1963, 31, 588–599.

Wright, B., & Tuska, S. The nature and origin of feeling feminine. *British Journal of Social and Clinical Psychology,* 1966, 5, 140–149.

Wylie, R. C. Some relationships between defensiveness and self-concept discrepancies. *Journal of Personality,* 1957, 25, 600–616.

Wylie, R. C. *The self concept: A critical survey of pertinent research literature.* Lincoln: University of Nebraska Press, 1961.

Wylie, R. C. The present status of self theory. In E. F. Borgatta, & W. W. Lambert (Eds.), *Handbook of personality theory and research.* Chicago: Rand McNally, 1968, Pp. 728–787.

Wysocki, B., & Whitney, E. Body image of crippled children as seen in Draw-A-Person Test behavior. *Perceptual and Motor Skills,* 1965, 21, 499–504.

Yamamoto, K.; Thomas, E. C.; & Karns, E. A. School-related attitudes in middle-school age students. *American Educational Research Journal,* 1969, 6, 191–206.

Yamamoto, K., & Wiersma, J. Rejection of self and of deviant others among student teachers. *Journal of Special Education,* 1967, 1, 401–408.

Young, H. H. A test of Witkin's field-dependence hypothesis. *Journal of Abnormal and Social Psychology,* 1959, 59, 188–192.

Young, H. H.; Holtzman, W. H.; & Bryant, N. D. Effects of item context and order on personality ratings. *Educational and Psychological Measurement,* 1954, 14, 499–517.

Zagona, S., & Babor, T. F. Adolescents' attitudes toward themselves and cigarette smokers. *Psychological Reports,* 1969, 25, 501–502.

Zahran, H. A. The self-concept in the psychological guidance of adolescents. *British Journal of Educational Psychology,* 1967, 37, 225–240.

Zavala, A. Development of the forced-choice rating scale technique. *Psychological Bulletin,* 1965, 63, 117–124.

Zax, M.; Cowen, E. L.; Budin, W.; & Biggs, C. F. The social desirability of trait descriptive terms: Applications to an alcoholic sample. *Journal of Social Psychology,* 1962, 56, 21–27.

Zelen, S. L. The relationship of peer acceptance, acceptance of others, and self acceptance. *Proceedings of the Iowa Academy of Science,* 1954, 61, 446–449. (a)

Zelen, S. L. Acceptance and acceptibility: An examination of social reciprocity. *Journal of Consulting Psychology,* 1954, 18, 316. (b)

Zelen, S. L.; Sheehan, J. G.; & Bugental, J. F. T. Self-perceptions in stuttering. *Journal of Clinical Psychology,* 1954, 10, 70–72.

Zellner, M. Self-esteem, reception, and influenceability. *Journal of Personality and Social Psychology,* 1970, 15, 87–93.

Ziller, R. C. The alienation syndrome: A triadic pattern of self-other orientation. *Sociometry,* 1969, 32, 287–300.

Ziller, R. C., & Golding, L. H. Political personality. *Proceedings of the 77th Annual Convention of the American Psychological Association,* 1969, 4, 441–442.

Ziller, R. C., & Grossman, S. A. A developmental study of the self-social constructs of normals and the neurotic personality. *Journal of Clinical Psychology,* 1967, 23, 15–21.

Ziller, R. C.; Hagey, J.; Smith, M. D.; & Long, B. Self-esteem: A self-social construct. *Journal of Consulting and Clinical Psychology,* 1969, 33, 84–95.

Ziller, R. C.; Long, B. H.; Kanisetti, R. V.; & Reddy, V. E. Self-other orientations of Indian and American adolescents. *Journal of Personality,* 1968, 36, 315–330.

Ziller, R. C.; Megas, J.; & DeCencio, D. Self-social constructs of normal and acute neuropsychiatric patients. *Journal of Consulting Psychology,* 1964, 28, 59–63.

Zimmer, H. Self-acceptance and its relation to conflict. *Journal of Consulting Psychology,* 1954, 18, 447–449.

Zimmer, H. Motivational factors in dyadic interaction. *Journal of Personality,* 1956, 24, 251–261.

Zimny, G. H. Body image and physiological responses. *Journal of Psychosomatic Research,* 1965, 9, 185–188.

Zion, L. C. Body concept as it relates to self-concept. *Research Quarterly,* 1965, 36, 490–495.

Zuckerman, M.; Levitt, E. E.; & Lubin, B. Concurrent and construct validity of direct and indirect measures of dependency. *Journal of Consulting Psychology,* 1961, 25, 316–323.

Zunich, M., & Ledwith, B. E. Self-concepts of visually handicapped and sighted children. *Perceptual and Motor Skills,* 1965, 21, 771–774.

Subject Matter Index

Variables studied as antecedents, correlates, or consequents of the self-concept (e.g., parental treatment, diagnostic categories, acceptance of others) are not indexed here, as they are alluded to in this volume only incidentally in connection with so-called assumed-validity studies.

Academic Self-Concept (Word Rating List), 106
   Achievement. *See* Murray need scores
   ACL. *See* Gough and Heilbrun Adjective Check List
Acquiescence response tendencies. *See under* Response or score determiners, irrelevant
Activity Vector Analysis (AVA), 97, 103
Adaptation-level theory, 80, 82
Adjective check lists
   Adjective Check List (ACL). *See* Gough and Heilbrun Adjective Check List
   Buss and Gerjuoy Scaled Adjectives, 96, 157, 158
   General Adaptability Adjective Check List (GAAL), 103
   Intellective Adjective Check List (IAL), 104
   Motivational Adjective Check List (MACL), 104
Adjustment
   scores for Q-sort items, 106–107, 132–134, 136, 139, 142–144, 167–168
   scores for SAI, 169
   self-regard and, 132–133
Affiliation. *See* Murray need scores
Aggression (hostility)
   nonphenomenal
     in Rorschach, 257
     in TAT, 252–253, 255

   phenomenal self-concept of
     Behavioral Hostility Test, 65
     Buss and Gerjuoy Adjectives, 96
     ICL (Lov), 215, 218, 220–223
     self-ratings, 252–253
     Siegel Manifest Hostility Scale, 82
     Worchel Self-Activity Inventory, 65–169
   See also Murray need scores
Allport-Odbert Adjectives, 62, 81, 150, 201
Allport-Vernon-Lindzey Study of Values, 80
Antecedent-inferred-consequent paradigm, 15–16, 28
Anxiety
   body. *See* Body attitude scores
   self-concept of. *See* Manifest anxiety scales; Murray need scores
   self-insight and, 10, 24–25, 288–289
Anxiety scales. *See* Manifest anxiety scales; Minnesota Multiphasic Personality Inventory
Approval need. *See* Marlowe-Crowne Social Desirability Scale Artifacts, 29–32
   contamination between measures, 27, 30, 88, 206, 231, 308
   dichotomous scoring and, 88
   ipsative scoring and, 78, 88, 100
   See also Insightfulness of self-concept; Reliability; Research design; Two-part indices; Validity,

Sophistication-of-Body-Concept score. *See* Witkin Sophistication-of-Body-Concept

Driscoll Play Kit, 256

Dual indices (difference scores) of individual differences. *See* two-part indices of individual differences

Dymond Adjustment Scores (for Butler-Haigh Q sort), 106–107, 132–134, 136, 139, 142–144, 167–168

Early School Personality Questionnaire, 103

Edwards Personality Inventory, 62

Edwards Personal Preference Schedule (EPPS), 53–55, 59, 62, 68, 79–80, 97, 100, 103, 116, 126, 298

Edwards Social Desirability Scale, 56–57, 62, 152, 204, 208

Ego, 2

Ego ideal, in ICL, 213

Ego Identity Measure, 116

Ego strength
inferred from Barron Ego Strength Scale, 96
inferred from DAP, 262

Embedded Figures Test, 264

EPPS. *See* Edwards Personal Preference Schedule

Essays for inferring
ideal self, 76–77, 86
self-concept, 76–77, 86

Ethics in self-concept research, 32–33, 330

Ethnocentrism. *See* California *E* Scale

Existential psychology, 12–14, 316

Eye, Hand, and Ear Test, 260

Eysenck Neuroticism Scale, 281. *See also* Maudsley Personality Inventory

Factor analysis
controversies re interpretation, 97, 99, 101
in construct validation, 97–102
of Edwards Personal Preference Schedule, 79
general self-regard factor and, 98, 101–102, 154, 177, 183–185, 207
Guttman scaling and, 183

of Holtzman Inkblot (including Barrier) scores, 273
of intraindividual correlation matrices from Q sort, 99, 103, 129
inverse, 103, 130
of ipsative scores, 88, 100
item analysis and, 98–101, 177, 183, 207–208
of multitrait-multimethod matrices, 112–114
recommendations, 102
of self-concept measures, 97, 99–107, 154, 168, 177, 183, 185, 189, 207–208, 218, 221, 231–233
of self-concept and other measures, 106–107, 161, 184
of semantic differential, 224–225, 227–228
subdivisions of self-concept and, 98–99

Femininity-masculinity. *See* Gough *Fe* Scale

Fisher Body Disturbance Score, 261

Forced choice
factor analysis, inapplicability of, 88, 100
as irrelevant response and score determiner, 59, 76–80
in Q sorts, 128–129, 137

Freudian theory, 2, 12, 201, 288, 321

F Scale. *See* California *F* Scale

Functionalist psychology, 2–3

GAAL. *See* General Adaptability Adjective Check List

Galvanic skin response (GSR)
generalization of, 23
as index of "subception," 24–25

GAMIN. *See* Guilford-Martin Inventory of Factors (GAMIN)

General Adaptability Adjective Check List (GAAL), 103

General psychology. *See* Behavioristic psychology; Gestalt, psychology; Perception

Gestalt
properties of phenomenal self-concept
inferred from Q sort, 132, 136, 138, 144
measurement status of, 324

contextual effects in, 82
empirical validity aim, 126
factor analyses including, 106
factors in, 74–75, 100, 104
K scale, 61, 161
as repressor-sensitizer measure, 219, 221
as self-concept index, 74
self-regard and, 161
social-desirability scale values for items, 54, 60, 62
Truax Anxiety Reaction Scale, 141
Welsh *A* Scale, 106
See also Taylor Manifest Anxiety Scale
Minnesota Percepto-Diagnostic Test, 264
MMPI. *See* Minnesota Multiphasic Personality Inventory
Mother-Child Relationships Questionnaire, 104
Motivational Adjective Check List (MACL), 104
Motivation Analysis Test, 96, 107
Multitrait-multimethod matrices, 107–116
ANOVA of, for estimating convergent and discriminant validity, 112–114
defined, 107
extent of use, 114–116
factor analysis of, for estimating convergent and discriminant validity, 112–114
methodological recommendations, 113–114, 116
of Murray need scores, 209–210
need for, 107–108
sample matrix, 109
of self-regard measures, 185–186
Murray need scores (for inferring self-concepts re Murray needs)
in ACL, 201–203, 206–207, 209–212
in Behavior Interpretation Inventory, 259–260
in EPPS. *See* Edwards Personal Preference Schedule
in Jackson Personality Research Form (PRF), 115
in self-ratings, 82, 116, 251, 259
in Thematic Apperception Test (TAT), 251, 253

Negative self-concept
nonphenomenal, 253
phenomenal, 221
Neo-Freudians
defensiveness, view of, 288
self-referent constructs and, 2
self-insight, view of, 288
Nomological psychology, 12, 14
Nonphenomenal self-concept, 5
behavior and, 10, 191, 248, 320–321
construct validity of measures of, 10, 248–249, 286–287, 324
extant measures of
Barrier scores for inferring body-image, 249–250, 265–287
Behavior Interpretation Inventory, 250, 259–260
doll play, 256
Draw-a-Person, 250–265
judgments of unrecognized self, 162, 250, 257–259
Rorschach test, 256–257. *See also* Barrier scores
sentence completion, 250
story-telling techniques, 250
Thematic Apperception Test (TAT), 140, 250–255
phenomenological theories and, 4–5, 8–12, 248–249, 320–322
preverbal learning and, 248
of self-regard, 253, 262
Nonphenomenal variables. *See* Phenomenological theories; Nonphenomenal self-concept

Opinionation (Left and Right) Scales, 106
Organization of self-concept. *See* Gestalt, properties of phenomenal self-concept
Osgood et al. Semantic Differential. *See* Semantic differential approach

Parent Attitude Research Instrument (PARI), 173
Patterning within self-concept. *See* Gestalt properties of phenomenal self-concept
Penetration score (of body image), 261, 266, 284

irrelevant response and score determiners, 184
multitrait-multimethod matrix,
185–186
description, 180–183
as overall self-regard measure, frequently used, 127
rationale, 180–183
recommendations, 188–189
reliability, 183
Rotter Incomplete Sentences Blank, 84,
97, 208
Rotter Internal-External Control Scale,
197

SAI. *See* Worchel Self-Activity Inventory
Sampling
of item populations, 41–42, 147–148
of person populations, 41
of situations, 44
Scaling, 42–49
of adverbs of degree, 46–48
Guttman, 181–183
interval, 43
of intimacy of topics, 72
need for, 42
psychophysical methods for, 45–48
of social desirability. *See* Social desirability
Schroeder and Streufert Sentence Completion Test (of cognitive complexity), 264
SDSVs. *See* Social desirability, items
from self-report instruments,
scaled social-desirability values
of
Sears Self-Concept Inventory for Children, 96
Secord Homonyms Test (of body anxiety), 239–240, 281
Security-Insecurity Inventory. *See* Maslow Security-Insecurity Inventory
SEI. *See* Coopersmith Self-Esteem Inventory
Self
actualization, 1, 320
as agent, object, 1
behaviorists and, 2–3, 15, 316, 318–
319
clinical psychology and, 2

concept of. *See* Self-regard; Self-concept
definitions of, 4–5
Freud and, 2, 12, 201, 288
functionalists and, 2–3
general psychology and. *See* Behavioristic psychology; Gestalt psychology; Perception
Gestalt psychology and. *See* Gestalt
history of interest in, 2–3, 316–317
inferred (Hilgard), 293
introspectionists and, 2
James, 2
meanings of, 1, 4–5
neo-Freudians and, 2, 288
organization or patterning in, 9–10,
132, 136, 138, 144, 319, 324
percept of. *See* Self-concept; Self-
regard
personality theories and, 3–4
real, 1
Self-acceptance. *See under* Self-regard
Self-Activity Inventory. *See* Worchel
Self-Activity Inventory (SAI)
Self-adequacy. *See under* Self-regard
Self-blame. *See under* Self-regard
Self-Cathexis Scale. *See* Jourard Self-
Cathexis Scale
Self-concept (phenomenal or conscious
self-concept)
of achievement, 166. *See also* Murray
need scores
of aggression (hostility), 65, 82, 166,
168–169, 215–218, 220–223, 252–
253
antecedents of (theoretical), 316–317
of anxiety. *See* Manifest anxiety
scales; Murray need scores
as behavior-influencing variable (s),
9–10, 19–20, 26–27, 316
body-image and. *See* Barrier scores;
Draw-a-Person; Jourard and Secord Body Cathexis Scale; Nonphenomenal self-concept, measures of
congruence with Ideal self. *See* Self-
regard, self-ideal correlations,
[Self — Ideal] discrepancies
as consequent (dependent) vari-
able(s), 17, 321–323
definitions of, 4–5, 9–10

Index of Proper Names

Proper names associated with measuring instruments are indexed in the Subject Matter Index as well as in the Index of Proper Names.

418